CAPITAL DRUG LAWS IN ASIA

Edited by

WING-CHEONG CHAN

Singapore Management University

MAI SATO

Birkbeck, University of London

MICHAEL HOR

The University of Hong Kong

CAMBRIDGE
UNIVERSITY PRESS

CAMBRIDGE
UNIVERSITY PRESS

Shaftesbury Road, Cambridge CB2 8EA, United Kingdom

One Liberty Plaza, 20th Floor, New York, NY 10006, USA

477 Williamstown Road, Port Melbourne, VIC 3207, Australia

314–321, 3rd Floor, Plot 3, Splendor Forum, Jasola District Centre, New Delhi – 110025, India

103 Penang Road, #05-06/07, Visioncrest Commercial, Singapore 238467

Cambridge University Press is part of Cambridge University Press & Assessment, a department of the University of Cambridge.

We share the University's mission to contribute to society through the pursuit of education, learning and research at the highest international levels of excellence.

www.cambridge.org
Information on this title: www.cambridge.org/9781009513517

DOI: 10.1017/9781009513555

When citing this work, please include a reference to the DOI 10.1017/9781009513555

First published 2025

A catalogue record for this publication is available from the British Library

A Cataloging-in-Publication data record for this book is available from the Library of Congress

ISBN 978-1-009-51351-7 Hardback

CONTENTS

List of Tables x
List of Charts xi
List of Contributors xii
Table of Cases xiv
Table of Statutes xviii
Table of International Treaties xxiii
List of Abbreviations xxiv

1 **Introduction** 1

MAI SATO, WING-CHEONG CHAN, AND MICHAEL HOR

1.1 Wrestling with the 'War on Drugs' in Asia 1
1.2 Structure of the Book 9

PART I **Executing States**

2 **China's 'Killing Less' Policy for Drug Crimes and the Role of the Judiciary** 21

XI LI

2.1 Introduction 21
2.2 Judicial Control of the Death Penalty for Drug-Related Crimes 23
2.2.1 Redefining 'The Most Heinous Criminals': Who Should Be Punished with Immediate Execution 23
2.2.2 Raising the Threshold Quantity of Drugs Triggering Execution in Practice 36
2.2.3 Establishing New Requirements for the Purity of Drugs 38
2.2.4 Developing New Rules on Determining Awareness of the Presence of Drugs 40
2.2.5 Impose Heavier Burden of Proof on the Prosecution 44
2.3 Conclusion 48

3 **Normative Legitimacy of Iran's Capital Drug Law and Its Application** 53

MAI SATO AND LEAVIDES DOMINGO-CABARRUBIAS

3.1 Introduction 53

3.2 Data 54

3.3 International Normative Standard: The ICCPR 55

3.4 Legislative Legitimacy: The 2017 Amendment to the Law for Combating Illicit Drugs 56

3.4.1 'Most Serious Crimes' 56

3.4.2 2017 Amendment 57

3.4.3 Impact of the 2017 Amendment? 60

3.5 Judicial Legitimacy: Input Justice 62

3.5.1 Independence and Selection of Judges 62

3.5.2 Fair and Public Hearing 64

3.6 Judicial Legitimacy: Output Justice 67

3.6.1 Transparency 67

3.6.2 Reasoned Judgments 68

3.6.3 Standard of Proof 70

3.7 Conclusion 72

4 **Debate and Contestation in Singapore's Death Penalty** 83

WING-CHEONG CHAN AND MICHAEL HOR

4.1 In the Spotlight Once Again 83

4.2 The Case for Deterrence and Public Support 84

4.3 Chilling Effect 86

4.4 Regional Reforms 88

4.5 Case Law Developments 90

4.5.1 *Mens rea* of Possession 91

4.5.2 Wilful Blindness and Evidential Presumptions 94

4.5.3 Defence of Safekeeping 97

4.5.4 Meaning of Cannabis Mixture 99

4.5.5 Discrimination against a Racial Minority 101

4.6 Conclusion 103

PART II **People on Death Row**

5 **From the Ghetto to the Gallows: Rights, Race, Class, and Drug Crimes in Malaysia** 111

THAATCHAAYINI KANANATU

5.1 Introduction 111

5.1.1 Theoretical Framework: Linking Rights, Race, Class, and Drug Crimes 112

5.2 Background and Historical Context 114

5.2.1 Race and Class in the Colonial Rubber Plantation 115
5.2.2 Race and Class in the Postcolonial Rubber Plantation 117
5.2.3 Race, Class, and Crime in the Ghettos 121
5.3 Drug Couriers on Death Row (the Gallows) 124
5.3.1 War on Drugs in Southeast Asia 125
5.3.2 Double Presumption Rule and the Mandatory Death Penalty 125
5.3.3 Fair Trial Rights and Standards 127
5.3.4 Abolition of the Death Penalty for Drug Trafficking 129
5.4 Concluding Remarks: Race, Class, and the Non-Rights Bearers 130

6 **Pathways to Prison: Economic, Personal, and Relational Motivations for Drug Offending in Indonesia** 135

CAROLYN HOYLE AND PARVAIS JABBAR

6.1 Introduction 135
6.2 Drug Laws and Policy in Southeast Asia 136
6.3 Indonesia: A Case Study 139
6.3.1 Indonesians Imprisoned for Drug Offences: Research Design and Sample 143
6.3.2 Structure and Agency in Pathways to Drug Crime 145
6.4 Conclusion 155

PART III **Actors and Agencies**

7 **National Narcotics Agencies in Southeast Asia: Relics of the Regional 'War on Drugs'** 167

DANIEL PASCOE

7.1 Introduction 167
7.2 Previous Literature 170
7.3 History 172
7.4 Organisation, Functions, and Powers 176
7.4.1 Common Themes 183
7.5 Severe Punishments, Including the Death Penalty, for Drug Crimes 185
7.6 Conclusion 187

8 **Leadership from Below? Networked Governance in Preventing the Reintroduction of the Death Penalty in the Philippines** 200

LEAVIDES DOMINGO-CABARRUBIAS AND MAI SATO

8.1 Introduction 200
8.2 Brief Review of Literature 202
8.3 Analytical Framework: Networked Governance 203

8.4 Data 205
8.5 Actors in the Anti-Death Penalty Movement 206
8.6 The Anti-Death Penalty Network: Synergies and Complementarities 209
8.6.1 Amplifying Voices to Counter Dominant Narratives by the State 209
8.6.2 Sharing Information and Expertise 211
8.6.3 Increasing Legitimacy and Improving Access to Finance 213
8.7 The Role of Anti-Death Penalty Network as a Check against Abuse of Power 214
8.8 Leadership from Below? 215
8.9 Conclusion 216

PART IV States in Transition

9 The New Narcotics Code of Thailand: A Promising Law? 225

RONNAKORN BUNMEE

9.1 Introduction 225
9.2 The Innovations 226
9.2.1 Unified Law 227
9.2.2 Systematic Committees 227
9.2.3 Allowing Drug Use and Possession 228
9.2.4 Targeted Criminal Sanctions 231
9.2.5 Criminals vs Patients 236
9.3 The Challenges Ahead 238
9.3.1 Operational Aspects 238
9.3.2 Death Penalty as Sentencing Option 239
9.4 Conclusion 243

10 The Undercurrent of the Death Penalty for Drug Trafficking in Southeast and East Asia for Abolitionist States: The Case of Hong Kong 246

KAREN JOE-LAIDLER AND KATE LOWE

10.1 Southeast Asia Penal Responses: Drugs, Death Penalty, and Imprisonment 246
10.1.1 Regional Context and Trends 248
10.1.2 Mandatory Minimum Sentences for Drug-Related Offences 250
10.1.3 Processes: Navigating Criminal Justice Systems Abroad 250
10.2 Hong Kong's Legal Response to Drug Trafficking 251
10.2.1 Step One: An Assessment of the Gravity of the Offence 252

10.2.2 Step Two: An Assessment of Role and Culpability 252
10.2.3 Step Three: Reference Bands in Guidelines 253
10.2.4 Step Four: Aggravating Factors 253
10.2.5 Step Five: Mitigating Factors 253
10.2.6 Step Six: Totality 254
10.3 The Influence of the 'Death Penalty' in Court of Appeal Cases 254
10.3.1 Protect and Deter Drug Trafficking in Hong Kong 255
10.3.2 National and Regional: Being a 'Good Neighbour' 257
10.3.3 China: 'One Country Two Systems' and a Border 257
10.4 The Death Penalty as a Tool to Convey a Consistent Message: Tough Yet Fair 258
10.5 Conclusion 260

Index 266

TABLES

1.1 Stance on death penalty in the jurisdictions covered in this book 10

3.1 Minimum quantities for capital drug offences: pre- and post-2017 amendment 59

6.1 Crimes and sentences of sample of prisoners 144

CHART

3.1 Number of known executions for drug offences 2013–2023 61

CONTRIBUTORS

RONNAKORN BUNMEE is Vice Rector and Assistant Professor of Law at Thammasat University.

WING-CHEONG CHAN is Professor of Law at the Yong Pung How School of Law, Singapore Management University.

LEAVIDES DOMINGO-CABARRUBIAS is a postdoctoral researcher at Eleos Justice, Monash University.

MICHAEL HOR is Professor at the Faculty of Law, University of Hong Kong.

CAROLYN HOYLE is Professor of Criminology and Director of the Death Penalty Research Unit at the University of Oxford.

PARVAIS JABBAR is the co-founder and co-executive director of the London-based legal charity, The Death Penalty Project, and Visiting Professor in Law at the University of Oxford.

KAREN JOE-LAIDLER is Professor in Sociology at the University of Hong Kong.

THAATCHAAYINI KANANATU is Senior Lecturer in Global Studies at the School of Arts and Social Sciences, Monash University Malaysia.

XI LI is Assistant Professor of Law at Nanning Normal University.

KATE LOWE is Lecturer in Criminology in the Department of Sociology at the University of Hong Kong.

DANIEL PASCOE is Associate Professor at the School of Law, City University of Hong Kong.

MAI SATO is Professor and Director of the Institute for Crime and Justice Policy Research, School of Social Sciences, Faculty of Humanities and Social Sciences, Birkbeck, University of London, UK.

TABLE OF CASES

Canada

Cox v. Canada, Communication No. 539/1993, U.N. Doc. CCPR/C/52/D/539/19930 (1994), 243

Hong Kong

AG v. Pedro Nel Rojas [1994] HKCA 54, 263
HKSAR v. Abdallah Anwar Abbas [2009] 2 HKLRD 437, 252, 254
HKSAR v. Abdallah Anwar Abbas [2009] HKCA 115, 263
HKSAR v. Chung Ping Kun [2014] HCCC 519 (2 July 2014, unreported), 252
HKSAR v. Conde Mamady [2012] HKCFI 508, 258
HKSAR v. Dewi Kartika Sari Binti Musli [2012] HKCU 2453 (29 November 2012, unreported), 252
HKSAR v. Herico Elsa Valencia [2012] HKCFI 1706, 258
HKSAR v. Herry Jane Yusuph [2020] HKCA 974, 252–5
HKSAR v. Herry Jane Yusuph [2021] 1 HKLRD 290, 254
HKSAR v. Jitsatta Chosita [2013] HKCFI 1658, 259
HKSAR v. Kilima Abubakar Abbas [2018] HKCA 602, 251, 256, 258
HKSAR v. Lam Kam-kwong [2002] 1 HKC 541, 253
HKSAR v. Leung Kwai Ping [2001] 4 HKC 383, 253
HKSAR v. Nganga Halfani Abdallah [2010] HKCFI 2250, 259
HKSAR v. Nwadiuto Samuel Joseph [2017] HKCA 64, 255
HKSAR v. Osisioma Emmanuel Emeka [2011] HKCFI 1428, 255, 257
HKSAR v. Raja Rajeswary P Kagasfaron [2020] HKCFI 2981, 255–6
HKSAR v. Tam Yi-chun [2014] HKCA 279, 263
HKSAR v. Torres Gomez Marino Enrique [2013] HKCFI 1653, 256
HKSAR v. Wong Yat-san [2008] HKCA 200, 264
HKSAR v. Zuberi Zuberi Mussa [2012] HKCFI 1028, 259
Queen v. Chan Chi-man [1986] HKCA 15, 264
Queen v. Chan Chi-ming [1979] HKCA 25, 265
Queen v. Lau Tak-ming [1990] HKCA 96, 263
Queen v. Lau Yiu-nam [1986] HKCA 88, 265
Queen v. Tuen Shui-ming [1995] HKCA 36, 264

R v. Lau Tak-ming & Others [1990] 2 HKLR 370, [1990] HKCU 399, 253
Secretary for Justice v. Hii Siew-cheng [2008] HKCA 197, 264
Secretary for Justice v. Tang King Wa [2023] 2 HKLRD 1440, 254

International

Soering v. the United Kingdom (1989) (Application no. 14038/88), 242

Iran

Ahmad Montahai (2012), 72, 81
Ali Sattari (2021), 66, 82
Alireza Madadpur (2012), 72, 74, 81
Behzad Qaffarzadeh (2014), 81
Cafe Houghough (2016), 60
Hamzeh Jamshidian (2014), 80
Khaleq Khezrzadeh (2021), 66, 70–2, 74, 82
Majid Parmasi (2013), 65–6, 79
Mehdi Rostami (2012), 72, 82
Mikael Shahbazi (2013), 65–6, 79
Mohammad Kia Kiamehr (2014), 81
Mohsen Danahur (2014), 81
Mohsen Nasiri Mojreh (2012), 79
Mohsen Nasiri Mojreh (2013), 68–70, 79
Mussa Shateranlu (2012), 72, 81
Pishro Bivarani (2013), 66, 72, 80
Raheem Zeyn (2021), 66, 82
Rahim Mohammadpur (2013), 66, 72, 79
Reza Hosseini (2014), 66, 80
Sa'eed Shokri (2014), 81

Malaysia

Alma Nudo Atenza v. PP and another appeal [2019] 5 CLJ 780, 126–7
Letitia Bosman v. PP and other appeals (No. 1) [2020] 5 MLJ 277, 90
Marlan Marpaung v. PP [2012] 8 CLJ 41, 126
PP v. Limneswaran Jegathesan [2019] 1 LNS 494, 128
Venkatesan Chinnasami v. PP [2011] 1 LNS 1736, 126

PRC

Li Changkui case, 48
Luo Xiaolin case, 42
Mo Weiqi case, 42
Yao Jiaxin case, 48

Singapore

Abdul Karim vin Mohamed Kuppai Khan v. PP [2021] 1 SLR 1390, 100
Abdul Raman bin Yusof v. PP [1996] 2 SLR(R) 538, 100
Adili Chibuike Ejike v. PP [2019] 2 SLR 254, 93–5
Ali bin Mohamad Bahashwan v. PP [2018] 1 SLR 610, 91
Arun Ramesh Kumar v. PP [2022] 1 SLR 1152, 99
Gobi a/l Avedian v. PP [2021] 1 SLR 180, 95
Iskandar bin Rahmat v. Attorney-General [2022] 2 SLR 1018, 86
Jingga bin Md Selamat v. PP [2001] SGCA 32, 98
Jumaat bin Mohamed Sayed v. Attorney-General [2022] SGHC 291, 87, 96
Jumaat bin Mohamed Sayed v. Attorney-General [2023] SGCA 16, 97
Law Society of Singapore v. Ravi s/o Madasamy [2023] SGHC 65, 87
Lee Yuan Kwang v. PP [1995] 1 SLR(R) 778, 98
Masoud Rahimi bin Mehrzad v. PP [2017] 1 SLR 257, 95
Muhammad Abdul Hadi bin Haron v. PP [2023] SGCA 4, 95
Muhammad Jeffry v. PP [1996] 2 SLR(R) 738, 91
Ong Ah Chuan v. PP [1979–80] SLR(R) 710, 96
PP v. Abdul Haleem bin Abdul Karim [2013] 3 SLR 734, 93
PP v. Adnan bin Kadir [2013] 3 SLR 1052, 91
PP v. Chijioke Stephen Obioha [2008] SGHC 243, 93
PP v. Goh Hock Huat [1994] 3 SLR(R) 375, 97
PP v. Manogaran s/o R Ramu [1996] 3 SLR(R) 390, 100
PP v. Rozman bin Jusoh [1994] SGHC 251, 93
Ramesh a/l Perumal v. PP [2019] 1 SLR 1003, 97–8
Roshdi bin Abdullah Altway v. PP [2022] 1 SLR 535, 98
Saravanan Chandaram v. PP [2020] 2 SLR 95, 100
Shan Kai Weng v. PP [2004] 1 SLR(R) 57, 92–3
Syed Suhail bin Syed Zin v. Attorney-General [2022] 4 SLR 934, 101
Syed Suhail bin Syed Zin v. Attorney-General [2022] 5 SLR 93, 86
Syed Suhail bin Syed Zin v. Attorney-General [2022] SGHC 140, 86
Sze Siew Luan v. PP [1997] 1 SLR(R) 806, 98
Tan Ah Tee v. PP [1979–1980] SLR(R) 311, 91–3
Tan Kiam Peng v. PP [2008] 1 SLR 1, 95
Tan Seng Kee v. Attorney-General [2022] 1 SLR 1347, 103
Tay Kah Tiang v. PP [2001] 1 SLR(R) 577, 98
Zainal bin Hamad v. PP [2018] 2 SLR 1119, 94

Thailand

1007/2554 (2010), 242
1212/2555 (2012), 242
4326/2554 (2011), 242

Uganda

Attorney General v. Susan Kigula & 417 Ors (Constitutional Appeal No. 3 of 2006) [2009] UGSC 6, 242

UK

Henfield v. Attorney General of the Commonwealth of The Bahamas [1996] UKPC 4, 242
Pratt and Morgan v. The Attorney General for Jamaica and another (Jamaica) [1993] UKPC 1, 242
R v. Warner [1969] 2 AC 256, 91–2

USA

Griggs v. Duke Power Co 401 US 424 (1971), 102
Washington v. Davis 426 US 229 (1976), 102

TABLE OF STATUTES

Indonesia

Criminal Code, 8, 140
Law No. 9/1976, 140
Law No. 35/2009
- Art. 112, 144
- Art. 114, 144
- Art. 132, 144

Iran

Code of Criminal Procedure (CCP), 64, 66, 68–9
- Art. 4, 70
- Art. 190, 64
- Art. 294, 64
- Art. 374, 69
- Art. 375, 69
- Art. 427, 66, 68
- Art. 428, 66, 68
- Art. 570, 68

Constitution, 65
- Art. 37, 70
- Art. 38, 65
- Art. 156, 63
- Art. 157, 63

Islamic Penal Code, 71
- Arts. 160–163, 71
- Art. 171, 71
- Art. 172, 71
- Art. 199, 71
- Art. 211, 71
- Arts. 211 and 212, 71
- Art. 213, 71
- Art. 286, 71

Law Amending the Law for Combating Narcotic Drugs
Art. 8, para. 6, 69
Law for Combating Illicit Drugs, 57
Art. 11, 59
Art. 32, 66, 68
Art. 38, 70
Art. 45, 58
Law for the Selection of Judges 1982, 63
para. 5, 63

Malaysia

Abolition of Mandatory Death Penalty Act 2023, 129
Commissions of Enquiry Act 1950, 122
Criminal Procedure Code
s. 28A(2)(b), 128
Dangerous Drugs Act 1952, 7, 125, 181
s. 37, 127
s. 37(d), 112, 125
s. 37A, 125–6
s. 39A, 130
s. 39B, 7, 123–4, 128
s. 39B(1), 123
Drug Dependants (Treatment and Rehabilitation) Act 1983, 180
Federal Constitution
Art. 5, 114, 126, 128
Art. 5(1), 127
Art. 5(3), 128
Art. 8, 117, 126
Art. 8(1), 117
Art. 10, 114
Art. 14, 117
Art. 14(1), 117
Art. 153, 117
Art. 153(1), 117
Art. 160, 119
Art. 160(2), 119
Misuse of Drugs and Substances (Prevention, Treatment and Rehabilitation) Act, 180
National Anti-Drugs Agency Act 2004, 174
ss. 4 and 5, 180
s. 6(a), 181

s. 6(i), 180
s. 7(2), 181
Revision of Sentence of Death and Imprisonment for Natural Life (Temporary Jurisdiction of The Federal Court) Act 2023, 130

Philippines

Comprehensive Dangerous Drugs Act 2002, 201
Constitution of the Republic of the Philippines 1987
Art. VI, s. 29, 206
Art. XIII, ss. 17 and 18, 206

PRC

Criminal Law 1997, 22, 24
Art. 347, 22, 36
Art. 357, 28
Death Penalty Evidence Rules 2010, 45

Singapore

Constitution, 102
Art. 9(1), 97
Criminal Procedure Code 2010
s. 307, 101
ss. 394F–394K, 86
Drug Trafficking (Confiscation of Benefits) Act 1993, 177
Misuse of Drugs Act 1973, 91, 93, 96–7, 103
s. 2, 98
s. 8A, 88
s. 17, 92
s. 18, 94
s. 18(1), 94–5
s. 18(2), 92–5
s. 33B, 103
Second Schedule, 7, 92–3
Misuse of Drugs Act 2020, 178
s. 3(1), 178
ss. 24–26, 178
s. 31, 178
s. 31A, 178
s. 31B, 178
s. 32, 178
s. 32A, 178

Penal Code 1871
s. 377A, 86
Post-appeal Applications in Capital Cases Act 2022, 86
Protection from Online Falsehoods and Manipulation Act 2019 (POFMA), 87

Thailand

Constitution, 234
Art. 28, 242
Constitution 1976, 174
Constitution 1977, 174
Constitution 1978, 174
Emergency Decree on Measures for the Prevention and Suppression of Technological Crimes, B.E. 2566 (2023), 235
s. 9, 235
Ministerial Regulation Specifying the Quantities of Narcotics and Controlled Substances Presumed to be Possessed for Consumption, B.E. 2567 (2024)
s. 2(1), 232
Narcotics Act (6th Amendment) B.E. 2560 (2017), 231
Narcotics Act 1979, 173
Narcotics Act B.E. 2522 (1979)
s. 15(2), 232
s. 65, 232
s. 67, 232
s. 91, 232
Narcotics Code 2021, 8, 174, 179, 226–7, 229–30, 233–4, 239, 241, 243
s. 1, 232
s. 4, 228
s. 25, 228
s. 29, 229
s. 30, 229
s. 33, 229
s. 33(2), 229
s. 34, 230
s. 35, 231
s. 63, 228
s. 79, 235
s. 85, 235
s. 90, 240
s. 107, 231
s. 109, 228, 236
s. 113, 236–7
s. 114, 236–7

s. 116, 238
s. 117, 238
s. 120, 237
s. 129, 235
s. 145, 232, 240
s. 152, 233
s. 162, 232, 236
s. 164, 232, 236
s. 165, 233
s. 166, 234
s. 167, 237
s. 168, 237
s. 169, 236
Narcotics Procedure Act (No. 2) B.E. 2564 (2021) (NPA 2021), 226–7
Penal Code
s. 3, 234
s. 19, 239
s. 20, 233
s. 39, 234
s. 56, 234
s. 78, 233
s.135/1, 241

USA

Civil Rights Act 1964, 102

Vietnam

Criminal Code of Viet Nam, 7
Art. 249(1)(c), 7
Art. 250(1)(c), 7
Art. 250(4b), 7

TABLE OF INTERNATIONAL TREATIES

Convention Against Illicit Traffic in Narcotic Drugs and Psychotropic Substances 1988, 1–2, 138, 168, 241
  Art. 3(5), 241
  Art. 3(2), 2
  Art. 4(c), 3
Convention on Psychotropic Substances 1971, 1–2, 168, 188
Geneva Opium Convention 1925, 2
Hague International Opium Convention 1912, 2
International Covenant on Civil and Political Rights (ICCPR), 4, 10, 54–7, 62, 64, 68, 73–4, 242
  Art. 2, 55
  Art. 6, 56
  Art. 6(2), 240, 242
  Art. 7, 65, 242
  Art. 14, 62, 64, 128
  Art. 14(1), 62, 68
  Art. 14(2), 128
  Art. 14(3), 128
  Art. 14(3)(b), 128
  Art. 14(3)(c), 129
  Art. 14(5), 68
  Art. 15, 242
  Second Optional Protocol, 10
Protocol amending the Single Convention on Narcotic Drugs 1972, 168
Single Convention on Narcotic Drugs 1961, 1–3, 168, 175, 188
Universal Declaration of Human Rights
  Art. 3, 114

ABBREVIATIONS

AADK	Agensi Antidadah Kebangsaan (National Anti-Drugs Agency)
ASEAN	Association of Southeast Asian Nations
BAKIN	Badan Koordinasi Intelijen Negara (National Intelligence Coordination Agency)
BKNN	Badan Koordinasi Narkotika Nasional (National Narcotics Coordinating Board)
BNN	Badan Narkotika Nasional (National Narcotics Board)
CADP	Coalition Against the Death Penalty
CBCP	Catholic Bishops Conference of the Philippines
CBN	cannabinol
CCP	Code of Criminal Procedure
CHRP	Commission on Human Rights of the Philippines
CNB	Central Narcotics Bureau
CSO	Civil Society Organisation
FLAG	Free Legal Assistance Group
GANNAS	National Movement Against Narcotics
GRANAT	National Movement Against Narcotics
ICCPR	International Covenant on Civil and Political Rights
IRI	Islamic Republic of Iran
KPK	Corruption Eradication Commission
MIC	Malaysian Indian Congress
NCB	Narcotics Control Board
NDP	National Development Policy
NEP	New Economic Policy
NGO	non-governmental organisation
NHRI	National Human Rights Institution
NPA	Narcotics Procedure Act (No. 2) B.E. 2564 (2021)
NPS	new psychoactive substances
NSB	Narcotics Suppression Bureau
ONCB	Office of the Narcotics Control Board
POFMA	Protection from Online Falsehoods and Manipulation Act 2019
PRC	People's Republic of China

SANA	Singapore Anti-Narcotics Association
THC	tetrahydrocannabinol
UNODC	United Nations Office on Drugs and Crime
UPR	Universal Periodic Review

1

Introduction

MAI SATO, WING-CHEONG CHAN, AND MICHAEL HOR

1.1 Wrestling with the 'War on Drugs' in Asia

This book provides an overview of the state of the debate on drug laws in Asia, with a focus on the use of the death penalty to control drug offending.[1] It documents, analyses, and makes accessible the law and policy related to illicit drugs in various Asian jurisdictions. The areas examined include developments in the law and policy relating to illicit drugs; use of criminal law measures to combat drug-related offences; motivations of drug offenders; public support for punitive punishments; structure of the laws; procedural rights of accused persons; mandatory and discretionary sentencing; and use of the death penalty. The 'war on drugs' in Thailand and the Philippines has been described as rife with egregious human rights violations that disproportionately affect the poor and marginalised,[2] while other countries in the region, such as China, Indonesia, Iran, Malaysia, and Singapore, regularly impose the death penalty for drug trafficking despite international criticism. However, the resistance to change is not as stubborn as before, and there are signs of a shift away from blanket criminalisation at the United Nations (UN) level and in some Asian jurisdictions.

International drug policy is primarily shaped by three treaties: the 1961 UN Single Convention on Narcotic Drugs, the 1971 UN Convention on Psychotropic Substances, and the 1988 UN Convention against Illicit Traffic in Narcotic Drugs and Psychotropic

This edited book, with contributions from twelve authors, is a collection of papers specially written for a workshop held at the Yong Pung How School of Law, Singapore Management University, in June 2023. We gratefully acknowledge the support from the Singapore Ministry of Education's Academic Research Fund and Eleos Justice at the Faculty of Law, Monash University, for making it possible to hold the workshop.

1 Drug offences that attract the death penalty are broad – generally, the death penalty is imposed for manufacturing, trafficking, and/or importing/exporting illicit drugs, but some countries also apply the death penalty for drug possession.

2 Human Rights Watch (2008, 2017).

Substances.[3] The 1961 UN Single Convention on Narcotic Drugs classified various substances as 'narcotic' drugs, ranking them according to the level of harm. Its requirements include drug misuse and trafficking to be managed in each country through national legislation. It not only recommends that serious offences relating to scheduled drugs, which include cannabis, should be punished by imprisonment but also allows those who use drugs to receive treatment and care as an alternative or in addition to punishment.[4] As new drugs became more prevalent, the 1971 UN Convention on Psychotropic Substances was created, dealing with 'psychotropic' drugs.[5]

The 1988 UN Convention against Illicit Traffic in Narcotic Drugs and Psychotropic Substances further solidified the enforcement-based approach, stating that the possession, purchase, or cultivation for personal use of illicit drugs should be criminal offences encompassed under the criminal legislation of each country.[6] The 1988 UN Convention also requires countries to confiscate proceeds of drug-related crime, facilitate extradition between countries for drug-related offences, and restrict the manufacture and distribution of precursor chemicals used to produce drugs scheduled under the 1961 and 1971 UN Conventions. In amplifying its requirements, however, the 1988 UN Convention states that countries may differentiate between those drugs that cause more harm from those that cause less harm by providing alternatives to

[3] International mechanisms for controlling opiates, cocaine, and cannabis were already in place under the 1912 Hague International Opium Convention and 1925 Geneva Opium Convention.

[4] While the Conventions endorse an enforcement-based approach, it is important to remember that the 1961 UN Single Convention on Narcotic Drugs made it clear that the ultimate objective of the drug control system was the improvement of the 'health and welfare of mankind'. Drug policies were therefore initially developed and implemented with the aim of 'achieving outcomes in terms of a reduction in harms to individuals and society – less crime, better health, and more economic and social development': Global Commission on Drug Policy (2011, p. 5).

[5] However, there is 'no conceptual basis' for a particular drug belonging in one Convention or the other and 'the legal definition of many psychotropic substances is entirely applicable to narcotic drugs, and in many cases, the reverse is true'. For example, cannabis appears under the 1961 UN Convention but tetrahydrocannabinol (THC) – the psychoactive element of cannabis – is controlled under the 1971 UN Convention: United Nations Drug Control Programme (2000, para. 27).

[6] Article 3(2) states: 'Subject to its constitutional principles and the basic concepts of its legal system, each Party shall adopt such measures as may be necessary to establish as a criminal offence under its domestic law when committed intentionally, the possession, purchase or cultivation of narcotic drugs or psychotropic substances for personal consumption . . .'.

criminal sanctions.[7] Similar to the 1961 UN Convention, there is considerable flexibility in the requirements of the 1988 UN Convention. It would be within the terms of the Convention to retain criminal sanctions for possession, but not to prosecute or punish the offender. In other words, decriminalisation may be consistent with the Conventions, but legalisation would be a stretch too far. In addition, current practices have been primarily measuring the 'success' of law enforcement, such as the number of arrests, the amounts seized, or the harshness of punishments; these measures may tell us how tough we are being, but they do not tell us how successful we are in improving the 'health and welfare of mankind'.[8]

A criminal justice response to drug problems may appear to be a logical step in controlling supply and demand through the threat of punishment – especially as the various UN Conventions on illicit drugs of the twentieth century, in fact, mainly required signatories to use criminal justice strategies to tackle drug distribution. However, it is now widely accepted among drug policy experts that the global war on illicit drugs has failed,[9] with devastating consequences adversely affecting vulnerable individuals and societies around the world.[10] The United Nations Office on Drugs and Crime (UNODC) – the very agency responsible for enforcing global prohibition of illicit drugs – in 2015 acknowledged that international drug policy based on criminal punishment has created 'a number of unintended negative consequences', including 'the creation of a lucrative and violent criminal black market for drugs'.[11] Criminalisation of drug offences simply leads to geographical and substance displacement, which is one of the reasons why a punitive response to drug problems does not often result in the elimination or the shrinking of the drug market. Drug policy at the international and domestic levels started shifting over the last twenty years, with more and more countries adopting some form of decriminalisation.[12] Indeed, in 2018, the UN

[7] Article 4(c) states: 'In appropriate cases of a minor nature, the Parties may provide, as alternatives to conviction or punishment, measures such as education, rehabilitation or social reintegration, as well as, when the offender is a drug abuser, treatment and aftercare.'

[8] See note 4. Also, refer to D. Pascoe in Chapter 7 in this volume.

[9] Global Commission on Drug Policy (2011, pp. 2, 4, 17).

[10] Punitive drug policies are known to disproportionately affect women, the poor, and foreign nationals: Hoyle and Harry (2020); Macaulay (2020).

[11] United Nations Development Programme (2015, p. 4).

[12] United Nations Office on Drugs and Crime (2008).

Chief Executives Board for Coordination[13] endorsed the following approach:[14]

> To promote alternatives to conviction and punishment in appropriate cases, including the decriminalization of drug possession for personal use, and to promote the principle of proportionality, to address prison overcrowding and overincarceration by people accused of drug crimes . . .

The recent decriminalisation of cannabis extracts and products with less than 0.2 per cent tetrahydrocannabinol (THC) in Thailand is a clear example of the changing landscape in drug policy.[15] More than forty countries have legalised cannabis fully or partially for medical and/or recreational use by adults,[16] showing that a shift away from a drug policy based on global prohibition (at least in 'soft' drugs) is happening at the country level.

The United Nations Human Rights Committee regards the application of the death penalty to drug-related offences as contrary to the International Covenant on Civil and Political Rights (ICCPR). While the ICCPR does not prohibit the death penalty, it restricts the death penalty to the 'most serious crimes' – understood as 'intentional killings' – which excludes drug offences:[17]

> The term 'the most serious crimes' must be read restrictively and appertain only to crimes of extreme gravity involving intentional killing. Crimes not resulting directly and intentionally in death, such as . . . drug and sexual offences, although serious in nature, can never serve as the basis, within the framework of article 6, for the imposition of the death penalty.

The ICCPR has near universal adherence, with 173 countries ratifying the treaty, though countries such as China, Malaysia, and Singapore, covered in this book, have yet to ratify it.[18] Despite developments in the interpretations of the 'most serious crimes' under the ICCPR, not all

[13] The UN System Chief Executives Board for Coordination (CEB) is the longest-standing and highest-level coordination forum of the United Nations system. Under the chairmanship of the United Nations Secretary-General, the Chief Executives Board brings together the Executive Heads of the United Nations, its twelve Funds and Programmes, the fifteen Specialized Agencies, and three Related Organizations.

[14] United Nations Chief Executives Board for Coordination (2019, p. 14).

[15] Refer to R. Bunmee in Chapter 9 in this volume.

[16] Maciver (2021).

[17] Human Rights Committee (2019, para. 35).

[18] United Nations Office of the High Commissioner for Human Rights (n.d.).

UN agencies have embraced this position consistently. For example, the UNODC has publicly stated its opposition to the death penalty, noting that drug offences do not meet the threshold of the 'most serious crimes' and that 'the use of the death penalty for those convicted solely of drug-related or economic offences raises grave human rights concerns'.[19] However, UNODC's annual reports fail to include any data on drug-related executions occurring in many countries.[20] Indeed, *The UNODC Strategy 2021–2025* is silent on the issue of the death penalty, even though it repeatedly stresses UNODC's mission to contribute to human rights and development.[21]

At the country level, thirty-four countries retain the death penalty for a range of drug offences.[22] However, there is no clear empirical evidence that the death penalty for drug-related crimes has reduced the volume of drugs available. Despite at least 3,113 executions carried out globally for drug-related offences in the decade between 2014 and 2024,[23] the drug market continues to expand. An upward trend in the number of executions for drug offences continues globally, from 30 in 2020,[24] 131 in 2021, 324 in 2022, and 467 in 2023.[25] Drug-related executions comprised an estimated 42 per cent of all confirmed executions in 2023.[26] Iran carried out at least 459 executions, a 79 per cent increase from 2022 and the highest since 2015.[27] Iran's executions accounted for 98 per cent of all the confirmed drug-related executions in 2023.[28] Singapore, after a two-year unofficial moratorium on executions during the COVID-19 pandemic, carried out eleven executions in 2022 and five more in 2023, including the first woman executed in the country in almost twenty years – all for drug-related offences.[29] Executions for drug offences are also assumed to

[19] United Nations Office on Drugs and Crime (2010, para 25; 2018).
[20] Amnesty International (2021).
[21] Ibid.
[22] Girelli, Jofré, and Larasati (2024, p. 10).
[23] Larasati and Jofré (2024, p. 12).
[24] The year with the lowest number of executions since Harm Reduction International (HRI) started monitoring the imposition of the death penalty and executions for drug offences: ibid, p. 13.
[25] Ibid.
[26] Ibid, p. 9.
[27] Girelli, Jofré, and Larasati (2024, p. 13); M. Sato and L. Domingo-Cabarrubias in Chapter 3 in this volume.
[28] Girelli, Jofré, and Larasati (2024, p. 13).
[29] Human Rights Watch (2024, p. 554); W. C. Chan and M. Hor in Chapter 4 in this volume.

have been carried out in China based on unofficial reports and past practice, but no accurate figures can be confirmed due to state secrecy.[30]

Execution is the obvious outcome of the death penalty, but to reduce the death penalty only to the infliction of lethal power by the State does not capture the full extent of the impact of the punishment. The number of countries actively imposing death sentences for drug offences has also steadily increased, from twelve in 2014 to sixteen in 2023.[31] There were 375 known death sentences for drug offences imposed in 2023, an increase from 312 in 2022 and 240 in 2021.[32] In 2023, at least 3,039 people were estimated to be on death row for drug offences.[33] Individuals live, often for years, under the sentence of death – a grim reality for persons in countries that have not carried out executions for over ten years, often referred to as de facto abolitionist States. The living conditions on death row have been found to amount to torture under certain circumstances.[34] In this book, the chapters by C. Hoyle and P. Jabbar (Chapter 6) and T. Kananatu (Chapter 5) describe the lives of those on death row and their motivations for offending. The 'war on drugs' has also been criticised as a 'war on the poor', targeting the slums but not the powerful criminal networks.[35] Instead of disrupting drug cartels, capital drug laws in practice operate to punish 'drug mules', who are typically recruited from marginalised groups with intersecting vulnerabilities and are easily replaced.[36]

In addition, although drug policies in these retentionist countries purport to impose harsh penalties *only* for drug traffickers while rehabilitating drug users, the difference between drug use and trafficking is often blurred. For example, Indonesia has expressed commitment to implement harm reduction approaches,[37] but ambiguous provisions in its Narcotics Act – which defines drug trafficking to encompass possession and storage of narcotics – have resulted in many drug users being

[30] Girelli, Jofré, and Larasati (2024, p. 14); X. Li in Chapter 2 in this volume.

[31] China, Indonesia, Iran, Malaysia, North Korea, Saudi Arabia, Singapore, Vietnam, Bangladesh, Egypt, Iraq, Lao PDR, Sri Lanka, State of Palestine, United Arab Emirates, and Yemen have been confirmed to impose death sentences on drug offences: Larasati and Jofré (2024, p. 15).

[32] Ibid.

[33] Ibid.

[34] Human Rights Council (2021, para. 67).

[35] Amnesty International (2017).

[36] Sato and Babcock (2023).

[37] Hagarty (2010, appendix C: Indonesia Matrix).

charged for trafficking.[38] Indonesia has actively imposed death sentences for drug offences in the past years, with 114 confirmed death sentences in 2023.[39] Vietnam has adopted 'harm reduction' interventions since late 2000 and decriminalised drug use in 2009, but the Criminal Code provides a very low threshold (less than 0.1 g) for the amount of heroin, cocaine, or methamphetamine that can be stored or transported without incurring criminal liability.[40] Transporting 100 g or more of heroin, cocaine, or methamphetamine is punishable by life imprisonment or death.[41] The threshold for incurring the death penalty for heroin trafficking is even lower in China (50 g),[42] Malaysia (15 g),[43] and Singapore (15 g).[44]

Despite the generally punitive drug policies, there have been efforts to reduce the use of the death penalty for drug offences in some parts of Asia. In July 2023, Pakistan removed the death penalty for drug offences under the Control of Narcotic Substances Act, making it 'the first country to abolish the death penalty for drug offences in over a decade'.[45] In April 2023, the Malaysian Parliament passed laws removing the *mandatory* death penalty for twelve offences, including drug trafficking.[46] However, although the mandatory application was removed, the law retains the death sentence as an option for drug trafficking under the Dangerous Drugs Act 1952.[47] As demonstrated in the case of Malaysia, political leadership plays a crucial role in moving away from the death penalty. Further, while the battle for the approval of the laws was largely fought in Parliament, the reform came after relentless efforts by activists, lawyers, and civil society organisations as well as transnational and international networks, all of which have actively campaigned against the death penalty in Malaysia for years.[48] Indonesia, which has long executed those convicted of offences such as drug trafficking, adopted a new Criminal

[38] Research by the Indonesia Judicial Research Society found that 44.6 per cent of those charged with trafficking were only 'end users': Nathanael *et al.* (2002).

[39] Larasati and Jofré (2024, p. 25).

[40] *The Criminal Code of Viet Nam* (as revised in 2015) Articles 249(1)(c) and 250(1)(c).

[41] Ibid, Article 250(4b).

[42] Statista (n.d.); X. Li in Chapter 2 in this volume.

[43] Dangerous Drugs Act 1952, s. 39B.

[44] Misuse of Drugs Act 1973, Second Schedule.

[45] Girelli, Jofré, and Larasati (2024, p. 19).

[46] The death penalty was also abolished entirely for seven offences, including attempted murder and kidnapping: Human Rights Watch (2023).

[47] Amnesty International (2023).

[48] Chew (2023).

Code in 2023 which no longer lists the death penalty as a 'principal punishment', but as a punishment to be applied 'alternatively, as a last resort'.[49] The new law also created a 'probationary period' of ten years, after which death sentences may be commuted if certain conditions are met.[50] Thailand's new Narcotics Code adopted in November 2021, while maintaining the death penalty as a sentencing option for some drug-related offences, directs the court to consider alternatives to incarceration such as rehabilitation at a drug treatment facility. Rather than maintaining a purely punitive approach to drug control, the law marks a shift towards public health initiatives that treat drug users as patients instead of offenders.[51]

In some countries, such as Thailand and the Philippines, punitive and repressive drug policies have led to state-sanctioned extrajudicial killings.[52] Indeed, nearly fifty years have passed since former US president Richard Nixon declared drug abuse the 'public enemy number one'.[53] Despite its failure in the US,[54] this 'war on drugs' is seeing a revival in some parts of Asia.[55] In the Philippines, where the death penalty has been abolished since 2006,[56] former President Rodrigo Duterte's anti-illicit drugs crackdown resulted in the death of 12,000 to 30,000 people from 2016 to 2019.[57] As of 2024, these deaths are being investigated by the International Criminal Court for crimes against humanity.[58] In addition to the extrajudicial killings, Duterte's administration attempted to reintroduce the death penalty as part of its zero-tolerance approach to illicit drugs.[59] By establishing drugs and people associated with drugs as the enemy, Duterte attempted to legitimise the

49 Pascoe (2023, p. 69). The new Criminal Code comes into effect in 2026.
50 Ibid, p. 100.
51 Bunmee in Chapter 9 in this volume.
52 See note 2.
53 Nixon (1971). Successive Malaysian Prime Ministers – Mahathir Mohamad in 1983 and Abdullah Badawi in 2007 – have also similarly declared the drug issue as the 'number one enemy', underlining the need for drastic punitive measures: Druis and Othman (2015).
54 Coyne and Hall (2017).
55 Lasco (2020). Singapore's official drug policy has also been described as a 'war': Shanmugam (2024).
56 The death penalty was first abolished in 1987 but reinstated in 1993, and abolished again in 2006.
57 International Criminal Court (2021, paras. 24, 67).
58 International Criminal Court (n.d.).
59 L. Domingo-Cabarrubias and M. Sato in Chapter 8 in this volume.

use of lethal violence to hunt, punish, and, in some cases, eliminate the 'deviant'.

Despite the country's failed attempts at reintroducing the death penalty, Duterte's rhetoric on the 'war on drugs' has spread to other parts of Asia. A study found that of the suspected drug dealers killed by the Indonesian police in the first six months of 2017, more than one-third occurred after the suspects had already surrendered to police.[60] In Sri Lanka, former president Maithripala Sirisena praised Duterte's war on drugs as an 'example to the world' and announced an end to the moratorium on the death penalty that has been in place for over forty years.[61] Bangladesh also followed and launched its own war against 'yaba' (methamphetamine with caffeine). Former Prime Minister Sheikh Hasina stated:[62]

> [W]e will rescue the country from the clutches of drugs . . . the war is on drug[s] now . . . We have delegated special responsibilities to all the law-enforcing agencies, intelligence agencies and RAB. Wherever there are drugs, tough measures will be taken . . . we are taking stringent measures.

Finally, in Indonesia, following a series of statements by senior government officials expressing support for Duterte's drug war, at least forty-nine suspected drug dealers were killed by the police in the first seven months of 2017.[63]

1.2 Structure of the Book

Of the thirty-four states that, as of 2023, retain the death penalty for drug offences, our book covers six of these jurisdictions – China, Indonesia, Iran, Malaysia, Singapore, and Thailand[64] – plus two that have abolished the death penalty, Hong Kong and the Philippines. This offers a comparative perspective on the implications of the 'war on drugs' in the region characterised by disproportionate penalties, denial of legal rights,

[60] Kine (2017).
[61] Ellis-Peterson (2019). To date, Sri Lanka remains an abolitionist de facto.
[62] Haider (2018).
[63] Mcrae (2017).
[64] China, Indonesia, Iran, Malaysia, and Singapore are five of the nine 'high application states' identified by Harm Reduction International for having carried out executions for drug offences and/or at least ten drug-related death sentences imposed per year in the last five years. The others are Kuwait, North Korea, Saudi Arabia, and Vietnam: Girelli, Jofré, and Larasati (2024, p. 6).

Table 1.1 *Stance on the death penalty in the jurisdictions covered in this book*

Jurisdiction	Death penalty status	Ratified ICCPR	Ratified second optional protocol to ICCPR	UN moratorium on the use of the death penalty (2022)[65]
China	Retentionist	No	No	Against
Indonesia	Retentionist	Yes	No	Abstained
Iran	Retentionist	Yes	No	Against
Malaysia	Retentionist	No	No	For
Philippines	Abolitionist	Yes	Yes	For
Singapore	Retentionist	No	No	Against
Thailand	Retentionist	Yes	No	Abstained
Hong Kong	Abolitionist	Yes	No	NA

exploding prison populations, and unquestioning faith in the deterrent effects of the death penalty. Information on some countries, such as China and Iran, are not readily available in English. We hope that this book will enhance the ability of public policy and lawmakers, NGOs, and the general population to engage in the debate on the appropriate approach towards illicit drugs. As can be seen from Table 1.1, there is a wide diversity among the jurisdictions covered.

This book is structured in four parts. Part I examines three countries that regularly execute individuals convicted of drug offences, namely, China, Iran, and Singapore. Although it is not possible to obtain accurate data on executions in China and Iran, both countries are believed to execute a significant number of drug offenders annually. At least 459 executions for drug offences have been recorded in 2023 alone in Iran.[66] On the contrary, Singapore is open about its executions, and all five executions in 2023 were for drug offences.[67]

The chapter by X. Li (Chapter 2) examines how the judiciary operates to restrict the use of the death penalty in China. Li notes that although China remains the most frequent user of the death penalty in

65 United Nations General Assembly (2022).
66 Girelli, Jofré, and Larasati (2024, p. 13).
67 Ibid.

the world – with drug offences attracting the highest number of executions in provinces such Yunnan and Guangdong – there has been a substantial decline in the number of executions in the past fifteen years. Since 2007, upon acquiring the exclusive power to review and approve death sentences from provincial courts, the Supreme People's Court implemented proactive measures to restrict the use of the death penalty, including enhancing due process in both pre-trial and trial proceedings. Measures to restrict the use of the death penalty for drug offences include setting out sentencing guidelines with aggravating and mitigating circumstances – encouraging provincial courts to set their own threshold quantity of drugs based on the local drug offending trends – and narrowing the scope of the death penalty to specific types of offenders who should be treated with severity (e.g., professional drug traffickers). Li concludes that the judiciary has succeeded in limiting the application of the death penalty to a very small number of drug offenders and that the overall reduction of the application of the death penalty has been achieved mainly through judicial leadership rather than legislative changes. As Chinese courts are allowed to develop a degree of institutional autonomy and professionalism, the judiciary will have the capacity to deepen the reform of China's death penalty system and further restrict the use of the death penalty.

In contrast, the chapter by M. Sato and L. Domingo-Cabarrubias (Chapter 3) describes that in the Islamic Republic of Iran, efforts to restrict the application of the death penalty for drug offences came from the legislature, though the long-term impact of the new law remains unclear. The authors examine the 2017 amendment to the capital drug law, noting that although the amendment sought to limit the application of the death penalty to major players in drug syndicates – such as by raising the minimum quantities of illicit drugs which would attract the death penalty – there remain serious issues that may hamper the realisation of the amendment's objective. The continued use of the mandatory death penalty, for instance, removes judges' discretion to consider circumstances that may spare those at the bottom of the drug chain from execution. The authors then investigate how judges apply drug laws in capital cases and the extent to which fair trial guarantees are observed. Using ten judgments handed down between 2014 and 2020, they demonstrate that while there have been positive developments in improving fair trial guarantees, certain judicial practices undermine procedural guarantees such as the right to fair and public hearing by a competent, independent, and impartial tribunal, the right to effective legal representation, and the right against self-incrimination.

In Singapore, despite the government's continued commitment to a 'zero-tolerance' approach to illicit drugs, there has been a dramatic reduction in the annual number of executions in recent decades. W. C. Chan and M. Hor, in their chapter (Chapter 4), examine recent social, political, judicial, and regional developments in Singapore's death penalty landscape and the extent to which these may shape Singapore's future death penalty policy and practice for drug offences. The authors analyse the rise of a local anti-death penalty movement, which has become increasingly vocal and organised; the greater interest in death penalty issues among the general public; the dramatic rise of death penalty litigation challenging many aspects of the death penalty; the judicial efforts to improve the fairness of death penalty proceedings; shifts in younger Singaporeans' attitudes towards recreational drug use; and regional moves to restrict, if not abolish, the death penalty. The authors argue that the Singapore government is at a critical juncture, requiring serious re-evaluation of its unrelentingly punitive approach to tackling illicit drugs.

Part II of the book turns to those living under the sentence of death, with an examination of death row prisoners in Malaysia and Indonesia. T. Kananatu's chapter (Chapter 5) explores the over-representation of Malaysian citizens of Indian descent facing the death penalty for drug trafficking in Malaysia. Marginalisation of the Malaysian Indian ethnic minority first began in the British colonial period and continued during and after independence. They were ignored and neglected by socio-economic policies from 1970 to 2000. On death row, they have been denied fair trial rights in the Malaysian criminal justice system. Due to the double-presumption rule that was in place until 2019 – where one can be presumed to be trafficking by being in control of anything, such as a bag containing certain amounts of illicit drugs – these drug couriers were not presumed innocent until proven guilty but were automatically subjected to the mandatory death penalty. Kananatu's historical analysis of the treatment of Malaysians of Indian descent puts into context their over-representation on death row, and how they continue to be vulnerable and powerless in the face of harsh drug trafficking laws in Malaysia that developed out of the 'war on drugs' in Southeast Asia. The abolition of the mandatory death penalty in Malaysia in 2023 may have the effect of reducing the number of individuals sentenced to death for drug trafficking, including Malaysian Indians.

In Chapter 6, C. Hoyle and P. Jabbar draw on interviews with fifty-seven prisoners convicted of drug offences. As of December 2021,

Indonesia has over 400 individuals on death row.[68] Understanding the motivations and factors that influenced people to be involved in the illicit drugs economy despite the harsh penal climate in Indonesia is crucial. Hoyle and Jabbar show that although financial reward is an important motivation for entry into the drug trade, it is not the only factor that motivates would-be drug offenders, given that most of the interviewees were not in absolute poverty when they decided to offend. Personal and relational motivations, particularly relationships of trust within their peer groups, and the desire to support their dependents – which is not only based on economic motivations but also relational imperatives – are also critical factors that need to be considered for future studies on drug offenders who have not been deterred by harsh punishments.

Part III shifts our attention from individuals facing the death penalty to actors who enforce national drug policies, on the one hand, and to non-state actors who have opposed punitive drug policies, on the other hand. In Chapter 7, D. Pascoe focuses on the role played by national narcotics agencies in Singapore, Thailand, Malaysia, and Indonesia in drug policy and enforcement. Noting that previous studies have neglected the inner workings of national narcotics agencies and their relative position within the state's policy power structure, Pascoe examines the functions and powers of each agency and their role vis-à-vis politicians and other public bodies in shaping drug policy. He demonstrates that the four agencies are mere 'cogs in the wheel' of national drug policymaking, and that, ultimately, the direction of drug policies is determined by political actors. As institutional relics of the 'war on drugs' in Southeast Asia, which began in the 1970s, the narcotics agencies and their staff argue for the necessity and the effectiveness of harsh punitive sanctions, including the death penalty for drug trafficking and manufacturing. Pascoe argues that without a mass turnover of staff, it will be difficult to change this aspect of the agencies' working culture.

The chapter by L. Domingo-Cabarrubias and M. Sato (Chapter 8) analyses how a network of small organisations from various sectors – lawyers' groups, church-based and civic groups, an independent government entity, academic institutions, and families of prisoners – played a pivotal part in preventing the reintroduction of the death penalty in the Philippines. Using the concept of 'networked governance' as a framework and drawing on interviews carried out with those involved in anti-death

[68] Cornell Center on the Death Penalty Worldwide (n.d.).

penalty advocacy on the ground, the authors examine how relatively powerless actors formed into a strong network to counter efforts to reintroduce the death penalty during 2016–2022. The authors note that important lessons can be drawn from the Philippines' networked governance experience, but caution that any attempt to replicate it should consider the factors that make the Philippine experience unique, such as the long history of anti-death penalty advocacy of many of the organisations involved, and the strong influence of the Catholic Church due to the large percentage of Catholics in the country.

Finally, Part IV of the book comprises two chapters which highlight the malleability of drug policy, using examples from Thailand and Hong Kong. In Chapter 9, R. Bunmee reviews Thailand's new anti-illicit drugs legislation, promulgated in 2021. He highlights the innovative aspects of the Narcotics Code, which adopts a public health approach to drug control. The law makes crucial amendments to sentencing policy to ensure that the brunt of punitive action is imposed on drug traffickers who profit from the drug trade, while individuals who use drugs are provided with alternatives to incarceration, such as rehabilitation at a drug treatment facility. Bunmee notes that this shift towards a public health approach marks a significant step towards a more compassionate, and hopefully a more effective, solution to Thailand's drug problem. However, he notes remaining challenges that need to be addressed, including the need to ensure equitable application of penalties, legal professionals' understanding of the law, and adequate resources for treatment and rehabilitation. Crucially, the Narcotics Code retains the death penalty as a sentencing option for some drug offences, which falls below international standards.

The chapter by K. Joe-Laidler and K. Lowe (Chapter 10) examines the other abolitionist country featured in this book. Unlike many of its neighbours, Hong Kong does not have the death penalty. Yet, the authors find that its legal response is framed within the broader prohibitionist, punitive approach in the region, in which a significant number of countries continue to apply the death penalty for drug offences. The authors examine court judgments to demonstrate that long prison sentences handed down to individuals convicted of drug trafficking are indicative of the desire to protect Hong Kong from being viewed as an easy location for trafficking. At the same time, judges appeared to be keen to impress upon the international community that Hong Kong is aligned with the rest of the region in the fight against the international drug trade. The chapter demonstrates that despite the death penalty being a matter of domestic criminal policy, and despite Hong Kong being an abolitionist country for decades, Hong Kong's legal response to drug trafficking is consistent with the generally punitive approach within the region, aligning itself with neighbouring countries that impose harsh punitive measures to protect their borders and deter drug trafficking.

References

Amnesty International. (2017) 'Philippines: Duterte's "War on Drugs" Is a War on the Poor'. www.amnesty.org/en/latest/news/2017/02/war-on-drugs-war-on-poor/.

(2021) 'World Drugs Day: UNODC Must Integrate Ending Drug-Related Executions in Its Work'. www.amnesty.org/en/wp-content/uploads/2023/08/ACT5043472021ENGLISH.pdf.

(2023) 'Reforms of Mandatory Death Penalty in Malaysia: What Do the Bills Say?' www.amnesty.my/wp-content/uploads/2023/03/Amnesty-International_Analysis-of-the-Bills-to-Abolish-The-Mandatory-Death-Penalty-in-Malaysia_March-2023-3.pdf.

Chew, D. (2023) 'A New Chapter: Malaysia's Journey toward Abolition', *Eleos Justice*. www.monash.edu/law/research/eleos/blog/eleos-justice-blog-posts/a-new-chapter-malaysias-journey-toward-abolition.

Cornell Center on the Death Penalty Worldwide. (n.d.) 'Republic of Indonesia (Indonesia)'. https://deathpenaltyworldwide.org/database/#/results/country?id=32.

Coyne, C. J. and Hall, A. R. (2017) 'Four Decades and Counting: The Continued Failure of the War on Drugs', Policy Analysis No. 811 (Washington, DC: Cato Institute).

Druis, M. D. and Othman, Z. (2015) 'Illicit Drugs as a Threat to National Security' 3(1) *Journal of Public Security and Safety* 139.

Ellis-Peterson, H. (2019) '"Example to the World": Sri Lanka President Plans to Copy Duterte's War on Drugs', *The Guardian* (18 January). www.theguardian.com/world/2019/jan/18/example-to-the-world-sri-lanka-president-plans-to-copy-dutertes-war-on-drugs.

Girelli, G., Jofré, M. and Larasati, A. (2024) *The Death Penalty for Drug Offences: Global Overview 2023* (London: Harm Reduction International).

Global Commission on Drug Policy. (2011) 'War on Drugs: Report of the Global Commission on Drug Policy'. www.globalcommissionondrugs.org/reports/the-war-on-drugs.

Hagarty, C. (2010) *Harm Reduction in Asia: Progress towards Universal Access to Harm Reduction Services* (Australia: Burnet Institute).

Haider, L. (2018) 'Bangladesh Has 7 Million Drug Addicts, "Over Half of Them Are Addicted to Yaba"', *bdnews24.com* (21 May). https://bdnews24.com/bangladesh/bangladesh-has-7-million-drug-addicts-over-half-of-them-are-addicted-to-yaba.

Hoyle, C. and Harry, L. (2020) 'Compounded Vulnerability: Foreign National Women and the Death Penalty in Southeast Asia' 40 *Amicus Journal* 15.

Human Rights Committee. (2019) *General Comment No. 36 – Article 6: Right to Life*, UN Doc CCPR/C/GC/36 (3 September).

Human Rights Council. (2021) *Overview of the Work Done by the Special Rapporteur on Extrajudicial, Summary or Arbitrary Executions during Her Tenure (2016–2021) – Report of the Special Rapporteur on Extrajudicial, Summary or Arbitrary Executions, Agnès Callamard* (A/HRC/47/33). https://documents.un.org/doc/undoc/gen/g23/099/99/pdf/g2309999.pdf?token=TMS9ETx2prGBjjlQgd&fe=true.

Human Rights Watch. (2008) 'Thailand's "War on Drugs"'. www.hrw.org/news/2008/03/12/thailands-war-drugs.

(2017) '"License to Kill": Philippine Police Killings in Duterte's "War on Drugs"'. www.hrw.org/report/2017/03/02/license-kill/philippine-police-killings-dutertes-war-drugs.

(2023) 'Malaysia Repeals Mandatory Death Penalty'. www.hrw.org/news/2023/04/11/malaysia-repeals-mandatory-death-penalty.

(2024) *World Report 2024: Events of 2023.*

International Criminal Court. (n.d.) *Republic of the Philippines* (ICC-01/21). www.icc-cpi.int/philippines.

(2021) *Situation in the Philippines: Decision on the Prosecutor's Request for Authorisation of an Investigation Pursuant to Article 15(3) of the Statute* (No. ICC-01/21). www.icc-cpi.int/sites/default/files/CourtRecords/CR2021_08044.PDF.

Kine, P. (2017) 'Duterte's "Drug War" Migrates to Indonesia', *Human Rights Watch* (23 August). www.hrw.org/news/2017/08/23/dutertes-drug-war-migrates-indonesia.

Larasati, A. and Jofré, M. (2024) *Special Issue: A Decade-Long Review on the Death Penalty for Drug Offences* (London: Harm Reduction International).

Lasco, G. (2020) 'Drugs and Drug Wars as Populist Tropes in Asia: Illustrative Examples and Implications for Drug Policy' 77 *International Journal of Drug Policy* 102668.

Macaulay, F. (2020) 'Gendering Drug Policy' in Buxton, J., Margo, G. and Burger, L. (eds.) *The Impact of Global Drug Policy on Women: Shifting the Needle* (Bingley: Emerald Publishing Limited).

Maciver, B. (2021) *Cannabis Legalization World Map: Updated.* www.cannabisbusinesstimes.com/article/cannabis-legalization-world-map/.

Mcrae, D. (2017) 'Is Indonesia Embarking on a Philippines-Style War on Drugs?' *University of Melbourne* (8 August). https://indonesiaatmelbourne.unimelb.edu.au/is-indonesia-embarking-on-a-philippines-style-war-on-drugs/.

Nathanael, M. *et al.* (2002) *Research on Sentencing Disparity and Criminal Policy of Narcotics Offence Cases in Indonesia* (Indonesia Judicial Research Society).

https://ijrs.or.id/en/publikasi-ijrs/research-on-sentencing-disparity-and-criminal-policy-of-narcotics-offence-cases-in-indonesia/.

Nixon, R. (1971) *Remarks about an Intensified Program for Drug Abuse Prevention and Control* (17 June). https://prhome.defense.gov/Portals/52/Documents/RFM/Readiness/DDRP/docs/41%20Nixon%20Remarks%20Intensified%20Program%20for%20Drug%20Abuse.pdf.

Pascoe, D. (2023) 'Indonesia's Revised Criminal Code and the Death Penalty – Progress Amid the Gloom?' 24(1) *Australian Journal of Asian Law* 67.

Sato, M. and Babcock, S. (2023) *Silently Silenced: State-Sanctioned Killing of Women* (Eleos Justice, Monash University and Cornell Center on the Death Penalty Worldwide).

Shanmugam, K. (2024) *Ministerial Statement on Singapore's National Drug Control Policy* (8 May). www.mha.gov.sg/mediaroom/parliamentary/ministerial-statement-on-singapore-national-drug-control-policy.

Statista. (n.d.) *Drug Use in China – Statistics & Facts*. www.statista.com/topics/11437/drug-use-in-china/#topicOverview.

United Nations Chief Executives Board for Coordination. (2019) *Summary of Deliberations* (CEB/2018/2) (18 January). https://unsceb.org/sites/default/files/imported_files/CEB-2018-2-SoD.pdf.

United Nations Development Programme. (2015) *Perspectives on the Development Dimensions of Drug Control Policy*. www.unodc.org/documents/ungass2016/Contributions/UN/UNDP/UNDP_paper_for_CND_March_2015.pdf.

United Nations Drug Control Programme. (2000) *UNDCP Model Drug Abuse Bill*. www.unodc.org/pdf/lap_drug-abuse-bill_commentary.pdf.

United Nations General Assembly. (2022) *Moratorium on the Use of the Death Penalty* (A/RES/77/222) (15 December). https://documents.un.org/doc/undoc/gen/n22/764/50/pdf/n2276450.pdf.

United Nations Office of the High Commissioner for Human Rights. (n.d.) *Status of Ratification Interactive Dashboard*. https://indicators.ohchr.org.

United Nations Office on Drugs and Crime. (2008) *Making Drug Control 'Fit for Purpose': Building on the UNGASS Decade – Report by the Executive Director of the United Nations Office on Drugs and Crime as a Contribution to the Review of the Twentieth Special Session of the General Assembly*. www.unodc.org/documents/commissions/CND/CND_Sessions/CND_51/1_CRPs/E-CN7-2008-CRP17_E.pdf.

(2010) *Drug Control, Crime Prevention and Criminal Justice: A Human Rights Perspective: Note by the Executive Director*. UN Doc E/CN.7/2010/CRP.6–E/CN.15/2010/CRP.1 (3 March). www.unodc.org/documents/commissions/CCPCJ/CCPCJ_Sessions/CCPCJ_19/E-CN15-2010-CRP1_E-CN7-2010-CRP6/E-CN15-2010-CRP1_E-CN7-2010-CRP6.pdf.

(2018) *The Death Penalty and Organized Crime*. www.unodc.org/e4j/zh/organized-crime/module-10/key-issues/death-penalty-and-organized-crime.html.

PART I

Executing States

2

China's 'Killing Less' Policy for Drug Crimes and the Role of the Judiciary

XI LI

2.1 Introduction

Since the People's Republic of China (PRC) was established more than seventy years ago, the death penalty has been used by the Chinese Communist Party as an important instrument to assert state control and crack down on what it considers to be the 'most serious crimes'. While the abolition of the death penalty has been an international trend in recent decades,[1] China remains the most frequent user of the death penalty and executes more people than the rest of the world combined.[2] Although the absolute execution numbers in China appear to remain very high, they have actually experienced a substantial decline since 2007, when the Party-state began to undertake a series of reforms to restrict and reduce the use of the death penalty.[3] These reforms include transferring the power to review and approve death sentences from provincial courts to the Supreme People's Court in 2007, introducing the softer criminal justice policy of 'balancing leniency and severity' in place of the 'punishing with severity and swiftness' policy of the 'Strike

[1] Miao (2013); Hood and Hoyle (2015, p. 26); Amnesty International (2019).

[2] Dui Hua Foundation (http://duihua.org/wp/wp/) released a report in October 2014, estimating that around 2,400 people were executed in China in 2013, far more than 778 people executed by the rest of the world combined. Accurate statistics regarding the death sentence and execution are not publicly accessible. It remains a state secret in China, disclosure of which will trigger serious criminal liability.

[3] Since the power of final review of death sentences was returned to the Supreme People's Court in 2007, the number of executions nationwide may have dropped by more than a third, with declines of nearly 50 per cent in some localities: Southern Weekly citing an expert familiar with the court system. Other experts have said that the national figure dropped by 50 per cent four years after 2007. Available at http://duihua.org/wp/?page_id=9270 accessed on 6 May 2023. In 2013 and 2014, the number who were executed was estimated to be only one-tenth of that at the height of the first 'Strike Hard' anti-crime campaign from 1983 to 1986.

Hard' era,[4] promoting the use of suspended death sentences as an alternative to immediate execution in lower courts, abolishing 13 non-violent capital offences in China's Criminal Law in 2011 and another 9 in 2015 (with 46 remaining), and further revising China's Criminal Procedural Law to provide suspects and defendants who are facing potential death sentence with enhanced procedural safeguards.

In China, there are two categories of crimes that are most likely to incur the death penalty: one is violent crimes resulting in the death of the victim, and the other is drug-related crimes, including drug trafficking, smuggling, manufacturing, and transportation. In the provinces of Yunnan and Guangdong, drug-related crimes in some years overtook violent crimes as the category attracting the highest number of executions.[5] Therefore, restricting the application of the death penalty for drug-related offences is of great significance in reducing the overall execution number in China. Unlike Singapore, China has no mandatory death penalty for drug-related offences. There is only one provision in the 1997 Criminal Law dealing with the application of the death penalty for drug-related crimes: 'offenders convicted of smuggling, trafficking, transporting, or manufacturing over 50g of heroin or amphetamines can be sentenced to 15 years' imprisonment, life imprisonment, or the death penalty'.[6] The vagueness of China's Criminal Law leaves judges with broad discretion in death penalty decision-making. Driven by the 'punishing with severity and swiftness' policy, judges at grassroots courts had a strong inclination to order the execution of the offender as long as the quantity of drugs involved in the case meets the threshold for the possible application of the death penalty. This resulted in an extremely high execution rate in drug-related cases during the 'Strike Hard' anti-crime campaign period.[7]

[4] Since 1949, the PRC has launched three waves of 'Strike Hard' anti-crime campaigns. The first campaign lasted from 1983 to 1986, the second from 1996 to 1999, and the third from 2001 to 2003. The first campaign targeted hooliganism, robbery, rape, murder, theft, and so on; the second 'Strike Hard' campaign focused on juvenile delinquency, human trafficking, drug-related crimes, and so on; and the third campaign focused on criminal syndicates, triad crimes, and economic-related crimes. The fundamental criminal policy during the 'Strike Hard' anti-crime period was the 'punishing with severity and swiftness' policy, which allowed police officers, prosecutors, and judges to handle cases in violation of legal procedures and encouraged judges to impose the heaviest penalties provided by law, to deter potential criminals and quickly restore the social order.

[5] Zui (2018).

[6] 1997 Criminal Law, Article 347.

[7] Chen (2006).

To check the over-zealous use of executions in drug-related crimes, and to pursue the new policy of 'killing less and killing cautiously', The Supreme People's Court and its reform-minded judges, upon acquiring the exclusive power to review and approve all death penalty cases across the country from provincial courts in 2007, have undertaken a series of proactive measures to guide the discretion of lower court judges and to steer their decision-making in individual death penalty-eligible cases. These include clarifying aggravating and mitigating circumstances, raising the standard of proof in potential death penalty cases, encouraging provincial courts to set their own threshold quantity of drugs for immediate execution based on 'the local crime situation of the province', and requiring judges to make judicial decisions on a case-to-case basis. These measures were typically effected by the Supreme People's Court by means of the issuance of judicial interpretations, handing down internal directives, and publishing 'guiding, typical and reference cases'.

After nearly fifteen years of continuous effort, the Chinese courts have succeeded in limiting the application of the death penalty to a much smaller range of drug crimes and far fewer categories of offenders. This has, to some extent, reversed China's hitherto extremely punitive criminal justice policy in dealing with drug-related offenders. The second part of the discussion will analyse in some detail the measures taken by the courts in limiting the application of the death penalty in drug-related criminal cases.

2.2 Judicial Control of the Death Penalty for Drug-Related Crimes

2.2.1 Redefining 'the Most Heinous Criminals': Who Should be Punished with Immediate Execution

In the vast majority, if not all, of the judicial interpretations and internal documents on the application of the death penalty, the Supreme People's Court urged lower court judges to 'treat different types of offenders differently' and be 'extremely cautious' in handing down a death sentence, to ensure that immediate execution is imposed only on 'a very small minority of the most heinous criminals'. To prevent the lower courts from interpreting 'the most heinous criminals' in an expansive manner, the '2008 Dalian Conference Minutes'[8] clearly enumerated the

[8] The full title of the '2008 Dalian Conference Summary' is 'Summary of the Work Conference on Trial of Drug Offence Cases in Selected Courts of the Country'. This judicial interpretation is commonly referred to in Chinese judicial practice as the '2008

following types of offenders who should be treated with relative severity: (1) professional drug traffickers; (2) recidivists, and habitual offenders; (3) principal offenders of joint crimes or leaders of organised criminal groups, who exhibit a high degree of subjective malice and whose actions have caused, particularly serious social harm; (4) offenders who smuggle drugs across the border, or who take part in organised cross-border drug smuggling or drug trafficking activities; (5) offenders who repeatedly sell large quantities of drugs, sell drugs to multiple persons, or induce multiple persons to take drugs; (6) offenders who resist lawful searches and arrests with the use of weapons or violence.[9]

To provide lower court judges with a better understanding of who should be executed and who should be spared in serious drug-related cases, the '2008 Dalian Conference Summary' and the '2015 Wuhan Conference Summary'[10] set out a series of aggravating and mitigating circumstances, and established the important sentencing principle that

Dalian Conference Summary'. For the full text of the '2008 Dalian Conference Summary', see www.pkulaw.com/chl/f278ab5d01b9428abdfb.html?keyword=&way=listView《全国部分法院审理毒品犯罪案件工作座谈会纪要》. The 'Dalian Conference Summary' and the subsequently mentioned 'Wuhan Conference Summary' are essentially judicial interpretations. In the PRC, judicial interpretations are authoritative explanations and clarifications of specific applications of legal issues in judicial practice. They are issued by the country's highest judicial authorities, namely the Supreme People's Court and the Supreme People's Procuratorate, based on the powers conferred by law. Only the Supreme People's Court and the Supreme People's Procuratorate have the authority to release judicial interpretations. These authorities can issue interpretations individually or jointly, addressing matters that involve the collaborative efforts of both institutions. They may also collaborate with other entities, such as the Political and Legal Affairs Committee, the Ministry of Justice, and the Ministry of Public Security to release relevant judicial interpretations. While judicial interpretations are not laws directly enacted by the legislative body, they carry legal force and provide specific interpretations within the existing legal framework regarding the meanings of legal provisions, their scope of application, and operational procedures. In China, judicial interpretations authorised by the legislative body (the National People's Congress and their Standing Committee) through a lawful process hold a status equivalent to laws and have a universal binding force nationwide. Judicial interpretations issued by the Supreme People's Court have a direct binding effect on the trial work of all levels of people's courts. This means that all lower courts should follow the interpretations of the Supreme People's Court when adjudicating individual cases. Similarly, judicial interpretations issued by the Supreme People's Procuratorate guide and constrain the work of procuratorates at various levels.

9 '2008 Dalian Conference Minutes', s. 2.

10 The full title of the '2015 Wuhan Conference Summary' is 'Summary of the Conference on Drug Offences Trials in all Courts of the Country'. This judicial interpretation is commonly referred to in China's judicial practice as the '2015 Wuhan Conference Summary'. For its full text, see www.pkulaw.com/chl/735e6374412f13b0bdfb.html?keyword=&way=listView《全国法院毒品犯罪审判工作座谈会纪要》.

judges should not take the quantity of drugs involved as the sole determining factor in sentencing, but should instead carefully weigh all possible mitigating and aggravating circumstances to assess whether the offender has 'demonstrated a high degree of subjective malice' and whether his actions have 'caused serious social harm'.[11] The aggravating circumstances that justify the death penalty, as set forth in the '2008 Dalian Conference Summary', include

(1) an offender who is the leader of a criminal gang, or who uses weapons to conceal drug-related offences, or who uses violence to resist inspection or apprehension, or who participates in organised international drug trafficking activities. Offenders in this category may be sentenced to death even if the total amount of drugs involved has not reached the threshold for execution;
(2) the overall quantity of drugs involved meets the threshold for execution, and the offender is a repeat offender of drug-related crimes, or uses or abets minors to smuggle, sell, transport or manufacture drugs, or sells drugs to minors;
(3) the overall quantity of drugs involved reaches the threshold for execution, and the offender has smuggled, sold, transported or manufactured drugs multiple times, or has trafficked drugs to multiple persons, or has induced other persons to take drugs, or has provided places for other persons to consume drugs in the course of committing a drug crime, or has trafficked drugs in drug rehabilitation center, or is a state employee who has used his official position or authority to commit drug-related crimes, a professional criminal, a recidivist or the principal offender of a joint crime;
(4) the overall quantity of drugs involved reaches the threshold for execution, and there are other aggravating circumstances;
(5) the overall quantity of drugs involved exceeds the threshold for execution, and there are no statutory or discretionary mitigating circumstances.

Compared with the sentencing practice in the 'Strike Hard' anti-crime campaign period, the perimeters of 'the most serious drug-related crimes' that may incur immediate execution have become clearer, and the scope of a lower court judges' discretion in death penalty decision-making has been narrowed. To encourage judges to treat the vast majority of

[11] '2008 Dalian Conference Summary', s. 2.

offenders in serious drug-related cases with relative leniency, the Supreme People's Court has listed a series of mitigating circumstances in detail in the '2008 Dalian Conference Summary' and the '2015 Wuhan Conference Summary', and made it clear that 'even if the overall quantity of drugs involved meets the threshold for execution, as long as there are one or more mitigating circumstances, judges can exempt the offender from the death penalty'. These mitigating circumstances have been frequently cited by lawyers in their defence briefs and by judges in their judgments as an important legal basis for avoiding the death penalty. The following is a summary and an analysis of the mitigating circumstances set out in the '2008 Dalian Conference Summary' and the '2015 Wuhan Conference Summary':

> (1) The offender has voluntarily surrendered to the police or has performed acts of merit, such as assisting the police in solving other criminal cases or in apprehending other criminal suspects, or has other mitigating circumstances provided for by law.

Under the 1997 Criminal Law, offenders who have surrendered or who have performed an 'act of merit' can be considered for a lighter punishment. However, the Criminal Law does not provide details on what constitutes 'surrender' and 'perform an act of merit'. The absence of detailed guidelines opened the way for inconsistency in determining voluntary surrender and performing a deed of merit within and across provinces. To address this issue, the Supreme People's Court issued an Opinion[12] in 2010, expanding the meaning of surrender and the 'act of merit' to include behaviours which were not recognised as such in the past, thereby further narrowing the scope of the use of the death penalty.

The circumstances that can currently be considered as 'voluntary surrender' include

> the perpetrator voluntarily reported the crime to the police, remained at the scene of the crime until the police arrived, and confessed to the crime when questioned by the police;

[12] The full title of this Opinion is *Zuigao renmin fayuan guanyu chuli zishou he ligong ruogan juti wenti de yijian* (The Supreme People's Court's Opinions on Several Specific Issues Concerning the Handling of Surrender and Meritorious Conduct). For details, see www.court.gov.cn/fabu/xiangqing/2484.html. Similar to the '2008 Dalian Conference Summary' and the '2015 Wuhan Conference Summary', this document is, in essence, a judicial interpretation issued by the Supreme People's Court. All lower courts must follow it when handling individual cases.

the perpetrator did not flee the scene of the crime or resist police apprehension after knowing that another person reported the crime to the police, and voluntarily confessed when questioned by the police;

the perpetrator voluntarily confessed while the police were still conducting a general investigation and had not yet identified a suspect;

the perpetrator voluntarily confessed to the crime when he was detained or arrested for commission of other offences;

the perpetrator voluntarily confessed when he was questioned by the police or other law enforcement agencies solely because of suspicious behaviour.

Judges were also encouraged to give offenders who involuntarily surrendered under certain circumstances the same treatment as those who voluntarily surrendered. For example, in dealing with cases where relatives of the offender assisted the police in arresting the offender, judges may impose a lighter punishment if the offender did not resist police arrest but voluntarily confessed to the crime. The Supreme People's Court has also lowered the requirement for a 'voluntary confession of guilt'. Here, 'guilt' refers only to the key facts of the crime. Even if the offender is unable to provide less important information such as his name, age, occupation, residential address, and so on, it does not affect the establishment of 'voluntary confession of guilt'.[13]

Similarly, the scope of an 'act of merit' has been expanded to include acts subsequent to the commission of the offence, such as persuading other suspects to come to a designated location by making phone calls or sending text messages, identifying other suspects on the spot, or assisting the police in making arrests by providing the police with the names, hiding places, and contact details of other suspects. When dealing with offenders who voluntarily surrender or who have done acts of merit, judges are required to be 'extremely cautious' in imposing the death penalty.[14] Only in an 'exceptionally' small minority of 'the most serious' cases, where the social harm caused by the crime is 'extremely grave', and

[13] The Supreme People's Court made these specific regulations because, in judicial practice, police officers and prosecutors often consider crime suspects and defendants who do not truthfully provide their name, age, occupation, and residential address as not voluntarily confessing.

[14] *Zuigao renmin fayuan guanyu chuli zishou he ligong ruogan juti wenti de yijian* (The Supreme People's Court's Opinions on Several Specific Issues Concerning the Handling of Surrender and Meritorious Conduct) and '2008 Dalian Conference Summary'.

the intent of the offender is 'extremely malicious', judges may consider immediate execution as a sentencing option.[15]

> (2) The quantity of drugs initially seized by the police did not reach the threshold for execution, and the offender, after being apprehended, confessed to the police that he had committed other undiscovered drug crimes. Acting on the offender's confession, the police seized more drugs. Eventually, the overall quantity of the drugs involved, exceeded the threshold for execution.
>
> (3) The drugs seized by the police have been identified as containing a very low drug content, and although the execution threshold in terms of quantity is technically met, the items concerned were adulterated with a large quantity of other non-drug substances; or, there is evidence indicating that the drugs were so adulterated with a large quantity of other non-drug substances to such an extent that it is not possible to determine the heroin content by means of the available identification techniques.

As mentioned earlier, Article 357 of the PRC Criminal Law explicitly specifies that the quantity of drugs involved is a decisive factor in sentencing. However, it does not stipulate whether judges should consider the purity of drugs during sentencing or to what extent they should take it into account. Prior to 2008, Chinese police officers, prosecutors, and judges, based on this legal provision, completely disregarded the purity of drugs involved when handling individual drug-related cases. During the investigation phase, police conduct qualitative tests only to determine the presence of drugs and identify the type of drugs. In the prosecution phase, prosecutors make sentencing recommendations based primarily on the quantity of drugs stated in the police investigation files.

[15] The death penalty with immediate execution and the death penalty with a two-year reprieve are two different methods of carrying out the death penalty in the PRC. Criminals sentenced to the death penalty with a two-year reprieve do not need to undergo review by the Supreme People's Court but are subject to review by a provincial-level court. Upon approval by the provincial-level court, the judgment of the death penalty with a two-year reprieve becomes effective, and the court sets a probationary period of two years for the criminal. If the criminal genuinely repents, after the expiration of the two years, his sentence will be commuted to life imprisonment. If there is genuine repentance and meritorious performance, after the two-year period, the criminal's sentence will be reduced to a fixed-term imprisonment of over fifteen years and up to twenty years. Once sentenced to the death penalty with a two-year reprieve, the criminal is highly likely to escape the fate of death. For criminals sentenced to the death penalty with immediate execution, their cases will be submitted to the Supreme People's Court for review. After the Supreme People's Court approves the sentence of immediate execution, the President of the Supreme People's Court will issue the order for execution. Upon receiving the execution order, lower courts must execute the criminals within seven days.

When judges determine the sentence, they only consider the total quantity of drugs involved and other sentencing factors, without taking into account the purity of the drugs (after all, there is no information regarding the purity of the drugs in the case materials). Despite the PRC Criminal Procedure Law granting the right to suspects or defendants, in case of objections to forensic examination conclusions, to apply for re-examination or supplementary examination to the public security organs, the procuratorates, and the courts responsible for the case, it is essential to note that such applications do not automatically trigger the process of re-examination or supplementary examination. The authority to decide whether to initiate such procedures remains firmly in the hands of the public security organs, the procuratorates, and the courts. Of course, these three criminal justice authorities also have the power to initiate the re-examination or supplementary examination procedure proactively. Unfortunately, in practice, whether initiated by the defendant's application or through the proactive exercise of power by these three criminal justice organs, the proportion of cases where the re-examination or supplementary examination procedure is actually carried out is very low.

There are three main reasons why the police, prosecutors, and judges focused only on the quantity of drugs. First, due to the vague sentencing provisions for drug-related crimes in the Criminal Law, prosecutors have significant discretion in seeking punishment, and judges enjoy considerable leeway in sentencing. Requiring prosecutors and judges at the local level to regard the overall quantity of drugs involved as a decisive sentencing factor may seem blunt, but it effectively prevented public perception of significant disparities in the types of penalties and lengths of sentences for defendants in different drug cases due to variations in drug purity. Such disparities might have otherwise led to public scepticism and criticism of the criminal justice authorities, thereby undermining the legitimacy of the Party. In addition, the Party-state had consistently adopted a policy of severely cracking down on drug crimes. By using the total quantity of drugs as the primary indicator to measure the societal harm of criminal behaviour and as a decisive factor in sentencing, the police, procuratorates, and courts could effectively prevent some criminals from evading stringent criminal sanctions by adding impurities to drugs in large quantities. This practice also allowed them to demonstrate their adherence to the Party policy in combating drug crimes. Second, in the real drug trade market in China, drugs are typically valued based on weight. In the view of the criminal justice authorities, the quantity of drugs more accurately reflected the market value of drugs and the illicit gains obtained or potentially obtainable by the suspect or defendant compared to the purity of drugs. Third, the cost of drug purity testing would have led to an increase in the investigation costs for the police. In China, qualitative analysis of poisons or drugs may require hundreds to thousands of Chinese Yuan, and more complex quantitative or compositional analysis would generate even greater additional expenses. For samples containing a mix of multiple drugs or complex components, the cost of conducting tests on them may well exceed tens of thousands of Yuan.

For the aforementioned reasons, in handling drug-related criminal cases, the three criminal justice authorities (the public security organs, the procuratorates, and the courts) tacitly focused only on the total quantity of drugs involved rather than purity. To bring down the execution number, the Supreme People's Court proactively broke this tacit understanding. In the '2008 Dalian Conference Summary', it explicitly required lower court judges, when adjudicating cases where the death penalty might be imposed, to take the purity of drugs into consideration. Even if the quantity of drugs involved reaches the statutory threshold for the death penalty, judges should exempt the defendant from death if there is evidence proving the actual or potential significant adulteration of drugs with non-drug substances. However, it is worth noting that this rule applies only to those cases where the defendants are facing the death penalty. For other ordinary drug-related cases, judges still make their sentencing decisions based on the quantity of drugs involved.

> (4)The drugs involved in the case is a new type of drug, which is used by a relatively small number of people and is relatively less harmful to the user.[16]
>
> (5) The quantity of the drugs seized meets the threshold for execution only because of the enticement of undercover enforcement agents.
>
> (6) In the case of drug trafficking, the overall quantity of drugs seized just reaches the threshold for execution, but the trafficker is also a drug user.[17]

[16] Unlike in some other jurisdictions, in the PRC, there is no classification of drugs based on their relative danger to those who use them in either the law or judicial interpretations.

[17] This situation is also known as 'quantity enticement' – the defendant would have committed the act of smuggling, manufacturing, trafficking, or transporting drugs even if he had not been induced to do so by an intelligence agent, but the quantity of the drugs involved would not have met the threshold for execution without the inducement of the

In the '2008 Dalian Conference Summary', this mitigating circumstance is expressed as 'the drug trafficker makes money by selling drugs and then uses that money to buy drugs for his own consumption'. In the '2015 Wuhan Conference Summary', this expression was changed to 'the drug dealer is also a drug user'. The reason for the change is that, in practice, it is much more difficult to prove the fact that 'the drug trafficker makes money by selling drugs and then used that money to buy drugs for his own consumption' than to prove the fact that 'the drug dealer is also a drug user'. To prove the latter, a simple blood or hair test on the drug dealer is all that is needed. After the '2015 Wuhan Conference Summary' was issued, this mitigating circumstance has been applied to an increasing number of drug trafficking cases, and many drug dealers who would have been executed in the past have escaped that fate.[18]

> (7) The overall quantity of the drugs seized just reaches the threshold for execution, but the offender is a first-time drug offender who has not caused any serious harm to anyone.
>
> (8) In the case of transporting drugs, if the overall quantity of the drugs seized exceeds the threshold for execution, but does not constitute a 'particularly large amount', and there is evidence that the offender is a first-time or occasional offender who is instructed or hired by others only to transport drugs, or if, on the basis of the available evidence, it is not possible to rule out the possibility of the offender being instructed or hired by another person only to transport the drug, judges should not sentence the offender to the death penalty with immediate execution.

This is a death penalty exemption rule specifically tailored for drug transporters by the Supreme People's Court. It was perfected through two revisions and played a crucial role in reducing the number of executions for drug trafficking crimes. The initial provision in the '2008 Dalian Conference Summary' stated that 'if the overall quantity of the drugs seized exceeds the threshold for execution, but does not constitute

undercover agent. In such cases, judges should not punish the defendant with immediate execution. There is also a situation called '*mens rea* enticement', which means that the defendant would not have had the intent to commit the crime in the first place if he had not been induced by the undercover agent. In cases of '*mens rea* enticement', judges are expected to find the defendant not guilty rather than convict and then give a lighter punishment. In dealing with those cases where the 'quantity enticement' or '*mens rea* enticement' can neither be proved nor ruled out, judges are required to 'leave some leeway' (留有余地) and exempt the defendant from execution.

[18] Li (2021).

a 'particularly large amount', and there is evidence that the offender is a first-time or occasional offender who is instructed or hired by others only to transport drugs, judges should not sentence the offender to the death penalty with immediate execution'. However, this provision remained inactive for a significant period after the release of the '2008 Dalian Conference Summary', with judges rarely invoking it as a basis for exempting defendants from the death penalty. The underlying reason was that Chinese police officers and prosecutors often prioritise seeking incriminating and aggravating evidence, paying less attention to potential exculpatory or mitigatory evidence. This is both a legacy of the 'Strike Hard' campaign and a consequence of the performance evaluation system within China's political–legal system. The prerequisite for judges to apply this rule, as clearly specified in the '2008 Dalian Conference Summary', is the existence of evidence indicating that the defendant is a first-time or occasional offender who was instructed or hired by others only to transport drugs. However, in reality, the prosecution lacked the incentive to collect such evidence and submit it to the court. There was even less motivation for the prosecution to persuade the court to apply this provision to spare the defendant from the death penalty. Therefore, if defendants wished the court to apply this provision and impose a lighter sentence, they must find ways to collect relevant evidence and submit it to the court themselves. The burden of proof, which should have been borne by the prosecution, had actually been shifted to the defence. The '2008 Dalian Conference Summary' provided a lifeline for drug transporters who are facing the death penalty, but it requires drug transporters to grasp this lifeline and rely on their own strength to climb up. In reality, unfortunately, the vast majority of drug transporters fail to do so and ultimately cannot escape the fate of being sentenced to death. Due to the high level of concealment involved in drug crimes, drug traffickers are very cautious to avoid leaving behind potentially 'tell-tale' evidence. Moreover, drug transporters typically have lower levels of education, leading to a lack of awareness in collecting and preserving evidence. Therefore, the vast majority of drug transporters are unable to provide evidence to prove that they have been instructed or hired solely to transport drugs.

This issue was quickly identified by the Supreme People's Court. To breathe life into this mitigating sentencing circumstance and make it effective in reducing the execution numbers in drug transportation cases, it added a clause in the '2015 Wuhan Conference Summary', allowing lower court judges to exempt drug transporters from immediate execution, 'as long as the prosecution evidence fails to rule out the possibility that the defendant was instructed or hired by others to merely transport drugs'. As a result, the burden of proof has been shifted back to the prosecution. Now, if prosecutors seek the death penalty for the defendant, they must provide sufficient and conclusive evidence to prove that there is no possibility that the offender is a 'drug mule' who is hired or instructed by others to merely transport drugs. Otherwise, the court will not support the prosecution's request for immediate execution of the offender and will impose a lighter sentence.

The vast majority of 'drug mules' or drug transporters in China are marginalised and vulnerable people with low education, no stable income, and who live under poor economic conditions.[19] The very low returns they receive for transporting drugs are clearly disproportionate to the enormous risks they have to bear. To punish them with severity, and even the death penalty, is clearly contrary to the principles of proportionality and fairness. Based on such considerations, in the '2015 Wuhan Conference Summary', the Supreme People's Court further clarifies that 'judges should generally not impose the death penalty with immediate execution on those offenders who passively participated in drug crimes, who played a subordinate or assisting role, and who received relatively small rewards'.

It is also common in reality that criminal groups often hire multiple individuals to transport the same batch of drugs. They assign each transporter to be responsible for transporting a portion of the drugs, aiming to avoid the police seizing all the drugs in one fell swoop. The drug transporters hired may not have any communication or cooperation with each other, or even be aware of each other's existence.[20] However, prior to 2008, when dealing with such cases, many judges tended to treat such cases as joint crimes, ruling that each transporter was responsible for the entire quantity of drugs involved, rather than for the portion of drugs they actually transported. To correct this way of thinking, the '2015 Wuhan Conference Summary' explicitly enjoins judges to accurately ascertain the division of labour between different drug transporters, the precise role each play, the extent of their respective involvement in the crime, and whether there is substantial cooperation

19 Chen (2009).

20 Each transporter may pick up the drugs at different times and deliver them to different locations.

between them. It also requires judges to be 'extremely cautious in executing more than one drug trafficker in the same case'.[21]

According to incomplete statistics, more than 70 per cent of all drug-related cases heard by courts in Yunnan province over the past fifteen years have been drug transporting cases, and the percentage may be higher in other parts of China.[22] The widespread application of this mitigatory circumstance has played a crucial role in bringing down the execution number for drug-related crimes in China.

> (9)In the case of a joint crime, when the overall quantity of the drugs seized just reaches the threshold for execution, and each offender plays an almost identical role in the crime or it is difficult to ascertain the exact proportion of criminal responsibility of each of the offenders ought to bear, judges should not impose a death sentence with immediate execution upon any of the offenders.
>
> (10)In the case of joint crimes, if it is possible to distinguish between principals and accomplices, judges shall not, simply because the quantity of drugs involved is particularly large, conclude that all the offenders are principals and impose relatively heavy penalties, even the death penalty; if all co-offenders are of equal status and play a similar role, or if the degree of culpability of each offender is indistinguishable from the other, judges can exempt all the offenders from immediate execution; if the culpability of the two principal offenders is very serious and they both have the legally stipulated aggravating circumstances, judges must carefully compare their respective subjective intents and motives and the likelihood of recidivism, and be 'particularly cautious' in imposing the death penalty with immediate execution upon both principals; if the offender apprehended does not deserve to be executed, judges should not sentence him to death simply because the other co-offender who should be executed has not been apprehended; if it is difficult to accurately determine the degree of culpability of the apprehended offender and the co-offender who has not been apprehended, judges should not impose the death penalty upon the offender apprehended; if a number of persons from the same family commit a joint offence and the offender who played a major role has been sentenced to the death penalty with immediate execution, the other offenders who played a minor or assisting role, and who are less culpable can be exempted from execution.

The reason why the Supreme People's Court has been so meticulous about the application of the death penalty in joint drug-related cases is its policy to completely change the prevailing 'kill more and kill swiftly'

[21] '2015 Wuhan Conference Summary', s. 4.

[22] Li (2021).

mindset of the lower courts in handling serious joint drug-related cases, a legacy of the 'Strike Hard' anti-crime campaign. During the 'Strike Hard' period, the usual practice of judges in dealing with joint drug-related cases in which the principals were not apprehended was to execute the apprehended non-principal offenders, as long as the total quantity of drugs involved meets the threshold for execution.[23] Similarly, lower court judges, when dealing with cases of joint offences in which the total quantity of drugs involved is 'extremely large', also tended to execute all the offenders without distinguishing between principal and non-principal offenders.[24]

To promote a 'kill less' atmosphere in the lower courts and to standardise judicial practice in handling joint drug-related criminal cases, the Supreme People's Court established a new sentencing principle in both the '2008 Dalian Conference Summary' and the '2015 Wuhan Conference Summary', namely, that judges must classify multiple offenders into different grades according to the degree of their culpability and reserve immediate execution only for the principal offenders of joint crimes and the leaders of criminal groups, including those who supply drugs or facilitate the purchase of drugs, those who initiate, plan, or arrange drug-related criminal activities, and those who hire or direct others to participate in drug-related crimes. It also urges lower court judges to be 'extremely cautious' in executing more than one offender in the same joint drug-related case; even if the overall quantity of drugs involved is 'extremely large', 'executing more than one offender in the same case should be the exception, not the rule'.[25]

From 2007 to 2015, until now, the Supreme People's Court's position and attitude toward the application of the death penalty in drug-related crimes has been clear and consistent, that is, 'when there is a choice to kill or not to kill, always choose not to kill'. This position and attitude of the Supreme People's Court was promptly adopted by lower court judges and reflected in the outcome of one drug-related criminal case after another; after all, the exclusive power to review and approve all death penalty cases across the country rests firmly in the hands of the Supreme People's Court. As is declared by Liu Jiachen, the former Deputy President of the Supreme People's Court in charge of criminal trials, by gaining the power to review and confirm all death sentences in China, the Supreme People's

23 Ibid.
24 Chen and Huang (2007).
25 '2015 Wuhan Conference Summary', s. 4.

Court has 'grabbed the horse (institution of punishment) by the hairs of its head so the rest of the body has no choice but to be dragged along (牵一发而动全身)'.[26]

2.2.2 *Raising the Threshold Quantity of Drugs Triggering Execution in Practice*

According to the PRC Criminal Law, the threshold quantity of drugs bringing the death penalty into play is 50 g. Offenders who smuggle, traffic, transport, or manufacture more than 50 g of heroin or amphetamine can be sentenced to over fifteen years' imprisonment, life imprisonment, or to death.[27] Since 2007, with the Supreme People's Court exercising exclusive authority to review and approve all death penalty cases across the country, much stricter conditions have been applied in confirming death sentences. As has been observed by many scholars, judges and lawyers, the Supreme People's Court, in the past five years, has rarely approved cases where the amount of heroin or amphetamines seized was less than 1 kg, and there were no aggravating circumstances.[28] Meanwhile, the Supreme People's Court has encouraged provincial courts to set their own benchmark so as to 'fit the local crime situations of the province'.[29] In general, the more rampant the drug crime, the higher the threshold quantity. In inland provinces with relatively low drug crime rates, such as Henan and Hubei, 300–500 g is routinely used as the benchmark for execution, while in drug crime prevalent provinces such as Guangdong and Guangxi, the figure increases to 1–2 kg; in Yunnan, China's top drug crime province, the benchmark is further raised to 3 kg.[30] Even within Yunnan province, the benchmark varies

[26] Xinhua News (2007).

[27] 1997 Criminal Law, Article 347.

[28] Hu and Chen (2020); Wang and Shao (2021); Li (2021); Zhang (2023).

[29] Supreme People's Court (2015).

[30] The rationale for this policy is that, in China, the death penalty has limited deterrent effects in regions with a high incidence of drug crimes, particularly in the southwestern parts near Myanmar, Laos, and Vietnam, where there are diverse ethnic populations and economic underdevelopment. Residents in these areas often face difficulties in employment and struggle with meagre daily labour income. Engaging in drug trafficking or manufacturing activities allows them to gain economic benefits far exceeding those of conventional jobs. The allure of substantial profits motivates many individuals to take the risky path of participating in such illegal activities, even at the cost of their lives. The drug crimes in these regions are intricately woven into the local social structure and cultural background, giving rise to a unique subculture of crime. In this environment, many

greatly from region to region, for example, in Xishuangbanna, which has a large ethnic minority population and is close to Myanmar, the benchmark is observed to be much higher than that of Kunming, the capital city of Yunnan province. In Xishuangbanna, trafficking even more than 5 kg of drugs does not necessarily incur the death penalty with immediate execution unless there are aggravating circumstances provided by law or judicial interpretation.

It is worth noting that the benchmarks in the same region or province are not fixed. China's local courts dynamically adjust the benchmark for execution according to the incidence of serious drug crimes in the region and the national criminal justice policy to avoid handing down too many death sentences, which might be overturned by provincial courts or disapproved by the Supreme People's Court. In China, death penalty decisions are not made by the judges handling the cases but are collectively determined by the Adjudication Committee of the court, which consists of the court president, vice president, division chief, vice division chief, and several senior judges.[31] In many cases, the court president may set the tone before the Adjudication Committee begins its deliberations

villagers have developed a high degree of numbness to the potential legal consequences of being sentenced to life imprisonment or the death penalty. Moreover, in China, criminal organisations involved in drug trafficking and manufacturing often have a tight organisational structure and a powerful network of personal connections locally, which can provide protection and a 'safety guarantee' for individuals involved in drug crimes. This easily leads villagers to develop a sense of luck, believing that they would not be easily caught by the police and sentenced to death by the court. In many regions, there is an unwritten rule that if the arrested criminals remain silent, taking sole responsibility for their crimes without revealing information about accomplices or crime organisation leaders, their families will receive financial compensation and ongoing livelihood support from the drug trafficking organisation. Therefore, there is a prevalent notion in many high-incidence drug crime areas in China that 'one person trafficking drugs, the entire family becoming wealthy'. Some villagers even feel proud as they believe they have secured a stable future for their families by sacrificing their lives. The results of China's 'Strike Hard' campaigns also demonstrate that relying solely on severe punishment, such as large-scale executions, cannot effectively curb the occurrence of drug crimes. Drug crime is fundamentally a complex social problem that requires a comprehensive strategy of social governance to address. Given the substantial number of drug crime cases and the consistently high annual count of executions in southwestern regions like Yunnan, the Supreme People's Court encourages lower courts to set their own threshold quantity of drugs for the death penalty based on the local drug-crime situation rather than uniformly applying statutory thresholds (50g) to reduce the overall execution number in China.

31 According to 'Interpretation of the Criminal Procedural Law', Article 178, issued by the Supreme People's Court, which is also a judicial interpretation that all courts in China must comply with, 'in cases where the death penalty (including death sentence with a two-year reprieve and death sentence with immediate execution) may be applied, the

or make the final decision when the Adjudication Committee cannot reach a unanimous opinion. In reality, the Adjudication Committee is strongly motivated to be prudent in making every death penalty decision because a revision by the provincial court or disapproval by the Supreme People's Court will have a negative impact on the performance assessment and ranking of the local court in the entire judicial system. This, in turn, affects the amount of year-end bonus for all judges in the court and the promotion prospects of the court's leaders. The Supreme People's Court may also select some cases where the death sentences are overturned or disapproved, to use as negative examples in the internal reference case compilations of the judicial system to instruct all lower courts 'under what circumstances the death penalty should not be imposed'. This is also something that the leadership and senior judges of each local court actively seek to avoid.

2.2.3 Establishing New Requirements for the Purity of Drugs

Prior to 2008, the total quantity of drugs involved was taken by Chinese lower court judges as the most important determinant of sentencing, while their purity was often overlooked.[32] When dealing with drug smuggling, manufacturing, trafficking or transport cases, as long as the total quantity of drugs involved meets the threshold for execution set out in the Criminal Law, judges are inclined to execute the offender even if the heroin content of the seized drugs is as low as 1 per cent.[33] Many drug traffickers and transporters often mix other non-drug substances with the drugs to change the physical form of the drugs and to increase the weight so as to avoid suspicion and to reap more profits. This occurs mostly in cross-border drug trafficking or transport situations. In some cases, the offenders dissolved heroin into red wine. When dealing with such cases, the usual practice of the police and judges was to consider the whole bottle of red wine as drugs and the weight of the red wine (liquid) as the quantity of the drugs involved. This resulted in the execution of many who did not really deserve the death penalty. This practice has been fundamentally changed since the issuance of the '2008 Dalian Conference Summary'. In this document, the Supreme People's Court,

collegiate panel should request the court president to submit it to the Adjudication Committee for discussion and decision'.

[32] Li (2021).

[33] Zhao and Li (2011). A similar observation was made by Li (2021).

for the first time, explicitly required lower court judges to ensure that the purity of the drugs involved is tested and confirmed by a legally authorised identification agent when dealing with cases in which the offender may be sentenced to death.[34]

For drugs with a heroin content of less than 25 per cent, judges are required to convert them to drugs with a heroin content of 25 per cent when calculating the total weight of the drugs.[35] The conversion formula is as follows: The quantity of drugs used for the purpose of the sentencing threshold = The total weight of drugs seized × The purity of heroin (X per cent) ÷ 25 per cent. For example, if the weight of the drugs seized is 1 kg, but the heroin content is only 1 per cent, the relevant weight is 40 g (1,000 × 0.01 ÷ 0.25). After conversion, the total quantity of drugs involved in the case is below the threshold quantity for execution as stipulated in the Criminal Law (50 g), and the offender should, therefore, be exempted from being sentenced to death.

In addition, the '2008 Dalian Conference Summary' also requires judges to exclude the waste generated in the drug manufacturing process when determining the total quantity of drugs for the death penalty threshold.[36] The practice of the police used to be to include the weight of all solid and liquid waste seized at the crime scene.[37] The incentives were such that the greater the quantity of drugs seized, the more honours and monetary rewards the public security organs would receive from the local government and the local party committee, and the more likely it would be that the leaders of the public security organ would be promoted. That is why, in the vast majority of drug manufacturing cases, the quantity of drugs reportedly involved easily exceeded 100 kg, which constitutes an 'extremely large' quantity of drugs (毒品数额特别巨大), and the offenders accused of drug manufacturing rarely escaped the fate of execution.[38]

To address this issue, the '2008 Dalian Conference Summary' stipulated in no uncertain terms for the first time that drug manufacturing waste, whether solid or liquid, which is too low in heroin content to be further extracted or refined as heroin, should not be included in the total

[34] '2008 Dalian Conference Summary', s. 5.

[35] It is an accepted practice by China's criminal justice institutions that when the drugs contain 25 per cent heroin, it can be deemed as pure heroin.

[36] '2008 Dalian Conference Summary', s. 4.

[37] Li (2021).

[38] Ibid.

weight of drugs involved. The threshold is set at less than 2 per cent by the Supreme People's Court, after conducting a year-long field study across the country which found that once the heroin content of the drug manufacturing waste is below 2 per cent, it is almost impossible, with the current technology available, to refine or extract heroin from it. Such drug manufacturing waste would not cause any harm to society and, therefore, should not and need not be recognised as drugs.[39] As has been observed by many judges and lawyers, this rule has played a critical role in reducing the number of executions in drug manufacturing cases.[40]

2.2.4 Developing New Rules on Determining Awareness of the Presence of Drugs

The defendant's full knowledge of the presence of drugs during the commission of the offence ought to be a necessary condition for a conviction. However, prior to 2008, neither the police nor the procuratorates was required to provide sufficient evidence to prove that a suspect or defendant had full knowledge that the items he was allegedly smuggling, manufacturing, selling, or transporting were drugs. Once the police had intercepted a drug shipment and apprehended the suspect, the courts tended to presume that the suspect had full knowledge of the presence of drugs, even if the suspect argued strenuously that he was deceived by others. From a large number of published judgments, we can see that in most, if not all, such cases, the courts have sided with the police and the procuratorates.[41] This practice is likely to have led to wrongful convictions and executions. To address this issue, the Supreme People's Court in the '2008 Dalian Conference Minutes' explicitly required judges of lower courts, when determining whether a defendant was fully aware of the presence of drugs, to carefully examine the relevant evidence to identify the process and manner in which the defendant committed the crime and the relevant circumstances at the time of the seizure of the drugs, and to take into serious consideration the

[39] Supreme People's Court (2018). *Criminal Trial Reference* is the only publication sponsored by the Supreme People's Court to guide the criminal trial work of all courts throughout the country.

[40] Wei (2018); Yu (2021); Li (2021).

[41] For details, search relevant cases on China Judgments Online: https://wenshu.court.gov.cn. A similar observation was made by Zhao (2023).

defendant's age, previous life experience, and level of intelligence, rather than relying solely on the defendant's confessions.[42]

To limit the relatively broad discretion that the local judges have in determining the knowledge, the '2008 Dalian Conference Minutes' listed the following ten situations in which 'the judge may presume that the defendant has full knowledge of the presence of drugs'. But there are two important prerequisites for such a presumption: first, the defendant cannot provide a reasonable explanation, and second, there is no evidence indicating that the defendant has been deceived by others.

These circumstances are as follows:

(1) When conducting an inspection at ports, airports, stations or other inspection sites, law enforcement officers requested the perpetrator to declare the items he was carrying for others and other items suspected of being drugs, and informed him of his legal responsibilities, but the perpetrator failed to make a truthful declaration, and the officers subsequently seized drugs in the items he was carrying;
(2) The perpetrator evaded customs or border control inspection by means which include a false declaration, concealment, or disguise, and law enforcement officers subsequently seized drugs in the items carried, transported or mailed by the perpetrator;
(3) In the course of inspection by law enforcement officers, the perpetrator fled, discarded items, evaded or resisted inspection, and law enforcement officers subsequently seized drugs from the items he is was carrying or discarding;
(4) The perpetrator concealed drugs in his body or in a hidden place close to his person;
(5) The perpetrator carried or transported items for others for a disproportionately high reward and law enforcement officers seized drugs from the items carried or transported by the perpetrator;
(6) The perpetrator carried or transported items in a highly concealed manner, and law enforcement officers seized drugs from the items carried or transported by the perpetrator;
(7) The perpetrator handed over the items to another person in a highly concealed manner which is clearly different from the usual way of handing over legitimate items, and law enforcement officers subsequently seized drugs from the items;

[42] '2008 Dalian Conference Summary', s. 5.

(8) The perpetrator's movements intentionally bypassed inspection sites, and law enforcement officers subsequently seized drugs in the items carried or transported by the perpetrator;
(9) The perpetrator checked in baggage under a false identity or address, and law enforcement officers seized drugs in the items checked in by the perpetrator;
(10) There was other evidence sufficient to prove that the perpetrator actually knew of the presence of the drugs.

Local courts and their judges have taken a relatively cautious approach in finding that 'the defendant has no knowledge of the presence of drugs'. Once the court has found that the defendant did not know of the existence of the drugs, it must find that the defendant did not have criminal intent, and this would result in an acquittal. Such a verdict would have been highly likely to provoke strong resentment from the police and the procuratorates, a situation Chinese courts and judges have tried to avoid. After the issuance of the '2015 Wuhan Conference Minutes', many Chinese courts and judges have adopted a compromise approach in determining whether a defendant was aware of the presence of drugs – as long as the defendant is able to provide a reasonable explanation or evidence to prove that there is a possibility that he had been deceived by another person, the court will exempt the defendant from the death penalty and give him a relatively lenient punishment. In recent years, however, even in the face of enormous pressure from the police and the procuratorates, some local courts have followed the legal rules and principles strictly and have found the defendant not guilty on the grounds of the defendant's lack of awareness of the presence of drugs.[43] But more courts have chosen to communicate privately with prosecutors to persuade them to withdraw their cases when the available evidence is insufficient to rule out the possibility that the defendant had been deceived by others, so as to avoid direct conflict with the procuratorates.[44]

Among all cases of acquittal, the most representative ones are the *Luo Xiaolin* case[45] and the *Mo Weiqi* case.[46] The defendants in both cases gave a reasonable explanation and provided circumstantial evidence of

[43] For further details of acquittal cases, see https://china.findlaw.cn/bianhu/sixingbianhu/gaipan/11068.html.
[44] Li (2021).
[45] See note 43.
[46] For further details, see www.chinanews.com/sh/news/2008/10-17/1415348.shtml.

deception and concealment by others. They were eventually acquitted by the court. In the *Luo Xiaolin case*, the police found 5,589 g of methamphetamine from the defendant's private car, but the defendant insisted that he knew nothing about it. Before the court, the defendant gave an explanation that he had lent his car to a friend for three days and it was highly likely that his friend had hidden the drugs in his car without his knowledge. In support of the defendant's claim, the defence lawyer submitted a notice of speeding penalty for *Luo Xiaolin*'s vehicle and a photo taken by a road camera a few days before the police search. The photo showed that the defendant was not in the car and the car was driven by someone else. The Yunnan Higher People's Court acquitted the defendant on the grounds of 'unclear facts and insufficient evidence'. The *Luo Xiaolin* case was later included in the 'Criminal Trial Reference' issued by the Supreme People's Court and has been frequently cited by defence lawyers.

In the *Mo Weiqi* case, the defendant, a migrant worker from Hunan, was hired by a businessman to transport jade samples from Yunnan province to Hunan province for a total of 10 days and was paid Renminbi (RMB) 100 (approximately USD 14) per day. During a baggage check at the airport, the defendant was found to be in possession of 1,027 g of heroin in a compartment of his baggage. The Dehong Intermediate People's Court, the court of first instance, sentenced the defendant to the death penalty with immediate execution. The defendant appealed to the Yunnan Higher People's Court. The Yunnan Higher People's Court, taking into account the fact that the defendant's fingerprints had not been found on the packaging of the drugs and that the defendant had not been overpaid (or even paid less than the market price for transporting legitimate goods), ultimately found the defendant not guilty on the grounds that the evidence was insufficient to prove that the defendant had full knowledge of the presence of drugs. Before receiving the not-guilty verdict, the defendant had been kept in custody for 451 days.

In another drug transportation case,[47] the defendant repeatedly claimed that he was only transporting a bag to his hometown for a friend who told him that the luggage contained a local specialty food item only, so he never opened the bag and was completely unaware that there were drugs in the bag. To counter this, the prosecutor presented ample evidence that the defendant took a detour during the drive, choosing a

[47] For details of the case, see the official website of the Tianjin No.1 Procuratorate: www.yftianjin.jcy.gov.cn/lldy/201507/t20150721_1643527.shtml.

much longer and more remote road and that he had hardly rested during the six-hour-long drive. The prosecutor submitted that the defendant had chosen to take the long detour in order to avoid police inspection, and, therefore, it could be presumed that the defendant knew that the luggage he transported contained drugs, based on circumstance (2) set out in the '2015 Wuhan Conference Summary'. The defendant offered a reasonable explanation for the detour – as it was during the National Day holiday, and the highway was very congested, the defendant chose a more remote road. Moreover, the defendant argued, there had been no fixed checkpoints on the more direct road, so the defendant could not foresee that the police would check vehicles passing along that road, so circumstance (2) should not apply. Since the defendant provided a reasonable explanation for the detour which convinced the court that he had no intention of bypassing the checkpoint, the court sentenced him to a suspended sentence for a period of time exactly equal to the time he had spent in detention prior to the trial, which is equivalent to a judgment of acquittal in China's judicial practice.

2.2.5 *Impose Heavier Burden of Proof on the Prosecution*

The three waves of the 'Strike Hard' anti-crime campaign have created a considerable number of wrongful convictions and executions,[48] seriously undermining the credibility of China's judicial system and even the legitimacy of the Party-state. To address this issue and restrict the use of the death penalty, the Supreme People's Court and some provincial courts have, since 2007, issued a series of judicial interpretations and internal directives to raise the standard of proof for both conviction in serious criminal cases and the application of the death penalty. Compared with the situation in the 1990s and early 2000s, Chinese courts have become more assertive and demanding as a result of institutional maturity and professional development. They are demanding more and better evidence from the prosecution. As a result, the public security organs and the procuratorates have to improve the quality of their evidence to meet the courts' requirements. Compared to the past, when dealing with potential death penalty cases, the public security organs and procuratorates bear a heavier burden of proof in persuading the courts to hand down a guilty verdict, and, in particular, a death sentence with immediate execution.

[48] Mühlhahn (2009).

In 2010, the Supreme People's Court, together with five other state organs, issued two important legal documents, namely, the '2010 Death Penalty Evidence Rules'[49] and the '2010 Provisions on Eliminating Illegally Obtained Evidence'.[50] In the 'Death Penalty Evidence Rules', the Supreme People's Court set a much higher standard of proof for death penalty-eligible cases than for ordinary criminal cases. It requires judges to ensure the case facts are ascertained based on conclusive and sufficient evidence. Here, 'conclusive and sufficient' means: (1) that all facts used for conviction and sentence are supported by evidence; (2) that all the evidence used for conviction and sentence has been verified for its authenticity and legality through a series of statutory procedures, including the presentation and scrutiny of evidence from both the prosecution and defence and the court's own investigation; (3) that there is no contradiction between the evidence and the facts of the case, or even if there is a contradiction, it has been reasonably explained or resolved; (4) the status and roles of the various defendants in a joint criminal offence have been ascertained; (5) the use of evidence to ascertain the facts of the case is in accordance with the laws of logic and experience, and the conclusions drawn from the evidence are conclusive, and, in particular, if the evidence consists only of the defendant's self-incriminating statement, a guilty verdict cannot be rendered.

In addition, the evidence used to prove the following facts must also be beyond reasonable doubt: (1) that a crime was committed; (2) that the crime was committed by the defendant, including the time, place, method, and consequences caused by the defendant; (3) aspects of the defendant's identity that may affect conviction and sentencing, such as whether the defendant is underage, a pregnant woman, a state employee, military personnel, or has committed the crime during probation or parole; (4) that the defendant is capable of bearing criminal responsibility, including the absence of a mental illness that completely impairs his ability to recognise or control his own behaviour, and he has reached the legally specified age (according to the PRC Criminal Law, if accused of drug trafficking, the defendant must be at least fourteen years old; for other drug-related offences, the defendant must be at least sixteen years old); (5) that the defendant, and not the victim, was at fault; (6) the defendant's precise role in the joint crime relied upon by the court; and (7) the mitigating or aggravating factors relied upon by the court.

[49] Supreme People's Court *et al.* (2010).
[50] Ibid.

To convict a defendant in the absence of direct evidence, judges are required to ensure that the following conditions are met: (1) all circumstantial evidence used to convict has been verified; (2) all circumstantial evidence used to convict corroborates each other and there are no contradictions that cannot be satisfactorily resolved; (3) the circumstantial evidence used to convict is sufficient to prove beyond reasonable doubt; (4) the circumstantial inferences drawn are compelling and beyond all reasonable doubt; and (5) the reasoning is in accordance with logic and empirical judgement. If the procuratorates fail to provide sufficient and solid evidence to meet the standard of proof, judges are required to exercise their power to deliver a verdict of acquittal or exempt the defendant from being executed.

The Supreme People's Court has also developed a series of evidential rules specifically for drug-related death penalty cases and enjoined the police and the prosecution to follow them. For instance, the 'Rules on the Procedures of Drugs Extraction, Seizure, Weighing, Sampling and Sending for Test in the Handling of Drug-related Cases'[51] issued by the Supreme People's Court, together with the Supreme People's Procuratorate and the Ministry of Public Security in 2016, clearly stipulates that the court and the procuratorates have the authority to review the legality of the process of extracting, seizing, weighing, and taking samples of drugs, as well as the sending of drugs for testing by the police. If the court or the procuratorates, after review, considers that there are flaws in the procedure that may seriously affect the conviction and sentence, they must request the police to make corrections or provide reasonable explanations. If the police fail to make corrections or give reasonable explanations, the evidence gathered in accordance with the flawed procedures cannot be used as the basis for conviction and sentencing.

Although remaining relatively weak in China's criminal justice system, the courts have stood firm by the legal rules in a number of drug-related cases, exempting the defendants from immediate execution on the

[51] The full title of its document is *Banli dupin fanzui anjian dupintiqu, kouya, chengliang, quyang he songjian chengxu ruogan wenti de guiding*. For its full text, see www.pkulaw.com/chl/fd3392598c850fd0bdfb.html?keyword=&way=listView《办理毒品犯罪案件毒品提取、扣押、称量、取样和送检程序若干问题的规定》. Similar to the 'Dalian Conference Summary' and the 'Wuhan Conference Summary', this document is also a judicial interpretation. According to China's political conventions, since this judicial interpretation is jointly issued by the Supreme People's Court, the Supreme People's Procuratorate, and the Ministry of Public Security, all levels of courts, procuratorates, and public security agencies in China must adhere to the provisions of this document.

grounds of irregularities in the process of weighing, seizing, and sampling drugs, as well as the sending the drugs for testing. For instance, the 'Rules on the Procedures of Drugs Extraction, Seizure, Weighing, Sampling and Sending for Test in the Handling of Drug-related Cases' requires the inclusion of the record of the investigating police officers collecting evidence and the inventory of seized drugs. Additionally, the seal of each bag used to contain seized drugs must be signed and stamped by three persons – the investigator, the suspect, and the witness. The absence of a suspect's or witness's signature may raise questions about the origin of the drugs. There was a case in 2020 in which the police seized five bags of methamphetamine tablets with similar outer packaging in different karaoke television (KTV) rooms and brought them back to the police station in one large bag. Since there were no signatures of suspects or witnesses on each of the sachets, the police were unable to determine the quantity of drugs each suspect was responsible for. During the court hearing, a heated debate erupted between the prosecution and defence, and the presiding judge had to adjourn the trial. With the judgment deadline approaching, the presiding judge eventually chose to communicate with the responsible prosecutor in private and convinced him to drop the charges through subtle pressure.

Other procedural irregularities that often occur in the handling of drug-related cases by the police include these situations: the electronic precision scales used for weighing the drugs involved was not regularly tested and maintained; the needle of the electronic scales was not reset to zero or there is no evidence to prove that the needle of the electronic scale was reset to zero before the drugs were weighed; the electronic scales was not placed on a horizontal floor when the drugs were weighed; the police stored the drugs in a warehouse after seizure and did not send them for testing within a specified period of time (within 3–5 days), resulting in reasonable doubt that the drugs may have been contaminated; when taking samples of liquid drugs, the police did not stir the drugs beforehand or only took the surface part of the liquid drugs as test samples without taking the middle and bottom parts of the liquid at the same time, resulting in the purity test results of the drugs being higher than the actual purity of the drugs; the police did not strictly follow the regulations on the proper storage of drugs after seizure, resulting in changes in the colour (e.g., from white to yellowish) and form (e.g., from powder to crystal) of the drugs, and the police are unable to provide a reasonable explanation, making it impossible to ascertain that the seized drugs were the same drugs as those sent for testing. When dealing with cases with such procedural irregularities, the vast majority of judges in the lower courts, while not daring to acquit, did not hesitate to exempt the defendants from immediate execution.[52]

2.3 Conclusion

Over the past fifteen years, despite being challenged and criticised from time to time by the public security organs (the police), the procuratorates, and even the political–legal committees for not being tough enough on drug crimes, the Supreme People's Court has consistently adhered to the 'kill less and kill cautiously' principle. It has developed innovative strategies to restrict and reduce the use of the death penalty in drug-related crimes. After the exclusive power to review and approve all death penalty cases across the country was handed back from the provincial court to the Supreme People's Court, courts and judges at the lower levels have quickly changed their 'strike hard' mindset of adjudication, handling the vast majority of criminal cases in strict accordance with the legal rules and the Supreme People's Court's directives (with the exception of serious violent crimes that have sparked public outrage nationwide),[53] individualizing the punishment for each offender, and flexibly using death sentence with two years' reprieve as an alternative to immediate execution. Through these unremitting efforts, the judiciary eventually succeeded in limiting the application of the death penalty to a very small number of drug offenders. It is fair to say that the substantial reduction of the application of the death penalty in China over the past fifteen years has been achieved mainly through judicial control rather than legislative changes.

At present, 'enhancing the substantiveness of trials'[54] and further reducing the number of death penalty cases have become an important

[52] Li (2021).

[53] Similar to many countries around the world, only a very small number of the most serious violent crimes, where the defendant employs extremely cruel methods resulting in the death of the victim, can trigger nationwide public outrage in China. When dealing with such cases, the court often faces significant pressure from the general public. Lacking independence, it is very difficult for the court to stand firm by the legal rules and spare the life of the defendant. The most representative examples are the *Li Changkui* case and the *Yao Jiaxin* case. For more details on these two cases, see https://baike.baidu.com/item/李昌奎案/9000529?fr=ge_ala and https://baike.baidu.com/item/药家鑫案?fromModule=lemma_search-box.

[54] In July 2016, the Supreme People's Court, the Supreme People's Procuratorate, the Ministry of Public Security, the Ministry of State Security, and the Ministry of Justice jointly issued a judicial interpretation titled '*Guanyu tuijin yi shenpan wei zhognxin de*

reform goal for China's judiciary. Li Xiao, head of the Research Office of the Supreme People's Court, delivered a speech at a press conference in June 2021, in which she emphasised that the following:

> Chinese courts will continue to adhere to the policy of 'retaining the death penalty, strictly controlling the death penalty, and applying the death penalty with caution', and ensure that the death penalty is only applied to a very small number of criminals who have committed extremely serious crimes that were highly detrimental to society, and that the evidence in whose case is sufficient and conclusive……[t]he court will make every death penalty case an 'iron case' (in which the findings of the fact and the application of the law are correct), so that the people can feel fairness and justice in every case and in every decision made by people's courts.[55]

The reform goals of the judiciary have been endorsed by the Party, largely accepted by the major stakeholders in the criminal justice system, including the police, and embraced by lawyers, and have gradually obtained the understanding of the general public. China's top leader, Xi Jinping, delivered a speech at the 35th Collective Study Session of the Political Bureau of the 19th Central Committee in December 2021, in which he stressed that:

> [p]arty organisations and leading cadres at all levels should unequivocally support the independent exercise of power by judicial organs in accordance with the law, and never allow cadres' interference with judicial organs' handling of individual cases.[56]

In the report of the 20th Party Congress in 2022, Xi Jinping again emphasised that 'we must build a modern socialist country on the track of the rule of law'.[57] As the Party-state remains committed to relying on

xingshi susong zhidu gaige de yijian (Opinions on Promoting the Reform of China's Criminal Procedure with Trial as the Center). This document clarifies the requirements for 'enhancing the substantiveness of trials', emphasising that the presentation of evidence, cross-examination, and debate by both the prosecution and defence should take place during the trial. The judge should ascertain the facts of the case during the trial, and the judge's decision on conviction and sentencing should be formed during the trial. The reform for 'substantive trials' aims to ensure that the courtroom is a crucial venue for judging the authenticity of evidence, determining the facts of the case, and forming judicial decisions. It seeks to safeguard the rights of defendants and other participants as prescribed by law, prevent the trial from being a mere formality, and thereby enhance the fairness of judicial decisions and the credibility of China's judicial system.

55 Shangyou News (2021).

56 www.cpcnews.cn (2016).

57 www.gov.cn (2022).

the rule of law to provide political legitimacy, promote economic development, and improve social governance, Chinese courts will be allowed to develop a degree of institutional autonomy and professionalism, and they will have the capacity and opportunity to deepen the reform of China's death penalty system and further reduce the use of the death penalty in individual criminal cases. For an authoritarian State like China, the institutional maturity and professional development of the court may be the best hope for an execution-rare state in the long term.

References

Amnesty International. (2019) *Death Penalty 2018: Dramatic Fall in Global Executions*. www.amnesty.org/en/latest/news/2019/04/death-penalty-dramatic-fall-in-global-execution/.

Chen, X. (2006) *Sixing beiwanglu* (Memorandum on the Death Penalty) (Wuhan: Wuhan University Press).

(2009) 'A Study of the Death Penalty as Applied to Those Engaged in the Transportation of Drugs' 41(4) *Chinese Sociology and Anthropology* 48.

Chen, Z. and Huang, K. (2007) 'Drug Problems in China: Recent Trends, Countermeasures, and Challenges' 51(7) *International Journal of Offender Therapy and Comparative Criminology* 98.

Hood, R. and Hoyle, C. (2015) *The Death Penalty: A Worldwide Perspective* (5th ed.) (Oxford: Oxford University Press).

Hu, J. and Chen, Y. (2020) *Dupin shuliang dui dupin fanzui rending de lixing sikao* (A Rational Reflection on the Significance of Drug Quantity in Determining Drug Crimes) *National Research Centre of Drug Issue Governance* (1 May). https://dcppc.swupl.edu.cn/zxcg/xzlw/282544.htm.

Li, X. (2021) 'Adjudication of Death Penalty Cases: Toward Professionalism and Leniency' in *Strong Court, Mild Punishment: The Death Penalty and the Role of Courts in Contemporary China* (Ph.D. Dissertation, The University of Hong Kong).

Miao, M. (2013) 'The Politics of China's Death Penalty Reform in the Context of Global Abolitionism' 53(3) *British Journal of Criminology* 500.

Mühlhahn, K. (2009) *Criminal Justice in China: A History* (Cambridge: Harvard University Press).

Shangyou News. (2021) *Guoxinban fabu | zuigao renmin fayuan yanjiushi: jinyibu yankong he shenzhong shiyong sixing* (State Council Information Office | Research Office of the Supreme People's Court: Further Strict Control and Cautious Apply the Death Penalty) (24 June). www.cqcb.com/xindiaocha/zhongguofabu/2021-06-24/4235826.html.

Supreme People's Court. (2015) *Zuigao renmin fayuan xingwuting fuzeren jiu 'quanguo fayuandupin fanzui shenpan gongzuo zuotanhui jiyao da jizhewen'*

(The Person in Charge of the Criminal Division Five of the Supreme People's Court Answers Questions from Reporters Regarding the 'Summary of the Conference on Drug Offences Trials in All Courts of the Country') (27 May). www.court.gov.cn/zixun/xiangqing/14580.html.

Supreme People's Court. (2018) 'Liu Shouhong fanmai zhizao dupin an-ruhe rending zhizaodupin xingwei yiji zhidu shuliang' (Liu Shouhong's Drug Trafficking and Manufacturing Case – How to Determine the Act of Manufacturing Drugs and the Quantity of Drugs Manufactured) 110 *Criminal Trial Reference* 23.

Supreme People's Court, Supreme People's Procuratorate, Ministry of Public Security, Ministry of State Security and Ministry of Justice. (2010) *Guanyu banli xingshi anjian paichu feifazhengju ruogan wenti de guiding* (Provisions on Several Issues Concerning the Exclusion of Illegal Evidence in Criminal Cases). www.court.gov.cn/shenpan/xiangqing/6617.html.

Wang, X. and Shao, X. S. (2021) 'Yunshu Dupin Fanzui de Xinfa Dingwei he Xingfa Shiyong' (Criminal Law Orientation and Criminal Punishment Adaptation over Drug Transportation Crime – An Empirical Study Based on 151 First-instance Criminal Verdicts in a Southwest City in China) 2 *Journal of Yunnan Police College* 11.

Wei, H. (2018) 'Dupin fanzui sihuan de piancha yu kuangzheng – jiyu 100 fen sihuan panjueshu de fenxi' (Judicial Deviation and Correction of Death Penalty in Drug Crimes: An Analysis of 100 Death Penalty Judgments) 5(40) *Xiandai Faxue (Modern Law)* 156.

www.cpcnews.cn. (2016) *Xi Jinping lun quanmian yifa zhiguo* (Xi Jinping's Comment on Promoting the Comprehensive Rule of Law) (27 April). http://cpc.people.com.cn/GB/http:/cpc.people.com.cn/n1/2016/0427/c64094-28307076.html?from=groupmessage&isappinstalled=1.

www.gov.cn. (2022) *Xi Jinping: Gaoju zhongguo tese shehuizhuyi weida qizhi wei quanmian jianshe shehuizhuyi xiandaihua guojia er tuanjie fendou* (Xi Jinping: Holding High the Great Banner of Socialism with Chinese Characteristics and Unitedly Striving for Building a Modern Socialist Country in All Respects – Report at the 20th National Congress of the Communist Party of China) (25 October). www.gov.cn/xinwen/2022-10/25/content_5721685.html.

Xinhua News. (2007) *Sixing hezhunquan shouhui buyong danxin xingfa guoqing wenti* (No Need to Worry About Lenient Penalties After the Power to Review and Approve All Death Penalty Cases Has Been Retrieved by the Supreme People's Court) (15 March). www.jiaodong.net/news/system/2007/03/15/000928989.shtml.

Yu, Z. (2021) *Xishuo dupin yu dupin fanzui diliu jiang-dupin fanzui de dingzui yu liangxing* (In-depth Discussion on Drugs and Drug Crimes Part Six – Conviction and Sentencing in Drug Crimes) *Shangquan lushi shiwusuo yanjiu* (Shangquan Law Firm Research). https://mp.weixin.qq.com/s/7Nev5691Y1vCngDFuseOMw.

Zhang, Z. (2023). 'Zhongda dupin fanzui liangxing guifan yanjiu' (Major Drug Crime Sentencing Guidelines – Analysis Based on 200 Major Drug Crime Judgments in Province A) 13 *People's Judicature* 30.

Zhao, B. and Li, Y. (2011) 'Lun Dupin Fanzui de Sixing Xianzhi' (On Restricting the Use of the Death Penalty in Drug Cases) 1 *Southern-Central Minorities University Journal* 111.

Zhao, M. (2023) *Dupin Fanzui Rending Biaozhun Yanjiu* (Study on the Criteria for Determining 'Knowledge of Presence of Drugs' in Drug-Related Offences) (Master of Laws Dissertation, Hubei University).

Zui, G. (2018) Yue Xiang Chuan Dian Cen, wudi shedupin fanzuiliang zhan quanguo 40% yishang (The Supreme People's Procuratorate: Guangdong, Hunan, Sichuan, Yunnan and Guizhou and Other Five Regions Account for More Than 40 Percent of the Country's Drug-Related Crimes). www.spp.gov.cn/spp/zdgz/201806/t20180626_382817.shtml.

3

Normative Legitimacy of Iran's Capital Drug Law and Its Application

MAI SATO AND LEAVIDES DOMINGO-CABARRUBIAS

3.1 Introduction

This chapter examines the legitimacy of the use of the death penalty for drug offences in Iran. Generally speaking, legitimacy is the right to rule and the recognition by the ruled of that right.[1] Hinsch distinguishes between 'normative' legitimacy and 'empirical' legitimacy.[2] The former is a term used to describe whether authorities meet certain desirable normative standards.[3] The latter is used to describe whether those who are subject to authority confer legitimacy on that authority.[4] This distinction between normative and empirical legitimacy is important because authorities that enjoy substantial popular support – which can be said to enjoy empirical legitimacy – can, at the same time, totally fail to meet basic standards of normative legitimacy. In sum, normative legitimacy is about justice, not widespread approval.[5]

In this chapter, we are interested in normative legitimacy concerning the use of the death penalty for drug offences.[6] A normative conception of legitimacy must justify the selection of specific criteria against which legitimacy is to be evaluated. In a Weberian framework, legitimacy is

We are extremely grateful to Roya Boroumand, executive director of Abdorrahman Boroumand Center (ABC) for Human Rights in Iran, for her detailed comments and suggestions on this chapter. This chapter is based on a policy brief published by ABC and Eleos Justice (2023). We would also like to thank Michael Hor and Daniel Pascoe for their insightful comments and feedback.

1 Sternberger (1968 p. 244); Beetham (1991); Tyler (2006); Bottoms and Tankebe (2012).

2 Hinsch (2008, 2010).

3 Hinsch (2008).

4 Ibid.

5 Mason (2022).

6 In this chapter, we do not focus on the empirical legitimacy of capital drug law, given the extent to which the Iranian public may be able to express their genuine consent to its authority, let alone being able to obtain reliable data.

found in public acceptance of the right of an institution to wield power and define behaviour. In theory, one could apply just this criterion, that people consent willingly to obey the decisions of authorities. However, many would be against accepting such a criterion as the only measure to evaluate an institution's normative legitimacy. Such a criterion pays little attention to the nature of social arrangements to which citizens are acquiescing in each country. A different type of criterion is necessary; normative legitimacy also resides in the extent to which institutions operate according to certain moral and ethical standards, according to accepted and justifiable standards of justice, accountability, transparency, and so forth.[7]

The use of the death penalty in law and practice involves at least two power holders: the legislature, which has the power to create and amend capital drug laws; and the judiciary, which has the power to apply the law and sentence individuals to death.[8] The normative legitimacy of these institutions, and their outputs – laws and judgments – are analysed against the principles enshrined in the International Covenant on Civil and Political Rights (ICCPR).

3.2 Data

This chapter uses in its analysis ten judgments[9] handed down in Iran during 2014–2020, involving nineteen defendants of whom sixteen were sentenced to death for drug offences.[10] Two judgments were handed down after the amendment to the capital drug law came into force. We make no claim about these judgments being representative of capital drug cases in Iran. As the total number of executions or death sentences for drug offences (or other capital offences) is not published regularly or systematically by official sources, we rely on estimates gathered by non-governmental organisations (NGOs). Using published estimates, our data – ten judgments – present a tiny proportion of a large number of known executions for drug offences. Our data are not collected systematically because judgments in Iran are not publicly available. This rules

[7] Beetham (1991).
[8] Other authorities also part of the operationalisation of the death penalty in Iran include the police, prosecution, and prisons.
[9] Judgments on file with ABC, translated into English by ABC and shared with Eleos Justice, Faculty of Law, Monash University. We received approval from the Monash University Human Research Ethics Committee (Project ID: 35771).
[10] See Appendix to this chapter.

out any form of representative sampling of cases. Despite these shortcomings, the judgments provide a rare insight into judicial decision-making in capital drug cases in Iran.

3.3 International Normative Standard: The ICCPR

The normative conception of legitimacy requires the selection and justification of a specific criterion against which legitimacy is to be evaluated. We must then justify our selection of the ICCPR. Critics of human rights or UN mechanisms may question the universality of human rights or the enforcement capabilities of the human rights apparatus.[11] Norms *per se* are not objective or universal; in international human rights, *jus cogens* may be the closest thing to a norm being universally accepted from which no derogation is permitted. However, for a norm to be regarded as *jus cogens*, a very large majority of states must agree to it, meaning that the power of a human rights norm depends on endorsement from governments to which such a norm would be subjected.[12]

The ICCPR has near universal adherence with 173 countries ratifying the treaty.[13] Iran ratified the ICCPR in 1975, binding itself to give effect to the Covenant in the domestic legal order.[14] Iran has expressed full support and cooperation with the United Nations (UN) human rights machinery and has been actively participating in the Universal Periodic Review (UPR) processes.[15] During the fourth UPR cycle, Iran affirmed the following:[16]

> On fulfilment of the country's obligations under Article 2 of the Covenant, The Islamic Republic of Iran (IRI) does not intend to invoke internal norms as justification for any failure to fulfil its obligations under the Covenant; we do commit ourselves to our international obligations as well as our Islamic commitments. IRI ratified the Convention in 1975 and thus it is an integral part of our legal system. As per Article 9 of the Civil Code, any international instrument which is ratified by IRI shall be treated as domestic laws.

11 Refer to Mason (2022, p. 1841) for a summary of the critique of human rights and United Nations (UN).
12 International Law Commission (2019).
13 UN Office of the High Commissioner for Human Rights (n.d.).
14 Ibid.
15 Human Rights Council (2010, para. 12; 2015, paras. 1 and 6).
16 Human Rights Committee (2023b, para. 1).

While indicating a full commitment to the ICCPR, Iran has been criticised by the UN concerning its use of the death penalty, particularly its application to many offences and to minors. This highlights one of the main critiques of the ICCPR – its enforcement powers. States are expected to provide remedies for any violations of the ICCPR, and enforcement relies on, besides international pressure, the UN Human Rights Committee, which can ask for updates on the remedies available.[17] Scholars have observed that judges and legislators in Iran tend to give precedence to domestic law, acknowledging the binding force of treaty provisions *only* if they are not contrary to domestic law or Islamic law.[18] Indeed, based on our data, none of the judgments referred to the ICCPR or any other human rights treaties that Iran had ratified.

In sum, we do not claim that the ICCPR is a universal norm on the death penalty; nor do we claim that the ICCPR always provides clear guidance on the use, restriction, or abolition of the death penalty. However, the ICCPR is an instrument that Iran has chosen to ratify, to recently reiterate its commitment to its principles over domestic norms, and to willingly continue to subject itself to external scrutiny over its compliance. For this reason, we use the ICCPR as a suitable norm to evaluate Iran's death penalty practice on drug offences.

3.4 Legislative Legitimacy: The 2017 Amendment to the Law for Combating Illicit Drugs

3.4.1 'Most Serious Crimes'

The ICCPR restricts the application of the death penalty to the 'most serious crimes'.[19] In 2018, the Human Rights Committee restricted its meaning to intentional killing and explicitly declared that crimes that are not resulting directly and intentionally in death, such as drug offences, can never serve as the basis for the imposition of the death penalty.[20] This definition of the most serious crimes has not been endorsed by Iran, which continues to maintain that death sentences are 'only issued for the *most serious crimes*' and that drug offences are 'most serious' – a common justification also given by other countries that retain the death

[17] Refer to Mason (2022).
[18] Azizi (2015, pp. 246 and 249); Ghaziani and Ghaziani (2020, pp. 103–104).
[19] ICCPR, Article 6.
[20] Human Rights Committee (2019, para. 35).

penalty for drug offences.[21] Iran is fully aware that General Comments are not legally binding: they are expert statements on the interpretation of the ICCPR and are 'secondary soft law instruments'.[22] Nevertheless, they remain 'norm generating instruments', consolidating the understanding of the ICCPR and 'over time could contribute to the emergence of customary international legal norms'.[23]

Despite the country's continued use of the death penalty for drug offences, in 2017, Iran amended its domestic law to restrict the application of the death penalty for drug offences. The change came after repeated calls by the UN and the unwillingness of some European states to fund anti-illegal drugs projects in Iran through the United Nations Office on Drugs and Crime to fund further projects due to the high number of executions for drug offences.[24] During the third cycle of the UPR, Iran explained the amendments as follows:[25]

> In the fight against narcotics, the law was amended. . .in which the limits for the amount of narcotics discovered from defendants who are subject to the death penalty, has expanded significantly and, in practice, the execution is only for heads of drug trafficking gangs, armed smuggling, or those who abuse children and people with mental disabilities for smuggling of high amounts of narcotics.

The UN bodies referred to the amendment as a positive development in limiting the application of the death penalty, to which we now turn.[26]

3.4.2 *2017 Amendment*

In November 2017, the amendment to the Law for Combating Illicit Drugs came into force.[27] The amendment added a single article, removing the death penalty for some less serious drug offences, reducing the

[21] Emphasis added. Iran reiterated this in 2019 and 2023: Human Rights Council (2020a, para. 5); Human Rights Committee (2023b, para. 13).
[22] Keller and Grover (2012, p. 129).
[23] Ibid.
[24] Iran Human Rights and ECPM (2022, p. 57).
[25] Human Rights Council (2020b, para. 85).
[26] Human Rights Council (2019a, pp. 18–19; 2019b, para. 69); Human Rights Committee (2023a, paras. 3(a) and 24).
[27] The Law for Combatting Illicit Drugs was drafted in 1988 and amended in 1997, 2011 and 2017. A copy of the law (as amended in 1997) is available in English at www.refworld.org/pdfid/4c35b0a52.pdf.

punishment to a maximum prison term of thirty years, while also retaining the mandatory death sentences for other drug offences.[28] The amendment was a compromise after a Bill attempting to abolish the death penalty for *all* unarmed drug offences had failed to pass.[29] The Bill was met with resistance from the judiciary and staff in the Interior Ministry's drug-control headquarters, who believed that removing capital drug offences would lead to more offending.[30] This resulted in the 2017 amendment, which passed with 183 voting in favour (out of 290 MPs).[31] In sum, the amendment sets out certain drug crimes as *Mofsed fel-Arz* (spreading corruption on earth) – an offence that carries the death penalty under Article 286 of the Iran Penal Code – and prescribes the death sentence and expropriation of assets obtained from activities related to illicit drugs.

First, the amendment restricted the application of the mandatory death penalty by raising the quantities of illicit drugs which would attract the death penalty.[32] It not only distinguishes 'production and trafficking' from 'possession and storing' but also distinguishes between different types of illicit drugs ('natural' and 'synthetic' substances) and applies varying minimum quantities sufficient to attract the death penalty. For example, before the amendment, producing more than 30 g of methamphetamine was a capital offence; now the new threshold is 2 kg. Based on our data, all ten judgments correctly applied the minimum quantity requirement to attract the death penalty, in accordance with the law pre- and post-amendment.

Second, the 2017 amendment introduced a series of circumstantial conditions under which the mandatory death penalty applies *even* where the quantities of illicit drugs are below the minimum. For example, one of the conditions is: 'If the main perpetrator or at least one of the accomplices draws a weapon during the commission of the crime, or carries a firearm or a hunting weapon with the intention of opposing law

28 Drug Reform Bill Version Approved by Majles on 4 October 2017, and Guardian Council on 18 October 2017 (www.iranrights.org/library/document/3262). While not the focus of this chapter, the Law for Combating Illicit Drugs treats drug use as an offence; people who use illicit drugs have been imprisoned and sent to compulsory drug treatment programmes: Barzin (2018, p. 4).

29 Drug Bill Reform Measure of Ninth Majles (www.iranrights.org/library/document/3224).

30 Library of Congress (2017).

31 Ibid.

32 See Table 3.1; Law for Combating Illicit Drugs, Article 45 (amended in 2017).

Table 3.1 *Minimum quantities for capital drug offences: pre- and post-2017 amendment*

Offences	Type of illicit drug	Minimum quantities Post-2017 amendment	Minimum quantities Pre-2017 amendment
Production and trafficking	'Natural' substances (cannabis, hashish, grass, opium, etc.)	50 kg	5 kg
	'Synthetic' substances (heroin, morphine, cocaine, and other chemical by-products)	2 kg	30 g
Possession and storing	'Natural' substances	Only applicable to repeat offenders 5–20 kg: for a third conviction 20 kg+: for a second conviction	Only applicable to repeat offenders 5–20 kg: for a third conviction 20 kg+: for a second conviction
	'Synthetic' substances	3 kg	30 g

Sources: ABC (2017); Harm Reduction International (2019).

Notes: a. 'Production and trafficking': 'importing, exporting, sending, producing, manufacturing, distributing, selling, making available for sale' according to the English translation of the 2017 amendment.

b. 'Possession and storing': 'purchasing, keeping, concealing, or carrying' according to the English translation of the 2017 amendment.

c. 'Natural' substances: 'traditional' substances according to the English translation of the 2017 amendment.

enforcement officials'.[33] This means that an individual shall be sentenced to death even if they trafficked below the minimum quantity if the individual – not just the principal offender but even a mere accomplice – drew a weapon during the commission of the offence.[34] Moreover,

[33] Under the 1997 law, Article 11, the punishment for 'armed smuggling of narcotic drugs' was the death penalty. What constitutes 'armed smuggling' is unclear in the legislation.

[34] Ibid, p. 3.

simply '*carrying* a firearm or a hunting weapon with the *intention* of opposing law enforcement officials' is enough for the judge to apply the death penalty. Hence, concerns have been raised about the circumstantial conditions being open to abuse.[35]

Third, under the amendment, individuals sentenced to death for drug offences *continue* to be subjected to expropriation of assets.[36] This provision ignores the reality of defendants convicted of drug offences, many of whom are driven to illicit drug activity by poverty and financial difficulties without complete knowledge of the law and are exploited by drug syndicates.[37] In this sense, the monetary punishment further exacerbates the economic hardship of offenders' families and dependents.

Finally, capital drug offences, according to the amendment, are considered '*Mofsed fel-Arz* (spreading corruption on earth)' under Sharia law. The jurisprudential basis – Quran, Prophetic Tradition, or Islamic belief – to justify the application of the death penalty for drug offences, using *Mofsed fel-Arz* (spreading corruption on earth), has been contested by religious experts and officials.[38] For example, retired Revolutionary Court judge Hossein Akbari argues that capital drug offences do not have any jurisprudence basis under Islamic teaching: the death penalty for a drug offence is neither '*hadd*' (punishment established by God) nor '*ta'zir*' (punishments administered at the discretion of a judge on *Sharia* grounds).[39]

3.4.3 *Impact of the 2017 Amendment?*

The amendment was introduced to restrict the application of the death penalty for drug offences, but such an aspiration was short lived. A dramatic reduction in the number of executions was recorded in 2018 compared to 2017, the year the amendment came into force (November). The known number of executions for drug offences

[35] Ibid. Based on our data, in the two cases that occurred after the 2017 amendment, the amount of illicit drug in question was above the minimum quantity to attract the death penalty.

[36] Others who are sentenced to a lesser punishment are also subjected to asset expropriation.

[37] Barzin (2018, p. 4); Drug Bill Reform Measure of Ninth Majles.

[38] Houghough (2016).

[39] Hossein Akbari relied on the opinions of Grand Ayatollahs Makarem Shirazi, Nuri Hamedani, Javad Tabrizi, and Abdolkarim Musavi Ardebili in reaching this conclusion: ibid.

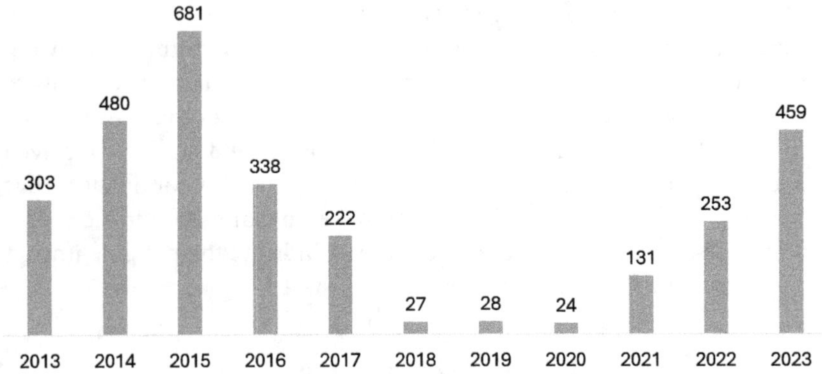

Chart 3.1 *Number of known executions for drug offences 2013–2023*
Source: Abdorrahman Boroumand Center (ABC) for Human Rights in Iran.

in 2017 was 222; in 2018, the figure dropped to twenty seven (see Chart 3.1). Despite the reduction in the known number of executions for drug offences during 2018–2020, execution numbers shot up after 2021. At least 131 executions were recorded for drug offences in 2021, almost doubled to 253 in 2022, and further increased to 459 in 2023.

Executions often take place several years after the original trial, and individuals convicted of a capital drug offence can appeal their convictions since 2015. Accordingly, it would be naive to assume that the 2017 amendment caused a sudden drop in executions a year after the amendment. As aforementioned, the amendment was likely a response to international pressure combined with the threat of funding for Iran being removed. Therefore, the most likely explanation is that the execution numbers dropped because a decision was made to reduce execution numbers. The increase in the number of executions after 2020 may have been caused by a backlog that was created. It may be a few more years before we see a decline in the number of executions *if* the amendment indeed had the effect of reducing the number of death sentences.[40] More broadly, so many factors influence the number of executions – including a policy decision not to execute while judges continue to hand down

[40] The number of death sentences for drug offences or other offences are not available and it is impossible to provide a reliable estimate.

death sentences, as observed by various countries that are considered 'abolitionist in practice'. Therefore, we must be mindful of drawing causal connections between execution numbers and the amended law.

Nevertheless, according to our data, out of eight cases that were judged before the 2017 amendment, it is likely that four would not have received the death penalty, based on the minimum quantity of illicit drugs attracting the death penalty. While we make no claims about the representativeness of our data, these cases at least indicate the possible impact the amendment may be having on cases post-2017.

3.5 Judicial Legitimacy: Input Justice

In this section, we make the distinction between input and output legitimacy.[41] We adopt the definition of input legitimacy as including 'all procedural and substantive considerations that form part of a decision-making process'.[42] Key procedural guarantees for a fair trial are enshrined in Article 14 of the ICCPR, which requires that individuals charged with a criminal offence be presumed innocent until proven guilty beyond reasonable doubt according to law, thus imposing on the prosecution the burden of proving the charge. We then analyse output legitimacy – 'any form of legitimacy that is validated on the basis of the practical consequences of such decision-making' – a clear example being the written judgments.[43]

3.5.1 Independence and Selection of Judges

Under the ICCPR, a fair trial requires a fair and public hearing by a competent, independent, and impartial tribunal.[44] The requirement of competence, independence, and impartiality refers to the establishment of a competent and independent tribunal to ensure the proper administration of justice. This includes a satisfactory process for the appointment of judges. Iran's Constitution guarantees the independence of the judiciary, but the same Constitution also stipulates that the supreme leader

[41] The distinction was originally introduced by David Easton and popularised by Fritz Scharpf: Scharpf (1999); Thomas (2014).

[42] Thomas (2014, p. 751).

[43] Ibid, pp. 751–752.

[44] ICCPR, Article 14(1).

appoints and *supervises* the head of judiciary.[45] Of course, institutional guarantees of independence do not always result in judges acting independently. However, in this case, Iran's judicial independence is directly undermined by the Constitution, putting the judiciary under the supervision of the head of state.

Concerning competency, a study into the standards and criteria for the selection of judges[46] explains that legal expertise is not a requirement to serve as a judge in Iran. Under Iranian law, individuals who are not law graduates can become judges if they fulfil certain conditions.[47] Indeed, many who have only had a religious education, including Sharia law (though not university-level education), have entered the judicial profession on that basis. The study showed that a significant number of high-ranking judges had been selected from individuals without a legal education. Based on Article 157 of Iran's Constitution, the two selection criteria for the Head of the Judiciary are to be a *religious* jurist knowledgeable in judicial matters and the ability to be a resourceful manager.

In 2021, Gholamhossein Mohseni-Ejei, an Islamic jurist, was appointed as the head of the judiciary. Mohseni-Ejei held several key positions in the executive and in the judiciary, including Minister of Intelligence (2005–2009), Attorney General of Iran (2009–2014), and Deputy Head of Judiciary (2014–2021).[48] When he was the deputy head of the judiciary, he was responsible for the final decisions in executing individuals sentenced to death for drug offences.[49] All death sentences are sent to the Supreme Court for final approval, but the head of judiciary, based on the powers delegated to him by the supreme leader, can make the final decision. Under Mohseni-Ejei's leadership, in 2015 alone, more than 600 individuals were executed for drug offences, the

[45] The supreme leader is the head of state and the highest ranking political and religious authority. Article 156 of the Constitution of the Islamic Republic of Iran states: 'The Judiciary shall be an independent power that protects individual and social rights' while Article 157 states: 'The Head of the Judiciary is directly appointed and supervised by the Supreme Leader'.

[46] The Law for the Selection of Judges of 1982 with subsequent amendments and the Guidelines for the Recruitment, Selection, and Apprenticeship of Applicants for Judgeship and Employment of Judges of 2013 were among the regulations that formed the basis of this analysis by Khalifeloo (2015).

[47] Paragraph 5 of the Law for the Selection of Judges provides guidelines on the selection of judges, such as that they should be selected from experts in religious jurisprudence (*Mojtahed*).

[48] Iran Human Rights and ECPM (2022, p. 20).

[49] BBC News (2014).

highest executions for drugs since the 1990s.[50] Again, Mohseni-Ejei's enthusiasm for executions provides a context for understanding the rise in execution numbers after the short-lived reduction.

3.5.2 *Fair and Public Hearing*

Under the ICCPR, a fair and public hearing refers to the transparency of the proceedings, participation of the accused through counsel of his own choosing, use of appropriate evidentiary requirements and standard of proof, and freedom from coercion.[51]

In Iran, drug offences are adjudicated in the Revolutionary Court, which was originally established in 1979 on the orders of the supreme leader, Ayatollah Khomeini.[52] All our judgments were delivered by the Revolutionary Court (or by a Revolutionary Court judge), which has been criticised for hearings often occurring behind closed doors, for being cursory, and for lawyers often not being given a chance to effectively defend their clients.[53] All our judgments show that the defendants were represented by their own counsel.[54] However, this does not necessarily indicate at what stage of the proceedings the defence counsel was present and how effectively they were able to assist the defendants. Iran's Code of Criminal Procedure (CCP), amended in 2015, provides that a defendant may be accompanied by counsel during the investigation phase.[55] According to the CCP, the right to legal counsel should be communicated to the defendant before the start of the investigation; failure to do so is punishable by law. However, a violation of this provision does not invalidate the results of the investigation.[56] In other words, if a defendant was not afforded counsel during the pretrial investigation, an official may be punished for not following the law, but the confession obtained without counsel remains admissible as long as the

[50] Ibid.
[51] ICCPR, Article 14.
[52] Under the Code of Criminal Procedure, Article 294, hearings are convened with one presiding judge and one associate judge.
[53] For example, Human Rights Council (2019b, para. 69); Human Rights Committee (2023a, paras. 3(a) and 24).
[54] See Appendix to this chapter.
[55] Code of Criminal Procedure, Article 190. A summary and English translation of the 2015 amendment is available at Iran Human Rights Documentation Center (2016).
[56] Iran Human Rights Documentation Center (2016).

confession was not obtained under duress.[57] NGO reports confirm that individuals, including those arrested for drug offences, are systematically subjected to torture following their arrest without access to a lawyer; often, by the time legal representatives are assigned, the accused would have already confessed to the crime.[58]

In our data, confessions played a large role in a conviction.[59] For example, the two defendants in Case 3 were sentenced to death for manufacturing and possessing 6.2 kg of crystal meth. They were convicted based on their multiple confessions and their presence at the location where the drugs were being manufactured. The judge sentenced them to death based on their confessions during the investigation phase – and by disregarding their subsequent retraction:

> In the preliminary investigations phase, the Defendants admitted and confessed to their activities regarding the manufacture of psychotropic drugs, and named other people as accomplices in the production of said drugs, even though said accomplices have not been identified and arrested thus far. In the subsequent phases of adjudication, however, including at trial, after they had come into contact with [and coached by] other criminals during their detention – criminals who are experienced in dealing with the judicial system – the Defendants denied manufacturing crystal meth and being in possession of the discovered psychotropic drugs, each claiming that the other one was the owner of said drugs, as is customary with drug traffickers.

The judge in this case dismissed the retraction without reservation, asserting that the defendants were coached by experienced criminals while in detention, without contemplating the possibility of the confessions being obtained through some form of coercion.[60]

In line with Article 7 of the ICCPR, Article 38 of Iran's Constitution forbids all forms of torture for the purpose of extracting confession or acquiring information.[61] It considers 'any testimony, confession, or oath obtained under duress' as 'devoid of value and credence' and violation of

[57] The 2015 amendment to the Code of Criminal Procedure, Article 190, removed the previous provision invalidating results of investigation if the defendant was not afforded counsel – which could have served as a safeguard against coerced 'confessions' – instead subjecting such breaches to disciplinary penalties: ibid. See also Amnesty International (2016).

[58] Iran Human Rights and ECPM (2022, pp. 57–58).

[59] See Appendix to this chapter under the column 'Evidence'.

[60] The judgment in this case is also silent as to whether a legal representative was present when defendants made their original confession.

[61] Constitution of the Islamic Republic of Iran.

this provision is punishable by law. However, UN and human rights groups have long documented the widespread use of torture and cruel, inhuman, or degrading treatment in detention facilities, and the use of coerced confessions as the primary evidence to obtain convictions in court.[62] The judgment in aforementioned Case 3 is silent on how the confession was obtained. However, information collected by ABC about this case strongly suggests that the defendant was subjected to torture: the defendant was arrested after he got into an argument with police officers who had intended to arrest Hosseini's neighbour.[63] In a published video statement, Hosseini's wife explained that the officers broke into the neighbour's apartment, took some boxes containing narcotics, and claimed that the discovered narcotics belonged to Hosseini. She also reported that he was interrogated and tortured for seventy days, during which he was denied visits. He was eventually transferred to Qezelhesar Prison, but his family was not allowed to visit him for another eleven months.

During the second UPR in 2014, the government accepted a recommendation to 'take measures to ensure due process and fair trial, particularly in any process that would lead to the application of the death penalty'.[64] While human rights bodies continue to express concern at the lack of fair trial guarantees in death penalty cases,[65] one positive change in fair trial guarantees may have been the availability of appeals for defendants since 2015. Article 32 of the Law for Combating Illicit Drugs is used to bar persons sentenced to death for drug-related offences from appealing their conviction; this has now been repealed by the new Code of Criminal Procedure.[66] Based on our data, the two judgments handed down after 2015 both make it clear that an appeal was available to defendants, including one case in which a death sentence was overturned on appeal by the Supreme Court (Cases 9 and 10).[67]

[62] For example, Human Rights Council (2011, para. 14; 2019b, para. 69); Human Rights Committee (2023a, paras. 3(a) and 24).

[63] ABC (n.d.) 'Reza Hosseini'.

[64] Human Rights Council (2015, paras. 138–213). However, Iran rejected most recommendations pertaining to the use of the death penalty.

[65] See note 62.

[66] According to the Code of Criminal Procedure, all persons have a right to appeal (Article 427). For capital offences, these appeals are heard by the Supreme Court (Article 428).

[67] See Appendix to this chapter. The judgment in Case 4 occurred before 2015. In this judgment, the judge tells one of the defendants that he cannot appeal his conviction.

3.6 Judicial Legitimacy: Output Justice

The concept of output legitimacy we adopt in this chapter is characterised as outcome-based legitimacy.[68] We shall examine the judgments for the availability of details and analyses of applicable laws relevant to the accused and their legal representatives preparing for an appeal, and to the wider society understanding the basis of the decision to apply the death penalty.

3.6.1 *Transparency*

Transparency is the key to achieving output legitimacy. The legitimacy of the judicial process requires outputs, such as the number of death sentences and executions as well as judgments, being readily available. Transparency in the administration of justice in Iran is not always guaranteed. For example, the *estimated* number of executions for drug offences was aforementioned because the figures are not published regularly or systematically by state authorities. *Some* judicial executions are officially reported on websites of the Iranian judiciary and police or in state-run media.[69] Accordingly, the *reported* number of executions represents the lowest estimate, meaning that the actual numbers are undoubtedly higher. Estimates from human rights organisations differ due to incomplete official data. The discrepancy is not huge: the overall trend captured by various organisations shows a similar pattern.[70] Nevertheless, not knowing the exact number of lives taken away by the state is not a trivial matter, and the discrepancy only underscores the authorities' control over the narrative of the death penalty in Iran. The pressure to release official data, however, does not come only from organisations outside of Iran. Jalil Rahimi Jahanabadi, a member of parliament, in 2017, called on the judiciary to release execution figures:[71]

[68] Thomas (2014, p. 752).

[69] According to Iran Human Rights, the estimated number of executions is largely dependent on unofficial sources: during 2016–2021, approximately 25 per cent of the total number of estimated executions came from official Iranian media. In 2022, this figure dropped to 12 per cent: Iran Human Rights and ECPM (2022, p. 17).

[70] For example, the number of executions for drug offences reported by Iran Human Rights is higher than ABC's figures (see Chart 3.1); however, both data follow the same trend. Figures reported by Iran Human Rights: 311 in 2013; 367 in 2014; 642 in 2015; 2966 in 2016; 231 in 2017; 24 in 2018; 30 in 2019; 25 in 202; 126 in 2021; and 256 in 2022: Iran Human Rights and ECPM (2022, p. 54).

[71] Iranian Students' News Agency (2017).

> The Judiciary should just announce the number of those executed and say how many [drug-related] executions have been carried out since the revolution. That has been done to some extent but the statistics are considered classified. As responsible officials, we must have a sense of responsibility toward the people.

Besides the number of executions, another aspect of Iran's judiciary that makes it difficult to gauge its output legitimacy is that, at least in the last decade, defendants do not always have access by default to their own judgment.[72] A copy of one's judgment is necessary if individuals wish to appeal against their conviction or sentence, a right granted to convicted drug offenders sentenced to death in 2015 with the reform of the Code of Criminal Procedure.[73] Indeed, the ICCPR guarantees the right to appeal,[74] requiring that convicted persons 'have, within a reasonable time, access to duly reasoned written judgments'.[75] The ICCPR also requires the judgment to be public.[76] They are key public records that can be used to understand trends and patterns of judicial decision-making and serve to keep the judiciary in check. Given the extensive power granted to the Iranian judiciary to take away liberty (imprisonment), property (fines and expropriation), physical integrity (corporal punishment), and life (death penalty), subjects of such power – the accused and society as a whole – ought to have access to an official record of how and why defendants were tried, convicted, and punished.

3.6.2 *Reasoned Judgments*

If defendants or their families manage to obtain a copy of the judgment, they may be disappointed by the level of detail offered. For example, in Case 1, the Revolutionary Court handed down a 400-word judgment, starting with a paragraph about the defendant and the offence for which

[72] Information provided by ABC based on their fieldwork.

[73] All persons have a right to appeal (Code of Criminal Procedure, Article 427). For capital offences, these appeals are heard by the Supreme Court (Article 428). Pre-2015, the Law for Combating Illicit Drugs, Article 32, barred persons sentenced to death for drug offences from appealing their conviction; this has now been repealed by the new Code of Criminal Procedure (Article 570).

[74] ICCPR, Article 14(5), states '[e]veryone convicted of a crime shall have the right to his conviction and sentence being reviewed by a higher tribunal according to law'.

[75] Office of the High Commissioner for Human Rights (2003, p. 307).

[76] ICCPR, Article 14(1), requires that any judgment rendered in a criminal case shall be made public, with certain exceptions.

he was charged, immediately followed by the decision to sentence the defendant to death:

> Regarding the charges brought against Mr. Mohsen Nasiri Mojreh, son of Nezamali, born in 1985–86, Identification Number 74 issued from [the town of] Khalkhall, single, literate, profession: sale of apparel, Shi'a Moslem, without a criminal record, national of Iran, from Khalkhal, residing at the Karaj Penitentiary, of possession of 4.4kg (approximately 10 pounds) of crystal meth.
>
> The Court,
>
> Having taken into consideration the report [of the relevant authorities], the discovered narcotic drugs, the Defendant's admission that said drugs had been left with him for safekeeping and that he had no knowledge that it was crystal meth, the Defendant's statements and admissions at various stages of the proceedings and his defence attorney's brief in his defence, and the totality of the contents of the case file; Finds that the charge against the Defendants has been *proven with certainty*; And pursuant to Article 8, Paragraph 6, of the Law Amending the Law for Combatting Narcotic Drugs, sentences the Defendant to death. (Emphasis added)

The judgment ends with three sentences indicating that the decision was issued in the presence of all concerned (though it is unclear who they are) and provides instructions on the expropriation of property derived from the crime.

According to the Code of Criminal Procedure, judgments should be well-reasoned and explicitly refer to the relevant legal provisions, mention the type of judgment (in person or in absentia), and mention potential retrial and appeal options and period.[77] All ten of our judgments cite the relevant law. Six out of ten judgments refer to the type of judgment,[78] but in the remaining four cases, the judgments do not mention whether the decision was issued in the presence of defendants or in absentia. Only in one judgment did the judge explicitly inform the defendant that he could not appeal his conviction.[79]

As to the requirement to provide a 'well-reasoned' judgment, the level of detail provided in Case 1 is not an outlier; other judgments are also

[77] Code of Criminal Procedure, Articles 374 and 375. See summary by The Norwegian Country of Origin Information Centre (Laninfo), The Office of the Commissioner General for Refugees and Stateless Persons (CGRS) and the State Secretariat for Migration (SEM) (2011, p 76).

[78] For example, 'This Decision was issued in the presence of [all or some of the individuals] concerned [at the trial stage, or who submitted briefs]'.

[79] Case 4.

similar in the level of detail provided. The short judgments may, to a certain extent, be explained by Iran's mandatory death penalty for some drug offences, which sets a minimum drug quantity.[80] Case 1 involved the possession of 4.4 kg of crystal meth, and the minimum quantity required to attract the death penalty for the possession of a synthetic drug was 30 g. Based on the judgment, it is unclear how the judge deemed that the defendant was in *possession* of the illicit drug. The judgment provides no detail about how the evidence was obtained, including how the drugs were 'discovered'; whether the defendant was assisted by counsel when he made his 'admissions at various stages of the proceedings', and the extent to which the judge considered the fact that the defendant's admission did not extend to his knowledge about possession of an illicit drug; and what arguments were presented by the legal counsel. Nevertheless, given the mandatory nature of the offence, *if* the court is satisfied with the defendant's possession of more than 30 g of crystal meth, the judge does not need to consider mitigating circumstances of the accused, as one would for a discretionary punishment. Perhaps this is why judgments rarely go into detail about the defendants' socio-economic or family circumstances.

Based on our data, almost all judgments end with the court's unwavering conviction – 'proven with certainty' – about the defendant's guilt. The phrase 'proven with certainty' is repeated also in other judgments, because it is the standard of proof required to convict an individual when invoking the 'knowledge of the judge' to which we now turn.

3.6.3 Standard of Proof

Although Iran's Constitution and the Code of Criminal Procedure recognise the presumption of innocence, Iranian law fails to clarify either the standard of proof or who bears the burden of proof.[81] Instead of setting an evidentiary standard for all criminal offences, such as 'beyond reasonable doubt', the Penal Code dictates the type of evidence required to convict various *hudud* offences. As noted earlier in the chapter, the

[80] Law for Combating Illicit Drugs, Article 38, indicates that judges may be able to exercise discretion 'if there are reasons by which the punishments subject to this act are mitigated'. However, according to the 'Note' linked to Article 38, the mitigation may be possible only when the accused cooperates with law enforcement, resulting in the arrest of drug networks.

[81] Constitution of the Islamic Republic of Iran, Article 37; Code of Criminal Procedure, Article 4.

Law Combating Illicit Drugs, amended in 2017, provides that capital drug crimes amount to 'spreading corruption on earth',[82] which may be proven by a single confession[83] or the testimony of two male witnesses.[84] This means that if an accused confesses to the commission of an offence, there is no need for the testimony.[85] If there is conflicting evidence, confessions must be given primacy over testimony, while testimony takes precedence over *qasameh* – the victims' relatives' oath as to the defendant's guilt.[86]

Finally, if the judge believes there is insufficient evidence to meet the Sharia requirements (namely, confession or testimony), he may invoke the concept of the 'knowledge of the judge',[87] which can be invoked by a judge when Sharia-based evidentiary requirement (e.g., a confession) is in doubt.[88] The judge may rely on 'other evidence', such as expert witness testimony, examination of the crime scene, the judge's own inquiries, police reports, and circumstantial and hearsay evidence.[89] In cases invoking the 'knowledge of the judge', the standard of proof is 'certainty', hence the phrase 'proven with certainty' used in the aforementioned cases examined. Knowledge of the judge is defined as:[90]

> [A] certainty resulting from manifest evidence in a matter brought before him. In cases where a judgment is based on the knowledge of the judge [as the proof of the offence], he is obliged to stipulate in the judgment the manifest circumstantial and hearsay evidence that has been the source of his knowledge.

'Certainty' is not defined anywhere, but the Penal Code stipulates that 'a mere perceptive knowledge... cannot be regarded as a deciding factor in delivering a judgment'.[91] As Sichani and Cheraghali observe, this signifies

[82] Corruption on Earth is a *hadd* (punishment established by God) offence under the Islamic Penal Code, Article 286.
[83] Islamic Penal Code, Article 172.
[84] Islamic Penal Code, Article 199.
[85] Islamic Penal Code, Article 171.
[86] Islamic Penal Code, Article 213.
[87] Islamic Penal Code, Articles 160–163.
[88] After the revision of the Islamic Penal Code in 2014, judges are obliged to stipulate in the judgment the source of their knowledge; before the revision, judges did not need to provide the basis for this insight or knowledge. Janghi and Rezazadeh (2013): [Under the old Penal Code], there [was] no criterion and standard to evaluate the judge's state of knowledge and when the judge mentions that he has acquired or has not acquired the required knowledge, he is just acknowledged.
[89] Islamic Penal Code, Articles 211 and 212.
[90] Islamic Penal Code, Article 211.
[91] Ibid., (under 'Note'); Alimardani (2018).

the legislature's refusal to allow 'personal' knowledge of the judge to influence proceedings.[92]

Confessions play a pivotal role in capital drug cases in law based on our data. The following comparison of the two cases further reinforces our finding on the centrality of confessions in securing a conviction as well as how confessions trump other evidence. Cases 4 and 8 both involve co-accused testifying that the defendants did not know about the drug offence in question, with the defendant in Case 4 not confessing and the defendant in Case 8 confessing to the alleged drug offence.

In Case 4, the defendant, Pishro Bivarani, and his co-accused were accused of manufacturing 1/58 kg of crystal meth. The co-accused was convicted and sentenced to death, but Bivarani was acquitted based on his vehement denial and his co-accused's repeated statements to the effect that Bivarani had no knowledge of the existence of the drugs, and that Bivarani was in the premises only to help irrigate the plants. In contrast, in Case 8, Alireza Madadpur, a student who worked part-time to make ends meet, was hired to perform janitorial jobs. As he waited outside the location where he was to work, police raided the house and found 990 g of methamphetamines and other substances used for meth manufacturing. Madadpur was arrested along with three co-accused. They all provided evidence that Madadpur had been on the premises for the first time on that day to perform janitorial work and that he had no knowledge of the activities conducted in the house. Despite these pleas from his co-accused, the judge sentenced all four defendants to death without explaining each defendant's role in the preparation and storage of methamphetamines. Madadpur was executed after his request for a retrial, and his request for a pardon was denied.[93]

The main difference between the two cases is the confession obtained in Case 8 despite the three co-accused stating otherwise. The two cases raise a strong suspicion that confession played a crucial role in one case, an acquittal, and in the other, a death sentence.

3.7 Conclusion

The legitimacy of state institutions ought not to be judged only by the governed conferring legitimacy on those institutions. Legitimacy also resides in the extent to which institutions operate according to justifiable

[92] Masoud, Sichani, and Cheraghali (2015).
[93] ABC (n.d.), 'Ali Reza Madadpur'.

normative standards. While acknowledging the political nature of international human rights treaties and the ambiguity in the language of the ICCPR, we used the Covenant as our normative framework on the basis that it has near-universal adherence, including ratification by Iran, and Iran's expressed, continued commitment in upholding its norms. This chapter aimed to do more than simply evaluate Iran's domestic capital drug law against the provisions of the ICCPR. It also examined the aims and likely motivations behind the 2017 amendment as well as how the law, before and after the amendment, was applied in practice by analysing judgments that are rarely in the public domain, including an assessment of the structure of the judiciary in which these judgments are delivered.

As the UN Human Rights Committee narrowed the definition of the 'most serious crimes' to intentional killing, Iran also appeared to be endorsing the UN's overall aim of progressive restriction of the death penalty, albeit short of complete abolition. Iran attempted to limit the scope of the death penalty to major players in major drug syndicates in 2017. Recognising that under the previous law, 'many of those sentenced to death [were] individuals who, due to poverty and life's financial difficulties, have been taken advantage of by the drug mafia, some without complete knowledge of the law,'[94] Iran amended its capital drug law by raising the minimum quantities of illicit drugs which would attract the death penalty among other provisions. Here, there was a normative alignment between the UN and Iran about reducing the scope of the death penalty.

Without access to the overall number of death sentences handed down by the trial courts before and after the amendment, it is difficult to assess the impact the amendment is having on the number of people sentenced to death. Nevertheless, our data suggested that some of the pre-2017 cases would not have attracted the death penalty, based on the increased minimum quantity of illicit drugs. However, based on our data, the overall aim of reducing the scope of the death penalty to major drug syndicates is unlikely to be realised due to the continued use of the mandatory death penalty under the amendment. Furthermore, the overreliance on confessions in sentencing individuals to death produces an additional problem of miscarriages of justice, risking wrongful executions.

First, while some defendants will avoid the death penalty based on the new minimum quantity of illicit drugs, any threshold based on a numeric

[94] Drug Bill Reform Measure of Ninth Majles.

indicator, albeit useful and clear, is arbitrary. This is why it is difficult to justify why possessing 3 kg of cocaine is a capital offence and not 2.9 kg. In these situations, judges' discretion becomes key in delivering a just outcome for the accused – 'just' referring to the purpose of the amended law. The amendment's mandatory imposition of the death penalty excludes defendants' personal circumstances, which means that the law does not allow judges to evaluate the motivations and socio-economic factors behind their offending. A comparison of two individuals sentenced to death before and after the amendment illustrates this. Alireza Madadpur (Case 8) was in his early thirties when convicted. He came from a poor family and was an accounting student in college and performed manual labour to pay for his tuition fees and to provide for his family. Khaleq Khezrzadeh (Case 9) also was sentenced to death in 2021 in his early thirties under the amended law; he also came from a poor family; after finishing his second year of high school, he worked as a truck driver. In sum, the law post-amendment continues to punish the same sort of individuals. Other than their age, the judgments are silent about their personal circumstances due to the mandatory nature of the law. Moreover, because the amendment continues to subject defendants to death *and* expropriation, the law is likely to further exacerbate the economic hardship of the offenders' families.

Second, the fact that Iran's approach to confession falls below the standard required under the ICCPR is well documented.[95] Given the supremacy of confession evidence under Iranian law, it is not surprising that the validity of confessions obtained was never questioned in our data. The significance of confessions was highlighted when the judge handed down a death sentence when a defendant retracted his confession, and when each of the three co-accused gave testimony that the defendant was not involved in the offence. Relying solely on confessions in securing a conviction might be observing legal validity by compliance with prescribed domestic legal and judicial processes. Under such conditions, however, its claim to be legitimate in a normative sense is in serious doubt.

The mandatory nature of the amended law removes discretion from the judiciary to consider circumstances that may spare those at the bottom of the drug chain from execution. The amendment, which operates within the existing judicial infrastructure that relies heavily on

[95] See, for example, Human Rights Council (2011, para. 14; 2019b, para. 69); Human Rights Committee (2023a, paras. 3(a) and 24).

confessions with limited safeguards, could result in a wrongful execution. In this sense, the amendment may limit the scope of the death penalty for some cases based on the increased minimum quantity to attract the death penalty. But whether the amended law really punishes only those at the top of the drug trade and spares vulnerable individuals at the bottom of the drug supply chain from execution remains uncertain.

References

ABC. (n.d.) 'Ali Reza Madadpur'. www.iranrights.org/memorial/story/-7968/ali-reza-madadpur.

'Darvish Monazami (Gulgani)'. www.iranrights.org/memorial/story/-8464/darvish-monazami-gulgani.

'Khaleq Khezrzadeh'. www.iranrights.org/memorial/story/-8586/khaleq-khezrzadeh.

'Majid Parmasi'. www.iranrights.org/memorial/story/-8575/majid-parmasi.

'Mika'il Shahbazi'. www.iranrights.org/memorial/story/-8576/mikail-shahbazi.

'Mohammad Kia Kiamehr'. www.iranrights.org/memorial/story/-8585/mohammad-kia-kiamehr.

'Mohsen Danahur'. www.iranrights.org/memorial/story/-8579/mohsen-danahur.

'Mohsen Nasiri'. www.iranrights.org/memorial/story/-7770/mohsen-nasiri.

'Musa Shateranlu'. www.iranrights.org/memorial/story/-8581/musa-shateranlu.

'Rahim Mohammadpur'. www.iranrights.org/memorial/story/-8577/rahim-mohammadpur.

'Reza Hosseini'. www.iranrights.org/memorial/story/-8578/reza-hosseini.

'Sa'id Shokri'. www.iranrights.org/memorial/story/-8580/said-shokri.

ABC and Eleos Justice. (2023) Proven With(out) Certainty: How Judges Sentence Defendants to Death for Drug Offences in Iran. www.iranrights.org/library/document/4034.

Alimardani, A. (2018) 'Neuroscience, Criminal Responsibility and Sentencing in an Islamic Country: Iran' 5(3) *Journal of Law and the Biosciences* 738.

Amnesty International. (2016) *Iran: Flawed Reforms: Iran's New Code of Criminal Procedure.* www.amnesty.org/en/wp-content/uploads/2021/05/MDE1327082016ENGLISH.pdf.

Azizi, S. M. M. (2015) 'Islamic Law and International Law in the Islamic Republic of Iran's Constitution' in Palmer, V. V. and Mattar, M. Y. (eds.) *Mixed Legal Systems, East and West* (London: Routledge).

Barzin, M. (2018) *A Review of Iran's Drug Law Reform* (Washington: Abdorrahman Boroumand Center for Human Rights in Iran).

BBC News. (2014) 'The Authority to Execute Part of the Death Sentences Was Delegated to Mohseni Ajei' (6 October). www.bbc.com/persian/iran/2014/10/141006_l39_execution_verdicts_mohseni_ejei.

Beetham, D. (1991) *The Legitimation of Power* (Basingstoke: Macmillan).

Bottoms, A. and Tankebe, J. (2012) 'Beyond Procedural Justice: A Dialogic Approach to Legitimacy in Criminal Justice' 102(1) *Journal of Criminal Law and Criminology* 119.

Ghaziani, M. A. and Ghaziani, M. A. (2020) 'Incorporation of Universal Human Rights' Norms in Public Municipal Law: An Analytical Study of Saudi Arabia, Iran, and India' 6(1) *Review of Human Rights* 98.

Harm Reduction International. (2019) *The Death Penalty for Drug Offences 2019.* www.hri.global/death-penalty-2019.

Hinsch, W. (2008) 'Legitimacy and Justice' in Kühnelt, J. (ed.) *Political Legitimation Without Morality?* (Berlin: Springer).

(2010) 'Justice, Legitimacy, and Constitutional Rights' 13(1) *Critical Review of International Social and Political Philosophy* 39.

Houghough, C. (2016) *Expert Conference on Drug Fight: Death Penalty Not Effective, Alternative Punishments Needed.* www.iranrights.org/library/document/3302.

Human Rights Committee. (2019) *General Comment No. 36* (CCPR/C/GC/36). www.ohchr.org/en/calls-for-input/general-comment-no-36-article-6-right-life.

(2023a) *Concluding Observations on Iran* (CCPR/C/IRN/CO/4). www.ohchr.org/en/documents/concluding-observations/ccprcirnco4-concluding-observations-fourth-periodic-report.

(2023b) *Replies of the Islamic Republic of Iran to the List of Issues in Relation to Its Fourth Periodic Report* (CCPR/C/IRN/RQ/4). 'https://tbinternet.ohchr.org/_layouts/15/treatybodyexternal/Download.aspx?symbolno=CCPR%2FC%2FIRN%2FRQ%2F4&Lang=en.

(2010) *Report of the Working Group on the Universal Periodic Review* (A/HRC/14/12). https://undocs.org/Home/Mobile?FinalSymbol=A%2FHRC%2F14%2F12&Language=E&DeviceType=Desktop&LangRequested=False.

(2011) *Compilation on the Islamic Republic of Iran* (CCPR/C/IRN/O/3). www.ohchr.org/en/documents/concluding-observations/ccprcirnco3-concluding-observations-human-rights-committee.

(2015) *Report of the Working Group on the Universal Periodic Review (Addendum)* (A/HRC/28/12/Add.1). https://undocs.org/Home/Mobile?FinalSymbol=A%2FHRC%2F28%2F12%2FAdd.1&Language=E&DeviceType=Desktop&LangRequested=False.

(2019a) *Compilation on the Islamic Republic of Iran* (A/HRC/WG.6/34/IRN/2). https://undocs.org/Home/Mobile?FinalSymbol=A%2FHRC%2FWG.6%2F34%2FIRN%2F2&Language=E&DeviceType=Desktop&LangRequested=False.

(2019b) *Report of the Special Rapporteur on the Situation of Human Rights in the Islamic Republic of Iran* (A/HRC/40/67). www.ohchr.org/en/documents/country-reports/ahrc4067-report-special-rapporteur-situation-human-rights-islamic.

(2020a) *Report of the Working Group on the Universal Periodic Review (Addendum)* (A/HRC/43/12/Add.1). www.ohchr.org/en/HRBodies/HRC/RegularSessions/Session43/Documents/A_HRC_43_12_Add.1_AV_Islamic RepublicofIran_E.docx.

(2020b). *National Report, Islamic Republic of Iran* (A/HRC/WG.6/34/IRN/1). https://undocs.org/Home/Mobile?FinalSymbol=A%2FHRC%2FWG.6%2F34%2FIRN%2F1&Language=E&DeviceType=Desktop&LangRequested=False.

International Law Commission. (2019) 'Chapter V. Peremptory Norms of General International Law (Jus Cogens)'. https://legal.un.org/ilc/reports/2019/english/chp5.pdf.

Iran Human Rights and ECPM. (2022) *Annual Report on the Death Penalty in Iran*. https://iranhr.net/media/files/Rapport_iran_2022_PirQr2V.pdf.

Iran Human Rights Documentation Center. (2016) *Amendments to the Islamic Republic of Iran's Code of Criminal Procedure – Part 2*. https://iranhrdc.org/amendments-to-the-islamic-republic-of-irans-code-of-criminal-procedure-part-2/.

Iranian Students' News Agency. (2017) *Majles Rep. Jahanabadi: Judiciary Should Announce Statistics on Drug-Related Executions*. www.iranrights.org/library/document/3207.

Janghi, A. and Rezazadeh, V. (2013) 'The Argumentum of Judge's Knowledge in Iranian and French Laws: A Brief Comparison of Iranian and French Legal Systems' 7(13) *Advances in Environmental Biology* 4280.

Keller, H. and Grover, L. (2012) 'General Comments of the Human Rights Committee and Their Legitimacy' in Keller, H. and Ulfstein, G. (eds.) *UN Human Rights Treaty Bodies* (Cambridge: Cambridge University Press).

Khalifeloo, M. B. (2015) *Iran Judges: A Selection Process That Paves the Way for Injustice*. www.iranrights.org/library/document/2877.

Library of Congress. (2017) *Iran: Drug Law Amended to Restrict Use of Capital Punishment*. www.loc.gov/item/global-legal-monitor/2017-08-31/iran-drug-law-amended-to-restrict-use-of-capital-punishment/#:~:text=The%20Amendment%20would%20increase%20the,and%20that%20of%20natural%20substances%2C.

Mason, B. M. (2022) 'The Legitimacy of International Human Rights Law – Addressing the Justification Gap' 47(6) *BYU Law Review* 1830.

Masoud, A., Sichani, A. M. and Cheraghali, M. H. (2015) 'The Position of Knowledge of the Judge in a Crime Evidence of Proof' 3(3) *Iranian Journal of Social Sciences and Humanities Research* 38. www.noormags.ir/view/fa/articlepage/1213242/the-position-of-knowledge-of-the-judge-in-a-crime-evidence-of-proof-with-theapproach-to-changes-on-islamic-penal-code-adopted-in-2013.

Office of the High Commissioner for Human Rights. (2003) *Human Rights in the Administration of Justice: A Manual on Human Rights for Judges, Prosecutors and Lawyers* (New York: United Nations Publication).

Scharpf, F. W. (1999) *Governing in Europe: Effective and Democratic?* (Oxford: Oxford University Press).

Sternberger, D. (1968) 'Legitimacy' in Sills, D. L. (ed.) *International Encyclopedia of the Social Sciences* (vol. 9) (New York: Macmillan).

The Norwegian Country of Origin Information Centre (Laninfo), The Office of the Commissioner General for Refugees and Stateless Persons (CGRS) and The State Secretariat for Migration (SEM). (2011) *Iran: Criminal Procedures and Documents.* https://landinfo.no/wp-content/uploads/2021/12/Iran-report-criminal-procedures-and-documents-122021-4.pdf.

Thomas, C. A. (2014) 'The Uses and Abuses of Legitimacy in International Law' 43(4) *Oxford Journal of Legal Studies* 751.

Tyler, T. R. (2006) 'Psychological Perspectives on Legitimacy and Legitimation' 57 *Annual Review of Psychology* 375.

UN Office of the High Commissioner for Human Rights. (n.d.) *Status of Ratification Interactive Dashboard.* https://indicators.ohchr.org.

Appendix

Judgments considered

	Name	Age	Date of Offence	Date of Judgment	Offence	Court	Legal Representation	Evidence	Penalty
1	Mohsen Nasiri Mojreh[1]	Estimated year of birth: 1985–1986	Not indicated	11 April 2013	Possession of 4.4 kg of crystal meth	Karaj Islamic Revolutionary Court	Represented by unnamed counsel	Defendant's admission; the discovered drugs in his possession; and the totality of the contents of the case file	Death
2	Darvish Monazami[2]	Estimated year of birth: 1957–1958	15 March 2012	(Illegible)	Procurement and possession of 5 kg of morphine	Orumieh County Islamic Revolutionary Court	Represented by Parviz Najafpur	Defendant's admission; Discovery of narcotic drugs at defendant's home	Death and expropriation of property derived from the crime
3	Majid Parmasi[3] Mikael Shahbazi[4]	Not indicated	Not indicated	7 June 2013	Manufacture and possession of 6.1 kg of crystal meth	Karaj Islamic Revolutionary Court	Parmasi: Represented by Rassul Azadbakht Shahbazi: Represented by Ahmad Khodayari	Defendants' admission; their presence at the location where drugs were being manufactured; discovery of the drugs and paraphernalia	Death and expropriation of property derived from the crime
4	Rahim Mohammadpur[5]	Not indicated	7 September 2013 (date of search in Mohammadpur's house)	19 December 2013	Manufacturing, transporting and possessing 1.5 kg crystal meth Possessing and manufacturing 3 L of acid acetone	Sardasht Revolutionary Court	Represented by Abdorrahman Mahmudi and Nasser Jamshidjam	Totality of content of the case file including police's preliminary report on the defendants' activities in cooking and manufacturing crystal meth; discovery of the drugs inside Mohammadpur's house; his record of a prior criminal conviction	Death by hanging inside Mahabad's prison Forty months imprisonment, forty lashes, and forty million rials monetary penalty

(*cont.*)

	Name	Age	Date of Offence	Date of Judgment	Offence	Court	Legal Representation	Evidence	Penalty
	Pishro Bivarani	Not indicated	7 September 2013	19 December 2013	Complicity in manufacturing, transporting and possessing 1.5 kg of crystal meth and 3 L of acid acetone		Represented by Khaled Paknam	Bivarani's vehement denial of the commission of the crime; Mohammadpur's statements that Bivarani had no knowledge of the drugs	Acquitted
5	Reza Hosseini[6]	Estimated year of birth: 1982–1983	Not indicated	16 February 2014	Possessing 140.3 kg of heroin and morphine		Represented by Omid Moghadasifar	Totality of the content of the case file including multiple-month surveillance in Hosseini's residence; discovery of drugs and 16.850 million Tumans in his rented apartment and his presence at the location	Death and expropriation of property derived from crime
	Hamzeh Jamshidian	Not indicated	Not indicated	16 February 2014	Possessing 18.4 kg of heroin	Tehran Islamic Revolutionary Court	Represented by Ebrahim Baboo	Discovery of drugs in Jamshidian's residence	Death and expropriation of property derived from crime
	Reza Hosseini objection to the Prosecutor General[7]	Not indicated		29 November 2014		Office of the State Prosecutor General			Objection of Hosseini's attorney denied; sentence affirmed
6	Mohsen Danahur[8] Mohammad Kia Kiamehr[9]	Estimated year of birth: 1990–1991 Estimated year of birth: 1982–1983	Not indicated	27 May 2014	Complicity in manufacturing psychotropic substances; possessing 2.8 kg of crystal meth	Karaj Islamic Revolutionary Court	Represented by Shamlu Ahmadi Represented by Mehrparvar and Azadbakht	Discovery of the drugs; Police's investigations; admissions of Danahur; statements of Kiamehr's fiancée re: delivery of a package from Danahur	Death and expropriation of property derived from the crime

7	Sa'eed Shokri[10]	23–24 estimated year of birth: 1990–1991	9 April 2014 (date of arrest)	20 July 2014	Purchasing and transporting 1.5 kg of heroin	Qom County Islamic Revolutionary Court	Represented by Mehdi Nasrollahi	Shokri's admission; Police investigations of his drug-related activities; discovery of 1.5 kg of heroin in his car	Death
	Behzad Qaffarzadeh	Estimated year of birth: 1986–1987	Not indicated	20 July 2014	Complicity in purchasing 1.5 kg of heroin		Represented by Mohammad Tahmassebi	Shokri's statement on Qaffarzadeh's role in procuring the heroin; Qaffarzadeh's presence at the site of the deal	Twenty-five years imprisonment
8	Mussa Shateranlu[11]	Estimated year of birth: 1983–1984	12 November 2011	17 July 2012	Participation in the preparation and storage of 990 g of methamphetamines	Karaj Islamic Revolutionary Court	Shateranlu: Represented by Jostani	Discovery of methamphetamines in Rostami's rented house; defendants' confessions (Note: Three defendants all claimed Madadpur's innocence)	Death expropriation of property derived from the crime
	Alireza Madadpur[12]	32–33 estimated year of birth: 1978–1979					Madadpur: Ms. Salarian		
	Ahmad Montahai	31–32 estimated year of birth: 1979–1980					Montahai: Zadeh		
	Mehdi Rostami	Not indicated					Rostami: Rezai		
9	Ali Sattari	Not indicated	13 December 2019	5 September 2021	Transporting and possessing 21.2 kg of crystal meth	Supreme Court (On appeal from Mashad Islamic Revolutionary Court dated 20 June 2021)		Discovery of drugs in Defendant's vehicle; admission that he transported containers with no knowledge that they contained drugs; laboratory result confirming that the contents are crystal meth	Death and expropriation of vehicle used transporting narcotics (upheld decision of trial court)

(cont.)

	Name	Age	Date of Offence	Date of Judgment	Offence	Court	Legal Representation	Evidence	Penalty
10	Khaleq Khezrzadeh[13]	Estimated year of birth: 1989–1990	1 June 2020	6 January 2021	Conspiracy in transporting 6.5 kg of crystal meth	Supreme Court (on appeal from Bandar Lengeh County Revolutionary Court dated 21 October 2020)	Represented by Hassan Azadbakht	Discovery of drugs in Defendant's vehicle; Khezrzadeh's admissions	Upheld the trial court decision sentencing Khezrzadeh to death
	Raheem Zeyn	Estimated year of birth: 1988–1989					Represented by Hassan Rias	Denial of the charges; Khezrzadeh's statements that Zeyn had no knowledge of the drugs	Overturned trial court's decision (remanded the case to lower court for *de novo* hearing)

[1] ABC. (n.d.) 'Mohsen Nasiri'.
[2] ABC. (n.d.) 'Darvish Monazami (Gulgani)'.
[3] ABC. (n.d.) 'Majid Parmasi'.
[4] ABC. (n.d.) 'Mika'il Shahbazi'.
[5] ABC. (n.d.) 'Rahim Mohammadpur'.
[6] ABC. (n.d.) 'Reza Hosseini'.
[7] Ibid.
[8] ABC. (n.d.) 'Mohsen Danahur'.
[9] ABC. (n.d.) 'Mohammad Kia Kiamehr'.
[10] ABC. (n.d.) 'Sa'id Shokri'.
[11] ABC. (n.d.) 'Musa Shateranlu'.
[12] ABC. (n.d.) 'Ali Reza Madadpur'.
[13] ABC. (n.d.) 'Khaleq Khezrzadeh'.

4

Debate and Contestation in Singapore's Death Penalty

WING-CHEONG CHAN AND MICHAEL HOR

4.1 In the Spotlight Once Again

Singapore's active death penalty regime, used primarily for drug offences, came under international scrutiny in 2004 when Amnesty International released a report revealing that the per capita execution rate in Singapore was the highest in the world.[1] This came as a shock to those not acquainted with Singapore (and, perhaps, to many locals as well). Execution rates in Singapore have dipped dramatically since then.[2] But suddenly, Singapore's death penalty was catapulted back onto the international stage when it resumed executions after a two-year unofficial moratorium during the COVID-19 pandemic.[3] A significant parallel development has been the evolution of an increasingly organised and sophisticated anti-death penalty activism and litigation movement within Singapore.[4] These two factors combined put the international spotlight once again on Singapore's death penalty, almost two decades after the 2004 Amnesty International Report.

What Singapore's death penalty critics, internal and external, have to say, and what the Singapore Government has put forward in defence of the practice are widely available. The purpose of this chapter is to sketch significant aspects of recent developments in Singapore's death penalty landscape with a view to continuing the necessary conversation of

1 Amnesty International (2004).

2 Hor (2013).

3 See, for example, the campaign by Amnesty International (2022). Officially, the absence of executions during the COVID-19 years was not because of the pandemic: Devaraj (2023).

4 A search on Singapore's legal database (LawNet) reveals some 20 death penalty related Court of Appeal decisions in 2022, which, for a small jurisdiction like Singapore, is quite an achievement. Perhaps the most active anti-death penalty group at present is the Transformative Justice Collective.

whether and how Singapore should retain the use of the death penalty, and for drug offences in particular.[5]

4.2 The Case for Deterrence and Public Support

The lynchpin of the Singapore Government's defence of capital drug laws is that they have effectively deterred would-be drug traffickers and have kept the country's drug problem firmly under control.[6] To quell critics who question the death penalty's effectiveness, the Singapore Government released its own studies in 2022.[7] One of these studies sought to assess public opinion, both within Singapore and in capitals of regional countries where visitors to Singapore are likely to come from, as to whether the respondents believed that the death penalty was an effective deterrent with respect to drug trafficking. Unsurprisingly, a vast majority of respondents in both Singapore and the selected foreign capitals said that they believed the death penalty to be an effective deterrent.

Although public opinion is a relevant factor in formulating criminal justice policy, it is also clear that much more work needs to be done to bridge the gap between what the public believe to be true and what is, in fact, true.[8] It would be natural for someone faced with general questions like that to put themselves into the shoes of a would-be offender. Would

[5] Changes were made to the mandatory death penalty regime for drug traffickers more than a decade earlier in 2012 to give judges the discretion to impose life imprisonment instead under certain circumstances, see Chan (2016).

[6] Articulations of this position are many and sustained. See, for example, Ministry of Home Affairs (2022b). The Singapore Government also frequently refers to the drop in kidnapping and firearms offences after the introduction of the death penalty for those offences in 1961 and 1973, respectively (see, e.g., Shanmugam 2020). The difficulties involved in attributing cause-and-effect in crime rates are well known among social scientists; see, for example, Levitt (2004). It cannot be discounted that violent crimes (whether capital or not) may well have dipped because of economic success and increased professionalism in, and resources for, law enforcement agencies. Another point to note is that kidnapping is only subject to a discretionary death penalty and not a mandatory death penalty as for drugs. A question naturally arises as to whether a discretionary death penalty for drugs would have the same effect.

[7] Ministry of Home Affairs (2022a). For a description and critical review of the studies, see Sato (2023).

[8] The studies also found that a majority believed that the death penalty effectively deters murder. But a study comparing Singapore and Hong Kong reached the conclusion that the murder rates over many years were more or less the same, notwithstanding Hong Kong's abolitionist position: Zimring, Fagan, and Johnson (2010).

they be deterred by the death penalty? Why, of course. Does the death penalty sound more terrifying than life imprisonment? Indeed, it does. But the problem is that (one hopes) a vast majority of these respondents would not traffic drugs in any event, even if the punishment were only a few years' imprisonment. The people the Singapore Government needs to ask are those who have trafficked drugs or would seriously consider doing so. Singapore's death penalty for drug trafficking is well-known, and yet there seems to be a cohort of people – both in and outside Singapore – who would still consider running the risk of being executed.

Quite apart from being evidence for deterrence, the survey serves as evidence of public opinion on drug policy based on deterrence. It is unfortunate that these studies did not engage with a 2018 study which was probably the first proper public opinion survey of the death penalty done in Singapore based on sound social science methods concerning sampling and question construction.[9] While the 2018 study yielded similar results for general questions concerning the death penalty, the picture was significantly different when respondents were given more detailed facts about situations where the death penalty would have been mandatory under the law. The initial general support for the death penalty fell significantly when respondents were faced with more contextual details and when presented with several penal options apart from the death penalty. It is trite that the kind of response elicited can depend a great deal on the way the question is posed. There is also a need to probe deeper into the reasons and sentiments which are behind the apparent popular support. Public opinion is only valuable if it is sufficiently well-informed.

In a 2020 Singapore Government study, it was claimed that the introduction of the mandatory death penalty for opium and cannabis in 1990 resulted in offenders trafficking in less than the quantities that would attract the death penalty.[10] However, care must be taken not to read too much into such 'restrictive deterrence'. We do not know if the lesser quantity was made up for by the offenders making more frequent runs, or by other offenders readily stepping in. In another Singapore Government study, coincidentally published in the same volume of the journal, it was found that other than knowledge of the punishment, the certainty of being caught, and other individual, contextual and situational factors are equally important in the decision whether to traffic

[9] Chan *et al.* (2018).

[10] Chia (2020). See Sato (2023) for a review of this study.

drugs.[11] That study, in fact, found evidence among drug traffickers that 'the certainty of being caught is a more powerful and effective deterrent than the punishment itself'.[12]

4.3 Chilling Effect

The years between the release of the 2004 Amnesty Report and the resumption of executions in 2022 have seen a remarkable advent of societal resistance to the death penalty.[13] The first broad development has been the dramatic rise of death penalty litigation, with many aspects of the death penalty being challenged in court. In the past, there would typically be a trial in the High Court, an appeal in the Court of Appeal, and a clemency petition, which would almost never succeed. Now it is common to see repeated court applications being filed to reopen concluded cases to challenge the constitutionality of the death penalty or the way the authorities have carried out their duties, sometimes delaying the execution for years. This has caused a degree of institutional stress because the principle of finality of the legal process could be undermined. The rise in litigations culminated in legislative amendments to severely restrict the availability of post-appeal applications.[14]

A corresponding development of greater import is the possibility of defence lawyers being called to account for 'abuse of process' by way of being made personally liable for costs.[15] It remains to be seen if there will be a 'chilling effect' in marginal cases where defence lawyers may be too cautious and refuse to act for fear of being slapped with costs personally, even when the application has some conceivable merit.[16]

[11] Kaur, Teo, and Samion (2020). Individual factors include thrill-seeking/impulsivity and criminal thinking patterns, contextual factors include having a deviant social network and exposure to people who use drugs, and situational factors include financial difficulties and the need to sustain their own drug behaviour.

[12] Ibid, p. 77. Also see C. Hoyle and P. Jabbar in Chapter 6 in this volume.

[13] Similar onslaughts against the Singapore law that criminalised sex between men, even in private (Penal Code 1871, s. 377A), occurred around the same time. Although that law had not been actively enforced since 2007, it remained in the law books until it was finally repealed in 2022.

[14] See Criminal Procedure Code 2010, ss. 394F–394K, and the new Post-appeal Applications in Capital Cases Act 2022 (Act 41 of 2022).

[15] Prominent death penalty lawyer M Ravi has been the subject of personal cost orders: *Syed Suhail bin Syed Zin v. Attorney-General* [2022] SGHC 140, and *Syed Suhail bin Syed Zin v. Attorney-General* [2022] 5 SLR 93.

[16] The constitutionality of the provision for personal costs was upheld in *Iskandar bin Rahmat v. Attorney-General* [2022] 2 SLR 1018, where the Court of Appeal felt that there were sufficient structural safeguards against such a 'chilling effect'.

Another parallel phenomenon has been the rise of a local anti-death penalty movement, which has become increasingly vocal and organised.[17] There is no doubt that the significant increase in post-appeal challenges where the defendant acts 'in person' without a lawyer has been enabled by this movement.[18] But the main anti-death penalty activism has been in the form of advocacy – the creation and dissemination of news and analysis critical of the death penalty. It is in this arena that anti-death penalty activists have come up against the controversial Protection from Online Falsehoods and Manipulation Act 2019 (POFMA),[19] legislation enacted to counter the dissemination of false news, which compels a creator or publisher of false news to post a Singapore Government-drafted warning,[20] much like the health warning on cigarette packs. There is once again the danger of the 'chilling' of speech, which may plausibly be considered an opinion rather than a false statement of fact. Although one may challenge a 'correction direction' in court, having to argue this in court is itself a significant deterrent. Another potential danger exists for lawyer activists: if their communication to the media is considered 'grossly improper conduct' or 'misconduct unbefitting', they risk censure, monetary penalty, or suspension from practice via disciplinary proceedings.[21]

[17] Support for the anti-death penalty movement has spread to the wider public. For example, a petition to halt the execution of Nagaenthran Dharmalingam netted more than 107,000 signatures (Change.org, 2021), and a candlelight vigil for Nagaenthran Dharmalingam and Datchinamurthy Kataiah on 25 April 2022 was attended by more than 300 people while many COVID-19 measures were still in place (Low, 2022).

[18] An example is *Jumaat bin Mohamed Sayed v. Attorney-General* [2022] SGHC 291, where four death row inmates, although formally appearing in person, most likely received considerable help from others in filing the application. Also see the court's questioning of Mdm Panchalai, Nagaenthran Dharmalingam's mother, who filed a last-minute appeal to stop her son's execution: Tang (2022).

[19] For comment on the law, refer to Ong (2019); Teo (2021).

[20] See, for example, the correction direction issued in relation to posts about Tangaruju s/o Suppiah's conviction for drug trafficking: Channel News Asia (2023).

[21] Prominent death penalty defence lawyer and anti-death penalty activist M. Ravi was suspended from practice for five years because of certain comments and allegations pertaining to the prosecution of a particular death penalty conviction and sentence which he successfully appealed against: *Law Society of Singapore v. Ravi s/o Madasamy* [2023] SGHC 65. The fact that the Court of Three Judges disagreed with both the Disciplinary Tribunal and a High Court Judge (who agreed with the Disciplinary Tribunal's finding) shows that what lawyers can and cannot say without risking suspension is not clear cut. We have no doubt that there can be litigation so egregious that lawyers ought to be made to pay costs personally, nor is there any doubt that fake news, especially on social media, can be a source of great harm. Striking the right balance is by no means a straightforward

Perhaps what has exercised the Singapore Government much more was a stunning admission in 2022 by three young national swimmers that they had consumed cannabis in Vietnam during a regional sports meet.[22] This was described as a 'setback' and 'swimming against the tide'[23] in the country's continuing 'war on drugs' by the minister of law and home affairs. First, the fact that the trio had consumed cannabis (a drug which would attract the death penalty in Singapore if trafficked over a certain quantity) without any apparent ill effects directly undermined the official message that all illicit drugs are evil substances that are extremely harmful.[24] Second, the trio were not just anyone off the streets. They were highly successful athletes, including Singapore's one and only Olympic Gold Medallist, whom many Singaporeans looked up to. Third, their views about cannabis may very well be representative of an attitudinal change by younger Singaporeans towards soft drugs.[25] In its response, the Singapore Government had to tread carefully by not alienating an entire generation by coming down too hard on the trio while at the same time avoid appearing to be going soft on illicit drug use by turning a blind eye to their activities.[26]

4.4 Regional Reforms

The generational change in attitudes towards cannabis in Singapore takes on an added significance in light of regional moves towards decriminalisation. Thailand decriminalised medical, and then recreational, marijuana use in recent years.[27] While it is not the first jurisdiction to do so, the proximity and availability of cheap travel between Singapore and Thailand make this policy change especially impactful.[28] Law

task. We sincerely hope that the law does no more than what is necessary to avert patently frivolous litigation or clearly false speech.

22 Ong (2022b). It is illegal for Singaporeans and Singapore permanent residents to consume controlled drugs even outside Singapore: Misuse of Drugs Act 1973, s. 8A.

23 Ong (2022a). We do not know if the pun on 'swimming' was intended.

24 See, for example, Central Narcotics Bureau (2014).

25 Iau and Lim (2022).

26 The response walked a tightrope between saying that no exceptions were made for them and yet recognising their immense contributions made to the country: Lee (2022). Perhaps what made this case different was that they also confessed to taking drugs and apologised for their mistakes.

27 Warr (2023). The Thai development has been controversial, and there are plans to re-criminalise recreational use of marijuana: Wongcha-um (2024).

28 Iau (2022).

enforcement will become even more challenging should next-door neighbour Malaysia, where close to half a million people cross the land border between the two countries every day, go the same way.[29]

The shift in regional attitudes towards cannabis comes in the context of significant moves to restrict, if not abolish, the death penalty in general.[30] Indonesia might well be on the cusp of major moves to limit the use of the death penalty. In 2023, Indonesian President Joko Widodo granted an 'unprecedented' clemency to Merri Utami, who was on death row for twenty years for drug trafficking.[31] This is the same Indonesian president who ended a moratorium on executions in 2014 to implement his 'war on drugs' policy (only to return to a moratorium two years later).[32] Equally significant is the introduction of an automatic 'probationary' death sentence in the revised Criminal Code under which death row inmates are on probation for ten years and, if they exhibit good behaviour in that period, their sentence of death may be commuted.[33] While none of this comes near abolition of the death penalty in Indonesia, they are clear reforms in favour of limiting or avoiding executions.

A growing divergence can also be seen between Malaysia and Singapore. The two former British possessions have much in common owing to their long-shared historical and cultural ties.[34] This extends to their legal systems and the use of the death penalty, including the mandatory death penalty for murder, kidnapping, and firearms offences. The death penalty policy for drug offences in Malaysia tracked Singapore's developments very closely, from mandatory death to a limited discretion to avoid the mandatory death penalty.[35] In recent years, however, Malaysia has taken steps to move away from the death penalty. A general moratorium on executions was announced in 2018, and the Malaysian Government announced an intention to abolish the death penalty altogether.[36] But barely five months later, apparently

[29] Malaysia announced plans to decriminalise the possession and use of small quantities of illicit drugs: Strangio (2023).

[30] D. Pascoe and R. Bunmee in Chapters 7 and 9, respectively, in this volume.

[31] AFP (2023).

[32] Kine (2016), although the Indonesian president did subsequently toy with the idea of extending the death penalty to corruption offences: Editorial (2019).

[33] The Jakarta Post (2023).

[34] Singapore was even part of Malaysia between 1963 to 1965.

[35] Tee (2023).

[36] NST Online (2018).

motivated by fear of a political backlash, the Malaysian Government changed its mind and decided to make the death penalty no longer mandatory instead.[37] In 2023, legislation to abolish the mandatory death penalty was passed in Malaysia.[38]

There can be no doubt that the Malaysian developments pose the most serious regional challenge to Singapore's insistence that the mandatory death penalty is necessary to deal adequately with drug trafficking.[39] Simply put, if it is unnecessary in Malaysia, why should it be in Singapore?[40] On a more technical level, the difference between the Singapore and Malaysian regimes raises a serious issue about whether the law enforcement agencies on both sides of the border can continue to cooperate the way they did before. Just as Singapore has had to give assurances that the death penalty would not be used to secure extradition from abolitionist jurisdictions,[41] similar assurances may have to be made before Malaysia agrees to continue to cooperate with Singapore enforcement agencies.

4.5 Case Law Developments

We now turn to analyse some case law developments, which, perhaps, have the greatest potential to affect the trajectory of the use of the death penalty in the near future.[42] In several instances dating from around

37 AP (2019). During this time, a constitutional challenge to the mandatory death penalty went all the way up to the Malaysian Federal Court in 2020: *Letitia Bosman v. PP and other appeals (No. 1)* [2020] 5 MLJ 277. The challenge failed by an 8–1 majority, with a very cogently argued dissent by Nallini Pathmanathan FCJ.

38 Tan, Rahimy, and Carvalho (2023). The death penalty was also removed for some offences, but not all.

39 Ong (2023).

40 Significantly, the sponsoring Minister was of the view that there was insufficient evidence of the efficacy of the death penalty in controlling crime – a position diametrically opposed to Singapore's official stance: Bernama (2023). In contrast, only three weeks earlier, Singapore passed amendments to impose heavier punishments for drug possession, including cannabis: Tang (2023).

41 Notably, in the McCrae case, where he was suspected of committing a double murder, the Singapore Government had to give an undertaking not to sentence him to death to secure his extradition from Australia: Shanmugam (2021). The Roach case itself had to do with similar assurances but with respect to corporal punishment for robbery in Singapore.

42 One example of the immense power that judges have is the long-standing practice that drug trafficking is not made out if the drug is meant for self-consumption. This defence is not stated anywhere in the legislation itself, although it has been referred to in parliament: Jayakumar (1993, col. 926). Also see X. Li in Chapter 2 in this volume on judiciary-led reforms in China.

2019,[43] the Court of Appeal departed from previous cases interpreting provisions in the Misuse of Drugs Act 1973.[44] It is not suggested that judges in Singapore have suddenly become soft on crime or that they are on a collision course with the legislature. In most respects, the Singapore Judiciary continues to enforce the country's strict drug policy,[45] but there are faint glimmers of easing at the margins.

4.5.1 Mens rea *of Possession*

A turning point in Singapore's drugs law came in 1979 when the Court of Criminal Appeal in *Tan Ah Tee v. PP*[46] adopted Lord Pearce's opinion of what 'possession' of an illicit drug entailed in *R v. Warner*.[47] In his speech, Lord Pearce said:[48]

> '[P]ossession' is satisfied by a knowledge only of the existence of the thing itself and not its qualities ... Though I reasonably believe the tablets which I possess to be aspirin, yet if they turn out to be heroin I am in possession of heroin tablets. This would be so ... even if I believed them to be sweets. It would be otherwise if I believed them to be something of a wholly different nature.

This very broad understanding of 'possession' (which does not require proof of knowledge of the nature of the illicit drug), when transplanted into Singapore soil had devastating consequences owing to the law's

43 There was also the earlier case of *Ali bin Mohamad Bahashwan v. PP* [2018] 1 SLR 610 but this dealt with the law of abetment rather than the offences in the Misuse of Drugs Act 1973 directly.

44 For examples of earlier cases where a literal interpretation of the Misuse of Drugs Act 1973 was taken which led to the mandatory sentences being applied, see *Muhammad Jeffry v. PP* [1996] 2 SLR(R) 738 ('give' includes those who give a drug gratuitously to another); *PP v. Adnan bin Kadir* [2013] 3 SLR 1052 ('import' includes those who bring a controlled drug into Singapore for their own consumption and not just those who intend to traffic the drug).

45 Hor (2011, paras. [40]–[82]); Chan (2023).

46 [1979–1980] SLR(R) 311. The former Chief Justice Wee Chong Jin said at [25]: 'In our opinion the word "possession" in the [Misuse of Drugs Act] should be construed as that word has been construed by Lord Pearce and we would respectfully adopt his reasons as contained in his speech'.

47 [1969] 2 AC 256.

48 Ibid, at 305. The speech 'has achieved near canonical status in Singapore': Hor (2001, p. 66).

harsh penalties.[49] In *Shan Kai Weng v. PP*,[50] for example, the defendant pleaded guilty to being in unlawful possession of one tablet found to contain nimetazepam. He did not deny possession of the tablet but claimed that he thought it was a sleeping pill. The court rejected the claim that the plea of guilt was invalid, saying:[51]

> The position under our law ... is that possession is proven once the accused knows of the existence of the thing itself. Ignorance or mistake as to its qualities is no excuse. The appellant knew the tablet was in his car. He believed it to be a sleeping pill, which, like the aspirin of the hypothetical in *Warner* and *Tan Ah Tee*, is a drug. As such, his ignorance as to the qualities of the tablet did not provide him a defence to the charge of possession, and his contention that he did not understand the nature of his plea could not stand.

One significant aspect of Singapore law that appears to have been overlooked is section 18(2) of the Misuse of Drugs Act 1973 where:

> Any person who is proved or presumed to have had a controlled drug in his or her possession is presumed, until the contrary is proved, to have known the nature of the drug.

Michael Hor commented:[52]

> The court in *Tan Ah Tee* ought to have realised at once that if knowledge of the nature of the contents of the bag were irrelevant (to liability), as Lord Pearce would have it, then it becomes pointless to prove that the accused did not have such knowledge.

In other words, the structure of the drugs law in Singapore clearly points towards a need for knowledge of the nature of the drug possessed. It is just that such knowledge is presumed unless proven otherwise on a balance of probabilities by the defendant.

[49] Michael Hor pointed out in 2001 that Lord Pearce's opinion in *Warner* ought not to have been adopted in the first place considering the very different structure of the drugs legislation in Singapore and the UK: Hor (2001, pp. 62–68).

[50] [2004] 1 SLR(R) 57.

[51] Ibid, at [24]. Fortunately, the court could exercise its discretion to impose an appropriate sentence. On account of the mitigating circumstances, the defendant was sentenced to one month's imprisonment. Other cases may not be so lucky: possession above quantities of certain drugs leads to a presumption of possession for the purpose of trafficking under the Misuse of Drugs Act 1973, s. 17, which could, in turn, lead to imprisonment (up to life imprisonment), caning (up to fifteen strokes), or death as well as mandatory minimum sentences under the Misuse of Drugs Act 1973, Second Schedule.

[52] Hor (2001, p. 67).

It was only in 2019 that the wrong turning made in *Tan Ah Tee* was finally laid to rest.[53] In *Adili Chibuike Ejike v. PP*,[54] the Court of Appeal clarified that there is a distinction between the fact of being in possession of a drug and the offence of drug possession. The former only requires that the defendant know the existence of the thing, later found to be a controlled drug under the Misuse of Drugs Act 1973; they do not need to know that the thing was, in fact, a controlled drug or its specific nature. This minimal requirement of knowledge is easily satisfied. An example where a defendant will not be found to be in possession of drugs even if they were in their physical custody of it is where the drugs were planted on them without their knowledge.[55]

On the contrary, it was held that the *offences* of drug possession (as well as of trafficking and importation) require proof that the defendant not only knew the existence of the thing but also knowledge of the specific nature of the drug in question: '[the offence of drug possession] is not a strict liability offence that is established simply by proof of the fact of possession'.[56] The earlier cases were found to have been wrongly decided because they conflated knowledge, which is required to establish the fact of possession, with the *mens rea* of the offence of drug possession.[57]

53 Prior case law was rather inconsistent. For example, *PP v. Chijioke Stephen Obioha* [2008] SGHC 243, decided by the Singapore High Court in 2008, had already departed from *Tan Ah Tee*, but the language was perhaps too subtle. At [171], the court pointed out:

> The concept of legal possession includes knowledge as physical possession without knowledge is not enough. It has generally been assumed in cases that the type of knowledge required is knowledge that the Accused was in possession of the specific drug, ie, cannabis in the present case (and not just knowledge that the drug is a controlled drug).

Other cases have also said that to prove a charge of drug trafficking, there must be (a) possession of a controlled drug (which may be proved or presumed under the Misuse of Drugs Act 1973, s. 18(1)); (b) knowledge of the nature of the drug (which may be proved or presumed under the Misuse of Drugs Act 1973, s. 18(2)); and (c) proof that the possession of the drug was for the purpose of trafficking. See, for example, *PP v. Abdul Haleem bin Abdul Karim* [2013] 3 SLR 734.

54 [2019] 2 SLR 254.

55 Ibid, at [31]–[34].

56 Ibid, at [35]. The punishment for illegal drug possession *simpliciter* is considerably lower than that for trafficking, import or export of illegal drugs under the Misuse of Drugs Act 1973, Second Schedule.

57 Ibid, at [38]–[40]. The two cases overruled were *PP v. Rozman bin Jusoh* [1994] SGHC 251 and *Shan Kai Weng v. PP* [2004] 1 SLR(R) 57.

4.5.2 *Wilful Blindness and Evidential Presumptions*

There are two presumptions relating to possession and knowledge of the controlled drug found in section 18 of the Misuse of Drugs Act 1973. Subsection 1 deals with the presumption of possession:

> Any person who is proved to have had in his or her possession or custody or under his or her control
>
> (a) anything containing a controlled drug;
> (b) the keys of anything containing a controlled drug;
> (c) the keys of any place or premises or any part thereof in which a controlled drug is found; or
> (d) a document of title relating to a controlled drug or any other document intended for the delivery of a controlled drug, is presumed, until the contrary is proved, to have had that drug in his or her possession.

Subsection 2 deals with the presumption of knowledge of the drug:

> Any person who is proved or presumed to have had a controlled drug in his or her possession is presumed, until the contrary is proved, to have known the nature of the drug.

These two presumptions are designed to mitigate practical difficulties encountered by the prosecution. Once the primary fact is satisfied, it is the defendant who bears the burden of proof to show that what is presumed is not true. On a charge of importing a controlled drug into Singapore, for example, the prosecution would have to show the following elements: (1) possession of the drug, (2) knowledge of the nature of the drug, and (3) intentional importation to Singapore without authorisation.[58] By invoking the presumptions, the prosecution would have an easier task in satisfying elements (1) and (2).[59] The defendant would then have to disprove (1) or (2) by showing that they did not have the drug in their possession or did not know the nature of the drug, as the case may be.

In *Adili Chibuike Ejike v. PP*,[60] the Court of Appeal clarified that the prosecution may not invoke section 18(1) of the Misuse of Drugs Act if

[58] If the defendant is charged with drug trafficking, the prosecution will not be able to use the Misuse of Drugs Act 1973, s. 17, to presume possession for the purpose of trafficking if it is using the presumptions in s. 18 as well: *Zainal bin Hamad v. PP* [2018] 2 SLR 1119.

[59] The prosecution could also choose not to rely on the presumptions and prove elements (1) and (2) beyond a reasonable doubt.

[60] [2019] 2 SLR 254.

its case is based on the defendant being wilfully blind[61] that the drugs were in his physical custody (in this case the drugs being hidden in the lining of a suitcase). This is because section 18(1) presumes actual knowledge by the defendant. If the prosecution's case is that the defendant was wilfully blind to the existence of the drug, it had to prove this beyond reasonable doubt.[62]

The same reasoning was extended to section 18(2) of the Misuse of Drugs Act 1973, which concerns knowledge of the nature of the drugs in a person's possession, by the Court of Appeal in *Gobi a/l Avedian v. PP*.[63] The defendant, in this case, knew that he was smuggling drugs into Singapore but claimed that he thought that the drugs were a mild form of 'disco drugs' mixed with chocolate rather than diamorphine (pure heroin). The issue was, therefore, whether the defendant knew the nature of the drugs for the charge of importing diamorphine.

The Court of Appeal held that section 18(2) also dealt with whether a person had actual knowledge of the nature of the drugs in his possession. It, therefore, followed that the prosecution could not invoke section 18(2) to presume that the defendant was wilfully blind to the nature of the drugs.[64]

These two decisions effectively erase any advantage served by the evidential presumptions. If the prosecution could prove that the defendant knew of the existence of the drugs such that he can be said to be in possession, the prosecution would not need the assistance of section 18 (1) in the first place. The same argument can be made for section 18(2). It is precisely because the prosecution's case is weak that it needs to utilise the rebuttable presumptions.[65] On the facts of *Adili*, the defendant

[61] Wilful blindness is used in the 'extended' sense to be the legal equivalent of knowledge – even if the defendant does not, in fact, know something but suspects what it is and deliberately refuses to investigate to avoid confirmation of their suspicions could, in certain circumstances, be treated as though they knew: ibid, at [47]. See the discussion in Hor (2011, paras. [14]–[39]).

[62] Ibid, at [70]. The prosecution was unable to do so because there were no reasonable means of inquiry available, which, if taken, would have led to the discovery of the truth, at [84]–[88].

[63] [2021] 1 SLR 180.

[64] Ibid, at [56]. There were statements to the contrary in previous cases, see *Tan Kiam Peng v. PP* [2008] 1 SLR 1 at [139] and *Masoud Rahimi bin Mehrzad v. PP* [2017] 1 SLR 257 at [50] and [55].

[65] An example of a strong case is *Muhammad Abdul Hadi bin Haron v. PP* [2023] SGCA 4, where the prosecution ran its case that the defendant had actual knowledge of the nature of the drugs. The presumption in Misuse of Drugs Act 1973, s. 18(2), was only used in the alternative.

was acquitted of the charge of drug importation since the prosecution could not establish that he knew about the drugs in the suitcase. In the case of *Gobi*, since the prosecution was unable to prove beyond reasonable doubt that the defendant either knew or was wilfully blind to the nature of the drugs, the court substituted his conviction for importing diamorphine (a capital charge) for one of attempting to import a Class C controlled drug[66] and sentenced him to fifteen years' imprisonment and ten strokes of the cane instead.

On a policy level, it seems odd that the Court of Appeal should decide that the presumptions apply only to actual knowledge and not wilful blindness, even though the *mens rea* of knowledge in drug offences comprises both actual knowledge and wilful blindness. If the prosecution wishes to rely on wilful blindness, then it has to prove its case beyond a reasonable doubt, without the aid of any presumption. The immediate anomaly is this – if presumptions are necessary for offenders who actually know what they are possessing or trafficking, why are the presumptions suddenly no longer necessary where they are wilfully blind? Conversely, if the presumptions are unnecessary for offenders who are wilfully blind, why are the presumptions not also unnecessary for offenders with actual knowledge? In comparison, no presumptions of *mens rea* exist at all for intentional murder, which is also punishable by mandatory death.

Furthermore, as a matter of policy and principle, the existence and employment of the drugs presumptions must mean that defendants are subjected to the mandatory death penalty even where a reasonable doubt may exist as to an essential element of the offence. A collateral challenge was made against the constitutionality of the drug presumptions in *Jumaat bin Mohamed Sayed v. Attorney-General*.[67] Justice Thean dismissed the challenge, holding that there was no arguable case. The Judge unfortunately cleaved to the jurisprudence of the late 1970s which declared that such presumptions do not violate the constitutional guarantee of a fair trial and of the presumption of innocence.[68] In the context of an actionable legal and constitutional right, the court is correct that the words of the Singapore Constitution do not expressly enshrine the presumption of innocence, nor do they clearly confer on the Judiciary the responsibility of assessing the justifiability of each and every

[66] This is the least serious drug category in the Misuse of Drugs Act 1973.
[67] [2022] SGHC 291.
[68] Primarily, *Ong Ah Chuan v. PP* [1979–80] SLR(R) 710.

presumption. Faced with a phalanx of common law persuasive authority that some presumptions may indeed fall foul of constitutional due process, the court observed that even in these jurisdictions, presumptions were not automatically unconstitutional and were eminently capable of justification.[69] So the case was not clear or strong enough to merit a post-appeal application. It is not the intent of this discussion to scrutinise the legal or constitutional merits of this view. Suffice it to say that equally strong arguments exist for the contrary view that the presumption of innocence is a constitutional right protected by the general constitutional right to a process 'in accordance with law',[70] that the presumption of innocence is violated by the drugs presumptions, and that whatever operational or law enforcement reason there might be for casting the burden on the defendant can be adequately met with placing the burden of production, and not the burden of persuasion, on the defendant.[71] We look forward to the matter being thoroughly debated by the Court of Appeal in the future.[72]

4.5.3 *Defence of Safekeeping*

The word 'traffic' in Singapore's Misuse of Drugs Act 1973 has an extremely broad definition, which includes 'to give' the drug to another. In *Ramesh a/l Perumal v. PP*,[73] the defendant was charged with possession of illicit drugs for the purpose of trafficking. He asserted that he was not trafficking the drugs because he was only safekeeping them with the intention of returning them to the person who originally entrusted the

[69] [2022] SGHC 291 at [76] and [77].

[70] Singapore Constitution, Article 9(1), provides: 'No person shall be deprived of his life or personal liberty save in accordance with law'.

[71] Hor (1995).

[72] An appeal against this judgment was filed, but certain documents were not filed within the prescribed time. An application for an extension of time was denied (*Jumaat bin Mohamed Sayed v. Attorney-General* [2023] SGCA 16). It is only a matter of time before the issue is raised again. Another aspect of due process to be challenged in the future is the use made during court proceedings of confessions and statements given while the drug offender was under custody. Safeguards like compulsory recording and the presence of defence lawyers, which are commonplace elsewhere, are not in place in Singapore. We do not doubt that drug offenders are accorded the criminal process prescribed by law, but the question remains whether the process can and ought to be improved, especially in the context of the death penalty.

[73] [2019] 1 SLR 1003.

drugs to him.[74] This did not seem to be a viable argument according to precedents. Past cases had consistently found that 'give' simply meant a physical transfer of the drug from one person to another; there was no further requirement that the defendant be a 'dealer' or 'supplier' of the drug. Returning the drugs to the owner would then amount to 'trafficking'.[75]

But in *Ramesh*, the Court of Appeal held that the word 'deliver' had to be interpreted purposively in light of the legislative policy behind the Misuse of Drugs Act 1973. 'Return' was not expressly within the definition of the term 'traffic'. The concern of the legislature was found to be the movement of drugs along the supply chain towards end-users, and not just the movement of the drugs *per se*.[76] The decision of the Court of Appeal could easily have gone the other way, considering that the response expected of people entrusted with drugs should be to hand over the drugs to the authorities as soon as possible instead of giving them back to the owner and facilitating their circulation in the community.

In *Roshdi bin Abdullah Altway v. PP*,[77] the Court of Appeal clarified that *Ramesh* did not stand for the general proposition that a person who safekeeps drugs to return them can never be liable for drug trafficking (or possession of drugs for the purpose of trafficking). The key inquiry is whether the person knew or intended that safekeeping the drugs was in some way part of the process of supply or distribution of the

[74] Owing to the way the prosecution ran its case, the prosecution had to prove beyond reasonable doubt that the defendant possessed the drug for the purpose of trafficking. It could not use the presumption of trafficking in Misuse of Drugs Act 1973, s. 17, because it had already relied on the presumption of knowledge of the nature of the drug under s. 18(2).

[75] *PP v. Goh Hock Huat* [1994] 3 SLR(R) 375 at [20]; *Lee Yuan Kwang v. PP* [1995] 1 SLR (R) 778 at [57] and [60]; *Jingga bin Md Selamat v. PP* [2001] SGCA 32 at [28]; *Tay Kah Tiang v. PP* [2001] 1 SLR(R) 577 at [35]. In *Sze Siew Luan v. PP* [1997] 1 SLR(R) 806 at [15], the former Chief Justice Yong Pung How characterised this argument as 'no defence at all'.

[76] [2019] 1 SLR 1003 at [110]. On the facts, the court did not think the defendant's acts amounted to abetting the offence of drug trafficking either, namely helping the primary offender to evade detection by safekeeping the drugs, at [115]. The defendant's original conviction for drug trafficking was therefore substituted for drug possession, and the sentence changed from life imprisonment and fifteen strokes of the cane to ten years' imprisonment, at [119]. However, the person who entrusted the drugs to another, even with a view to taking them back, is within the meaning of 'giving' and 'delivering'. This is because they have moved the drugs to a third party and facilitated the dissemination of drugs, at [123]–[125]. A distinction is, therefore, made between the person who receives the drugs and the person who gives the drugs.

[77] [2022] 1 SLR 535.

drugs.[78] On the facts of the case, it was found that the defendant knew that the person who entrusted the drugs to him was engaged in trafficking drugs and that if any customer wanted the drugs, he would return the drugs that he was safekeeping.[79] Hence, he was aware that by safekeeping the drugs, he was facilitating the process of their sale and distribution. In *Arun Ramesh Kumar v. PP*,[80] the Singapore Court of Appeal also observed that the defence would not ordinarily apply to the return of the drugs via a third party. This is because doing so would move the drugs along the chain of supply and distribution, thus coming within the definition of 'traffic'.

The clarifications in *Roshdi* and *Arun* have therefore restricted the 'safekeeping defence' to a very small group where the defendant can show that they did not know that safekeeping the drugs and their eventual return would lead to the distribution of the drugs, and return had to be made directly to the person who gave them the drugs. However, the important point remains that *Ramesh* reversed 'settled law'[81] and created a very narrow exception to the meaning of drug trafficking by allowing the presumption of possession of a drug for purposes of trafficking to be successfully rebutted.

4.5.4 *Meaning of Cannabis Mixture*

'Cannabis' and 'cannabis mixture' are both controlled drugs under the Misuse of Drugs Act. The former is defined as 'any part of a plant of the genus Cannabis, or any part of such plant, by whatever name it is called', while the latter is defined as 'any mixture of vegetable matter containing tetrahydrocannabinol ["THC"] and cannabinol ["CBN"] in any quantity'.[82] A question arose as to whether 'cannabis mixture' could include a mixture of various parts of the same cannabis plant or whether it only

[78] Ibid, at [115] and [184].

[79] The degree of knowledge is crucial. In *Ramesh*, the defence applied even though the defendant 'must have known that he was committing some act that was connected . . . to the illicit circulation of the drugs', at [118]. Whether the defendant 'collected' the drugs or the drugs were 'deposited' with the defendant could also make a difference. In *Arun Ramesh Kumar v. PP* [2022] 1 SLR 1152 at [28]–[30], the Singapore Court of Appeal held that the former may show that the defendant knew or intended the arrangement to be part of the supply or distribution of drugs.

[80] [2022] 1 SLR 1152 at [34].

[81] *Sze Siew Luan v. PP* [1997] 1 SLR(R) 806 at [15].

[82] Misuse of Drugs Act 1973, s. 2.

meant a mixture of cannabis and non-cannabis vegetable matter. In 1996, the Court of Appeal in *PP v. Manogaran s/o R Ramu*[83] decided that parliament could not have intended to exclude a mixture of vegetable matter of entirely cannabis origin from the term 'cannabis mixture'.

Referring to the same Legislative material as *Manogaran*, the Court of Appeal in *Saravanan Chandaram v. PP*[84] came to a completely different conclusion regarding the purpose behind the words 'cannabis mixture', which was purely to deter offences relating to cannabis when it was mixed with other vegetable matter such as tobacco. The court, therefore, overruled *Manogaran*and held that 'cannabis mixture' can only mean 'a mixture where cannabis plant matter is commingled with the vegetable matter of indeterminate origin or known to be of non-cannabis origin, where the components cannot be easily distinguished or separated from each other'.[85]

This may seem to be an argument in semantics, but it does have real implications in cases. The most common way in which cannabis is trafficked is in the form of a compressed block of plant material. To analyse its contents, the analyst breaks up the block, and in doing so, vegetable fragments (which contain THC and CBN) are created. For twenty-four years after *Manogaran*, a 'dual charging practice' was developed by the prosecution: for a single block of cannabis-related plant material, a charge will be preferred relating to 'cannabis' for the portion certified to consist purely of cannabis,[86] and a charge relating to 'cannabis mixture' for the portion consisting of fragmented vegetable matter that was found to contain THC and CBN. This was so even though on visual observation, all the material in the latter were from the cannabis plant.

With the change in the law, a charge relating to cannabis mixture cannot be used unless it complies with the definition of the term as stated

[83] [1996] 3 SLR(R) 390 at [43]. In doing so, the court overruled its decision made just three months earlier in *Abdul Raman bin Yusof v. PP* [1996] 2 SLR(R) 538, which held otherwise and was said to be 'clearly erroneous', at [50].

[84] [2020] 2 SLR 95. The decision was affirmed in *Abdul Karim vin Mohamed Kuppai Khan v. PP* [2021] 1 SLR 1390.

[85] [2020] 2 SLR 95 at [119].

[86] To be certified to be cannabis, a rigorous standard was imposed by the analyst such that the plant material must exhibit the botanical features of cannabis under both a macroscopic and microscopic examination as well as to be found to contain THC or CBN. Failure to satisfy any one of the three criteria would mean that the material cannot be certified as cannabis. The testing criteria are in accordance with the guidance from the United Nations Office on Drugs and Crime, ibid, at [61] and [105].

in *Saravanan*.[87] The prosecution can no longer use dual charges: it has to either charge as cannabis mixture for the entire block, or charge as cannabis only for the portion that can be certified to be cannabis. This has real implications because the gross weight of cannabis mixture trafficked, imported or exported must be double that of pure cannabis for the same punishment to be imposed.[88] For example, the death penalty applies to a person who traffics more than 500g of pure cannabis, but if it is cannabis mixture, the quantity must be more than 1,000g. Furthermore, if the defendant is convicted of fewer charges, it could also mean lower sentences because consecutive sentences may be avoided.[89]

4.5.5 *Discrimination against a Racial Minority*

Syed Suhail bin Syed Zin v. Attorney-General,[90] decided in 2022 by the High Court, threw into focus a particularly sensitive aspect of the death penalty – that of its disproportionate impact on a racial minority (Malays) in Singapore.[91] The defendants sought to challenge the death penalty because its use violated constitutional equality guarantees. Justice Thean refused to allow the challenge to proceed because there was neither direct discrimination (or disparate treatment) nor indirect discrimination (or disparate impact). There was no evidence of direct discrimination but indirect discrimination is rather more contestable. The plaintiffs gave evidence of statistical over-representation of Malays among those who were prosecuted for capital drug offences and that they were also more likely to be sentenced to death.[92] Justice Thean concluded as follows:

> [T]he plaintiffs 'categorically reject' the suggestion that Malay persons are more likely to commit capital drug offences than persons of other

[87] In any case, a charge of cannabis mixture for the fragmented vegetable matter was also found not to be correct because this did not exist at the time of the offence. It was created by the analyst, and so the *mens rea* for the offence did not exist at the time, ibid, at [184] and [185].

[88] The Misuse of Drugs Act 1973, Second Schedule.

[89] Under Criminal Procedure Code 2010, s. 307, a court is required to impose consecutive imprisonment sentences on at least two offences if a person is convicted of at least three 'distinct offences' at one trial.

[90] [2022] 4 SLR 934.

[91] Malaysians on the Singapore death row are also disproportionately of a particular racial minority (Indians): Loheswar (2022). The Government does not make publicly available the racial breakdown of the prison population or offenders in general: Shanmugam (2022a). Also see T. Kananatu in Chapter 5 in this volume.

[92] [2022] 4 SLR 934 at [43].

> ethnicities. They have also not identified any particular policy or criterion that, while appearing to apply indiscriminately to all, has the effect of putting Malay persons at a disadvantage by subjecting them to requirements that they are less able to meet.[93]

It is difficult to fault the reasoning. However, the statistical disparity nevertheless calls into question the facially neutral law prescribing the death penalty for drug trafficking itself. Unlike direct discrimination, which is *ipso facto* unconstitutional under Article 12(2) of the Constitution,[94] indirect discrimination is not explicitly dealt with in *Syed Suhail bin Syed Zin*. Most legal systems do not outlaw indirect discrimination but allow those defending it to justify the indirectly discriminatory measure.[95] It is here that there are interpretive choices to be made about the kind and degree of scrutiny of the proffered justification for the indirectly discriminatory measure. The reason for the measure is obvious – it is to deter and punish the trafficking of dangerous and illicit drugs. A 'light touch' scrutiny might well end the inquiry here – since these drugs, according to the Singapore Government, are a great menace to society, the highest penalty known to the law can be employed to deal with them. A more searching scrutiny might drill further down to ask if it is indeed necessary to use the mandatory death penalty to deal with drug trafficking, given the possibility of indirect discrimination on the racial minority owing to their lower socio-economic and educational status. It is no secret that those on death row in Singapore are unlikely to be 'kingpins'.[96] They are more likely

[93] Ibid, at [91].

[94] This provision reads: 'Except as expressly authorised by this Constitution, there shall be no discrimination against citizens of Singapore on the ground only of religion, race, descent or place of birth in any law . . .'.

[95] *Griggs v. Duke Power Co* 401 US 424 (1971) is the United States Supreme Court decision which is the grandfather of this line of jurisprudence. Measures with a disproportionate impact on certain racial groups may nonetheless be justified if they are reasonably job related. This decision was, no doubt, about the Civil Rights Act 1964, Title VII. United States constitutional jurisprudence requires not just disproportionate impact, but discriminatory intent to establish unconstitutional discrimination (*Washington v. Davis* 426 US 229 (1976)). When faced squarely with the issue, Singapore courts will have to decide which standard they wish to apply. If the *Davis* test is adopted, a constitutional challenge is unlikely to succeed. The discussion proceeds on the assumption that the *Griggs* test is chosen.

[96] The Minister of Home Affairs and Law observed, 'The kingpins sit in Malaysia and Thailand and other places. And so what are we supposed to do about that?': Shanmugam (2022b).

to be very far down the hierarchy. It remains to be seen how the Court of Appeal may decide should the issue come before it.[97]

4.6 Conclusion

The Singapore Government has repeatedly stated that it takes a 'zero tolerance' approach against illicit drugs[98] and adopts deterrence as a core sentencing principle towards drug offences.[99] The Misuse of Drugs Act 1973, which prescribes the mandatory death penalty for some drug offences, was described as 'one of the most successful pieces of legislation in the world in the control of the misuse of drugs'.[100] But in contrast to the depiction of a Singapore hell-bent on executing drug traffickers, there has, in fact, been a dramatic reduction in the per capita annual execution rate for drug traffickers, from fifty-four and fifty-two in 1994 and 1995, respectively, to mostly single digits since 2004.[101] At the same time, it seems clear that the Singapore Government is not prepared to abolish the death penalty completely or remove the mandatory death penalty.[102]

It is in this context that some of the recent case law developments are notable. The judicial efforts to improve the fairness of death penalty proceedings have even led one commentator to claim that the courts are 'willing to engage in outcome-based reasoning to mitigate the effect of a disproportionate and unjust result'.[103] Coupled with better organisation among anti-death penalty activists, greater interest in death penalty issues among the general public, shifts in younger Singaporeans' attitudes towards recreational drug use, and regional reforms concerning decriminalisation and the move away from the death penalty, the Singapore

97 A possible sea-change in judicial attitudes towards scrutiny of official measures was hinted at in *Tan Seng Kee v. Attorney-General* [2022] 1 SLR 1347 at [328], where the Court of Appeal discussed two possible levels of scrutiny on constitutional equal protection but left the decision open on which to take.

98 Masagos (2012, cols. 1220 and 1225); Teo (2012, col. 1244).

99 Chua (1984, col. 1867); Teo (2012, col. 1242).

100 Chua (1984, col. 1867).

101 But eleven persons were executed for drug offences in 2018 and 2022: Devaraj (2023). None were executed for drug trafficking in 2010, 2012, 2013, 2020, and 2021.

102 Chan (2016, p. 179). Although the death penalty is no longer mandatory for drug couriers who suffer from diminished responsibility or render substantive assistance to disrupt drug trafficking activities (Misuse of Drugs Act 1973, s. 33B, introduced in 2012), the thrust of Singapore's drug policy has not changed over the years: Chan (2023).

103 Yang (2021, p. 94).

Government will need to seriously reconsider its unremittingly punitive stance towards illicit drugs sooner rather than later.

References

AFP. (2023) 'Indonesian President grants 'unprecedented' clemency to death row drug convict' *The Straits Times* (25 April). www.straitstimes.com/asia/se-asia/indonesian-president-grants-unprecedented-clemency-to-death-row-drug-convict.

Amnesty International. (2004) *Singapore: The Death Penalty – A Hidden Toll of Executions*. www.amnesty.org/en/documents/asa36/001/2004/en/.

(2022) *Singapore: Halt Resumption of Unlawful Executions*. www.amnesty.org/en/documents/asa36/5264/2022/en/.

AP. (2019) 'Malaysia Backtracks on Plans to Abolish Death Penalty', *AP News* (14 March). https://apnews.com/article/–9823fa5ca16f498f9961bac2c37ae4a6.

Bernama. (2023) 'Death Penalty Not Proven as Best Preventive Measure: Ramkarpal', *New Straits Times* (11 April). ww.nst.com.my/news/nation/2023/04/898627/death-penalty-not-proven-best-preventive-measure-ramkarpal-nsttv.

Central Narcotics Bureau. (2014) *CNB statement on assessment of the Singapore Cannabis Awareness website to be objectionable* (18 February). www.cnb.gov.sg/NewsAndEvents/News/Index/cnb-statement-on-assessment-of-the-singapore-cannabis-awareness-website-to-be-objectionable.

Chan, W. C. (2016) 'The Death Penalty in Singapore: in Decline but Still Too Soon for Optimism' 11 *Asian Journal of Criminology* 179.

(2023) 'Escape from the Hangman's Noose? Singapore's Discretionary Death Penalty for Drug Traffickers' 24(1) *Australian Journal of Asian Law* 83.

Chan, W. C., Tan, E. S., Lee, J. T. T. and Mathi, B. (2018) 'How Strong is Public Support for the Death Penalty in Singapore?' 13(2) *Asian Journal of Criminology* 91.

Change.org. (2021) *Pardon the Death Sentence of an Intellectually Disabled Man*. www.change.org/p/pardon-the-death-sentence-of-an-intellectually-disabled-man.

Channel News Asia. (2023) 'Authorities Reject Activist Group's POFMA Appeal Over Facebook Post on Drug Trafficker's Death Sentence' (30 May). www.channelnewsasia.com/singapore/pofma-transformative-justice-collective-tjc-death-sentence-tangaraju-suppiah-3524656.

Chia, Y. F. (2020) 'Deterrent Effect of Historical Amendments to Singapore's Sanction Regime for Drug Trafficking' *Home Team Journal* 56. www.mha.gov.sg/docs/hta_libraries/publications/ht-journale-jan-2020-(special-edition).pdf.

Chua, S. C. (1984) 'Penal Code (Amendment) Bill', *Singapore Parliamentary Debates* (26 July). https://sprs.parl.gov.sg/search/#/topic?reportid=003_19840726_S0002_T0010.

Devaraj, S. (2023) '11 Judicial Executions in 2022: None in Previous Two Years', *The Straits Times* (9 February). www.straitstimes.com/singapore/courts-crime/11-judicial-executions-in-2022-none-in-previous-two-years.

Editorial. (2019) 'Death Does Not Become Us', *The Jakarta Post* (17 December). www.thejakartapost.com/academia/2019/12/17/death-does-not-become-us.html.

Hor, M. (1995) 'The Presumption of Innocence: A Constitutional Discourse for Singapore' *Singapore Journal of Legal Studies*365. www.jstor.org/stable/24866862.

(2001) 'Misuse of Drugs and Aberrations in the Criminal Law' 13 *Singapore Academy of Law Journal* 54.

(2011) 'Criminal Justice in the Chan Court: Change, Contestation and Conservatism in the Court of Appeal' in Yeo, T. M., Tjio, H. and Tang, H. W. (eds.) *SAL Conference 2011: Developments in Singapore Law between 2006 and 2010* (Singapore: Academy Publishing).

(2013) 'Singapore's Death Penalty: The Beginning of the End?' in Hood, R. and Deva, S. (eds.) *Confronting Capital Punishment in Asia* (Oxford: Oxford University Press).

Iau, J. (2022) 'Thailand Legalising Cannabis Poses More Challenges to S'pore's Anti-drug Stance: Shanmugam', *The Straits Times* (1 September). www.straitstimes.com/singapore/courts-crime/thailand-legalising-cannabis-poses-more-challenges-to-spores-anti-drug-stance-shanmugam.

Iau, J. and Lim, M. Z. (2022) 'Generational Shift in S'pore on Cannabis Use Overseas: Survey', *The Straits Times* (2 October). www.straitstimes.com/singapore/generational-split-among-sporeans-on-whether-consuming-cannabis-abroad-should-be-illegal-survey.

Jayakumar, S. (1993) 'Misuse of Drugs (Amendment) Bill', *Singapore Parliamentary Debates* (10 November). https://sprs.parl.gov.sg/search/#/topic?reportid=020_19931110_S0003_T0006.

Kaur, J., Teo, K. S. and Samion, S. (2020) 'The Impact of Deterrence on the Decision-Making Process of Drug Traffickers' *Home Team Journal* 65.

Kine, P. (2016) 'Indonesia President Jokowi May Rethink Death Penalty Policy', *Human Rights Watch* (10 November), www.hrw.org/news/2016/11/10/indonesia-president-jokowi-may-rethink-death-penalty-policy.

Lee, D. (2022) 'Schooling, Lim Treated "in the Same Way" as Others in Cannabis Use Investigation: Shanmugam', *The New Paper* (31 August). https://tnp.straitstimes.com/sports/swimming/schooling-lim-treated-same-way-others-cannabis-use-investigation-shanmugam.

Levitt, S. D. (2004) 'Understanding Why Crime Fell in the 1990s' 18(1) *Journal of Economic Perspectives* 163.

Loheswar, R. (2022) 'Five Hanged in Last Decade, Nine More in Line: A Look at Malaysians Facing Gallows in Singapore for Drug Offences' *Malay Mail* (29 April), www.malaymail.com/news/malaysia/2022/04/29/five-hanged-in-last-decade-nine-more-in-line-a-look-at-malaysians-facing-ga/2056200.

Low, J. Y. (2022) '300–400 People Attend Candlelight Vigil at Hong Lim Park for M'sian Drug Traffickers on Death Row', *Mothership* (26 April). https://mothership.sg/2022/04/candlelight-vigil-nagaenthran-datchinamurthy/.

Masagos, Z. (2012) 'Misuse of Drugs (Amendment) Bill', *Singapore Parliamentary Debates* (14 November). https://sprs.parl.gov.sg/search/#/sprs3topic?reportid=bill-32.

Ministry of Home Affairs. (2022a) *Findings from Recent Studies on the Death Penalty in Singapore* (19 October). www.mha.gov.sg/mediaroom/press-releases/findings-from-recent-studies-on-the-death-penalty-in-singapore/.

(2022b) *Statement by the Ministry of Home Affairs in Response to the International Drug Policy Consortium's Article on the Use of Capital Punishment Against Drug-Related Offences* (25 November). www.mha.gov.sg/mediaroom/press-releases/statement-by-the-ministry-of-home-affairs-in-response-to-the-international-drug-policy-consortium-article-on-the-use-of-capital-punishment-against-drug-related-offences.

NST Online. (2018) 'Death Penalty to be abolished', *New Straits Times* (10 October). www.nst.com.my/news/nation/2018/10/419931/death-penalty-be-abolished.

Ong, B. J. (2019) 'Looking Beyond the Vague Terms in Singapore's Fake News Laws', *Today* (14 May). www.todayonline.com/commentary/looking-beyond-vague-terms-fake-news-laws.

Ong, J. (2022a) "Joseph Schooling's Confession to Cannabis Use a 'Setback' for Singapore's Fight Against Drugs: Shanmugam", *Today* (1 September). www.todayonline.com/singapore/joseph-schooling-cannabis-singapore-fight-against-drugs-shanmugam-1982146.

(2022b) '3rd National Swimmer, Teong Tzen Wei, Took Drugs Overseas; SportSG Suspends Support to Errant Swimmers', *Today* (28 September). www.todayonline.com/singapore/third-national-swimmer-used-drugs-abroad-sportsg-2005276.

(2023) 'Explainer: How Will Malaysia's Abolition of Mandatory Death Penalty Affect Crime Rates, and Will S'pore Face Pressure to Follow Suit?', *Today* (4 April). www.todayonline.com/singapore/explainer-msia-mandatory-death-penalty-abolish-crime-rates-2144491.

Sato, M. (2023) *Singapore's Death Penalty for Drug Trafficking: What the Research Says and Doesn't.* www.academia.sg/academic-views/review-of-death-penalty-research/.

Shanmugam, K. (2020) *Written Reply to Parliamentary Question on Studies on the Deterrent Effect of a Life Sentence Relative to the Death Penalty.* www.mha.gov.sg/mediaroom/parliamentary/written-reply-to-parliamentary-question-on-studies-on-the-deterrent-effect-of-a-life-sentence-relative-to-the-death-penalty-by-mr-k-shanmugam-minister-for-home-affairs-and-minister-for-law/.

(2021) *Written Reply to Parliamentary Question on the Case of Mr David Roach.* www.mha.gov.sg/mediaroom/parliamentary/written-reply-to-pq-on-the-case-of-mr-david-roach/.

(2022a) 'Reasons for Not Disclosing Racial Composition of Prison Inmate Population and Criminal Offender Figures', *Singapore Parliamentary Debates* (4 July). https://sprs.parl.gov.sg/search/#/sprs3topic?reportid=oral-answer-2842.

(2022b) *Transcript of Sydney Morning Herald's Interview with Mr K Shanmugam, Minister for Home Affairs and Minister for Law, on 15 September 2022.* www.mha.gov.sg/mediaroom/speeches/transcript-of-sydney-morning-herald-interview-with-mr-k-shanmugam-on-15-september-2022/.

Strangio, S. (2023) 'Malaysia Announces Plans to Decriminalize Minor Drug Offenses', *The Diplomat* (17 May). https://thediplomat.com/2023/05/malaysia-announces-plans-to-decriminalize-minor-drug-offenses/.

Tan, T., Rahimy, R. and Carvalho, M. (2023) '"Nay" to Mandatory Death Penalty', *The Star* (4 April). www.thestar.com.my/news/nation/2023/04/04/nay-to-mandatory-death-penalty.

Tang, L. (2022) 'AGC Flags Possible Contempt of Court Action Over 'False Claims' in Failed Bid to Halt Drug Trafficker's Execution', *Today* (27 April). www.todayonline.com/singapore/agc-contempt-court-action-false-claims-drug-trafficker-execution-1884306.

(2023) 'New Laws Passed to Increase Penalties for Drug Possession, Better Tackle Psychoactive Substances', *Channel News Asia* (21 March). www.channelnewsasia.com/singapore/new-laws-passed-increase-penalties-drug-possession-better-tackle-psychoactive-substances-3362596.

Tee, K. (2023) 'A Brief History of Malaysia's Capital Punishment and Death Row Inmates', *Malay Mail* (3 April). www.malaymail.com/news/malaysia/2023/04/03/a-brief-history-of-malaysias-capital-punishment-and-death-row-inmates/62376.

Teo, C. H. (2012) 'Misuse of Drugs (Amendment) Bill', *Singapore Parliamentary Debates* (14 November). https://sprs.parl.gov.sg/search/#/sprs3topic?reportid=bill-38.

Teo, K. X. (2021) 'Civil Society Responses to Singapore's Online "Fake News' Law"' 15 *International Journal of Communication* 4795.

The Jakarta Post. (2023) 'New Penal Code Offers Hope of Abolishing Death Penalty in Indonesia', *The Star* (17 May). www.thestar.com.my/aseanplus/aseanplus-news/2023/05/17/new-penal-code-offers-hope-of-abolishing-death-penalty-in-indonesia.

Warr, P. (2023) 'Thailand's Cannabis Decriminalisation and Subsequent Unregulated Industry', *Thailand Business News* (25 March). www.thailand-business-news.com/opinion/97257-thailands-cannabis-decriminalisation-and-subsequent-unregulated-industry.

Wongcha-um, P. (2024) 'Thailand's Flourishing Cannabis Culture to End as Government Seeks Ban', *Reuters* (15 March). www.reuters.com/investigates/special-report/thailand-cannabis/.

Yang, K. (2021) 'Is Safekeeping Drug Trafficking? The Singapore Court of Appeal's Attempt to Delineate Role and Culpability in Drug Trafficking Offenses' 24(1) *New Criminal Law Review* 90.

Zimring, F. E., Fagan, J. and Johnson, D. T. (2010) 'Executions, Deterrence and Homicide: A Tale of Two Cities' 7(1) *Journal of Empirical Legal Studies* 1.

PART II

People on Death Row

5

From the Ghetto to the Gallows: Rights, Race, Class, and Drug Crimes in Malaysia

THAATCHAAYINI KANANATU

5.1 Introduction

In 2019, Amnesty International reported that:[1]

> [O]ut of the 713 Malaysian nationals on death row [in Malaysia], 48% belonged to the Malay ethnic group; 24% to the Chinese group; 25% to the Indian group; and 4% to other ethnic groups. This indicates that the Indian population and people belonging to other ethnic minorities are overrepresented on death row, while the Malay ethnicity has a lower proportion compared to its national comparative.

The 2018 Population Census of Malaysia reports that the ethnic breakdown of Malaysian citizens is 69 per cent Malay, 23 per cent Chinese, 7 per cent Indian, and 1 per cent Others.[2] This shows that Indians in Malaysia are an ethnic minority and are overrepresented on death row.

In the report, Amnesty International indicated that these figures were provided to them by 'official sources' with a caveat that the figures do not directly prove the existence of any ethnic or race-based and/or class-based discrimination in the Malaysian criminal justice system.[3] The report, however, gives a clear indication that the majority of those convicted under the mandatory capital drug laws come from less advantaged communities, that is, lower socioeconomic background or social class. This was based on the observation that the majority of individuals caught for drug trafficking are drug couriers, meaning that these individuals are at the bottom rung of the drug trafficking chain with less power, lack agency, and are from the least economically advantaged communities. These individuals can be argued to be in a vulnerable position as there have been reports of a high incidence of judicial errors in death

1 Amnesty International (2019).
2 Department of Statistics Malaysia (2018).
3 Amnesty International (2019).

penalty cases,[4] and increasing concerns regarding the lack of intellectual capacity and/or mental disabilities being considered in the decisions.[5]

This chapter takes the 2019 Amnesty International report as a starting point in exploring the overrepresentation of Malaysian citizens of Indian descent or race (hereinafter referred to as Malaysian Indians) on death row for drug trafficking in Malaysia. Using group-differentiated rights theory,[6] this study unpacks the overrepresentation of Malaysian Indians indicated in the Amnesty International report by applying the concept of a 'non-rights bearer group'. Malaysian Indians on death row are comprised of lower-class Malaysian Indians who can historically be traced back to Indian agricultural labourers or Indian indentured labourers brought into Malaya (as Malaysia was known then) by British colonial planters to work in British-owned rubber plantations. The argument that they are a non-rights bearer group is made by reference to the serious grievances and neglect that the group experienced because of the postcolonial socioeconomic policies from 1970 to 2000, primarily the 1971 New Economic Policy (NEP) and the 1990 National Development Policy.[7]

This chapter also argues that the drug couriers convicted of drug trafficking and sentenced to death prior to the abolition of the mandatory death sentence in 2023 are another 'non-rights bearer group' as they were not accorded the rights that come with international fair trial standards. Due to the nature of the drug trafficking laws, which carried the 'double presumption rule' under section 37(d) of the Dangerous Drugs Act 1952, drug couriers were not presumed innocent until proven guilty, but rather presumed guilty and automatically subject to the mandatory death penalty. This phenomenon was due to the strict and harsh drug trafficking laws in Malaysia which developed out of the 'war on drugs' policy in Southeast Asia.

This chapter will proceed to explain the theoretical framework that links the two aforementioned propositions.

5.1.1 *Theoretical Framework: Linking Rights, Race, Class, and Drug Crimes*

Eric Mitnick, in describing the group-differentiated rights theory, stated that the denial of legal rights creates a group or collective identity and

[4] Lim, Ngeow, and Arivananthan (2018).
[5] Amnesty International (2019); Antolak-Saper *et al.* (2020).
[6] Mitnick (1999, 2000, 2006).
[7] Kananatu (2020).

shared grievances, referred to as a 'non-rights bearer group'. Mitnick's argument is based on the constitutive theory of rights, which enunciates that legal rights constitute or create connections based on individuals' shared cultural or social identity. These aspects of shared identity or 'investitive criteria',[8] may include specific conditions or cultural markers – such as sex, ethnicity, economic status, or disability. These group-differentiated rights can create 'spheres of membership'[9] as rights bearers or non-bearers.

Conversely, the absence or denial of legal rights constitutes or forms a collective identity between individuals who share the grievance of rights denied. The process by which rights bearers are constructed also creates a non-rights bearer group that is denied the legal rights (due to the absence of the 'investitive criteria') and/or excluded from the sphere of privileges or entitlements accorded by that legal right. Mitnick elucidates that by denying rights, the law may stir a 'group consciousness', which may indeed lead to 'a roar'.[10] In other words, the creation of an aggrieved non-rights bearer group may lead to collective action, where the aggrieved collective may make claims against the duty bearers (those who have given the entitlements or privileges to the rights bearers).

Mitnick's group differentiated theory is used in this chapter for two purposes: first, to make a case that Malaysian Indians, particularly those from the lower socioeconomic class, are descendants of the Indian agricultural labourers or Indian indentured labourers during the colonial period in Malaya (1890s onwards), and were excluded from the post-colonial socioeconomic and national development policies (1970s to 1990s), which sought to eradicate poverty and socioeconomic disparities in Malaysia. As law and policy turned a blind eye to the grievances of this social underclass, it created race-based and class-based grievances that led to the formation of a non-rights bearer group.[11] Furthermore, the aggrieved were mobilised and took collective action once during the colonial period (the 1941 Klang Strikes), and again during the post-colonial period (the 2007 Hindraf or Hindu Rights Action Force), discussed in Section 5.2.

The second proposition focuses on the drug couriers who form an overwhelming majority of death row prisoners convicted of drug

[8] Mitnick (2000, p. 189).
[9] Mitnick (1999).
[10] Mitnick (2000, pp. 192–193).
[11] Kananatu (2020).

trafficking.[12] Under Malaysian law, drug couriers who may also be 'innocent carriers' were denied the legal rights that should be accorded to them by international fair trial standards, including the right to be presumed innocent until proven guilty.[13] This was due to the double-presumption rule that was in place until 2019, where one was presumed to be trafficking if caught in possession of a bag containing what turns out to be 'dangerous drugs'. The drug trafficking law not only thwarted the presumption of innocence but also meant that the convict would be automatically sentenced to death. This was the nature of the mandatory death sentence, which impeded the judge's discretion in sentencing, further explained in Section 5.3.

Using Mitnick's group differentiated theory, it is proposed here that the nature of the drug trafficking laws carrying the mandatory death penalty and the absence of fair trial rights had worked to constitute a non-rights bearer group – the members of which were denied basic rights, including the right to life and fair trial rights, as enshrined under international human rights law (Article 3 of the Universal Declaration of Human Rights) and the Malaysian Constitution (Articles 5 and 10 of the Federal Constitution).

Hence, Malaysian Indians convicted of drug trafficking do, as an overrepresented population on Malaysian death row, belong to *both* these non-rights bearer groups: first, as an ethnic minority that has been denied socioeconomic entitlements under the national laws and policies, and second, as drug couriers or innocent carriers denied fair trial rights under the Malaysian criminal justice system. It is proposed here that by virtue of falling into both the non-rights bearer groups, the Malaysian Indians on death row convicted of drug crimes face double discrimination as a marginalised group (to be explained in Section 5.3).

5.2 Background and Historical Context

This section traces the Malaysian Indian community from the British colonial period (1890s to 1956) to the postcolonial period (1957 onwards) to show the gradual construction of a race-based and class-based non-rights bearer group that was both socially and economically marginalised.

[12] Amnesty International (2019); Antolak-Saper *et al.* (2020); and Malaysian Parliament (2022).

[13] Antolak-Saper *et al.* (2020).

5.2.1 Race and Class in the Colonial Rubber Plantation

In the 1890s, British Malaya was the epicentre of colonialism and capitalism, as the British-ruled Straits Settlements (which included Malaya and Singapore) thrived due to the tin mining and rubber industries. As the native population, consisting mostly of the Malays, was predominantly located in rural areas and involved in paddy planting and fishing, the British sought to import cheap and affordable labour to work in the country's tin mines and rubber plantations. The British employed a strict divide-and-rule labour policy to control and manage the labour population, as well as to facilitate economic growth. The tin mining industry was manned by Chinese migrants and mostly located near towns and urban centres, while the rubber plantations in rural areas were predominantly worked on by Indian indentured labourers (that is, lower caste agricultural workers from the state of Tamil Nadu in British India). This created a legal and geographical segregation of the three main races – Malays, Chinese, and Indians – according to their economic roles.

Sandhu (1969) described that the British colonials found the typical Indian Tamil plantation worker 'docile and malleable'. The British planters chose them specifically as they were reverent to higher authority and were physically capable of working hard long hours in the plantations. Indian Tamil plantation workers spoke the Tamil language and were predominantly Hindu, and several authors[14] have described this group as having come from a lower caste in Tamil Nadu, India, mostly illiterate or with very little education. Recruitment of this group was necessary to keep them under the strict hierarchical control of both the British planters and the higher caste Indians who were recruited to manage them.

The mass migration of Indian Tamil labourers into Malaya occurred in two phases: the first phase (1890s to 1920s) witnessed the migration of indentured labourers (based on the indenture contract) involving direct recruitment of labourers by British planters.[15] The indentured labourer was akin to a slave as the indentured labourer system was described by Tinker (1974) as a 'new system of slavery'. The second phase of migration (1920s to 1950s) was through the *kangany* system of recruitment, where a *kangany* or head recruiter acted as an intermediary between the British planters and the labourers. This system also ensured that the labourers

[14] Sandhu (1969, 1993); Tate (2008); and Manickam (2012).
[15] Stenson (1980).

were managed by the *kangany* or foreman and often under a strict punitive management system involving physical punishment. The punishment for insubordinate behaviour involved flogging or whipping with a cat-o-nine-tails which sometimes led to death.[16]

The key labour issues that emerged at that time were extremely low wages, the strict and harsh treatment of the labourers, and poor basic amenities, especially for health and education for the children of labourers. Despite the strict hierarchy and control, the rubber plantation community developed and grew with the British establishment of basic housing, a basic primary school for the children of the labourers (vernacular or Tamil schools), and a temple for religious and cultural activities. As Indian Tamils were brought in as agricultural labourers, the intention was that their children would eventually become labourers themselves. This system seems to have persisted for decades, as it ultimately created a backward class lacking in education and with little or no opportunities for social mobility.

The 1940s witnessed a rising labour movement, as unions and organisations were set up and run by more educated Indians who had independently migrated to Malaya in the 1930s.[17] These individuals included journalists, clerks, and administrators in the British colonial administration. For instance, the 1941 Klang Strikes, which occurred in the urban town of Klang in the state of Selangor, involved several leaders who represented the plantation workers demanding better working and living conditions. However, labour movements and strikes were quickly stomped down by the British using military troops, while the Indian leaders were ousted and deported back to India. The British High Commissioner for the Federated Malay States, 'Sir Shenton Thomas accepted the view taken by the United Planting Association of Malaya (an association of British planters in Malaya) that "the strikers" demands were ridiculous'.[18]

This left the plantation workers at the mercy of the British planters until there was a rise in political activity after the Second World War. A new Indian movement was rising in Malaya, which sought to liberate British India and British Malaya from colonial rule. As Indians were beginning to collectivise, the leaders consisting of journalists, lawyers, administrators, and traders, attempted to mobilise and lead the plantation labourers into an Independent Malaya in 1957. As a politically

[16] Amrith (2010).
[17] Stenson (1980).
[18] Ibid, p. 64.

mobilised group moving towards independence and the possibility of new citizenship in Malaya, the Indian community in Malaya was heavily influenced by the anti-caste movement and the anti-colonial movement in India, creating a temporary unity among the Indian community in Malaya (cutting across caste, class, language, and religious divisions). The emancipation of the lower-caste labourers was a key agenda in the overall independence movement.

Once independence was achieved, the labour group's grievances were again forgotten. In essence, this group lacked agency, leverage, legal rights – either as citizens of British India or British Malaya – and legal protection as indentured servants of the British planters. The key issues remained, particularly those related to wages, living conditions, health, and educational facilities.

5.2.2 Race and Class in the Postcolonial Rubber Plantation

From 1957 to 1963, Malaya, as a newly independent state, was focused on building a strong nation and transitioning into a multicultural and multiracial society with new citizenships offered to the Chinese, Indians, and other races. The 1957 Federal Constitution included an equality provision (Article 8),[19] which ensured equality of all races; a citizenship provision (Article 14),[20] which allowed for automatic citizenship by virtue of being born in Malaya; and a provision on the special position of the Malays (Article 153),[21] which established special rights

[19] Article 8(1) of the Federal Constitution states that: '[a]ll persons are equal before the law and entitled to the equal protection of the law'. Article 8(2) states: '[e]xcept as expressly authorised by this Constitution, there shall be no discrimination against citizens on the ground only of religion, race, descent, place of birth or gender in any law or in the appointment to any office or employment under a public authority or in the administration of any law relating to the acquisition, holding or disposition of property or the establishing or carrying on of any trade, business, profession, vocation or employment'.

[20] Article 14(1) of the Federal Constitution states: '[s]ubject to the provisions of this Part, the following persons are citizens by operation of law, that is to say

(a) every person born before Malaysia Day who is a citizen of the Federation by virtue of the provisions contained in Part I of the Second Schedule and
(b) every person born on or after Malaysia Day, and having any of the qualifications specified in Part II of the Second Schedule'.

[21] Article 153(1) of the Federal Constitution states: '[i]t shall be the responsibility of the Yang di-Pertuan Agong to safeguard the special position of the Malays and natives of any of the States of Sabah and Sarawak and the legitimate interests of other communities in accordance with the provisions of this Article'.

and quotas in tertiary education, certain business licences and positions in the public service. The special position was redressed by ensuring the 'legitimate interests of other communities' and was safeguarded under the same provision. In 1963, Malaya transformed into Malaysia, incorporating North Borneo or Sabah, Sarawak, and Singapore (the latter of which left Malaysia in 1965). While this created further cultural and geographical diversity, native rights were beginning to play a dominant role in law, policy, and politics.

Within the new postcolonial multicultural milieu, Indians formed a minority and a large percentage of them were still located in the rural rubber plantations. It is crucial to note that there existed social class and economic cleavages among the Malaysian Indians themselves, and this chapter is focused on the Malaysian Indians who are descendants of the colonial indentured labourers in the aforementioned discussion on rubber plantations.

The socioeconomic plans and policy changes that came during this period greatly influenced and affected Malaysian Indian plantation labour. Malaysia was the world's largest producer of rubber and tin, and while heavily reliant on the tin mining and rubber industries, was looking to redress the problem of falling rubber prices and rapid depletion of tin.[22] One of the key economic moves was to shift from rubber to oil palm plantations, a change which would directly affect the Indian plantation labour. While economic planning was underway, 1969 witnessed political and social unrest which led to a 'race riot' between the Malays and the Chinese.[23] This event left the nation at a standstill, and issues pertaining to racial politics and the nation's economic position drove the agenda in new policies coming into play.

In 1971, the 'NEP'[24] was set in place in order to redress economic imbalance and bring social unity among the three main races (Malays, Chinese, and Indians). At this point, the racial classifications were formalised and legalised in population census categories, registration laws, affirmative action policies and programmes.[25] Under the NEP, the term 'Bumiputera' (translated to 'sons of the soil') was introduced, incorporating the native people of Sabah and Sarawak. The indigenous people or

[22] First Malaysia Plan (1966–1970).
[23] Kua (2008).
[24] Second Malaysia Plan (1971–1975).
[25] Kananatu (2020).

aboriginals of Peninsula Malaysia were captured under a separate provision under the Federal Constitution (Article 160).[26]

The dual purpose of the NEP was to eradicate poverty regardless of race and to rectify the economic and social imbalances created by the colonial economy as a result of the colonial divide-and-rule policy where labour was segregated according to economic function (Indians in rubber plantations, Chinese in tin mining, and Malays in paddy plantations). Due to the special focus on Malay and Bumiputera special privileges and affirmative action programmes, the NEP is often characterised as an affirmative action policy. However, the general focus of the NEP was to eradicate poverty and remedy economic imbalances.

The NEP should, in theory, have included the hardcore poverty experienced by the Malaysian Indian rubber plantation labour group. However, this group was neglected by the NEP and disregarded in all government poverty reduction initiatives because they were labourers situated in privately owned plantations or corporations (half of which were British-owned, such as Guthrie and Harrison & Crosfield). Due to this discrepancy, this group lost out on many of the poverty eradication schemes rolled out by the government under the NEP. Private corporations that owned the plantations lacked interest in addressing the grievances experienced by the Malaysian Indian plantation labourers, so continued to pay them low wages and disregarded their socioeconomic welfare. Many self-help groups and cooperatives from the more middle-class educated members of the Malaysian Indian community tried to alleviate the poverty and welfare issues faced by plantation labourers, but this was a gigantic task and was not sustainable in the long run.

Leaders of the Malaysian Indian Congress ('MIC'), the political party that was part of the ruling government coalition Barisan Nasional, voiced out grievances of the community and produced a Blueprint (1974) containing policy recommendations to address the problem faced by the Malaysian Indian plantation labourers. The Blueprint described the grievances of the rubber plantation workers and suggested solutions and recommendations to ensure that this group would not continue to be marginalised by the NEP. The four main issues identified were 'the economic position of Malaysian Indians, employment issues and

[26] Article 160(2) of the Federal Constitution defines 'aborigine' as 'an aborigine of the Malay Peninsula'.

problems, land development, and education problems'.[27] One of the main contentions was to counter the race-based approach taken by the NEP, which centred around the Malay affirmative action policy. Despite the strong approach taken in producing the MIC Blueprint, the recommendations were not taken further in parliament or in the MIC's political lobbying, due to 'the lack of political clout and leverage of the MIC leadership' within the government coalition.[28]

The calls to the government to address the problems faced by the Indian plantation labourer group were often neglected because the plantations were in private land and owned by foreign companies. However, in the mid-1980s, it became clear that most of the multinational corporations owning the plantations were, in fact, linked to the ruling government. In September 1981, due to an event called the 'London Dawn Raid', the previously British-owned plantation company Guthrie was aggressively bought overnight by a Malaysian government-linked Bumiputera trust agency called Permodalan Nasional Berhad.[29] Because the Malaysian Indian plantation labourer's grievance had rested on the fact that they were on privately owned plantations, they had hoped for security in terms of tenure, better wages, and working conditions. Their hopes were crushed as the new management was only interested in multiplying profits and ensuring wages remained low.[30] Hence, they were marginalised by both government policy (the NEP) and employers – rendering them a non-rights bearer group.

From 1990 to 2000, the National Development Policy ('NDP')[31] was launched as a successor to the NEP. The NDP was positioned to rapidly develop rural land and improve the nation's economy by focusing on urban development and technological advancement. The process of urbanisation involved the fragmentation (splicing plantation land to sell at a higher market price) of plantations and redevelopment of the land. The NDP neglected to consider the plight of the Indian plantation labourers, the majority of whom were now facing rural displacement, forced urbanisation and, ultimately, urban poverty. Many were gradually retrenched, and families were evicted from the plantation land. As the government focus shifted to the more lucrative palm oil industry, the

27 Malaysian Indian Congress Blueprint (1974).
28 Kananatu (2020).
29 Sivachandralingam (2012).
30 Ibid.
31 Sixth Malaysia Plan (1990–1995); Seventh Malaysia Plan (1996–2000).

government-linked companies opted to hire cheaper migrant workers from Indonesia and Bangladesh. The unemployed and evicted former Indian plantation labourers now faced the perils of urban poverty, as most were pushed to urban squatter settlements or ghettos.

5.2.3 *Race, Class, and Crime in the Ghettos*

This section discusses the creation of an Indian urban underclass in urban squatter settlements or ghettos, due to (1) the eviction of the Indian plantation labourers from the estates as these rubber plantations were subdivided, sold, and redeveloped for other purposes and (2) the loss of jobs due to the replacement of labourers with cheaper migrant workers from Bangladesh and Indonesia.

The eviction of the former Indian plantation workers effectively meant that they were forcibly removed from the plantation community and placed in makeshift urban squatter settlements. The social displacement that occurred led to more serious social problems, including overcrowded living conditions (in mostly low-cost flats, slums, and squatters), a high unemployment rate, and problems among the uneducated and unemployed youth – including criminal activities and gangsterism. These places where they were forcibly moved to include temporary flats like Taman Permata, in Dengkil,[32] and squatter areas like Kampung Medan (that became the site of a racial riot in 2001 resulting in the racial stigmatisation of Indians as a criminalised problematic group.[33] In essence, this gradual process of marginalisation of former Indian plantation labourers led to the creation of an Indian underclass.[34] As Bunnell, Nagarajan and Willford argue, '[c]onfined to a national ex-plantation periphery, this group was increasingly characterised as a criminalised and socially problematic sub-class'.[35]

In the case of the 2001 Kampung Medan incident, the differential treatment accorded to Indian victims by the police and state authorities led to outrage among human rights activists and lawyers. A memorandum signed by fifty-one non-governmental organisations in 2001 was sent to the prime minister, indicating that this incident called for a Royal Commission of Inquiry. This call was supported by the

[32] Bunnell, Nagarajan, and Willford (2010).
[33] Nagarajan and Arumugam (2012).
[34] Lian (2002, 2006); Loh (2003, p. 223).
[35] Bunnell, Nagarajan, and Willford (2010, p. 1264).

Malaysian Bar Council, which requested an enquiry under the Commissions of Enquiry Act 1950. The main contention was the differential treatment accorded to the Indian victims by the police force. The failure to set up an inquiry had triggered and fuelled further outrage. This event was instrumental in the culmination of the 2007 Hindraf movement and demonstrations and later led to the electoral mobilisation of Indians in the 2008 General Elections.[36]

Civil society groups began to emerge requesting investigations of other issues such as the high number of Indian victims of police shootings and deaths in police custody. The issues with the police were related to the rise in youth crime and gangsterism that was becoming prevalent in the ghettos.

These squatter settlements or ghettos attracted social problems, including increased participation in drug-related crimes.[37] A 2019 study conducted by Durairaja *et al.*, involving interviews of ex-gangsters and the police, linked such criminality with psychological factors such as negative emotional responses, low self-control, and high impulsivity; criminogenic factors, such as substance abuse; and having antisocial peers and dysfunctional families. The authors contended that due to the background of this group (coming from urban squatters and urban poverty), the Indian gangsters involved in crime (including drug crimes) were reluctant to part from 'benefits deriving from illegal monetary gains'.[38]

Studies have examined the overrepresentation of Indians from a lower socioeconomic background among victims of deaths in custody[39] and those involved in gangsterism related to drug crimes.[40] However, there have been no studies or official figures provided on the possible overrepresentation of this group on death row due to drug crimes. As mentioned in Section 5.1, Amnesty International (2019) reported that there is an overrepresentation of Indians on death row. Following this report, in 2020, the then minister in the prime minister's department (parliament and law), Dato' Takiyuddin bin Hassan,[41] indicated that there were 1,324 death row prisoners, out of which 788 or 60 per cent

36 Kananatu (2018).
37 Durairaja, Mat Saat, and Kamaluddin (2019).
38 Ibid, p. 84.
39 Mahamad Arif *et al.* (2021, pp. 305–307).
40 Durairaja, Mat Saat, and Kamaluddin (2019).
41 Malaysian Parliament (2020).

were Malaysian citizens. When requested for an ethnic breakdown, the minister presented that there were 405 Malays (51 per cent), 210 (27 per cent) Indians, and 173 (22 per cent) Chinese. This clearly shows an overrepresentation of Indians on death row, but it does not indicate the ethnic percentage of those on death row for drug crimes.

As of 2022, based on the data provided by the then minister in the prime minister's department (parliament and law) Dato Sri Dr. Haji Wan Junaidi bin Tuanku Jaafar,[42] there were 1,343 death row prisoners in Malaysia. At the session, the former member of parliament of Batu Kawan, Mrs Kasthuriraani Patto, requested a breakdown of the prisoners according to race (*kaum* or *bangsa* in Malay), age, sex, economic status (whether in the economic grouping of the top twenty, middle forty, or bottom forty), type of crime, nationality, and their prison location. Mrs Kasthuriraani also requested information on the government's efforts to head towards a rehabilitative system and the timeline for the abolition of the mandatory death penalty.

The minister responded that out of the 1,343 death row prisoners in Malaysia, 67 per cent of these prisoners were charged under section 39B of the Dangerous Drugs Act 1952.[43] Of this number, the minister indicated that 62.3 per cent were Malaysians and 36.7 per cent foreign nationals; 821 were Malaysian men and twenty-eight Malaysian women; 396 were foreign national men and ninety-eight foreign national women; 328 were aged between twenty-one and thirty years, 546 aged between thirty-one and forty years; and 355 aged between forty-one and fifty years. While information was given pertaining to the citizenship, sex, and age demographics of the death row prisoners, the minister failed to provide the numbers according to race and socioeconomic status.

In the author's ongoing study of drug crimes and the death penalty in Malaysia from 1980 until 2023, it has been found that of the 914 legal cases involving persons charged with drug trafficking under section 39B

[42] Malaysian Parliament (2022).

[43] Section 39B(1) of the Dangerous Drugs Act 1952 states:

> No person shall, on his own behalf or on behalf of any other person, whether or not such other person is in Malaysia
>
> (a) traffic in a dangerous drug;
> (b) offer to traffic a dangerous drug; or
> (c) do or offer to do an act preparatory to or for the purpose of trafficking in a dangerous drug.

of the Dangerous Drugs Act 1952, 125 involved Malaysian Indians (14 per cent), 175 involved Malaysian Chinese (19 per cent), and 286 involved Malaysian Malays (31 per cent). It is clear that Malaysian Indians are overrepresented, given that they comprise 14 per cent of those charged under section 39B of the Dangerous Drugs Act 1952 despite amounting to only 6.7 per cent of the country's population according to the latest 2020 Population Census. Out of the 914 cases, 603 involved Malaysian citizens and 311 involved foreign nationals. A comparison of ethnic or racial percentages among Malaysian nationals indicates that Malaysian Indians account for 21 per cent of Malaysians charged under section 39B of the Dangerous Drugs Act 1952. Of the 125 cases involving Malaysian Indians, 120 of them involved Malaysian Indian men and five involved Malaysian Indian women; hence, there is an overrepresentation of Malaysian Indian males among those charged with drug trafficking in Malaysia.

The study also found that from 1980 (when an amendment was made to incorporate the mandatory death penalty for drug trafficking under section 39B of the Dangerous Drugs Act 1952) to 1986, there were no cases that involved Malaysian Indians. From 1987 to 1997, there were only three cases that involved Malaysian Indians. Whereas, from 1998 to 2008, there were seventeen Malaysian Indians charged under section 39B of the Dangerous Drugs Act 1952. A sudden increase was seen from 2009 to 2019, when seventy-three Malaysian Indians were charged under the provision. From 2020 to 2023, there were thirty-one Malaysian Indians charged under section 39B of the Dangerous Drugs Act 1952. The spike in the number of cases involving Malaysian Indians from 1998 to 2019 (104 cases in a span of almost twenty years) correlates with the forced migration of the Indian plantation labourers to the ghettos from the mid-1990s (as discussed in subsection 5.2.3).

As an overrepresented ethnic minority on death row, these individuals are also members of the non-rights bearer group who have been marginalised and neglected by the government socioeconomic policies from the 1970s to 1990s. The next section will discuss the construction of the *second* non-rights bearer group that they fall into: the drug couriers on death row.

5.3 Drug Couriers on Death Row (the Gallows)

The formation of this non-rights bearer group is intimately tied to the nature of drug trafficking laws in Malaysia and the drug law amendments and anti-narcotics policies that were put in place in Malaysia, following suit with Singapore, Indonesia, and Thailand.

5.3.1 *War on drugs in Southeast Asia*

Within the geopolitics of the Southeast Asian region, the mid-1970s witnessed a strong call by Malaysia and Singapore to declare a 'war on drugs'[44] and emphasis on the need to safeguard national security and national sovereignty.[45] The Malaysian government sought to frame the drug trafficking issue as a 'foreign' threat to the nation, which was in its infancy in terms of national and economic development.[46] The national threat was the drug trafficker, who, in most cases highlighted by the media at that time, involved foreign nationals from Western liberal democracies.[47] This played into the political emphasis of the 'Asian Values' rhetoric which undermined the value of an individual's human rights and civil liberties in favour of the community and nation. In sum, the United States-inspired 'war on drugs' was used as a political tool to dissuade drug crime, legitimised by the Asian Values rhetoric, national security concerns, and national development policies.

The geopolitics and national security concerns explain the nature of the amendments made to the Dangerous Drugs Act in 1980 to incorporate the double presumption rule in tandem with the disproportionately harsh punishment of the mandatory death penalty for drug trafficking.

5.3.2 *Double Presumption Rule and the Mandatory Death Penalty*

The double presumption rule found in the now abolished section 37A and section 37(d) of the Dangerous Drugs Act 1952[48] provided that if a person were to be caught with any 'dangerous drug', that person would be presumed to be in possession of that drug, which would trigger the

[44] Novak (2014, p. 303).
[45] Harring (1991, p. 371).
[46] Kananatu (2022).
[47] Anderson and Van Atta (1990); Deans (1990).
[48] Section 37(d) of the Dangerous Drugs Act 1952 reads: 'any person who is found to have had in his custody or under his control anything whatsoever containing any dangerous drug shall, until the contrary is proved, be deemed to have been in possession of such drug and shall, until the contrary is proved, be deemed to have known the nature of such drug . . .'.

second presumption that the person was, in fact, trafficking in the drug. Under the Malaysian common law, there is something known as the defence of innocent carrier, which is defined as 'a state of affairs where an accused person acknowledges carrying for example a bag or a box . . . containing the dangerous drugs but disputes having knowledge of the drugs'.[49] N. Antolak-Saper *et al.* found that out of the 24 cases where the defence was raised fifteen times (from 1978 to 2019), it was never accepted.[50]

The courts are generally reluctant to accept the innocent carrier defence, as the courts find it unconvincing. If an accused, for instance, flees from the scene or attempts to evade an arrest, it can 'whittle away the presumption of innocence'.[51] Hence, even if the person had not, in fact, trafficked a dangerous drug, being found in possession of such a drug and not being able to explain why may potentially lead the individual to the gallows.

Criminologists[52] have focused on the unfairness of these laws that have sent drug couriers (many of whom may be innocent carriers) to death while disregarding factors such as citizenship, age, sex, and socioeconomic backgrounds that make these individuals vulnerable and disadvantaged. Hoyle argues that 'characteristics such as race, religion and citizenship status are not protective and are sites of discrimination in the administration of the death penalty'.[53] However, the rule led to a total disregard for the accused's vulnerabilities, as judicial discretion in determining mitigating circumstances had been removed.

Human rights scholars have argued for a more proportionate punishment, taking into consideration the accused's socioeconomic status as a mitigating circumstance. Lawyers and legal activists centred upon the human rights argument: that section 37A of the Dangerous Drugs Act 1952 contravened the constitutional prohibition on arbitrary deprivation of life or liberty (Article 5) and the right to equality before the law (Article 8). This argument was successfully brought up in the 2019 Federal Court decision of *Alma Nudo Atenza v. PP and another appeal*.[54]

[49] *Venkatesan Chinnasami v. PP* [2011] 1 LNS 1736.
[50] Antolak-Saper *et al.* (2020).
[51] *Marlan Marpaung v. PP* [2012] 8 CLJ 41; Evidence Act 1950, s. 8.
[52] Hoyle (2019); Harry (2021).
[53] Hoyle (2019, p. 177).
[54] *Alma Nudo Atenza v. PP and another appeal* [2019] 5 CLJ 780.

The legal argument of the defence rested on the 'double presumption rule' which operated to remove the judge's discretion to consider mitigating factors during the sentencing process. The *Alma Nudo* case successfully removed this rule, allowing for the judge's discretion to consider mitigating circumstances. The court considered whether using the presumption of possession to invoke the presumption of trafficking under section 37 of the Dangerous Drugs Act 1952 was 'harsh, oppressive and thus impermissible'.[55] In addressing the effect of the double presumption rule on the presumption of innocence, the Federal Court judgment in the *Alma Nudo case* stated that:[56]

> Drug trafficking has been a major problem in the country. It needs to be curbed. One way is to secure convictions of drug traffickers which can be considered a sufficiently important objective and one which is substantial and pressing.

Nevertheless, while remaining cognisant of the importance of curtailing drug crime, the court ultimately found the double presumption rule to be a 'grave erosion to the presumption of innocence housed in Article 5(1) of the [Federal Constitution]'.[57]

These arguments and reasonings made by scholars, lawyers, and judges, emphasise the draconian nature of the double presumption rule – which ultimately left the accused or drug mule without recourse and certain death. Further to this, there was a clear absence of fair trial rights and standards that were normally accorded to a person accused of a criminal offence. The following arguments will show that drug couriers are a non-rights bearer group that had been robbed of their basic human rights.

5.3.3 *Fair Trial Rights and Standards*

Several reports have identified various fair trial rights as being absent from drug trafficking cases in Malaysia.[58] These fair trial rights are discussed in the following and linked to the creation of a non-rights bearer group due to the absence of these rights for the drug couriers.

[55] Ibid, at 782.

[56] Ibid, at 832.

[57] Ibid.

[58] Lim, Ngeow, and Arivananthan (2018); Amnesty International (2019); Antolak-Saper *et al.* (2020); and Anti Death Penalty Asia Network (2022).

According to Article 14 of the International Covenant on Civil and Political Rights 1966 ('ICCPR'), every person is entitled to a fair and public hearing by a competent, independent, and impartial tribunal established by the law. This provision applies to all, regardless of whether the state is party to the ICCPR or not, by virtue of it being part of customary international law.[59] Malaysia is not a signatory to the ICCPR, but nevertheless, adheres to this provision through Article 5 of the Federal Constitution. The most significant provision is Article 14(2) ICCPR which states that 'everyone charged with a criminal offence shall have the right to be presumed innocent until proved guilty according to law'. As drug offenders were subject to the double presumption rule, it meant that they were robbed of this significant legal right. Instead, they were presumed guilty until proven innocent.

Further issues can be seen in terms of Article 14(3) which lists the rights to (*a*) be informed of the nature and cause of any criminal charge in the language which one understands and (*f*) be given the assistance of an interpreter where necessary. The national language in Malaysia is Bahasa Malaysia or the Malay language, which is the language that most law enforcement officers are conversant in. The rights enumerated in Article 14(3) are undermined in many cases, mostly those involving foreign nationals as well as Malaysian Indians, as evident in the case of *PP v. Limneswaran Jegathesan*.[60] In this case, Limneswaran, a Malaysian citizen unable to speak Bahasa Malaysia, was charged with the offence of trafficking in dangerous drugs (736.6g of methamphetamine) under section 39B of the Dangerous Drugs Act 1952. Limneswaran stated that 'he was never given the opportunity to explain himself fluently in Tamil with the aid of an interpreter, right from the time he was arrested until he was charged'. He was also required to sign on a piece of paper which he had no knowledge of its contents.

Additionally, Article 14(3)(b) of the ICCPR ensures that the accused has adequate time and facility to prepare his or her defence and communicate with his or her own counsel of choice. While this is embedded in section 28A(2)(b) of the Criminal Procedure Code and Article 5(3) of the Federal Constitution, the reality for most accused who cannot afford a lawyer is that one is provided under legal aid schemes. According to Amnesty International (2019), there are three legal aid schemes for death penalty cases: schemes provided by the courts (providing free

[59] Human Rights Committee (1994, para. 8).
[60] [2019] 1 LNS 494; Antolak-Saper *et al.* (2020).

representation), the National Legal Aid Foundation (providing aid during the pre-trial stage and pardon applications for Malaysians), and the Bar Council Legal Aid Centre (providing pro bono legal assistance from the remand stage regardless of the accused's nationality).

Despite these avenues for legal aid, one major issue highlighted is the insufficient funding provided to the pro bono lawyer working on the case. The lack of funding impedes the lawyer from getting adequate independent expert witnesses and barely covers the cost.[61] The problem of lack of funding for legal aid works against the drug couriers who are mostly from a lower socioeconomic background. This is the group that is being disadvantaged from the very start of the process.

Other fundamental fair trial rights which have been denied include the right to be tried without undue delay (Article 14(3)(c) of the ICCPR), the privilege against self-incrimination (which in theory is against the double presumption rule that requires the accused to rebut the presumption), and the right to appeal conviction and sentence.[62] Undue delays in the process can particularly be a problem as death row inmates may experience psychological issues known as the 'death row phenomenon' when they are incarcerated for a prolonged period anticipating their death.[63]

The denial of these fair trial rights rendered drug couriers, particularly those with low education (including language skills) from the lower socioeconomic group, powerless and without adequate recourse to justice.

5.3.4 *Abolition of the Death Penalty for Drug Trafficking*

This chapter's focus on specific drug trafficking laws is due to the mandatory death penalty that was in place for the last forty-three years, from 1980 to 2023. The mandatory death penalty was abolished under the Abolition of Mandatory Death Penalty Act 2023 ('2023 Abolition Act') for twelve crimes, including drug trafficking, under section 39B of the Dangerous Drugs Act 1952. After a long battle fought by human rights lawyers, anti-death penalty organisations, and human rights non-governmental organisations (international and local), both the ruling government and opposition parties were agreeable to the 2023 Abolition Act.

[61] Antolak-Saper *et al.* (2020).
[62] Ibid.
[63] Ibid.

Currently, those who were previously convicted and sentenced to death, await the potential revision of their sentences. The Revision of Sentence of Death and Imprisonment for Natural Life (Temporary Jurisdiction of The Federal Court) Act 2023 (Act 847) has initiated the resentencing process. Under the Act, the Federal Court has been given jurisdiction to review the sentences of death and life imprisonment for natural life imposed on convicted persons. According to the current minister of Law and Institutional Reform, Datuk Azalina Othman said: '[t]he implementation of the handling mechanism of court proceedings will allow all 1,020 prisoners who have been sentenced to mandatory death and life imprisonment, to file an application in court to review their respective sentences'.[64]

As part of the resentencing process, the courts are now allowed to look at mitigating circumstances and factors and may revise the death sentence at their discretion. The question remains if factors such as socioeconomic position coming from a marginalised community can be considered in determining mitigating circumstances. It remains to be seen if the courts can remedy the wrongs that have been meted out to the non-rights bearer groups in particular.

5.4 Concluding Remarks: Race, Class, and the Non-Rights Bearers

This chapter started with the premise that Malaysian Indians are over-represented on death row. Various international human rights reports and information obtained from the parliament question and answer sessions with the minister of law have indicated this to be true. While there is still a lack of official statistics on the ethnic breakdown, particularly of those on death row for drug trafficking offences, this chapter proceeded with data obtained through human rights organisations' reports, and a study was done on legal cases involving section 39B of the Dangerous Drugs Act 1952 from 1980–2023.

This chapter has presented two main arguments. The first argument is that the majority of Malaysian Indians who ended up on death row are from the Indian underclass that was marginalised from the British colonial period (the 1890s) to the postcolonial period (1957 onwards). The gradual process of marginalisation had led to this formerly rubber

[64] Hilmy (2023).

plantation labour group being socially displaced, ostracised, and criminalised in the urban squatters or ghettos. Chan and Hor also noted that Malaysians on Singapore's death row are also disproportionately of a particular racial minority – in that case, the Malaysian Indian minority.[65] This merits further study on the impact of drug laws in both Malaysia and Singapore on marginalised groups – particularly those who are generationally trapped between the intersections of race and economic colonisation.

The second argument is that the drug trafficking laws that provided for the mandatory death penalty until its recent abolition disregarded fair trial rights and standards, which has had an impact on drug couriers who come from lower educational and socioeconomic communities, including the Indian underclass. The disregard for their fair trial rights had rendered them powerless in the face of harsh and draconian drug trafficking laws that were put in place due to the war on drugs in Southeast Asia.

Essentially, the Malaysian Indians who are overrepresented on death row for drug crimes fall into both non-rights bearer groups: the Indian underclass and the drug couriers. This made them particularly vulnerable and discriminated against in the criminal justice system.

References

Amnesty International. (2019) *Fatally Flawed: Why Malaysia Must Abolish the Death Penalty*. www.amnesty.org/en/documents/act50/1078/2019/en/.

Amrith, S. S. (2010) 'Indians Overseas? Governing Tamil Migration in Malaya 1870–1941' 208 *Past and Present* 231.

Anderson, J. and Van Atta, D. (1990) 'American Faces Death Row in Malaysia' *The Washington Post* (19 September). www.proquest.com/historical-newspapers/american-faces-death-row-malaysia/docview/89072539/se-2?accountid=12528.

Anti Death Penalty Asia Network. (2022) *Report on the Death Penalty in Malaysia: Reform in Limbo*. https://adpan.org/wp-content/uploads/2021/06/ADPAN-Malaysia-Report-Reform-in-Limbo.pdf.

Antolak-Saper, N., Kowal, S., Lindsey, S., Ngeow, C. Y. and Kananatu, T. (2020) *Drug Offences and the Death Penalty in Malaysia: Fair Trial Rights and Ramifications* (Monash University). www.monash.edu/__data/assets/pdf_file/0011/2213867/MU_ADPAN_report_v6.pdf.

[65] W. C. Chan and M. Hor in Chapter 4 in this volume.

Bunnell, T., Nagarajan, S. and Willford, A. (2010) 'From the Margins to Centre Stage: "Indian" Demonstration Effects in Malaysia's Political Landscape' 47(6) *Urban Studies* 1257.

Deans, B. (1990) 'Dadah Means Death: Even for Foreigners' *Edmonton Journal* (18 March). www.proquest.com/newspapers/dadah-means-death-even-foreigners/docview/250537225/se-2?accountid=12528.

Department of Statistics Malaysia. (2018) *Current Population Estimates, Malaysia, 2017–2018.* https://v1.dosm.gov.my/v1/index.php?r=column/cthemeByCat&cat=155&bul_id=c1pqTnFjb29HSnNYNUpiTmNWZHArdz09&menu_id=L0pheU43NWJwRWVSZklWdzQ4TlhUUT09.

Durairaja, S., Mat Saat, G. A. and Kamaluddin, M. R. (2019) 'Psychological and Criminogenic Factors Underlying Gangsterism Among Indians in Malaysia from the Perspective of Ex-gangsters and Police Personnel' 12(1) *Psychological Thought* 74.

First Malaysia Plan. (1966–1970) 'First Malaysia Plan, 1966–1970'. www.ekonomi.gov.my/en/economic-developments/development-plans/rmk/first-malaysia-plan-1966-1970.

Harring, S. L. (1991) 'Death, Drugs and Development: Malaysia's Mandatory Death Penalty for Traffickers and the International War on Drugs' 29(2) *Columbia Journal of Transnational Law* 365.

Harry, L. (2021) 'Rethinking the Relationship between Women, Crime and Economic Factors: The Case-Study of Women Sentenced to Death for Drug Trafficking in Malaysia' 10(1) *Laws* 9.

Hilmy, I. (2023) 'Law on Revision of Death Sentences and Life Imprisonment Comes Into Force on Sept 12', *The Star* (11 September). www.thestar.com.my/news/nation/2023/09/11/law-on-revision-of-death-sentences-and-life-imprisonment-comes-into-force-on-sept-12.

Hoyle, C. (2019) 'Capital Punishment at the Intersections of Discrimination and Disadvantage: The Plight of Foreign Nationals' in Steiker, C. S. and Steiker, J. M. (eds.) *Comparative Capital Punishment* (Cheltenham: Edward Elgar Publishing).

Human Rights Committee. (1994) *General Comment No. 24* (CCPR/C/21/Rev.1/Add.6). https://digitallibrary.un.org/record/200963?v=pdf.

Kananatu, T. (2018) 'The Politico-Legal Mobilisation of Ethnic Indians Before Malaysia's 2018 Election' 107(6) *The Round Table* 703.

(2020) *Minorities, Rights and the Law in Malaysia* (Abingdon: Routledge).

(2022) 'Framing Death Penalty Politics in Malaysia' 11(3) *International Journal for Crime, Justice and Social Democracy* 57.

Kua, K. S. (2008) 'Racial Conflict in Malaysia: Against the Official History' 49(3) *Race & Class* 33.

Lian, K. F. (2002) 'The Political and Economic Marginalisation of Tamils in Malaysia' 26(3) *Asian Studies Review* 309.

(2006) *Race, Ethnicity, and the State in Malaysia and Singapore* (Leiden: Brill).

Lim, C. H., Ngeow, C. Y. and Arivananthan, H. (2018) 'High Incidence of Judicial Errors in Capital Punishment Cases in Malaysia' *Penang Institute Issues* (30 October). https://penanginstitute.org/wp-content/uploads/2018/10/oct_30_2018_CHTEAM_download.pdf.

Loh, F. (2003) 'The Marginalization of the Indians in Malaysia' in Siegel, J. T. and Kahin, A. R. (eds.) *Southeast Asia Over Three Generations: Essays Presented to Benedict R. O'G. Anderson* (Ithaca: Cornell Southeast Asia Program).

Mahamad Arif, A. N. F., Syed Alwee Al'aidrus, S. S., Shafee, M. S. and Mohd Nor, F. (2021) 'A 15-Year Study of Death in Custody in Tuanku Ja'afar Hospital Seremban' 43(2) *The Malaysian Journal of Pathology* 303.

Malaysian Indian Congress Blueprint. (1974) First Malaysian Indian Economic Seminar on 'The New Economic Policy, the Second Malaysia Plan, and the Mid-Term Review, and the Role of the MIC' (Kuala Lumpur, 11–12 May).

Malaysian Parliament. (2020) 14th Parliament, Third Session, Third Meeting (26 November) (Kasthuriraani Patto, Question 20). www.parlimen.gov.my/files/jindex/pdf/JDR26112020.pdf.

(2022) 14th Parliament, Fifth Session, Second Meeting (2 August) (Kasthuriraani Patto, Question 71). www.parlimen.gov.my/files/jindex/pdf/JDR02082022.pdf.

Manickam, J. R. (2012) *The Malaysian Indian Dilemma: The Struggles and Agony of the Indian Community in Malaysia* (Klang: Nationwide Human Development and Research Centre).

Mitnick, E. J. (1999) 'Taking Rights Spherically: Formal and Collective Aspects of Legal Rights' 34 *Wake Forest Law Review* 409.

(2000) 'Constitutive Rights' 20(2) *Oxford Journal of Legal Studies* 185.

(2006) *Rights, Groups, and Self-Invention: Group Differentiated Rights in Liberal Theory* (Aldershot: Ashgate).

Nagarajan, S. and Arumugam, K. (2012) *Violence Against an Ethnic Minority in Malaysia: Kampung Medan, 2001* (Petaling Jaya: SUARAM).

Novak, A. (2014) 'The Future of the Mandatory Death Penalty in Malaysia and Singapore: "Asian Values" and Abolition in Comparative Perspective, with Implications for Indonesia' 1(1) *Indonesian Journal of International and Comparative Law* 303.

Sandhu, K. S. (1969) *Indians in Malaya: Some Aspects of Their Immigration and Settlement (1786–1957)* (Cambridge: Cambridge University Press).

(1993) 'The Coming of the Indians to Malaysia' in Sandhu, K. S. and Mani, A. (eds.) *Indian Communities in Southeast Asia* (Singapore: Institute of Southeast Asian Studies).

Second Malaysia Plan. (1971–1975) 'Second Malaysia Plan, 1971–1975'. www.ekonomi.gov.my/en/economic-developments/development-plans/rmk/second-malaysia-plan-1971-1975.

Seventh Malaysia Plan. (1996–2000) 'Seventh Malaysia Plan, 1996–2000'. www.ekonomi.gov.my/en/economic-developments/development-plans/rmk/seventh-malaysia-plan-1996-2000.

Sivachandralingam, S. R. (2012) 'The London Dawn Raid and Its Effect on Malaysian Plantation Workers' 40(116) *Indonesia and the Malay World* 74.

Sixth Malaysia Plan. (1990–1995) 'Sixth Malaysia Plan, 1990–1995'. www.ekonomi.gov.my/en/economic-developments/development-plans/rmk/sixth-malaysia-plan-1990-1995.

Stenson, M. R. (1980) *Class, Race and Colonialism in West Malaysia: The Indian Case* (St Lucia: University of Queensland Press).

Tate, M. D. (2008) *The Malaysian Indians: History, Problems and Future* (Petaling Jaya: Strategic Information and Research Development Centre).

Tinker, H. (1974) *A New System of Slavery: The Export of Indian Labour Overseas, 1830–1920* (New York: Oxford University Press, for the Institute of Race Relations).

CAPITAL DRUG LAWS IN ASIA

The book documents, analyses and makes accessible the law and policy related to illicit drugs in various Asian jurisdictions. The focus is specifically on the measures undertaken in Asia to combat drug offences and, in particular, the use of the death penalty for such offences. It will enhance the ability of public policy and lawmakers, non-governmental organisations and the general population to engage in the debate on the appropriate approach towards illicit drugs. A wide range of Asian jurisdictions, particularly in Southeast Asia, have been intentionally selected to show a diversity of approaches in the 'war on drugs' debate. The areas examined include developments in the law and policy relating to illicit drugs; use of criminal law measures to combat drug-related offences; motivations of drug offenders; public support for punitive punishments; structure of the laws; procedural rights of accused persons; mandatory/discretionary sentencing; and use of the death penalty.

WING-CHEONG CHAN is Professor at the Singapore Management University. He teaches and researches mainly in the areas of criminal law and family law. His recent projects examine the criminal laws in various Asian countries. Book publications that he has been involved in include *Criminal Law in Singapore* (2022), *Criminal Law in Sri Lanka* (2020), *Criminal Law in Myanmar* (2016), *Codification, Macaulay and the Indian Penal Code* (2011), and *Support for Victims of Crime in Asia* (2008).

MAI SATO is Professor and Director of the Institute for Crime and Justice Policy Research, School of Social Sciences, Faculty of Humanities and Social Sciences, Birkbeck, University of London, UK. In August 2024, she was appointed as the UN Special Rapporteur on the situation of human rights in the Islamic Republic of Iran. She was the inaugural director of Eleos Justice – a research initiative on state-sanctioned killing, including the death penalty.

MICHAEL HOR is Professor at the University of Hong Kong. He was formerly Dean of the Faculty of Law at the University of Hong Kong and was Professor at the Faculty of Law, National University of Singapore. He has taught, researched and published in criminal law, criminal procedure and criminal justice for more than thirty-five years. He was co-editor of and contributor to *Global Anti-Terrorism Law and Policy* (2009 and 2012 (2nd ed.)) and most recently *The National Security Law of Hong Kong* (2022).

6

Pathways to Prison

Economic, Personal, and Relational Motivations for Drug Offending in Indonesia

CAROLYN HOYLE AND PARVAIS JABBAR

6.1 Introduction

Harsh drug policies across Southeast Asia are premised on the notion of deterrence, that those contemplating entry into the drug trade will be dissuaded by the threat of compulsory drug treatment centres, prison, and perhaps the death penalty. Deterrence research has typically been framed by rational-choice theory, drawing on econometric perspectives.[1] A behavioural economic approach presumes that people rationally balance the incentives and risks of crime, as determined by the criminal justice system, and that by heightening the risk through harsh punishments and thereby reducing the incentives of crimes, crime will decrease.[2] While rational choice theory is not solely about economic choices and can be driven by emotional gains, it, nonetheless, assumes the potential offender is a rational, self-interested actor whose key incentives for entry into the drug trade are economic and who can express preferences from a range of choices.

There are few studies of deterrence in the global south and no robust deterrence studies on drug offending that we know of.[3] We recently commenced research to test deterrence theory for drugs in Indonesia, aimed at gathering a large, representative sample of prisoners convicted of drug offences and sentenced to life or death, as well as a sample of

We are grateful to Lucrezia Rizzelli and Jocelyn Hutton in Oxford and to our colleagues at Atma Jaya Catholic University, Indonesia for research assistance.

1 Ehrlich (1975); Sunstein and Vermeule (2006); for a review of the literature, see Hood and Hoyle (2015, chapter 9).

2 Becker (1968).

3 Fagan (2015).

drug trading networks in the community.[4] However, before embarking on this research programme, we conducted a preliminary study of fifty-seven prisoners in Jakarta who had been convicted of drug offences, people who had, necessarily, not been deterred from involvement in the illicit drug trade.[5] We sought information on what influenced their choices and why the risks of punishment had not deterred them. Here, we do not focus on risks, but on the perceived rewards and, therefore, the motivations for entry into the illicit drug trade. We draw on the wider literature based on community studies of people's motivations for drug use and drug trading to see if our data provide support for studies which emphasise economic motivations, which could fit within a deterrence model.

Indonesia and most of its neighbours across Southeast Asia impose particularly harsh penalties for drug offences, which speak to the issue of deterrence and choices about entry into the drug trade. Therefore, we situate our research in a discussion of drug policy across the region, before moving on to describe the laws and policies of Indonesia. We start with a brief exposition of the drug laws and policies in Southeast Asia.

6.2 Drug Laws and Policy in Southeast Asia

Drug production and trafficking are increasing each year, and drug markets are becoming more complex, with over thirty-five million people experiencing drug use disorders globally, disproportionately the socially and economically disadvantaged.[6] The illicit production and trafficking of drugs in Southeast Asia is at record levels, with a market value of more than USD 61 billion, while the types and quantities of drugs multiply within and around the 'Golden Triangle' – traditionally a source of opiates,[7] though seizures of synthetic drugs in the region have increased year-on-year over the last decade.[8] The United Nations Office on Drugs and Crime (UNODC) states that 'drugs cost lives', with half a million people killed globally in 2019 as a result of drug use,[9] though some of

[4] Mapping the Political Economy of Drugs and the Death Penalty in Southeast Asia, Death Penalty Research Unit (www.law.ox.ac.uk/esrc-project-mapping-political-economy-drugs-and-death-penalty-southeast-asia).

[5] Hoyle *et al.* (2023).

[6] United Nations Office on Drugs and Crime (2021).

[7] Wojcik (2020).

[8] United Nations Office on Drugs and Crime (2020).

[9] United Nations Office on Drugs and Crime (2021).

those people die as a result of severe human rights violations associated with efforts to control the illicit drug trade.[10]

Many countries in Southeast Asia have become key players in the international 'war on drugs', with trading in drugs presented as an issue of security that threatens acceptable ways of living. There are variations in enforcement policies and legal thresholds for the amount and types of drugs sold between the region's states,[11] but overall, the focus is not on protecting individuals from the excesses of penal power, but on protecting society from drug misuse through increased law enforcement and criminal penalties. Indeed, the Association of Southeast Asian Nations (ASEAN) rather optimistically agreed in 1998 to eradicate the production, trafficking, and use of illicit drugs by 2020.[12]

While in 2022, Thailand became the first country in Southeast Asia to decriminalise cannabis; the new prime minister declared that his government would change policy to restrict its use to medical purposes.[13] Furthermore, the consumption and distribution of other widely available psychoactive substances continue to be subject to severe penal sanctions there, with some drug offenders still sentenced to death.[14] Elsewhere across the region, the 1980s through the early 2010s saw the emergence of laws and policies that include compulsory detention for treatment for those who use drugs, including marijuana. The treatment institutions have been subject to critical scrutiny from international organisations such as the United Nations, with criticisms focusing on the treatment of people without consent, the lack of due process protections for compulsory detention, poor healthcare, forced labour, and physical and sexual abuse.[15] Nevertheless, they continue to remain popular among governments whose harsh penal policies for drugs, including long-term imprisonment,[16] have created prison overcrowding, particularly in the Philippines, Thailand, and Indonesia,[17] and the disproportionate use of capital punishment.

[10] Fordham and Fernández (2021).

[11] Raffle (2021).

[12] Pushpanathan (1999).

[13] Lopez (2023).

[14] R. Bunmee in Chapter 9 in this volume.

[15] United Nations Joint Programme on HIV/AIDS (2012), cited in Kamarulzaman and McBrayer (2015).

[16] K. Joe-Laidler and K. Lowe in Chapter 10 in this volume.

[17] Walmsley (2017).

Indeed, although the pace of death penalty abolition elsewhere has increased since the end of the 1980s, notably in sub-Saharan Africa, many countries in Southeast Asia have responded to international concern about the growth of trafficking in illicit drugs by introducing the death penalty for drug offences that fall short of drug-related homicide. They include the manufacture, importation, and 'possession for sale' of specific amounts – often arbitrarily determined – of particular drugs, and in some jurisdictions, they have made the death penalty mandatory for offences where it was previously discretionary.[18]

While the colonial history of Southeast Asia has had a lasting impact on drug crime policies,[19] the imposition of the death penalty for drug crimes is a clear response to the global war on drugs, with many retentionist states having adopted these laws since the 1970s and 1980s, particularly following the 1988 United Nations Convention against Illicit Traffic in Narcotic Drugs and Psychotic Substances, which established obligations in international law on states to enact harsh punishment for drug offenders.[20] For example, Singapore and Malaysia enacted laws applying the death penalty for drug offences in the 1970s, and Indonesia first executed someone for drug offences in 1995. Although Malaysia is in the sixth year of an execution moratorium,[21] and has recently abolished the *mandatory* death penalty,[22] and is currently in the process of resentencing those on death row, it retains a discretionary death penalty for drug offences. When the death penalty is not applicable, long prison sentences are common in Southeast Asia, even for relatively low-level drug offences.[23] Furthermore, other abuses of human rights occur alongside the death penalty: Singapore inflicts a range of harsh penalties for drug-selling and trafficking, including imprisonment and caning,[24] primarily in the name of deterrence,[25] notwithstanding the lack of empirical evidence for such a claim.[26]

[18] Harm Reduction International (2023).

[19] Harry (2023); Lindsey and Nicholson (2016).

[20] Lines, Barrett, and Gallahue (2015).

[21] Its last execution was in 2017, but the moratorium was not announced until 2018.

[22] United Nations (2023).

[23] This can include personal drug consumption, drug possession for personal use, and possession of equipment used in drug preparation and consumption. Some countries in the region criminalise the latter, even in settings where harm-reduction programmes distribute sterile injecting equipment to reduce the risk of disease.

[24] Clift-Matthews and Jabbar (2020).

[25] W. C. Chan and M. Hor in Chapter 4 in this volume.

[26] Zimring, Fagan, and Johnson (2010); also refer to Yap and Tan (2020).

While socioeconomic and political conditions across jurisdictions vary somewhat, there are common features to states' efforts to control the production, sale, and use of drugs by resorting to punitive judicial and extra-judicial measures. Most notably, states have justified policies by persistently focusing on the dangers and disruptive qualities of drugs and by exaggerating or providing misinformation about the health and social impacts of the illicit drug trade.[27] Moreover, different states' drug enforcement policies have tended to target ethnic minority groups and the socially and economically marginalised,[28] including women who can find it difficult to find work in the legal economies of many countries due to the feminisation of poverty.[29] Drawing on historical evidence from the Philippines in the 1970s and Thailand in the 2000s and from contemporary sources from Bangladesh and Indonesia, Lasco finds evidence of the conflation of the 'drug menace' with ethnic, economic 'others'.[30]

However, too little is known about those people who are incarcerated across Asia for their drug use or involvement in the illicit drug trade. Policies are based on assumptions about motivations to commit drug offences and about the extent to which harsh punishments will deter potential drug offenders. These beliefs are thus far unsupported by scientific research.[31] There have been studies that have told us something about the economic motivations for drug crime within the wider political economy of drugs, but many do not also consider the personal and relational motivations nor the extent – if any – to which the existence of harsh judicial and extrajudicial sanctions exerts a deterrent effect. This chapter will draw on interviews conducted in a prison in Indonesia with people convicted of drug offences to explore the economic, personal, and relational drivers of drug crime.

6.3 Indonesia: A Case Study

Attention to Southeast Asia's drug trade has historically focused on the 'Golden Triangle', an area between Thailand, Laos, and Myanmar prominent in opium production. More recently, neighbouring countries, such as Indonesia, have begun local production of drugs, often synthetic,

[27] Seddon (2023).
[28] Lasco (2020); T. Kananatu in Chapter 5 in this volume.
[29] Fleetwood and Leban (2023); Macaulay (2020, pp. 23–32).
[30] Lasco (2020, p. 77).
[31] Fagan (2015).

contributing to increasing rates of drug disorders. Nonetheless, the drug emergency is portrayed by governments of countries outside the Golden Triangle as an external threat. In Indonesia, harsh punishments are justified as a necessary weapon in the government's arsenal for eradicating drug crimes.[32] Law No. 9/1976 introduced the death penalty for drug offences in the early years of the global 'war on drugs', with further legislation in 1997 and 2009 a clear response to the failure of those tough laws to reduce the illicit drug trade,[33] notwithstanding the United Nations admission, in 2009, that such laws had failed to reduce drug crime.[34] In December 2022, Indonesia passed a new, long-awaited Criminal Code which provides some limited scope for optimism. Judges can decide to sentence an offender to a ten-year 'probationary' death sentence, given certain mitigating circumstances (if the defendant has played a minor role in the criminal act and if there is evidence of remorse and the potential for rehabilitation). At the end of the ten-year period, conditions would need to be met for a commutation of the sentence, and that would be subject to presidential approval following consideration by the Supreme Court.[35]

Nevertheless, Indonesia is set to continue its zero-tolerance approach to drugs that have been visible in the steady pace of death sentences.[36] Since the start of the twenty-first century, drug convictions have put over 300 people on death row and led to twenty-four executions. President Joko Widodo's pro-death penalty stance for drug offences was evinced in 2014, when he refused clemency to drug offenders on death row, arguing that capital punishment was a necessary deterrent to the 'narcotic emergency'.[37] Similarly, the government justified the eighteen executions for drug offences in 2015 and 2016 by reference to a 'state of emergency'.[38]

Political rhetoric and judicial sentencing in Indonesia, as elsewhere in the region, rely on official statistics on high rates of drug-related deaths that suggest drug misuse has devastating consequences for the health of the nation, though the statistics are based on questionable methods and measures.[39] Indeed, there is no workable or precise definition of

[32] Edwards *et al.* (2010).
[33] Stoicescu and Palmer (2019).
[34] United Nations Office on Drugs and Crime (2009).
[35] Rancangan Kitab Undang-undang Hukum Pidana 2022.
[36] Gunawan and Pamintori (2019).
[37] Nasir (2016).
[38] Maulana (2018).
[39] Maulana (2018); Stoicescu (2015).

'drug-related death'.[40] Not surprisingly, there is no evidence of a reduction in drug trafficking subsequent to the executions between 2015 and 2018.[41]

Public funding has been directed towards drug control and punishment, rather than public-health-oriented programmes, though harsh penalties appear to have had no impact on trafficking.[42] However, what little diversion there has been has not escaped the punitive rationale. In Indonesia, as elsewhere in the region, the move towards a bifurcated justice response to drug crime, with an expansion of drug policy into health and community spaces, is recognised by many in civil society as being driven principally not by concerns for harm reduction and human rights but the need to reduce overcrowding in prisons.[43]

Indeed, rather than removing people who use drugs from carceral settings, the policy of diversion into compulsory drug treatment centres may be increasing the scale and social concentration of penal control in non-penal settings, without procedural safeguards.[44] Objections are raised about the *compulsory* nature of detention in drug treatment institutions in Indonesia, and other countries such as Thailand. But concerns also focus on the *nature* of control within such places, which is punitive and intensive.[45] As in other Southeast Asian countries including Cambodia, Laos, Malaysia, Thailand, Vietnam, Myanmar, and the Philippines, in Indonesia, the treatment approach is focused on abstinence. The compulsory treatment facilities closely resemble prisons, are usually in remote areas, and their 'inmates' are often compelled to engage in forced labour.[46] Thus, in the name of the war on drugs, it appears that Indonesia and other Southeast Asian states now administer punishment in what are purportedly care settings,[47] with such institutions characterised by the same coercive, stigmatising, and restrictive mechanisms for control as are apparent in prisons.[48]

[40] The metrics of international drug policy are simplistic and much of the data is unreliable because of the weak epidemiological capacity in many countries and the inevitable challenges of surveying criminalised and hidden populations: Buxton and Burger (2020).
[41] Winarso, Irawati, and Handoyo (2019).
[42] Rowe (2019).
[43] Cullen and Hoyle (2024).
[44] Bottoms (2017).
[45] Ibid.
[46] Ritter (2022, chapter 4).
[47] Miller and Stuart (2017).
[48] Ritter (2022, chapter 1).

Meanwhile, methamphetamine consumption continues unabated across Southeast Asia,[49] while punitive approaches are associated with greater health and social risk and the increased marginalisation, criminalisation, and stigmatisation of people who use drugs,[50] not least women.[51] The Indonesian government has set aside around USD 25 million per year to address the public health needs of drug users, but is spending more than five times as much on drug-control measures that punish drug use.[52] Indonesia's harsh eradication and punishment policies, which have criminalised drug users and sentenced to death or to long prison terms some of those who traffic drugs, have had the collateral effect of increasing 'violence, crime, marginalisation and other harmful outcomes for vulnerable people',[53] entrenching poverty and inequalities.[54]

Such an approach speaks to the political economy of the drug trade with the economically marginalised being excluded from society, punished, incarcerated, and even killed. While political economy is but one component in a complex web of forces including crime, culture, institutions, and economics, that shape penal policy, it is an important one.[55] Furthermore, drug policy is rooted in racist assumptions about immoral 'foreigners' entering the country with drugs from afar.[56] This moral agenda creates drug policy enforcement in many countries that targets those deemed dangerous based on factors such as race, ethnicity, religion, and even ideological belief.[57] For example, there is some evidence that border controls in Indonesia are permeable, with drug kingpins able to avoid detection by bribing police and thereby continuing a lucrative business unimpeded by drug control policies. Meanwhile, less powerful, 'disposable' drug mules are apprehended and punished.[58] Moreover, most people executed for drug trafficking by the current Widodo administration have been foreign nationals – a reversal of the position under its predecessor, led by Suslio Yudhoyono. This shift underlines the

[49] United Nations Office on Drugs and Crime (2020).
[50] Csete *et al.* (2016).
[51] Macaulay (2020).
[52] Rowe (2019).
[53] Havenhand (2020, p. 7).
[54] Ibid.
[55] Tonry (2007).
[56] Buxton and Burger (2020).
[57] Fellner (2009).
[58] Cullen and Hoyle (2024).

significance of foreign nationality and minority ethnicity as risk factors for capital punishment, not least for women,[59] and manifests an arbitrariness that violates the constitutionality of capital punishment.[60] In Indonesia, therefore, the evidence suggests that the state governs and controls through crime policy and punishment, justified by a culture of fear and a rhetoric of war.[61]

To explore the relative disadvantage among those subject to penal power in Indonesia's war on drugs and to better understand why people continue to commit drug offences notwithstanding the harsh penal climate, we conducted a small, in-depth study of the economic, personal, and relational motivations for drug crimes.

6.3.1 Indonesians Imprisoned for Drug Offences: Research Design and Sample

Having secured permission from the Directorate General of the Correctional Facility in Indonesia to interview people convicted of drug offences within a prison in Jakarta, we were assisted in conducting interviews by researchers from Atma Jaya Catholic University. Prisoners were approached, provided with information about the project, and invited to participate in interviews.[62] Sixty-four prisoners expressed interest, but seven were ineligible; one changed his mind about participating, and six were shown by our Mental Health Screening Tool to be suffering from mental health or cognitive problems that precluded them on ethical grounds. All interviews were conducted in 2021, face to face, as the COVID-19 pandemic restrictions were easing. While there was a prison officer in the room during the interviews, he was not sufficiently close to hear the exchange between the interviewer and the prisoner, and all but two interviews were recorded, fully transcribed, and translated into English.[63]

Our qualitative, semi-structured interviews with fifty-seven prisoners cannot tell us about the drug 'kingpins'. As Table 6.1 shows, our interviewees were convicted of a range of drug-related crimes but were

[59] Hoyle and Harry (2020).
[60] McRae (2017).
[61] Simon (2009).
[62] Ethical protocols for the study were approved by the 'Central University Research Ethics Committee' of the University of Oxford (reference No. R74247/RE001) and Atma Jaya Catholic University's Research Ethics Board.
[63] Two prisoners asked not to be recorded. In these cases, detailed hand-written notes were taken.

Table 6.1 *Crimes and sentences of sample of prisoners*

Crimes		
	Possession	16%
	Storage	7%
	Delivering	32%
	Selling	19%
	Dealing	25%
Sentence		
	5–7 years	22%
	8–10 years	52%
	11+ years	26%

reasonably low down the supply chain, though as such, they are likely representative of the majority of drug offenders within the Indonesian prison complex. Our interviewees had been sentenced to prison for between five and fifteen years for a range of drug offences; most had been sentenced to between eight and twelve years, with an average sentence of nine years, reflecting the harsh punishments discussed in this chapter.

That said, our relatively small sample cannot claim to be representative of the total population of prisoners serving sentences for drug offences in Jakarta or across Indonesia. It is neither random nor sufficiently large to generalise from. Rather, it might indicate what would be found in a large, random, and representative population of drug-convicted prisoners across Indonesia, but it may be different on two key issues. First, we have not interviewed prisoners in a woman's prison and their routes to drug offending may be somewhat different to men's.[64] Furthermore, while we were prepared to interview foreign nationals – with our research materials translated into other languages that the research team was able to converse in – only Indonesian nationals agreed to be interviewed.

Almost all (91 per cent) of the interviewees had been charged with Article 114 of Law 35 of 2009,[65] 66 per cent were charged with Article 112[66] (which does not require *mens rea* [intention] if someone has drugs in their possession), but only 8 per cent were charged with Article 132,

[64] Fleetwood and Leban (2023).

[65] Article 114: Offering to be sold, selling, purchasing, receiving, being an intermediary within a transaction, exchanging, or delivering Narcotics Group 1.

[66] Article 112: Planting, maintaining, owning, keeping, controlling, or providing Narcotics Group 1 (not in the form of a plant).

which requires the prosecution to demonstrate that there are other people involved in the criminal activity. This was somewhat surprising given that many interviewees mentioned they worked with several people in the illicit drug trade. Indeed, many of their responses referred to people higher up in the drug network who had authority over them. A third of the participants estimated their network to consist of three or fewer people, but two-thirds said it was more than four, and three of those thought it was more than ten people. The majority (38) of participants' offences related to amphetamine-type stimulants, such as methamphetamines, with four arrests relating to ecstasy and one to heroin. Eleven involved cannabis only.

6.3.2 *Structure and Agency in Pathways to Drug Crime*

Research that attempts to identify the risk factors for entry into the illicit drug trade suggests they are a product of a dynamic, 'complex system'[67] and are difficult to predict, with pathways 'virtually infinite' and interactions between factors 'greater than the sum of their parts'.[68] Indeed, it has been argued that interactions between people and background environmental factors create 'transformative . . . moments of "assemblage"'.[69] That said, across the literature some models focus on structural factors, others on agency. Those that emphasise agency have been criticised for a tendency towards 'risk individualization',[70] given that structural and cultural constraints limit individual capacity to calculate and manage risk.[71] Risk, it is argued, should be understood as being significantly shaped by and situated within particular settings and contexts.[72] But just as some have cautioned against the use of models that give an inadequate account of objective, structural forces,[73] others have criticised those that underplay individual agency in decision-making.[74]

[67] Galea, Hall, and Kaplan (2009).
[68] Resnicow and Page (2008, p. 1382). Also refer to Galea, Hall, and Kaplan (2009); Rhodes (2009).
[69] Rhodes (2009).
[70] Blackenship *et al.* (2006); Bourgois (2003); Moore (2004); Nasir (2006); Nasir and Rosenthal (2009a).
[71] Moore (2004). This is, in part, Fleetwood and Leban's criticism of 'emancipation thesis' in relation to women's involvement in the drugs trade: Fleetwood and Leban (2023).
[72] Rhodes (2002).
[73] Duff (2007).
[74] Fitzgerald (2009).

Factors contributing to the initiation and maintenance of drug use can be personal, relational, and contextual.[75] Personal factors include low self-esteem, impulsivity, emotional distress, chronic anger, and lack of future orientation.[76] Relational factors speak to issues, such as poor family bonding and conflict, peer pressure, and peer deviance.[77] Meanwhile, and perhaps more predictably, contextual factors include low educational opportunities and socioeconomic marginalisation.[78] The research suggests we should not look for linear causal relationships between these factors and drug use but should explore the interaction between individual choice, microsocial context, and macrosocial change.[79] While individuals can make a personal choice to use drugs or to become involved in the illicit drug economy, this choice will be subject to structural constraints and interactional influences. It will be a product of social conditions and social relationships, especially those with peer groups among the young.[80] Indeed, theories concerning the individualisation of risk have been thought to underestimate the influence of friendship groups since the American criminologist, Edwin Sutherland, first suggested in 1939, that criminal behaviour is learned through interactions with others, particularly in close peer groups.[81] Thus, the motivations for drug use and drug trading are multidimensional, a product of the interaction of many structural, social or relational, and personal dynamics.[82] We explored their influence with the people we interviewed, turning first to the primarily structural elements.

6.3.2.1 Structural conditions

Around the world, drug use and drug crime appear to be associated with socioeconomic marginalisation, disadvantage, and social exclusion,[83] especially in urban poor neighbourhoods,[84] areas of high

[75] Kim, Zane, and Hong (2002).
[76] Newcomb and Locke (2005).
[77] Boys, Marsden, and Strang (2001). Theories of peer pressure hark back to Sutherland's differential association theory which proposes that people learn values, attitudes, and motivations for crime through interactions with their peers (Sutherland (1939)).
[78] Barker (2005); Bourgois (2003); Hunt (2006); Mayock (2005); Seddon (2006).
[79] Pilkington (2007a).
[80] Pilkington (2007b).
[81] Sutherland (1939); also refer to Pilkington (2007b).
[82] Grund (2005).
[83] MacDonald and Marsh (2002).
[84] Fitzgerald (2009); Mayock (2005); McIlwaine and Moser (2001).

unemployment,[85] and social deprivation, particularly for those with poor educational experiences.[86]

Drug use can lead to drug-selling as a way to generate the income needed to keep buying drugs, and often results in the spread of drug use amongst peers.[87] Just as drug cultivation on land unsuitable for legal crops can be related to efforts by farming communities to mitigate poverty and livelihood insecurity,[88] inner-city drug use and selling are similarly associated with poverty and can be central to the economic viability of such communities.[89] Indeed, some regard such drug use as responding to traumatic stress disorder or 'social suffering'[90] caused by the structural violence of poverty among marginalised people.[91]

As elsewhere, drug use in Asia is influenced by poor educational attainment, low economic status, and peer pressure.[92] The first two are highly correlated; while some people with little formal education do well, most do not achieve economic success.[93] For this reason, we sought information on participants' educational attainment and employment at the time of arrest. Of the fifty-seven prisoners we interviewed, most had completed high school or received vocational training, but only three had completed postsecondary education and 14 per cent had only completed elementary school. These rates appear to be lower than in the general population of Indonesia, of which 30 per cent complete junior high school and 10 per cent go to university.[94]

Just over half (55 per cent) of our interviewees were employed at the time of arrest. Of this group, 43 per cent (twelve) were in a permanent job or on a long-term contract, with others in temporary employment. Many were drivers (mainly motorcycle drivers), others worked in retail (four), in offices (seven), in hospitality (three), in other customer service industries (two), or in a range of manual or security jobs (eleven). Several of those who had been unemployed at the time of arrest said they had

85 Pearson (1987, p. 74).
86 Parker, Bakx, and Newcombe (1988, p. 22).
87 Meehan *et al.* (2022).
88 Meehan (2021).
89 Fitzgerald (2009).
90 Kleinman, Das, and Lock (1997); Simmonds and Coomber (2009).
91 Singer (2004).
92 Kokkevi *et al.* (2007).
93 Valero (2021).
94 Statista, *Share of Indonesian population in 2022, by highest education level* (www.statista.com/statistics/1298842/indonesia-share-of-population-by-highest-education-level/).

become involved with the illegal drug trade because they were *'between jobs'*: *'I became involved with drugs because I was fired from my previous job'*. At arrest, some had only recently been released from prison and were finding it difficult to secure legitimate employment: *'I had just been released [from prison] so my activities were limited'*.

While over half of the interviewees were in employment at the time of arrest, and the majority of those reported that their financial situation was 'good' (twenty-two) or 'more than good' (eight), further inquiry about participants' earnings showed that most were not making a decent wage from their lawful employment. Without drug income, almost half the interviewees did not have enough money.

Among the twenty-two participants who were in a good or 'more than good' financial position, half were in that financial situation because of earnings from the illicit drug trade, and seven of the eight who had *more* than enough money considered themselves to be financially secure *because of* the drug trade. Overall, three-quarters did not have enough money to get by without the income they received from the drug trade.

Based on both illicit and legal earnings across those in the sample who provided details,[95] the mean average *legal* income per month at the time of arrest[96] was Indonesian Rupiah (IDR) 5.30 million (approximately USD 400). While this is not a high income by the standards of the developed world, it is almost double the average for Indonesia.[97] This suggests that our sample of prisoners was not among those in the direst financial need. What is much more interesting is the mean average for *illicit* income. This was IDR 39.34 million a month (approximately USD 2,500), more than seven times as much as our interviewees were earning legally. Some of our participants were significantly enhancing their incomes, although they were relatively minor players in the illicit drug trade and certainly not 'kingpins'.

While only eight of the prisoners had been in debt when arrested, nine people reported not being able to afford basic necessities, two said they were only able to afford them some of the time, and a further nine said

[95] We did not ask interviewees about their illicit income, so we do not have data for the full sample. However, in answering a question about income at the time of the offence, twenty-nine of our participants provided further information about illicit earnings.

[96] This is an adjusted mean income, after removing two 'outliers' (with the two outliers, the average is IDR 6.81 million – approximately USD 430).

[97] The average monthly net wage of employees in Indonesia from 2010 to 2023 was IDR 2.94 million Indonesian rupiah (approximately USD 189) (see www.statista.com/statistics/1065801/indonesia-average-monthly-net-wage-of-employees/).

they could only take care of their basic needs because of their illicit earnings. Half said they could not afford luxuries of any kind, and some of those who could made it clear that this was only possible through drug money.[98]

These data uncover the social structures and contextual features that perpetuate drug use and drug crime.[99] They help us to understand the wider 'risk environment',[100] as distinct from dominant narratives in Asia that blame rising drug use on deviant individual behaviours.[101] But while drug use can be seen as a means of survival in settings characterised by poverty, lack of education and unemployment,[102] focusing on structural forces can leave uncharted the specific pathways through which macro forces lead to drug use and crime.[103] Structuralist approaches can also overlook how people actively shape the environments in which they live.[104] As Rhodes observes, 'risk environments should be understood as emerging out of an "assemblage" of manifold interactions between individuals and environments'.[105]

Just because many of our participants were not financially comfortable without involvement in drug crime does not mean they were involved exclusively or even primarily for economic reasons, nor does it explain why very many people in Indonesia do not commit drug crimes notwithstanding similar living and working conditions. To better distinguish causation from correlation, we asked our participants a series of questions about motivation towards drug offending.

6.3.2.2 Economic motivations

None of the prisoners we interviewed were coerced by threats of violence into drug offending; they had agency, and the vast majority (84 per cent) said they were motivated by financial gain. Several interviewees needed the higher income that drug offending brought to support their own drug use, which would not have been sustainable on their earnings from legal

[98] The data on this question were missing in many cases. Answers to other questions suggest that a significant number, probably a majority of those who could afford luxuries, could only do so on account of drug earnings.

[99] Pilkington (2007b).

[100] Rhodes (2009).

[101] Zoccatelli (2014).

[102] Nasir and Rosenthal (2009b); Singer (2006).

[103] Duff (2007).

[104] Cohen (2014); Lasco (2014).

[105] Rhodes (2009).

work. One commented: *'I was already addicted to [drugs]. It was the only reason'*, while another explained: *'Because at that time, I was addicted to drugs, and I needed to fulfil my basic needs'.* Indeed, for many, the opportunity to become part of a drug network came while they were heavily involved in drug use, with the promise of alleviating financial difficulties: to *'pay my debts'.*

More than half (57 per cent), however, committed drug offences to help someone else, typically members of their families. The majority (forty-three) of our participants had dependents, on average three dependents (children, siblings, and parents), though ten had five or more. Not surprisingly, some referred to their financial difficulties: *'We lived from hand to mouth... I had financial issues'; 'I was part of the less fortunate'.* A few were explicit that their responsibilities for dependents encouraged them to commit offences: *'I have responsibility to provide for my wife and child. Finally, I took a shortcut [became involved in drug crimes] even though my life was decent'.* And another explained: *'At first, I was working to fulfil my wife's needs ... I was tempted with the profits ... We were using drugs too. Instead of buying, which cost money, we buy more and sell some drugs to get profit'.*

Basic necessities were mentioned by interviewees in relation to providing for their family: *'I saw my kids who wanted to buy things [...] My kids' needs [...] Yes, and my family. I was financially responsible for them'.* Several wanted to fund their child's education (*'I want to pay for my kid's graduation'*), as well as making their parents comfortable, including, for one man, paying for his mother's medical treatment: *'I actually had a desire to make my mother happy'.* While these accounts of meeting dependents' needs are clearly economic rationales, they also speak to relational motivations, with the prisoners wanting to support families and sustain relationships, in part, through fiscal generosity.

Many were mindful of the lack of other profitable opportunities, speaking of the difficulties of finding legal employment, especially if they already had a criminal record. Indeed, three of our interviewees explained that they had no other option but to accept involvement in drug crimes because of the lack of alternative job opportunities:

> *'It was fairly hard for me to find jobs'.*
>
> *'I didn't actually choose, but I had to [commit drug offences] because it was hard to get a job outside prison'.*
>
> *'Well, the money's good [...] I thought to myself, what else can I do? I'm a junior high school graduate. There's nothing I can do'.*

A few participants were explicit that they wanted to acquire wealth, and saw the drug trade as a good way to make quick and easy profits. They spoke about their aspirations to own things beyond their reach, such as a car. They distinguished between the high profits of the drug trade and their less-than-fortunate situation, with many experiencing unemployment and a consequent inability to provide for their families or support their drug use:

> *'At that time, I was only a user. So maybe my salary wasn't enough'.*
>
> *'I had many dependents, and I was also chased by the debt collectors'.*
>
> *'I was just tempted. Drugs easily yield money'.*

The last quotation complicates the narrative about poverty and drug dealing. Drug-selling as an occupation 'can be characterized by many of the same work problems, motivations, rewards, and experiences found in the legitimate world'.[106] However, for a few, it is valued for its 'distinct working conditions': flexible, exciting, entrepreneurial; thrilling work that people can derive status from and make large sums of money in short periods. If people then get used to a high standard of living, which they could not maintain with legal work, they may be persuaded to continue, notwithstanding the risks. Alternatively, they can become immersed in the drug world and seduced into continuing, losing patience for the slower rewards of lawful employment.[107] As one of our participants explained: *'I was doing great at the hotel. The job was great. How stupid was I? I ended up being involved in drugs again. I wonder why people are never satisfied with anything?'*

A study in Myanmar identified a range of structural factors for engaging in the illicit drug trade that are likely to be common across the region: economic hardship, limited social safety nets, challenges of finding work, providing for families, dealing with sudden emergencies, and trying to fulfil aspirations to improve their lives, while at the same time dealing with the exhaustion, drudgery, and physical and mental depletion that these challenges generate.[108] In such circumstances, drug use and drug-selling can be ways to cope with the trials of everyday life and exert agency within a wider environment of poverty, insecurity and minimal welfare provision.[109] To consider further the agency and choices

[106] Adler (1993, p. 147).
[107] Ibid.
[108] Meehan *et al.* (2022).
[109] Ibid.

exercised by our participants within the similar structural constraints of their everyday lives, we turn now to personal and relational motivations for involvement in the illicit drug economy.

6.3.2.3 Personal and relational motivations

Research suggests that entry into the illicit drug trade is often tied to people's social networks and drug use within them.[110] People typically start using and trading drugs through contact with peers who have already become involved, and so become part of networks that provide opportunities for jobs in the informal economy when legal options may be limited, especially for those with little formal education. Drug use can also alleviate boredom and frustration among young, disenfranchised people with limited life chances, strengthening bonds within peer groups.[111]

Perhaps not surprisingly, the great majority (forty-four) of our interviewees said they used drugs before their arrest, with ten having been in compulsory rehabilitation at some point. Peer influence is considered to be the most consistent and influential factor in drug use,[112] so it is unsurprising that most (thirty-six) first became involved in drug crimes before the age of 25 years, with eight starting before they were fourteen, and many were part of a drug using and drug trading community. This speaks to their pathways to drug offending. Drug trading communities provide social solidarity, companionship, and, sometimes, financial support for their members, with 'friendship networks of "users–dealers" supporting each other and trading within the group in a reciprocal fashion'.[113] Those with friends or family within a local drug network are more likely to be involved in the trade, as people are enticed into the drug economy through these relationships,[114] with young people in particular attracted to the lifestyle and subculture.[115] Drugs are also often taken as part of a shared experience in which people, often young men, seek to establish social bonds. Sharing drugs can be a way of establishing friendships and social networks that others may get from their working roles in the legal economy.[116]

110 Taylor and Potter (2013); Windle and Briggs (2015).
111 Lasco (2014).
112 Newcomb and Bentler (1989).
113 Dorn, Murji, and South (1992, p. xiii).
114 Coomber, Moyle, and South (2016).
115 Higgins and Butler (1982, p. 192).
116 Meehan *et al.* (2022).

It was no surprise to us, therefore, that most of our participants were recruited into drug crime by a friend, and while ten of them had only relatively recently become acquainted with the recruiter (one year or less), nine had known their recruiter for more than twenty years. The mean average length of the relationship was eight-and-a-half years – more than enough time to develop a meaningful relationship, one characterised by mutual trust. Indeed, consistent with the findings of ethnographies of drug communities, trust emerged as a significant feature of recruitment, with just under half of our interviewees saying that they were recruited because of mutual trust and more than one in five because the recruiter had known them for a long time, suggesting that they had become involved in the illicit drug trade through a somewhat organic social process.[117]

When asked *why* they may have been recruited, five interviewees referred to their recruiter's knowledge of their financial needs, but almost half of those who answered (nineteen of forty-two) said it was because they were considered to be 'trustworthy', with a further nine referring to the fact that they had known their recruiter for a long time, implying this was a relationship characterised by mutual trust:

> *'We were regular friends who hung out together, and then this person introduced me to their boss'.*
>
> *'He was like my brother. We were together during the hard times. After I got released, he was still in prison. One week after that, he told me that he wanted to offer me a job. I said that I wanted to rest first, and that I would contact him when I was ready. Then, I contacted him because, well, I was unemployed, and I needed to eat. He was the one who directed me if I had to pick up'.*
>
> *'It started from a friend who saw me unemployed. We used [drugs] together and [he] asked if I wanted to [become involved in drug dealing]'.*

Pathways to drug-selling are varied[118] but ethnographic studies suggest some commit drug crimes for the thrills, as a way to avoid the dreariness of low-wage legal work.[119] A few of our participants spoke about the lure of the illicit drug trade, the pursuit of excitement, and the avoidance of boring low-wage legal work:[120]

117 For example, refer to Adler (1993).
118 Paternoster and Bachman (2012).
119 Bourgois (2003); Fagan and Freeman (1999).
120 Ibid; Fitzgerald (2005).

> *'It was fun'.*
>
> *'I wanted to become a mafia [...] a cartel – just like how it is in other countries'.*
>
> *'I wanted to be famous at the time'.*
>
> One respondent wryly commented: *'It was my passion. Imagine being asked what your passion was and answering 'drugs'. Damn, that's insane'.*

One study of drug use in Indonesia shows that some seek only pleasure and mood enhancement[121] as was reflected in the comments by a few of our participants: *'I used it because it made me feel more relaxed, and I enjoyed it'.* Other research has found that some use drugs, especially methamphetamines, to boost stamina if working hard in manual labour or to stay awake when working hours are irregular, or to self-medicate when life feels hard but expectations of masculinity require young men to be confident and assertive, and to forge trust, loyalty, and camaraderie.[122] As one of our participants put it: *'My body was tired, and I needed the dopamine to work'.* Another two described the beneficial effects of marijuana in alleviating the symptoms of cancer.

Drug use can instigate drug-selling as a way to generate the income needed to keep buying drugs, often resulting in the spread of drug use among peers, perpetuating the risk environment of drug use.[123] One of the main benefits of drug dealing mentioned by our participants was the possibility of using the drugs 'for free':

> *'I could use drugs freely'.*
>
> *'I could have the leftovers to myself'.*
>
> *'I did it on my own, because I need to use and [it] would be free if I became a dealer'.*

It is clear that pathways to drug use and trading are connected to people's social and relational networks,[124] but studies also show that using drugs in peer groups enhances participants' enjoyment and friendship bonds. It also augments their social status and respect derived from others.[125] In this regard, personal and relational motivations are interdependent. Many participants talked about their use of drugs as simply part of their

[121] Hardon, Idrus, and Hymans (2013).
[122] Cohen (2014).
[123] Meehan *et al.* (2022).
[124] Taylor and Potter (2013); Windle and Briggs (2015).
[125] Bourgois (2003).

lifestyle, making clear that they were not dependent on drugs, but just '*having fun*'; '*I wasn't an addict, and I did that just for fun and entertainment. That was just living in a metropolitan city . . .*'.

In Asia, there are many purposes for which people turn to drugs: to feel happy, confident, strong, alert, energetic, modern, sophisticated, and cosmopolitan. People also use drugs to bond with friends, transform their bodies, lose weight, stay warm, alleviate hunger, fall asleep, escape from their troubles, and gain status among peers. Sometimes using drugs has an overtly economic logic, increasing their capacity to earn, at other times drug use just helps them get by,[126] to navigate the structural constraints they face.[127] It is hard to explain all these varied positive and negative reasons for drug use and involvement in the drug trade by reference to *either* economic *or* personal and relational motivations. In most cases, probably all features, just as most people have agency, but their choices are bounded by their structural conditions and wider environments.

6.4 Conclusion

Across Southeast Asia, thousands of people are sentenced to imprisonment for sometimes quite minor drug crimes in an effort to eradicate drug crime, an effort that has coincided with the proliferation of drug consumption and trafficking, suggesting an expensive and immiserating policy failure. In Indonesia, as elsewhere, the violation of fundamental human rights is, in part, a result of the impunity with which 'drug wars' are conducted by state authorities.[128] We have considered why, given the harsh punishments meted out in Indonesia, the fifty-seven prisoners we interviewed had made choices that put them at risk of incarceration.

A few of those we interviewed articulated pathways to drug offending that suggest little control over their actions. For example, one man described himself as 'out of control' following the death of his wife:

> '*Before I got married, I . . . had sold drugs like ecstasy. I stopped everything when I got married in 2009. . . . because it's impossible to give illegal money to my child and wife. . . . My wife died, and I got into drugs again. My friend invited me to use. I became addicted, and I became a drug user once more. I could get 3 million per day in 2017, but that money was spent on nightclubs and on drugs. I was out of control*'.

[126] Hardon and Hymans (2014).
[127] Lasco (2014).
[128] Lines *et al.* (2017).

Most of our interviewees did not describe being in such a fragile emotional state. Nevertheless, it could not be said that they had the full range of choices available to them that would be accessible for others differently situated and, furthermore, it could not be said that they were all capable of making fully rational decisions based on those choices.

International drug treaties and regional and national drug policies and laws steer narratives, action, and strategy towards high-level and transnational criminality, the drug kingpins. By so doing, they justify expensive, brutal and, it would seem, ineffective policy responses.[129] It was clear that those we interviewed were not the drug 'kingpins' targeted in the regional war on drugs, but expendable 'foot soldiers'. Most had relatively limited access to lucrative legal employment and yet considerable financial responsibilities. They felt they could not meet those responsibilities, or even live comfortably themselves, without illicit earnings. For most, then, financial rewards featured significantly in their decisions to commit drug offences. As Buxton and Burger argue, 'the travesty of drug policy is that rather than operationalised as a 'war on drugs', it has instead been a war on the poor – the poorest individuals and the poorest communities – and it has been most aggressively operationalised in the poorest and most unequal countries of the world'.[130] Our data provide further evidence for that position and in that regard, the war on drugs needs to be understood within the political economy of drug crime and drug policy. However, our interviews do not fit neatly into a narrative of drug crime which leaves no room for personal and relational motivations for drug offending, nor for agency within these structures of relative poverty and limited opportunities.

Our interviews suggest that while structural accounts are helpful, and while many people may have primarily economic motivations for entry into the drug trade, the body of literature that has considered the social, contextual, and personal motivations for drug use and drug trading must not be ignored. Those we interviewed were deeply influenced by their peer groups. Their entry into the drug trade was motivated to a great extent by relationships of trust within those peer groups and by the desire to support their dependents. Such support speaks not only to economic motivations but also relational imperatives, given that most of our participants were not in absolute poverty when they decided to enter the drug trade. Hence, economic, personal, and relational theories are

[129] Buxton and Burger (2020, p. 20).
[130] Ibid, p. 22.

critical to future studies on drug offenders who have not been deterred by harsh punishments.

This chapter has presented the results of a preliminary study. Participants were not a representative sample and further work will be done to collect more data from which we can draw inferences to the wider population. However, as preliminary as the study is, it suggests both a direction of travel for further research and a theoretical framework within which it can be placed. Previous studies of the drug trade and drug use – not only in Southeast Asia but also around the world – have tried to identify the routes participants follow into drug crime. Many emphasise socioeconomic, structural theories. Our analysis suggests a nuanced and complementary approach is required, one that can account for the interaction of structures and agency and the role of personal and relational factors, as well as economic motivations.

References

Adler, P. A. (1993) *Wheeling and Dealing: An Ethnography of an Upper-Level Drug Dealing and Smuggling Community* (New York: University of Columbia Press).

Barker, G. T. (2005) *Dying to Be Men: Youth, Masculinity and Social Exclusion* (London: Routledge).

Becker, G. S. (1968) 'Crime and Punishment: An Economic Perspective' 76(2) *Journal of Political Economy* 169.

Blackenship, K. M., Friedman, S. R., Dworkin, S. and Mantell, J. E. (2006) 'Structural Interventions: Concepts, Challenges and Opportunities for Research' 83(1) *Journal of Urban Health* 59.

Bottoms, A. E. (2017) 'Punishment' in Non-Custodial Sentences: A Critical Analysis' 28 *Criminal Law Forum* 563.

Bourgois, P. (2003) *In Search of Respect: Selling Crack in El Barrio* (Cambridge: Cambridge University Press).

Boys, A., Marsden, J. and Strang, J. (2001) 'Understanding Reasons for Drug Use Amongst Young People: A Functional Perspective' 16(4) *Health Education Research* 457.

Buxton, J. and Burger, L. (2020) 'International Drug Policy in Context' in Buxton, J., Margo, G. and Burger, L. (eds.) *The Impact of Global Drug Policy on Women: Shifting the Needle* (Bingley: Emerald Publishing Limited).

Clift-Matthews, A. and Jabbar, P. (2020) 'Singapore Should Be Ashamed of Lashings' *The Times* (3 September). www.thetimes.com/uk/article/singapore-should-be-ashamed-of-lashings-kxndjlcfs?region=global.

Cohen, A. (2014) 'Crazy for *Ya Ba*: Methamphetamine Use Among Northern Thai Youth' 25(4) *International Journal of Drug Policy* 776.

Coomber, R., Moyle, L. and South, N. (2016) 'The Normalisation of Drug Supply: The Social *Supply* of Drugs as the "Other Side" of the History of Normalisation' 23(3) *Drugs: Education, Prevention and Policy* 255.

Csete, J., Kamarulzaman, A., Kazatchkine, M., Altice, F., Balicki, M., Buxton, J., Cepeda, J., Comfort, M., Goosby, E., Goulão, J., Hart, C., Kerr, T., Lajous, A. M., Lewis, S., Martin, N., Mejía, D., Camacho, A., Mathieson, D., Obot, I., Ogunrombi, A., Sherman, S., Stone, J., Vallath, N., Vickerman, P., Zábranský, T. and Beyrer, C. (2016) 'Public Health and International Drug Policy' 387(10026) *The Lancet* 1427.

Cullen, D. and Hoyle, C. (2024) *The Role of Socioeconomic Factors in Indonesia's Punitive Drug Policy Regime* (Oxford: Death Penalty Research Unit).

Dorn, N., Murji, K. and South, N. (1992) *Traffickers: Drug Markets and Law Enforcement* (London: Routledge).

Duff, C. (2007) 'Towards a Theory of Drug Use Contexts: Space, Embodiment and Practice' 15(5) *Addiction Research & Theory* 503.

Edwards, G., Barbor, T., Darke, S., Hall, W., Marsden, J., Miller, P. and West, R. (2010) 'Drug Trafficking: Time to Abolish the Death Penalty' 8(4) *International Journal of Mental Health and Addiction* 1267.

Ehrlich, I. (1975) 'The Deterrent Effect of Capital Punishment: A Question of Life and Death' 65 *American Economic Review* 397.

Fagan, J. (2015) 'Deterrence and the Death Penalty in International Perspective' in Šimonović, I. (ed.) *Moving Away from the Death Penalty: Arguments, Trends and Perspectives* (New York: United Nations).

Fagan, J. and Freeman, R. B. (1999) 'Crime and Work' 25 *Crime and Justice* 225.

Fellner, J. (2009) 'Race, Drugs, and Law Enforcement in the United States' 20(2) *Stanford Law and Policy Review* 257.

Fitzgerald, J. (2005) 'Illegal Drug Markets in Transitional Economies' 13(6) *Addiction Research and Theory* 563.

Fitzgerald, J. L. (2009) 'Mapping the Experience of Drug Dealing Risk Environments: An Ethnographic Case Study' 20(3) *International Journal of Drug Policy* 261.

Fleetwood, J. and Leban, L. (2023) 'Women's Involvement in the Drug Trade: Revisiting the Emancipation Thesis in Global Perspective' 44(2) *Deviant Behavior* 238.

Fordham, A. and Fernández, A. C. (2021) 'Silence Costs Lives: The World Drug Report 2021 and the Importance of Political Courage' *International Drug Policy Consortium* (12 July). https://idpc.net/blog/2021/07/silence-costs-lives-the-world-drug-report-2021-and-the-importance-of-political-courage.

Galea, S., Hall, C. and Kaplan, G. A. (2009) 'Social Epidemiology and Complex System Dynamic Modelling as Applied to Health Behaviour and Drug Use Research' 20(3) *International Journal of Drug Policy* 209.

Grund, J. P. C. (2005) 'The Eye of the Needle: An Ethno-Epidemiological Analysis of Injecting Drug Use' in Pates, R., McBride, A. and Arnold, K. (eds.) *Injecting Illicit Drugs* (London: Blackwell Publishing).

Gunawan, R. and Pamintori, R. T. (2019) 'Populism Versus Justice' 137 *Inside Indonesia* (14 October). www.insideindonesia.org/editions/edition-137-drugs/populism-versus-justice.

Hardon, A. and Hymans, T. D. (2014) 'Ethnographies of Youth Drug Use in Asia' 25(4) *International Journal on Drug Policy* 749.

Hardon, A., Idrus, N. I. and Hymans, T. D. (2013) 'Chemical Sexualities: The Use of Pharmaceutical and Cosmetic Products by Youth in South Sulawesi, Indonesia' 21(41) *Reproductive Health Matters* 214.

Harm Reduction International. (2023) *The Death Penalty for Drug Offences: Global Overview 2022* (London: Harm Reduction International).

Harry, L. (2023) 'The Legacy of Colonial Patriarchy in the Current Administration of the Malaysian Death Penalty: The Hyper-Sentencing of Foreign National Women to Death for Drug Trafficking' in Aliverti, A., Carvalho, H., Chamberlen, A. and Sozzo, M. (eds.) *Decolonizing the Criminal: Colonial Legacies, Contemporary Problems* (Oxford: Oxford University Press).

Havenhand, G. (2020) *Reorienting Drug Policy in Indonesia: Pathways to the Sustainable Development Goals* (Lembaga Bantuan Hukum Masyarakat and Reprieve). https://lbhmasyarakat.org/wp-content/uploads/2020/06/Pathways-to-the-Sustainable-Development-Goals-1.pdf.

Higgins, P. C. and Butler, R. R. (1982) *Understanding Deviance* (New York: McGraw-Hill).

Hood, R. and Hoyle, C. (2015) *The Death Penalty: A Worldwide Perspective* (Oxford: Oxford University Press).

Hoyle, C. and Harry, L. (2020) 'Compounded Vulnerability: Foreign National Women and the Death Penalty in Southeast Asia' 40 *Amicus Journal* 15.

Hoyle, C. (with Rahadi, A., Rizzelli, L. and Handayani, P.) (2023) *Dealing with Punishment: Risks and Rewards in Indonesia's Illicit Drug Trade* (London: The Death Penalty Project). https://deathpenaltyproject.org/wp-content/uploads/2023/03/DPP-Indonesia-Deterrance-Report_final.pdf.

Hunt, N. (2006) 'Young People and Illicit Drug Use' in Aggleton, P., Ball, A. and Mane, P. (eds.) *Sex, Drugs and Young People: International Perspectives* (Abingdon: Routledge).

Kamarulzaman, A. and McBrayer, J. L. (2015) 'Compulsory Drug Treatment Centers in East and Southeast Asia' 26(Suppl. 1) *International Journal of Drug Policy* S33.

Kim, I. J., Zane, N. W. S. and Hong, S. (2002) 'Protective Factors Against Substance Use Among Asian American Youth: A Test of the Peer Cluster Theory' 30(5) *Journal of Community Psychology* 565.

Kleinman, A., Das, V. and Lock, M. M. (eds.) (1997) *Social Suffering* (Berkeley: University of California Press).

Kokkevi, A., Richardson, C., Florescu, S., Kuzman, M. and Stergar, E. (2007) 'Psychosocial Correlates of Substance Use in Adolescence: A Cross-National Study in Six Countries' 86(1) *Drug and Alcohol Dependence* 67.

Lasco, G. (2014) '*Pampagilas*: Methamphetamine in the Everyday Economic Lives of Underclass Male Youths in a Philippine Port' 25(4) *International Journal of Drug Policy* 783.

(2020) 'Drugs and Drug Wars as Populist Tropes in Asia: Illustrative Examples and Implications for Drug Policy' 77 *International Journal of Drug Policy* 102668.

Lindsey, T. and Nicholson, P. (2016) *Drugs Law and Legal Practice in Southeast Asia: Indonesia, Singapore and Vietnam* (London: Bloomsbury Publishing).

Lines, R., Barrett, D. and Gallahue, P. (2015) 'The Death Penalty for Drug Offences: "Asian Values" or Drug Treaty Influence?' *Opinio Juris* (21 May). http://opiniojuris.org/2015/05/21/guest-post-the-death-penalty-for-drug-offences-asian-values-or-drug-treaty-influence/.

Lines, R., Elliott, R., Hannah, J., Schleifer, R., Avafia, T. and Barrett, D. (2017) 'The Case for International Guidelines on Human Rights and Drug Control' 19(1) *Health and Human Rights* 231.

Lopez, R. (2023) 'Thailand to Clamp Down on Cannabis Use in Major U-Turn on Drug Policy', *The Guardian* (22 September). www.theguardian.com/world/2023/sep/22/thailand-to-clamp-down-on-cannabis-use-in-major-u-turn-on-drug-policy.

Macaulay, F. (2020) 'Gendering Drug Policy' in Buxton, J., Margo, G. and Burger, L. (eds.) *The Impact of Global Drug Policy on Women: Shifting the Needle* (Bingley: Emerald Publishing Limited).

MacDonald, R. and Marsh, J. (2002) 'Crossing the Rubicon: Youth Transitions, Poverty, Drugs and Social Exclusion' 13(1) *International Journal of Drug Policy* 27.

Maulana, A. (2018) 'Indonesia: Indonesian Death Row and Problems of Unfair Trial', *Asian Human Rights Commission* (9 April). www.humanrights.asia/news/ahrc-news/AHRC-PAP-002-2018/.

Mayock, P. (2005) '"Scripting" Risk: Young People and the Construction of Drug Journeys' 12(5) *Drugs: Education, Prevention and Policy* 349.

McIlwaine, C. and Moser, C. O. N. (2001) 'Violence and Social Capital in Urban Poor Communities: Perspectives from Colombia and Guatemala' 13 *Journal of International Development* 965.

McRae, D. (2017) 'Indonesian Capital Punishment in Comparative Perspective' 173(1) *Journal of the Humanities and Social Sciences of Southeast Asia* 1.

Meehan, P. (2021) 'Precarity, Poverty and Poppy: Encountering Development in the Uplands of Shan State, Myanmar' 89 *International Journal of Drug Policy* 103064.

Meehan, P., Sadan, M., Hla, S. A., Phu, S. K. and Oo, N. M. (2022) 'Young People's Everyday Pathways Into Drug Harms in Shan State, Myanmar' 43(11) *Third World Quarterly* 2712.

Miller, R. J. and Stuart, F. (2017) 'Carceral Citizenship: Race, Rights and Responsibility in the Age of Mass Supervision' 21(4) *Theoretical Criminology* 532.

Moore, D. (2004) 'Governing Street-Based Injecting Drug Users: A Critique of Heroin Overdose Prevention in Australia' 59(7) *Social Science and Medicine* 1547.

Nasir, S. (2006) *Stories from the Lorong: Drug Subculture and the Social Context of HIV-Risk Behaviours Among Intravenous Drug Users in Makassar, Indonesia.* Unpublished thesis of Master of Women's Health (by research) at the Key Centre for Women's Health in Society, School of Population Health, the University of Melbourne.

(2016). 'Behind Jokowi and Duterte's "War on Drugs"', *Policy Forum* (21 September). www.policyforum.net/behind-jokowi-dutertes-war-drugs.

Nasir, S. and Rosenthal, D. (2009a) 'The Social Context of Initiation Into Injecting Drugs in the Slums of Makassar, Indonesia' 20(3) *International Journal on Drug Policy* 237.

(2009b) 'The *Lorong* as a Risk Environment: Drug Use and Gangs Among Young Men in the Slums of Makassar, Indonesia' 36(1–2) *Contemporary Drug Problems* 193.

Newcomb, M. D. and Bentler, P. M. (1989) 'Substance Use and Abuse Among Children and Teenagers' 44(2) *American Psychologist* 242.

Newcomb, M. D. and Locke, T. (2005) 'Health, Social and Psychological Consequences of Drug Use and Abuse' in Sloboda, Z. (ed.) *Epidemiology of Drug Abuse* (New York: Springer).

Parker, H. J., Bakx, K. and Newcombe, R. (1988) *Living with Heroin: The Impact of a Drugs 'Epidemic' on an English Community* (Milton Keynes: Open University Press).

Paternoster, R. and Bachman, R. (2012) 'Perceptual Deterrence Theory' in Cullen, F. T. and Wilcox, P. (eds.) *The Oxford Handbook of Criminological Theory* (Oxford: Oxford University Press).

Pearson, G. (1987) *The New Heroin Users* (Oxford: Basil Blackwell).

Pilkington, H. (2007a) 'In Good Company: Risk, Security and Choice in Young People's Drug Decisions' 55(2) *The Sociological Review* 373.

(2007b) 'Beyond "Peer Pressure": Rethinking Drug Use and "Youth Culture"' 18(3) *International Journal on Drug Policy* 213.

Pushpanathan, S. (1999) *Combating Transnational Crime in ASEAN.* https://asean.org/combating-transnational-crime-in-asean-by-s-pushpanathan/.

Raffle, E. (2021) 'The War on Drugs in Southeast Asia as 'State Vigilantism' 92 *International Journal of Drug Policy* 103114.

Resnicow, K. and Page, S. E. (2008) 'Embracing Chaos and Complexity: A Quantum Change for Public Health' 98(8) *American Journal of Public Health* 1382.

Rhodes, T. (2002) 'The "Risk Environment": A Framework for Understanding and Reducing Drug-Related Harm' 13(2) *International Journal of Drug Policy* 85.

(2009) 'Risk Environments and Drug Harms: A Social Science for Harm Reduction Approach' 20(3) *International Journal on Drug Policy* 193.

Ritter, A. (2022) *Drug Policy* (Abingdon: Routledge).

Rowe, E. (2019) 'From Drug Control to Harm Reduction' 137 *Inside Indonesia* (15 October). www.insideindonesia.org/editions/edition-137-drugs/from-drug-control-to-harm-reduction.

Seddon, T. (2006) 'Drugs, Crime and Social Exclusion: Social Context and Social Theory in British Drugs-Crime Research' 46 *British Journal of Criminology* 680.

(2023) *Rethinking Drug Laws: Theory, History, Politics* (Oxford: Oxford University Press).

Simmonds, L. and Coomber, R. (2009) 'Injecting Drug Users: A Stigmatised and Stigmatising Population' 20(2) *International Journal of Drug Policy* 121.

Simon, J. (2009) *Governing Through Crime: How the War on Crime Transformed American Democracy and Created a Culture of Fear* (New York: Oxford University Press).

Singer, M. (2004) 'The Social Origins and Expressions of Illness' 69(1) *British Medical Bulletin* 9.

(2006) *Something Dangerous: Emergent and Changing Illicit Drug Use and Community Health* (Long Grove: Waveland Press).

Stoicescu, C. (2015) 'Indonesia Uses Faulty Stats on 'Drug Crisis' to Justify Death Penalty', *The Conversation* (5 February). https://theconversation.com/indonesia-uses-faulty-stats-on-drug-crisis-to-justify-death-penalty-36512.

Stoicescu, C. and Palmer, W. (2019) 'Drugs and Drug Policy' 137 *Inside Indonesia* (15 October). www.insideindonesia.org/editions/edition-137-drugs/drugs-and-drug-policy.

Sunstein, C. R. and Vermeule, A. (2006) 'Is Capital Punishment Morally Required? Acts, Omissions, and Life–Life Tradeoffs' 58 *Stanford Law Review* 703.

Sutherland, E. H. (1939) *Principles of Criminology* (3rd ed.) (Chicago: J.B. Lippincott Company).

Taylor, M. and Potter, G. R. (2013) 'From "Social Supply" to "Real Dealing" Drift, Friendship, and Trust in Drug-Dealing Careers' 43(4) *Journal of Drug Issues* 392.

Tonry, M. (2007) 'Determinants of Penal Policies' 36(1) *Crime and Justice* 1.

United Nations. (2023) *Malaysia: UN Experts Hail Parliamentary Decision to End Mandatory Death Penalty*. (11 April). www.ohchr.org/en/press-releases/2023/04/malaysia-un-experts-hail-parliamentary-decision-end-mandatory-death-penalty#:~:text=GENEVA%20(11%20April%202023)%20–,1300%20prisoners%20on%20death%20row.

United Nations Joint Programme on HIV/AIDS. (2012) *Joint Statement: Compulsory Drug Detention and Rehabilitation Centres*. www.unodc.org/roseap/uploads/archive/documents/2012/03/drug-detention-centre/JC2310_Joint_Statement6March12FINAL_En.pdf.

United Nations Office on Drugs and Crime. (2009) *Political Declaration and Plan of Action on International Cooperation Towards an Integrated and Balanced Strategy by Counter the World Drug Problem*. www.unodc.org/documents/drug-prevention-and-treatment/High-level_segment_Commission_on_Narcotic_Drugs_11-12_March_2209.pdf.

(2020) *Synthetic Drugs in East and Southeast Asia: Latest Developments and Challenges* (Bangkok: United Nations Office on Drugs and Crime). www.unodc.org/documents/scientific/ATS/2020_ESEA_Regonal_Synthetic_Drug_Report_web.pdf.

(2021) *World Drug Report 2021* (Vienna: United Nations). www.unodc.org/unodc/en/data-and-analysis/wdr2021.html.

Valero, A. (2021) *Education and Economic Growth (Discussion Paper No. 1764)* (London: Centre for Economic Performance).

Walmsley, R. (2017) *World Prison Brief* (London: Institute for Criminal Policy Research).

Winarso, I., Irawati, I. and Handoyo, P. (2019) *Country Report on Drugs, Indonesia: 1976–2016*. www.researchgate.net/publication/332186973_COUNTRY_REPORT_ON_DRUGS_INDONESIA_1976-2016.

Windle, J. and Briggs, D. (2015) 'Going Solo: The Social Organisation of Drug Dealing Within a London Street Gang' 18(9) *Journal of Youth Studies* 1170.

Wojcik, J. (2020) 'Southeast Asia Has a Synthetic Drug Problem, China Has Key Stake in Fixing It' *Oxford Political Review* (15 August). https://oxfordpoliticalreview.com/2020/08/15/southeast-asia-has-a-synthetic-drug-problem-china-has-key-stake-in-fixing-it/.

Yap, A. and Tan, S. J. (2020) 'Capital Punishment in Singapore: A Critical Analysis of State Justifications from 2004 to 2018' 9(2) *International Journal for Crime, Justice and Social Democracy* 133.

Zimring, F. E., Fagan, J. and Johnson, D. T. (2010) 'Executions, Deterrence and Homicide: A Tale of Two Cities' 7(1) *Journal of Empirical Legal Studies* 1.

Zoccatelli, G. (2014) '"It Was Fun, It Was Dangerous": Heroin, Young Urbanities and Opening Reforms in China's Borderlands' 25(4) *International Journal of Drug Policy* 762.

PART III

Actors and Agencies

7

National Narcotics Agencies in Southeast Asia

Relics of the Regional 'War on Drugs'

DANIEL PASCOE

7.1 Introduction

From the 1990s to the early 2000s, Southeast Asia was unique as a world region where penal laws on drugs tended to become more, rather than less, punitive.[1] During that period, the work of national narcotics agencies was central to the public discourse in Southeast Asia, flooding the region's visual, virtual, and news media spaces.[2]

This chapter focuses on the role played by Southeast Asia's national narcotics agencies in drug policy and enforcement in the region. The four most prominent national narcotics agencies within the Association of Southeast Asian Nations (ASEAN)[3] are the Central Narcotics Bureau

I would like to thank Sara Kowal and the Eleos Justice Anti-Death Penalty Clinic at Monash University for helping with the preliminary research for this chapter. Ahmad Sabirin also provided research assistance for the Indonesian leg of the project. Thank you also to Gloria Lai and Ricky Gunawan for their comments on a draft version.

1 Baldwin (2013); Coca (2018).

2 During my first (2004) and second (2011) ever trips to Singapore, anti-drug advertisements featuring the national agency's name were a frequent sight by the roadside. I saw the same during fieldwork travel to Indonesia's capital, Jakarta, in 2013, whether at the city's international airport or on giant billboards beside highways. Further striking examples from the web are the following: Badan Narkotika Nasional (2023) (anti-drug fun run, advertised on Instagram, Indonesia); Shofa (2022) (press conference proudly announcing drug seizures); Ebay (2022) (set of Central Narcotics Bureau 50th anniversary commemorative stamps reading 'stay away from drugs'); Central Narcotics Bureau (2021c) (glossy television advert); Zulkifli (2019) (militarised photo op); Government of Malaysia (2020) (downloadable application to volunteer for the AADK-backed NGO 'Skuad Antidadah'); Facebook (2020) (sponsorship of the national youth football league); Arayasukawat (2021) (auction of anime figures seized in drug cases).

3 National anti-narcotics agencies or committees also exist in Brunei, Cambodia, Laos, Myanmar, Philippines, and Vietnam. The leaders of these bodies form part of ASEAN's Senior Officials on Drug Matters (ASOD) grouping: see ASEAN (2022).

(CNB) in Singapore, the Office of the Narcotics Control Board (ONCB) in Thailand, the Agensi Antidadah Kebangsaan (AADK) in Malaysia,[4] and the Badan Narkotika Nasional (BNN, National Narcotics Board) in Indonesia. Each plays a role in law enforcement, rehabilitation, and anti-drug education. Although there are some nuances between countries, this chapter will show that (1) these four national narcotics agencies, counter-intuitively given their powers and public prominence, are mere 'cogs in the wheel' of national drug policymaking, the direction of which is instead determined by political actors; and (2) these agencies and their staff support the death penalty for narcotics crimes and more generally espouse a punitive approach towards drug offenders, reflecting the Southeast Asian agencies' standing as institutional relics of the region's 'War on Drugs' which began in the 1970s.

The CNB, ONCB, AADK, and BNN were chosen for analysis for three reasons. First, Singapore, Thailand, Malaysia, and Indonesia together make up around 57 per cent of ASEAN's population. Second, these four states, as compared with remaining ASEAN members Brunei, Cambodia, Laos, Myanmar, the Philippines, and Vietnam, are each right-of-centre 'flawed' democracies and, most importantly, all still retain and use the death penalty for drug offences.[5] Third, the four states' anti-narcotics policies and institutions are also broadly comparable arising from their common ratification of the three United Nations (UN) drug control treaties, concluded in 1961, 1971, and 1988.[6] The need to adopt a

[4] Sometimes, the Malaysian agency is referred to in English as the National Anti-Drug Agency (NADA).

[5] Each are classified by Amnesty International as 'retentionist' states: Amnesty International (2023). The most recent execution for drug offences took place in Indonesia in 2016, in Malaysia in 2017, in Singapore in 2023, and in Thailand in 2009. Vietnam is also classified as a retentionist state. However, Vietnam's criminal justice system is more closely comparable with those of other hard-line socialist nations, China, Laos, and North Korea within the Asian continent: Johnson and Zimring (2009); Pascoe (2019).

[6] These are the Single Convention on Narcotic Drugs 1961, as amended by the Protocol amending the Single Convention on Narcotic Drugs 1972 (both being ratified by Singapore in 1975, Thailand in 1975, Malaysia in 1978 and Indonesia in 1976); the Convention on Psychotropic Substances 1971 (ratified by Singapore in 1990, Thailand in 1975, Malaysia in 1986 and Indonesia in 1996); and the Convention against Illicit Traffic in Narcotic Drugs and Psychotropic Substances 1988 (ratified by Singapore in 1997, Thailand in 2002, Malaysia in 1993, and Indonesia in 1999). Jelsma and Armenta (2015, p. 1) summarise the effect of the three multilateral treaties:

regionally comparative approach in criminal justice research is well established:[7] comparison between the different national agencies creates context, demonstrating what is normal and what is exceptional.[8] Comparison aids explanation, and even cautious prediction of social phenomena.[9] Finally, comparison can also assist policy assessment such that agencies may learn from the best practices of others.[10]

The research presented in this chapter relies upon different sources, including legislation, policy statements, media reports, and in-country fieldwork interviews with 'elites' conducted between June and September 2023.[11] Arguably, previous non-governmental organization (NGO) reports and academic studies on comparative Asian and Southeast Asian drug policy, while serving as important starting points and advocacy tools,[12] have neglected the inner workings of national narcotics control bodies and their relative position within the state's policy power structure. This chapter aims to rectify this blind spot in the literature. 'Elite' interviews are a key means to this end, helping to reveal the reasons behind the official decisions and agendas of those

> The purpose of these treaties is to establish internationally applicable control measures with the aim of ensuring that psychoactive substances are available for medical and scientific purposes, while preventing them from being diverted into illegal channels. The treaties also include general provisions on the trafficking and use of psychoactive substances.
>
> The 1961 and 1971 Conventions classify controlled substances in four lists or Schedules, according to their perceived therapeutic value and potential risk of abuse. Included in an annex to the 1988 Convention are two tables listing precursor chemicals, reagents and solvents which are frequently used in the illicit manufacture of narcotic drugs and psychotropic substances. This treaty also significantly reinforced the obligation of countries to establish criminal offences in order to combat all aspects of the illicit production, possession and trafficking of psychoactive substances.

[7] Johnson and Zimring (2009).

[8] Nelken (2011).

[9] Kohli *et al.* (1995); Steinmo (2008).

[10] Pakes (2015).

[11] Ethics approval for the interviews was granted by the Human and Artefacts Ethics Sub-Committee of the City University of Hong Kong, with the application number HU-STA-00000399. After obtaining informed consent from participants, interviews were conducted face-to-face with manual note-taking. See Appendix to this chapter for the list of interviewees.

[12] For example, refer to Rahman and Crofts (2013); Baldwin (2013); Lasco (2020); Miao (2017); Miao and Lai (2023); Pardo, Kilmer, and Huang (2019); Sachsenröder (2022).

individuals from politics, law, and the civil service who shape government policy.[13]

The chapter proceeds as follows: After the present introduction, Section 7.2 summarises the findings from the relevant academic literature on law enforcement agencies and their internal culture, with a particular focus on drug policing. Section 7.3 proceeds to relay the history of each of the four Southeast Asian anti-narcotics agencies, together with the origins of their punitive policies on drugs. Section 7.4 describes the present organisation, functions, and powers of each agency, to address their relative power vis-à-vis politicians and other public bodies in shaping drug policy. Section 7.5 then discusses agency and officer views on punitive approaches to drug offending. Finally, the conclusion in Section 7.6 summarises the research findings and discusses the related policy implications.

7.2 Previous Literature

The academic literature covering police and other law enforcement agencies is the most relevant frame through which to consider the position of Southeast Asia's national narcotics agencies within the state's power structure. Law enforcement bodies, together with social services and public health agencies are typically located in the executive branch of government, with their staff being public employees. Within their operational discretion, they implement the policy priorities of the government of the day.[14] Occasionally, specialised law enforcement agencies such as anti-corruption bodies may be established outside this typical structure and even form their own distinct 'fourth branch' of government, to maintain their financial and structural independence, to keep watch over misconduct within the police, military, civil service and by elected politicians.[15] Yet such 'fourth branch' institutions are typically limited to those with an 'integrity' function and are usually still beholden to the authority of the head of state and to the courts via judicial review.[16]

With politicians more directly accountable to the public as they make decisions,[17] police and related government departments do not see their

[13] Lilleker (2003).

[14] Caplan (1971); Ritter and Lancaster (2013).

[15] Howe and Haigh (2016); Quah (2014).

[16] Howe and Haigh (2016).

[17] Even though Singapore, Thailand, Malaysia, and Indonesia hold regular elections for national and sub-national political offices, each of them are (sometimes very) flawed democracies. In 2023, NGO Freedom House classified Singapore, Malaysia, and

role to lead in terms of policy, but rather to follow. Law enforcement agencies generally have little room to come up with criminal justice policies themselves, with national-level politicians from the executive or legislative branch instead playing the leading role in setting policy priorities in response to state security concerns.[18] Southeast Asia's national narcotics agencies provide an important test of these assumptions due to their prominent public profile and the vast powers and responsibilities that they have accumulated since the early 1970s.

Furthermore, recent policing literature has emphasised the organisational missions of law enforcement agencies and the personal viewpoints of law enforcement staffers as being pro-'law and order' or as focused on 'crime control',[19] including when policing drugs.[20] On specific punishments, previous literature from both retentionist and abolitionist nations tends to have found that law enforcement officers favour maintaining or re-establishing capital punishment for murder, if not for other crimes.[21] A less-punitive self-image, seeing such agencies as community-rooted providers of public services, is popular within the writings of policing theorists but tends to be less popular within the agencies themselves.[22]

What explains the discrepancy between theory and practice? Law enforcement bodies are institutions which develop their own working culture within which new recruits are socialised.[23] Rational self-interest plays a part in developing such 'law and order' views: supporting harsher punishments for crimes and a lesser use of lenient discretion are the most risk-averse positions to take vis-à-vis one's superiors within the organisation and in relation to the law-abiding public,[24] a majority of whom might not closely identify with the suspects targeted by police investigations, particularly in light of ethnic, class, and age differences. An established agency staff member or new recruit who publicly espoused a view contrary to that of the majority would likely find his or her path to promotion more difficult.[25]

Indonesia as 'Partly Free' jurisdictions: Freedom House (2023). Thailand was classified as 'Not Free', although a May 2023 election has since ended direct military rule.

18 Babor *et al.* (2018); Sacco (2014).

19 Loftus (2009); O'Sullivan (2005); Prenzler (1997); Silvestri (2003).

20 Bacon (2022); Burris and Burrows (2009); Crofts *et al.* (2013).

21 Bedau (1973); Colman and Gorman (1982); Fagan (1986); Mapstone (1992); Wallace (2024).

22 For example, refer to Loader and Mulcahy (2003); Ponsaers (2001).

23 O'Sullivan (2005); Silvestri (2003).

24 Burris and Burrows (2009); Crofts *et al.* (2013).

25 Crofts *et al.* (2013).

Rational self-interest also extends to the mission of the institution as a whole. A law enforcement organisation whose official position on the death penalty or other harsh punishment approaches was at odds with that of politicians from the executive or legislative branch would soon risk budget cuts, dismissal of its personnel or its decisions being undermined or reversed. Furthermore, promoting and enforcing harsh punishments for drug crimes arguably feeds into the 'prison industrial complex' in the modern state, whereby the prison economy justifies more arrests and convictions, which in turn justifies ever more money being spent on corrections.[26]

In short, there are powerful incentives for individuals to toe the line within law enforcement organisations, and for the organisations themselves to adopt a position, often punitive, that accords with the government of the day.[27] In jurisdictions where officers are ordered to take on a multifaceted role in dealing with drugs, incorporating law enforcement, rehabilitation, education, and harm reduction, such as within a national narcotics agency, mission confusion may result. As N. Crofts *et al.* observe:

> Where this has been studied, the overwhelming finding is of a perceived and often severe conflict between unresolved and competing imperatives of the dual roles police are asked to fulfil – drug crime policing and support for harm reduction.[28]

In the Southeast Asian context, Section 7.5 of this chapter considers the available evidence for punitive views on the part of the agencies and their staff. Nevertheless, brandishing punitive views towards drug offenders and users is not quite the same as pulling the key policy levers that determine how punitive the criminal justice system can be in practice.

7.3 History

Since the 1970s, the decade during which the first permanent national narcotics agencies were founded in Southeast Asia, drug crimes have been seen by Southeast Asian governments as some of the most serious crimes in the statute book, if not *the* most serious category.[29] The

[26] Cummings (2012).
[27] Prenzler (1997).
[28] Crofts *et al.* (2013, p. 73).
[29] Petcharamesree (2023).

regional political consensus was that widespread illicit drug use would form a kind of wider sabotage of productivity and family values, and create a countercultural threat to state survival.[30] In all four jurisdictions discussed in this chapter, the establishment of the current national narcotics agency or a precursor institution embodied government desires to incorporate the most coercive components of the 1960s to 1980s UN narcotics control treaties.[31] Across the ASEAN bloc, accession to these multilateral agreements eventually led to mass anti-drug education efforts in schools and universities, confined rehabilitation for regular users, the destruction of drug crops such as opium and cannabis, and legislation to allow or mandate the death penalty for drug traffickers and manufacturers.[32] In the aftermath of the American war in Vietnam, Southeast Asia had begun its very own 'War on Drugs'.

Southeast Asia's oldest surviving anti-narcotics agency was established in Singapore. The CNB's origin story is typical of counternarcotics efforts across the region. As part of an effort to deal with opium, cannabis, and methaqualone from the Golden Triangle entering the region during the Vietnam War, the Singaporean government established the CNB as a specialised anti-narcotics law enforcement and preventive agency in November 1971.[33] Parliament thereafter increased the penalties for drug offences by enacting the Misuse of Drugs Act in 1973. The culmination of Singapore's punitive turn was the Misuse of Drugs (Amendment) Act 1975 which imposed the mandatory death penalty for drug crimes for the first time. On the CNB's fiftieth anniversary in 2021,[34] the Singaporean government was quick to praise the agency's work as a reason that the country is 'largely drug free. They [CNB officers] have saved tens of thousands of young people from a life of drugs and crime'.[35]

In Thailand, although a police-led Central Narcotics Board was established as far back as 1961, it had no permanent legislative mandate and was abolished and reconstituted with every following government.[36] With the Narcotics Control Act 1976, the cabinet-level Narcotics Control Board (NCB) and its secretariat, the ONCB, were established. Shortly afterwards, the Narcotics Act 1979 first introduced the judicial

30 Pascoe (2019).
31 Gunawan and Lai (2018).
32 Baldwin (2013); C. Hoyle and P. Jabbar in Chapter 6 in this volume.
33 Central Narcotics Bureau (2021a); Sachsenröder (2022).
34 Also see note 2.
35 Central Narcotics Bureau (2021a, p. 5).
36 Ministry of Justice (n.d.).

death penalty for narcotics crimes, although the Constitutions of Thailand 1976, 1977, and 1978 had each made provision for arbitrary executions (that is, executions without trial) which could be applied to drug dealers.[37] It is significant that both Singapore and Thailand were, effectively, authoritarian states at the time their narcotics agencies came into being. Singapore's politics was dominated by its founder and first prime minister, Lee Kuan Yew. Thailand's was a military dictatorship headed by a caretaker prime minister, Thanin Kraivichien.[38] While at its foundation the ONCB was formed as an independent department under the office of the prime minister, a ministerial reorganisation in 2002 affiliated the agency with the ministry of justice.[39] In more recent years, whereas disrupting methamphetamine importation and repurposing rural opium plantations remain as ONCB law enforcement priorities,[40] the agency has supported the legalisation of kratom[41] and cannabis for medicinal (but not recreational) use.[42] It has become the only regional agency of those under study in this chapter to adopt both positions. The new Narcotics Code of Thailand, purportedly consistent with the result of the UN General Assembly Special Session on the World Drug Problem (2016), was passed in November 2021.[43]

In Malaysia, an anti-drugs committee has existed at the cabinet level in one form or another since 1975.[44] However, it was not until 1996, following a Ministry of Home Affairs proposal, that a National Drug Agency was established by amalgamating several agencies which focused separately on enforcement, prevention, and rehabilitation for drug crimes and drug use across separate government departments.[45] It was only some years after its founding that the newly-named AADK received its own dedicated statute, in 2004, with the National Anti-Drugs Agency Act. In one key respect, Malaysia is the odd nation out within those

37 Pascoe (2019).
38 In 1961, Thailand was also run by a military government, headed by Field Marshal Sarit Thanarat.
39 United Nations Office on Drugs and Crime (2008).
40 Laohong (2016); Tangsathaporn (2022).
41 Tanguay (2011).
42 Laohong (2018).
43 Office of the Narcotics Control Board (n.d.b); R. Bunmee in Chapter 9 in this volume.
44 National Anti-Drugs Agency (n.d.a).
45 Azizan *et al.* (2018); National Anti-Drugs Agency (n.d.a); Muniandy and Jalil (2010). A Central Narcotics Bureau, although established in 1972 and sharing a name with its Singaporean counterpart, had an enforcement focus and was accordingly based within the ministry of law: National Anti-Drugs Agency (n.d.a); United Nations (1974).

considered in this chapter: its current national agency was formed long after the country's peak in terms of drug punitiveness. In the other three jurisdictions, the establishment of the present agency or a national precursor came before the nation's most punitive period, which its enforcement work then contributed to, whether that was the mid-1990s (Singapore), the late 1990s to early 2000s (Thailand), or the mid-2010s (Indonesia).[46] Malaysia reached its own punitive apex under Prime Minister Mahathir Mohamad as the chair of the UN's International Conference on Drug Abuse and Illicit Trafficking, held in Vienna in 1987,[47] without the input of an integrated national agency for implementing drug policy.

The example of Malaysia shows that putting into practice a strongly coercive drug policy does not necessarily require an all-encompassing national drugs agency. Separate government departments and agencies in the fields of health, law enforcement, corrections, education and prosecutions can implement policies such as compulsory rehabilitation for users, fervent anti-drug education in schools, and, most strikingly, enforce the mandatory death penalty for traffickers and manufacturers.[48] Today, the AADK is mainly known for its rehabilitation and education work,[49] with its law enforcement functions primarily limited to actions against individual drug users.[50] Nevertheless, as will be shown in Sections 7.4 and 7.5, the way the AADK carries out its functions still reflects a 'War on Drugs' mentality.

The history of Indonesia's national narcotics board, BNN, is longer than it first appears. The present agency was only established in 2002. However, the BNN's conceptual origins are, as with its Singaporean and Thai equivalents, in Indonesia's 1970s reforms to drug laws under an authoritarian government, that of President Suharto. By the 1970s, Indonesia had started to see drugs as a threat to individuals, communities, and the state.[51] The death penalty for narcotics crimes was introduced by legislation in 1976, directly after Indonesia's ratification of the UN Single Convention; however, no trafficker was executed until 1995.[52]

46 Pascoe (2019).
47 Harring (1991).
48 Ibid.
49 Interviews (Malaysia: 25 July 2023, 26 July 2023, and 28 July 2023b).
50 The Malaysian Administrative Modernisation and Management Planning Unit (n.d.).
51 Havenhand (2020); Lindsey and Nicholson (2016).
52 Pascoe (2019).

From 1971, the mitigation of drug use in Indonesia fell under the authority of the National Intelligence Coordination Agency (Badan Koordinasi Intelijen Negara – BAKIN), a small coordinating body made up of representatives from the ministries of health, social affairs, foreign affairs, and the attorney-general's office, among others. However, this BNN antecedent agency had no direct funding via the national budget, and limited authority to conduct its own operations.[53] A national narcotics coordinating board (Badan Koordinasi Narkotika Nasional – BKNN) combining representatives from twenty-five government agencies was established by presidential decree in 1999, but the BNN was not founded as a separate institution with its own budget and its own staff until 2002.[54]

BNN was initially governed by presidential decrees and regulations rather than by its own dedicated statute,[55] and was first headed by the serving Chief of Indonesian Police, rather than by an in-house leader.[56] Its institutional evolution only became complete with the passage of Law 35/2009 on Narcotics. Since then, its authority has grown rapidly. BNN is now one of the most powerful and vocal non-ministerial agencies in Indonesia.[57] Its two founding purposes are to coordinate (1) relevant executive agencies in the formulation and implementation of the national drug prevention policy and (2) the implementation of the national drug control policy.[58]

7.4 Organisation, Functions, and Powers

Unlike the more specialised US drug agencies[59] or those found in other regions, a common distinguishing feature of the four most prominent Southeast Asian agencies is the extremely wide powers that they enjoy, extending on paper to prevention not only through law enforcement but also through publicity, education, community empowerment, and rehabilitation. In jurisdictions around the world, these functions are often divided among different ministries and agencies,[60] whose

53 Badan Narkotika Nasional (2022a).
54 Ibid.
55 Lindsey and Nicholson (2016).
56 Baldwin (2013).
57 Honna (2011); International Drug Policy Consortium (2017).
58 Badan Narkotika Nasional (2022a).
59 US Department of Justice (n.d.).
60 Greenwald (2009); Scorzelli (1992).

conflicting priorities and competition with one another may, in some cases, compromise the effectiveness of drug control or harm-reduction efforts. In contrast, the four Southeast Asian narcotics agencies considered in this chapter possess a (mostly) all-encompassing agenda, often achieved through the amalgamation of smaller precursor agencies that dealt with more specific policy areas. They are not merely specialised law enforcement vehicles analogous to anti-corruption bodies, customs and excise agents, or even 'morality police' in Islamic-majority countries, but rather institutions that aim to coordinate entire governmental and societal responses to illicit drugs and their use. At first glance, the vast array of responsibilities accorded to the Southeast Asian agencies appears to challenge the conception that such bodies are merely 'cogs in the wheel' bringing to life drug policies that are devised by political actors. Yet, the agencies' decision-making reality is far more circumscribed than their widespread powers suggest on paper.

In Singapore, the CNB's stated functions are to enforce the nation's narcotics laws, to train its own enforcement officers, to run publicity campaigns aiming to create public opinion against illicit drug use and trafficking, to collect intelligence on drug trafficking in coordination with Singapore's other law enforcement agencies, and to act as a liaison with the international drug control bodies.[61] When it was first established in 1971, the Bureau consisted of just three sections: enforcement; administration; and research, training, and publicity. Thereafter, its responsibilities expanded over time, concomitant with the rise of Singapore's now pervasive anti-drug 'ideology'.[62] Five years after its founding, the agency's powers expanded by subordinate legislation to reflect the importance of rehabilitating drug users and minimising their relapse rate. The director of the CNB was empowered to seek confined treatment for arrested drug users.[63] In November 1993, the CNB was further entrusted with additional powers by the Drug Trafficking (Confiscation of Benefits) Act, allowing the agency to trace, freeze, and confiscate assets identified as proceeds from drug trafficking.

As the CNB's powers have expanded, it is also notable that, over the years, its primacy in anti-drug education has waned. This function is now shared with the Singapore Anti-Narcotics Association (SANA) (an NGO), the Ministry of Education, and the Singapore Armed Forces,

[61] Central Narcotics Bureau (2021b); United Nations Office on Drugs and Crime (2008).
[62] Miao (2017, p. 64).
[63] Central Narcotics Bureau (2021a); Chok (2017).

although the CNB retains a coordinating role.[64] The overall vision is for the CNB to play a central role in a 'whole of society' strategy to combat illicit drug use and distribution in Singapore, albeit in cooperation with other government agencies and closely regulated by primary and subordinate legislation. Drug policy is initially formulated by the minister of home affairs, with input from fellow cabinet ministers. It is the CNB which is tasked with implementing this policy, albeit within a reasonable margin of professional judgment.[65]

The director of the CNB is appointed by the Singaporean minister of home affairs and has significant powers under the Misuse of Drugs Act in its most recent (2020) iteration.[66] CNB agents possess all the same powers available to police officers to investigate an offence under the Act, including entrapment, searching suspects, and the ability to conduct random drug tests in public places.[67] Legislation specifically states that its officers shall be armed.[68] However, the CNB's law enforcement operations against drug traffickers and users are shared with other law agencies, particularly the Singapore Police Force, Singapore Customs, and the Immigration & Checkpoints Authority.[69] The CNB also works closely with foreign drug enforcement agencies, with the International Criminal Police Organization (INTERPOL), and with industry leaders to control access to precursor chemicals.[70] Despite its prominent public reputation, the CNB is but one facet of the Singaporean government's eradication-centred response to drugs in the city-state.

In Thailand, day-to-day work on drug control is carried out by the ONCB, which acts as a secretariat for the more powerful NCB, the committee which controls drug policy and strategy.[71] While the ONCB is made up of civil service professionals across various fields, the NCB is formulated as essentially an 'anti-drugs cabinet', headed by the prime minister. Among the NCB's other members are key government ministers, the attorney general, the leaders of the Thai police force and

64 Central Narcotics Bureau (2018); Lim (2022); Quah (2008).

65 Interviews (Singapore: 23 June 2023, 28 June 2023, and 30 June 2023).

66 Misuse of Drugs Act 2020, ss. 3(1), 24–26.

67 Misuse of Drugs Act 2020, ss. 31, 31A, 31B, and 32; Interviews (Singapore: 28 June 2023 and 30 June 2023).

68 Misuse of Drugs Act 2020, s. 32A.

69 ASEAN (1991); Lindsey and Nicholson (2016).

70 Ibid; Quah (2008).

71 Office of the Narcotics Control Board (n.d.c); Narcotics Control Act 1976, ss. 5, 11–13; R. Bunmee in Chapter 9 in this volume.

Customs Department, and the NCB secretary-general. The latter concurrently supervises the activities of the ONCB.[72] Thai drug policy, ultimately directed from the political level, has until recently been criticised as being conservative and anti-scientific.[73]

In contrast with the NCB, the ONCB is tasked with narcotics policy implementation, including inter-agency coordination, surveillance, and intelligence, conducting arrests, forcible rehabilitation, preventive education, minimising the transmission of HIV through intravenous drug use, drug research, and also coordinating with its international equivalents and with local NGOs.[74] That is not to say, though, that the ONCB plays no role at all in policy formulation. The NCB has, in the past, approved or endorsed policy ideas originating from the ONCB.[75] One prominent recent example was kratom decriminalisation in 2021.[76] The new Narcotics Code of Thailand (2021) was first drafted by the ONCB, before its ratification by cabinet and parliament.[77] Increasingly, Thailand's political decision-makers seem more willing to trust the ONCB's subject-specific expertise in devising drug policy.

One of the ONCB's major functions remains law enforcement. While the agency's focus is on transnational cases, the Narcotics Suppression Bureau (NSB) of the Royal Thai Police is responsible for domestic (street-level) drug crimes. Both agencies work closely together, with the police force providing manpower when necessary.[78] The NSB is just one of the many executive agencies working alongside the ONCB to pursue drug control in Thailand.[79]

Moving to Malaysia, the AADK is directly responsible to the cabinet's committee on the eradication of drugs and acts as its secretariat,[80] with much the same relationship as the ONCB and NCB, respectively, in Thailand. The cabinet committee is chaired by Malaysia's deputy prime minister and includes the AADK's director in its membership,[81] along

72 Ministry of Justice (n.d.).

73 Pardo, Kilmer, and Huang (2019); Windle (2016). Corroborated by Interview (Thailand: 23 August 2023).

74 ASEAN (1991); Office of the Narcotics Control Board (n.d.a).

75 Interviews (Thailand: 24 August 2023 and 28 August 2023).

76 Interviews (Thailand: 23 August 2023). Also refer to Office of the Narcotics Control Board (n.d.c); Tanguay (2011).

77 Office of the Narcotics Control Board (n.d.c).

78 GlobalSecurity.org (n.d.). Corroborated by Interview (Thailand: 24 August 2023).

79 US Department of State (2001). Corroborated by Interview (Thailand: 23 August 2023).

80 United Nations Office on Drugs and Crime (2008).

81 Chan (2023).

with the minister of home affairs, whose portfolio includes responsibility for the AADK.[82] The agency's director general is appointed by the Malaysian King on the advice of the prime minister.[83] Although the AADK provides expert policy advice to the minister of home affairs and to the members of parliament on new legislation,[84] the ultimate balance between reducing supply and demand, between law enforcement, education, and rehabilitation is carved out at the cabinet level.[85] Any major changes in direction are achieved by the passage of new primary or subordinate legislation, rather than the agency working within the existing legislative framework.[86] Prominent examples are the mooted reforms towards decriminalisation of minor drug possession and voluntary rather than mandatory rehabilitative detention for drug users. Both may soon be realised with the replacement of the Drug Dependants (Treatment and Rehabilitation) Act 1983, enacted during Malaysia's most punitive era on drugs under Prime Minister Mahathir, with the Misuse of Drugs and Substances (Prevention, Treatment, and Rehabilitation) Act, which is being debated at the time of writing.

Malaysia's stated National Drug Policy aims to 'create a Malaysian nation and society that is free from the threat of [narcotic] drugs to ensure the well-being of community life, [and to] maintain national stability and resilience'.[87] The main method through which AADK tries to achieve this is through illicit drug use prevention, via both reductions in drug demand and in drug supply.[88] Like the other national agencies, the AADK does not act alone in pursuing the state's narcotics policy goals. As part of its work, it organises interdepartmental and international cooperation to counterdrug production and distribution.[89] As with their CNB equivalents, AADK agents have all the same powers and immunities as police officers in dealing with drug cases, yet their law enforcement role is circumscribed by legislation, so as to focus on

[82] National Anti-Drugs Agency (n.d.c).
[83] National Anti-Drugs Agency Act 2004, ss. 4–5.
[84] Interviews (Malaysia: 27 July 2023a, 29 July 2023a). The agency advises the minister of home affairs 'on policies relating to prevention of misuse of dangerous drugs, treatment and rehabilitation of drug dependants, special preventive measures of persons associated with trafficking in dangerous drugs and the forfeiture of property connected with dangerous drugs offences': National Anti-Drugs Agency Act 2004, s. 6(i).
[85] Abdullah (2023); Al Jazeera (2019).
[86] Interviews (Malaysia: 24 July 2023 and 25 August 2023).
[87] Agensi Antidadah Kebangsaan (2019, p. 1).
[88] International Society of Substance Abuse Professionals (n.d.).
[89] United Nations Office on Drugs and Crime (2008).

individual users.[90] It is instead the Royal Malaysia Police's Narcotics Division that investigates and enforces major drug crimes under the Dangerous Drugs Act 1952.[91]

One component of the AADK's agenda already exhibits an important difference from the other three agencies under study. It is only the AADK whose mission statement currently extends to harm reduction,[92] which is broadly defined as a recognition that drug use cannot be eliminated but that its harms to human health and social and legal wellbeing can be lessened by shifting the focus of operations.[93] In cooperation with the Royal Malaysia Police, Ministry of Health, Prisons Department, academics, and NGOs, the AADK's harm reduction strategy began in 2005 with a methadone therapy programme,[94] but has not yet progressed beyond this to encompass needle exchanges, for example. Nevertheless, in an apparent contradiction, the stated goals of the AADK still include freeing Malaysia from narcotic drugs entirely,[95] starting with anti-drug education for preschool-age children.[96] In practice, the agency continues to favour a coercive, abstinence-based approach to drug control while merely paying lip service to the international discourse on harm reduction.[97]

Finally, in Indonesia, the BNN's main role is to prevent and eradicate the use and illicit trafficking of narcotics, psychotropics, drug precursors, and other addictive substances, excluding tobacco and alcohol. To this end, apart from law enforcement, BNN also conducts work towards community empowerment, education, rehabilitation of users, and drug research.[98] As examples of its work practices, BNN has, in the recent past, conducted user surveys, drug seizures, assessments of international

[90] National Anti-Drugs Agency Act 2004, ss. 6(a), 7(2); Interviews (Malaysia: 24 July 2023 and 27 July 2023a).

[91] Interviews (Malaysia: 24 July 2023 and 27 July 2023a).

[92] 'Harm reduction' can be contrasted with references to 'harm prevention' found within materials published by other agencies. For example, see Central Narcotics Bureau (2018, p. 2 and 2023). Thailand's ONCB has also moved in the direction of harm reduction, although it does not form part of the organisation's mission statement: Interviews (Thailand: 23 August 2023, 28 August 2023). Also refer to Baldwin (2013); Pardo *et al.* (2019).

[93] Miao and Lai (2023); Pardo, Kilmer, and Huang (2019).

[94] Lee, Jacka, and Crofts (2013).

[95] National Anti-Drugs Agency (n.d.b).

[96] Agensi Antidadah Kebangsaan (2019).

[97] Interviews (Malaysia: 26 July 2023, 27 July 2023a, and 27 July 2023b).

[98] Alam *et al.* (2020); Badan Narkotika Nasional (2022b); Law 35/2009 on Narcotics, Articles 67 and 70.

trafficking routes, bilateral cooperation with other nations' narcotics agencies, and assessments of the impact of illicit drugs on the Indonesian economy.[99]

As a non-ministerial government institution, BNN is independent of all government ministries and is directly accountable to the president of Indonesia.[100] BNN officials provide advice directly to the president,[101] including clemency applications in drug cases.[102] There have even been occasions where BNN leaders have criticised the president for commuting the death sentences of convicted drug traffickers, and for failing to prioritise drug enforcement within the national political agenda.[103]

Incorporating its provincial and district components,[104] BNN is an organisational behemoth, with more than 3,000 staff, regional offices in thirty-three provinces, and more than 100 offices at a local level. Broadly speaking, BNN's status is comparable to that of the national police, armed forces, state intelligence agency, public prosecution service, and the Corruption Eradication Commission (KPK). Despite being formally separate from the Indonesian National Police, both work closely together through a memorandum of understanding.[105] On drug enforcement, the BNN tends to handle large-scale trafficking cases whereas the police handle street-level cases, although their overall responsibilities substantially overlap.[106] BNN also cooperates with the Ministry of Health as the latter classifies drugs and sets standards for rehabilitation and treatment programmes.[107] Moreover, as with several of the other agencies under study, BNN's educational and preventive functions are shared with volunteers from anti-drugs NGOs – most prominently GRANAT and GANNAS (both Indonesian acronyms translated as the National Movement Against Narcotics).[108]

When assessing BNN's broader impact on Indonesia's drug policy, it is notable that its founding functions focus on coordination between

99 Lindsey and Nicholson (2016).
100 Ibid.
101 International Drug Policy Consortium (2017).
102 Pascoe (2019).
103 McRae (2013).
104 United Nations Office on Drugs and Crime (2008).
105 Lindsey and Nicholson (2016).
106 Interviews (Indonesia: 10 August 2023b, 14 August 2023, and 15 August 2023a).
107 Lindsey and Nicholson (2016); Havenhand (2020).
108 Interviews (Indonesia: 10 August 2023c, 18 August 2023, and 5 September 2023). Also refer to Kantor Kementerian Agama Kabupaten Purbalingga (2021); Ministry of Social Affairs (2019).

different government agencies to implement policy, rather than solely devising the policy itself.[109] While BNN is required to provide its own input to the presidency and Indonesia's legislature when developing narcotics policy,[110] the agency's often shrill public messaging on illicit drugs masks a concerted political plan of action emanating from the elected executive, rather than the other way around.[111] This is a situation replicated in the other three agencies under study.

7.4.1 Common Themes

In terms of functions and powers, one initial commonality is that all four agencies focus their attention on illicit drugs (narcotics), to the exclusion of tobacco, alcohol, and prescription drug abuse. This reflects their primary role in law enforcement, rather than a deeper concern with human health and the substances which actually cause the most harm in each jurisdiction. At present, harm reduction from tobacco and alcohol use in Southeast Asia falls within the province of separate government departments (such as health ministries) and community and religious-based NGOs.[112] Whereas tobacco and alcohol (mis)use are largely normalised across the non-Muslim populations of the region, the national narcotics agencies exist in their current form to perpetuate the coercive goals of the American-led and narcotics-focused 'War on Drugs', starting from the 1970s. Lasting change on this front will likely require the relocation of the Singaporean, Thai, Malaysian, and even Indonesian agencies to their respective governments' Ministries of Health, a move that will surely prompt fierce internal resistance.[113] For example, in Indonesia, every chair of BNN has thus far come from a police background, rather than from a health background.[114]

Nevertheless, the most significant common theme across all four agencies is that major changes to the scope of their responsibilities and the policies that they are tasked with implementing must come from the political level. This is readily explicable in Southeast Asia, a region where

[109] Badan Narkotika Nasional (2022a).

[110] United Nations Office on Drugs and Crime (2008). Corroborated by Interviews (Indonesia: 10 August 2023b, 10 August 2023c, and 15 August 2023b).

[111] Interviews (Indonesia: 10 August 2023a, 11 August 2023, and 18 August 2023).

[112] Amul and Pang (2018); World Health Organization (2017).

[113] Interviews (Malaysia: 26 July 2023 and 27 July 2023a; Thailand: 23 August 2023; Indonesia: 10 August 2023b and 11 August 2023).

[114] Badan Narkotika Nasional (2020).

drug control is often portrayed as an issue of national importance – a threat to the survival of the state, according to prominent current or former leaders, namely, Lee Kuan Yew (Singapore, 1965–1990), Thaksin Shinawatra (Thailand, 2001–2006), Mahathir Mohamad (Malaysia, 1981–2003; 2018–2020), and Joko Widodo (Indonesia, 2014–2024).[115] Whereas agency staff often supply data or direct drafting input into the early stages of a new policy proposal or in helping to tweak existing laws, the final decision on an issue of such magnitude could never be delegated to the unelected civil servants staffing an executive agency. A clear concern with this approach is that political leaders may have different short-term objectives, such as ensuring their continued popularity and re-election, and catering to donors and vested business or political interests, rather than formulating an evidence-based drug policy that best meets the needs of the public.

Four specific ways in which the political dependence of national narcotics agencies plays out are the following: first is the very detailed legislative regulation of the agencies concerned, with their responsibilities, powers, and their limits spelled out precisely in primary or subordinate legislation, and subject to amendment from time to time. While their powers are wide, they are not plenary. Significantly, none of the agencies are afforded any constitutional recognition, either as a 'fourth branch' of government or otherwise. Second are the various veto points in the system still accorded to political actors. Examples include ministerial or presidential appointment of agency leadership plus ultimate oversight of agency activities and budgets,[116] and even executive discretion in granting clemency to 'thwart' an agency's desired case outcome. Third is the cooperation necessary with other law enforcement bodies (for example, overlapping responsibilities with the police force and customs agents), prosecutors, and government ministries in fields, such as health and social welfare, each of whom is helping to implement a political programme of action, albeit through a division of labour across government. Fourth, although national narcotics agencies cooperate closely with their counterparts abroad and with INTERPOL, the

[115] Human Rights Watch (2004); Pascoe (2019); Sachsenröder (2022).

[116] Whereas there are national agencies accountable to the relevant minister of home affairs (Singapore and Malaysia), the minister of justice (Thailand), and/or a cabinet-level anti-drugs committee (Thailand and Malaysia), Indonesia's is the only agency under study that is *not* similarly accountable through its relevant institutional arrangements. The BNN reports directly to the president of Indonesia, which may explain its relative assertiveness in recent years.

framework for international cooperation in drug control is set mainly through bilateral and multilateral treaties,[117] which fall within the prerogative authority of the elected executive. In each of these ways, the capacity of the national agencies to operate truly autonomously is circumscribed by national laws and policies.

7.5 Severe Punishments, Including the Death Penalty, for Drug Crimes

In each of the four jurisdictions under study, the death penalty, life or long terms of imprisonment, detention without trial, and confined rehabilitation for users are or were, until recently, standard state responses to drug crimes.[118] Singapore and Malaysia remain two of the few nation-states that also impose corporal punishment on drug offenders, through caning or whipping.[119] Agency views on punishment are important, given their initial input into policy formulation as discussed in this chapter, and their role as law enforcers for serious drug crimes, either on their own or in conjunction with the relevant national police force.

Thus, an unexpected starting point is that, according to several interviewees, for each of the four agencies, their official position is *neutral* with regard to capital punishment.[120] The agencies' role, in accordance with this official position, is to enforce the law of the land, and if that includes the death penalty for drug crimes, then they will devote their resources to ensuring that drug traffickers and manufacturers are punished in this manner.[121] The same logic applies to life without parole,[122] corporal punishment, confined treatment for users, or administrative detention in cases where these are authorised by national law.

117 See note 6.

118 Baldwin (2013); Rahman *et al.* (2016); United Nations Office of the High Commissioner for Human Rights (2018).

119 Farrell (2021).

120 Interviews (Singapore: 30 June 2023; Malaysia: 25 July 2023 and 26 July 2023; Thailand: 23 August 2023 and 24 August 2023; and Indonesia: 10 August 2023c). Also see Havenhand (2020); Taher (2018) on Indonesia's BNN. Nevertheless, on several occasions around the time of controversial executions, the CNB has issued statements signalling that the death penalty is an essential part of Singapore's deterrence strategy. See, for example, Central Narcotics Bureau (2023).

121 Interviews (Singapore: 28 June 2023; Malaysia: 25 July 2023 and 26 July 2023; Indonesia: 10 August 2023c and 15 August 2023a). On Thailand, refer to Frankel (2001).

122 As of April 2023, the natural life sentence has now been abolished in Malaysia.

Officially, the agencies are each concerned with drug control, rather than with the method by which this is achieved. For advocates of a more parsimonious approach toward punishment, this is both a blessing and a curse. It is good news in the sense that there is apparent room for evolution in the way these organisations carry out their mission, but bad news because the agencies and their staff have been so used to putting into practice maximally punitive approaches to narcotics control ever since their foundation.

Although the agencies do not officially take sides in Southeast Asia's polemical death penalty debate; in practical terms, it is clear that they still support capital punishment for drug offences, or at least do not morally oppose it, in cases where that sentence is available.[123] Socialisation and rational self-interest within a pro-death penalty culture and a selection bias in hiring, including recruitment from national police forces, ensure the agency employees have the same views.[124] Above all, agency employees see their law enforcement function as the main priority, and the drug problem through a purely criminal lens, emphasising deterrence.[125] Two interviewees in Singapore described the self-image of CNB officers as 'guys on the ground just doing their jobs', with little time to question the morality of punishments such as the death penalty.[126] For officers in more senior positions in the various agencies, their presumptive security background and proximity to the country's political establishment usually help to engender the same set of punitive views.[127]

As part of their work, there are even twenty-first-century examples of Southeast Asian agencies aiding extrajudicial killing schemes first initiated by politicians. In Thailand, the ONCB helped to compile blacklists of people involved in the drugs trade for summary execution by police officers in 2003, under the policy of former Prime Minister Thaksin Shinawatra.[128] In Indonesia, BNN leaders gave enthusiastic support to

[123] Interviews (Singapore: 28 June 2023; Malaysia: 26 July 2023; Indonesia: 10 August 2023a and 18 August 2023). On Thailand, refer to Frankel (2001); Pascoe (2019).

[124] Interviews (Singapore: 23 June 2023 and 30 June 2023; Malaysia: 29 July 2023a; Indonesia: 10 August 2023b).

[125] Interviews (Singapore: 28 June 2023 and 30 June 2023; Malaysia: 26 July 2023 and 29 July 2023a; Indonesia: 10 August 2023b and 15 August 2023a; Thailand: 23 August 2023).

[126] Interviews (Singapore: 23 June 2023 and 30 June 2023).

[127] Interviews (Singapore: 23 June 2023; Malaysia: 28 July 2023b; Thailand: 23 August 2023 and, 24 August 2023; Indonesia: 10 August 2023b and 14 August 2023).

[128] Dorabjee, Zakaria, and Lewis (2013).

President Joko Widodo's infamous 2017 exhortation for law enforcement officers (including BNN officers themselves) to kill drug traffickers if they resist arrest,[129] mirroring the position of former Philippines President Rodrigo Duterte.[130] This is not the work of organisations and individuals who conscientiously reject premeditated state killing.

It remains to be seen whether the agencies and their employees, having committed for so long to punitive tactics, will find it possible to pivot to a different model within countries such as Thailand and Malaysia as they move to abolish the death penalty for drug crimes in its entirety and to refocus on voluntary rather than court-ordered rehabilitation.[131]

7.6 Conclusion

While Southeast Asian politicians do rely on the advice and expertise of national narcotics agencies in first developing and then tinkering with drug policies, the chapter's first major finding is that national narcotics agencies are simply 'cogs in the wheel' of a politically chosen direction on narcotics control. This finding is significant for future advocacy. Progressive change toward a harm reduction-based model, potentially including a shift in the agencies' main focus to alcohol and tobacco as legal yet harmful drugs, must ultimately come from Southeast Asia's political leadership. One of the more radical suggestions posed by several interviewees across jurisdictions would be to reconstitute the agencies within their respective national health ministries. Such significant reorientations away from the established 'War on Drugs' approach are unlikely to be supported by agencies which are housed in the law and security-focused government ministries (CNB, ONCB, and AADK), or indeed by BNN, a non-ministerial body whose senior staff all possess a law enforcement background and mindset. Any lasting change must come from the top.

129 McRae (2017); The Jakarta Post (2017).

130 L. Domingo-Cabarrubias and M. Sato in Chapter 8 in this volume. In a remarkable contrast with Indonesia and Thailand, the Philippines' own agency, the Dangerous Drugs Board, bravely opposed Duterte's 'shoot to kill' policy in 2017: Kine (2017).

131 Malaysia has already done so for the mandatory death penalty but retains the discretionary death penalty, corporal punishment, and administrative detention as punitive tools against drug offenders: Human Rights Watch (2023). Thailand retains the death penalty for drug crimes, but in 2022, the country decriminalised the recreational use of cannabis (R. Bunmee in Chapter 9 in this volume).

In turn, Southeast Asia's political leadership may be inclined to adopt a less punitive approach if the multilateral consensus changes, either at the ASEAN level or, more likely, at the UN.[132] Ultimately, it is from the 1961 and 1971 UN drug control conventions that Southeast Asia's current, punitive, model first originated, a drug control model that was officially endorsed at the regional level in 1976 with the ASEAN Declaration of Principles to Combat the Abuse of Narcotics Drugs.[133] Notably, the 1976 declaration and its successor statements promoting an eradication-centred position in 1997, 1998, 2000, and 2012 were all made by ASEAN heads of state, government, or foreign ministers.[134]

The finding that Southeast Asia's key national narcotics agencies are bureaucratic bodies implementing priorities set at the political level broadly resonates with the existing academic literature on policing and law enforcement. What, then, explains the apparent mismatch between their ubiquitous public profile as leaders of the fight against drugs and their reality as lower-level policy advisors and implementers? Partly it is due to their very status as national coordinating agencies, playing a multidimensional role in reducing drug supply and demand and thus appearing more often in the public discourse. A useful contrast can be made between the specialised narcotics divisions of Southeast Asian police forces,[135] and with volunteer-staffed anti-drugs NGOs.[136] Each possess a far lower profile both domestically and internationally.

A second likely explanation is the political legitimacy that the regional 'War on Drugs' has brought for Southeast Asian politicians since the 1970s. Drug traffickers and users have, until recent years, largely served to replace communist insurgents as convenient state enemies for Southeast Asian governments.[137] Absent democratic legitimacy through

[132] Baldwin (2013).

[133] Gunawan and Lai (2018); Pardo, Kilmer, and Huang (2019). The Declaration 'calls for [ASEAN member states] to strengthen cooperation on vigilance and preventive and penal measures, drug research and education and improvements in national legislation in the fight against drug abuse': ASEAN Secretariat (n.d.).

[134] ASEAN Secretariat (n.d.).

[135] For example, the Narcotics Suppression Bureau of the Royal Thai Police; the Narcotics Crime Investigation Department of the Royal Malaysia Police; and the Directorate of Drug Investigation of the Indonesian Regional Police. Each of the seven land divisions of the Singapore Police Force conducts drug operations alongside the CNB in addition to their other work.

[136] For example, SANA in Singapore, GRANAT and GANNAS in Indonesia, and SKUAD Antidadah in Malaysia.

[137] Pascoe (2019).

winning free and fair elections against credible opposition, combatting drugs in a very public way both contributes towards a perceived 'performance legitimacy' in governance,[138] and helps to distract voters from policy shortcomings in other areas. The national narcotics agencies are the institutional face of Southeast Asian governments' drug-fighting efforts on the ground,[139] in jurisdictions where there is already an outsized political focus on narcotics.

This apparent mismatch between public profile and policy-setting powers may serve as a starting point for future reforms. Two clear solutions present themselves. The national narcotics agencies could either share the public limelight more widely if they are not really masters of the state's drug control agenda, or else could demand and be granted more autonomy from political leaders, to pursue their own specialised vision for drug policy.

In the way they are structured, conceive of, and conduct their work, the Southeast Asian national narcotics agencies are institutional relics of the region's 'War on Drugs', the political consensus for which is now fraying.[140] Across all four jurisdictions under study, one of these organisational attributes still appears to be a belief in the necessity and effectiveness of harsh coercive measures against drug crimes. Such measures extend to confined rehabilitation for drug users, to corporal punishment, long-term imprisonment, and the death penalty in trafficking and manufacturing cases, and even to extrajudicial killings where judicial punishment is assumed to have failed to deter. Absent a mass turnover of staff, this aspect of the agencies' working culture will be extremely difficult to change. Training or retraining narcotics officers 'to ensure that positive policy change and law reform is translated into [their] operational consciousness' is a minimum prerequisite for organisational evolution.[141]

Of the four nations under study in this chapter, Thailand and Malaysia are furthest along the path to abolishing the death penalty for drug crimes and adopting a harm reduction model for users of drugs.[142] In Indonesia and Singapore, there are no imminent plans to abolish capital punishment, whether for drug trafficking and manufacturing or

138 Dupont (2001); Miao (2017).
139 United Nations Office on Drugs and Crime (2008).
140 Interviews (Thailand: 23 August 2023; Malaysia, 25 August 2023).
141 Crofts *et al.* (2013, p. 75).
142 Mayberry (2018).

for other crimes.[143] Indonesia has just passed a new penal code, the nation's first since independence in 1945, which still provides for the death penalty as a punishment of last resort. Although Indonesian death sentences are now imposed with a mandatory ten-year suspension period, the new penal code may have strengthened capital punishment as a 'normal' judicial remedy, including for drug crimes.[144] Aside from a methadone programme and risk-based needle exchanges,[145] the Indonesian executive is yet to favourably consider harm reduction as a policy response to narcotics use.[146] In Singapore, the Prison Service continues to make up for 'lost time' during the COVID-19 pandemic by executing a backlog of drug prisoners on death row at a rapid rate.[147] Moreover, any steps towards harm reduction tend to be scorned by the Singaporean government as 'enabling' drug use.[148]

Based on the findings presented in this chapter, in countries such as Indonesia and Singapore, limited mitigative measures are ironically best placed to come from *within* the existing narcotics control bureaucracy, rather than from intransient politicians. Although national narcotics agencies and the departments they work alongside cannot directly abolish the death penalty, sympathetic insiders can at least 'throw sand in the machine' of death,[149] including through the use of discretion in arresting and charging. It is also within the agencies' considerable power to moderate their public statements on illicit drugs and drug users, to treat users ordered to undertake compulsory rehabilitation with dignity, to work with civil society and other government departments to obtain data supporting harm-reductive policies on narcotics and likewise to lobby political decision-makers to reallocate their resources to tobacco and alcohol – the two recreational drugs that cause by far the most harm to consumers in Southeast Asia. Whether the agencies' long-established coercive internal culture and careerist leadership will permit such modest changes is another matter entirely.

[143] Pascoe (2023); W. C. Chan and M. Hor in Chapter 4 in this volume.

[144] Pascoe (2023).

[145] Havenhand (2020).

[146] Interviews (Indonesia: 10 August 2023c and 11 August 2023).

[147] The Standard (2023).

[148] Ministry of Home Affairs (2020). Corroborated by Interview (Singapore: 23 June 2023).

[149] This is the phrase Sarat and Scheingold (1998, p. 20) attribute to anti-death penalty lawyers in the United States when faced with a hostile political situation that prevents abolition.

References

Abdullah, S. A. (2023) 'Thailand Praises Malaysia's National Drug Policy' *New Straits Times* (11 May). www.nst.com.my/news/nation/2023/05/908159/thailand-praises-malaysias-national-drug-policy.

Agensi Antidadah Kebangsaan. (2019) *Dasar Dadah Negara* (Agensi Antidadah Kebangsaan, Kementerian Dalam Negeri). https://web.archive.org/web/20240208122158/https://www.adk.gov.my/wp-content/uploads/Dasar-Dadah-Negara-BM_compressed.pdf.

Alam, W. Y., Marijan, K., Aminah, S. and Putranto, T. D. (2020) 'Drug Eradication in Indonesia Millennials Through School Visits' 9(1) *Journal of Drug and Alcohol Research* 1. https://web.archive.org/web/20220308114010; www.ashdin.com/articles/drug-eradication-in-indonesian-millennials-through-school-visits.pdf/.

Al Jazeera. (2019) 'Malaysia to Decriminalise Drug Use, Says Health Minister' (28 June). www.aljazeera.com/news/2019/6/28/malaysia-to-decriminalise-drug-use-says-health-minister.

Amnesty International. (2023) *Death Sentences and Executions 2022* (London: Amnesty International). www.amnesty.org/en/wp-content/uploads/2023/05/ACT5065482023ENGLISH.pdf.

Amul, G. G. H. and Pang, T. (2018) 'The State of Tobacco Control in ASEAN: Framing the Implementation of the FCTC from a Health Systems Perspective' 5(1) *Asia and the Pacific Policy Studies* 47.

Arayasukawat, P. (2021) 'ONCB Auctions Off Anime Figures Seized in Drug Cases' *Thai News* (7 February). https://thainews.prd.go.th/en/news/detail/TCATG210207094754143.

ASEAN. (1991) *Report: The 14th Meeting of ASEAN Senior Officials on Drug Matters, Jakarta, Indonesia 26–29 August 1991* (Jakarta: ASEAN).

(2022) 'ASEAN Senior Officials on Drug Matters (ASOD) Directory' (23 December). https://asean.org/wp-content/uploads/2022/12/ASOD_Directory_as_of_23_December_2022.pdf.

ASEAN Secretariat. (n.d.) *Illicit Drugs*. https://asean.org/our-communities/asean-political-security-community/peaceful-secure-and-stable-region/illicit-drugs/.

Azizan, I. A., Juahir, H., Toriman, M. I. and Mohamad, M. (2018) 'Trend Detection of Drug Abuse Using Multivariate Analysis in Malaysia During the Years 2005 to 2015' 7(3) *International Journal of Engineering and Technology* 147.

Babor, T., Caulkins, J., Fischer, B., Foxcroft, D., Humphreys, K., Medina-Mora, M. E., Obot, I., Rehm, J., Reuter, P., Room, R., Rossow, I. and Strang, J. (2018) *Drug Policy and the Public Good* (2nd ed.) (Oxford: Oxford University Press).

Bacon, M. (2022) 'Desistance from Criminalisation: Police Culture and New Directions in Drugs Policing' 32(4) *Policing and Society* 522.

Badan Narkotika Nasional. (2020) *Kepala BNN dari Masa ke Masa*. https://bnn.go.id/kepala/.

(2022a) *Sejarah*. https://jakarta.bnn.go.id/sejarah/.

(2022b) *Satuan Kerja*. https://bnn.go.id/satuan-kerja/.

(2023) 'BNN Run' *Instagram* (3 May). www.instagram.com/p/CrxsEnALj8U/.

Baldwin, S. (2013) 'Drug Policy Advocacy in Asia: Challenges, Opportunities and Prospects' *International Drugs Policy Consortium*. www.aidsdatahub.org/sites/default/files/resource/idpc-drug-policy-advocacy-asia-challenges-opportunities-prospects.pdf.

Bedau, H. A. (1973) 'The Nixon Administration and the Deterrent Effect of the Death Penalty' 34 *University of Pittsburgh Law Review* 557.

Burris, S. and Burrows, D. (2009) 'Drug Policing, Harm Reduction and Health: Directions for Advocacy' 20(4) *International Journal of Drug Policy* 293.

Caplan, G. M. (1971) 'The Case for Rulemaking by Law Enforcement Agencies' 36(4) *Law and Contemporary Problems* 500.

Central Narcotics Bureau. (2018) *Preventive Drug Education in Singapore* (25 September 2018). www.unodc.org/documents/commissions/CND/2019/Contributions/Panellists/25_Sept/4.CHERN_HONG_Singapore.pdf.

(2021a) *The Bureau's Fight for a #DrugFree SG*. www.cnb.gov.sg/docs/default-source/pdfs/a_mha_cnb_commemorativebook_r6_fa_r1_lowres.pdf.

(2021b) *Annual Report* (Singapore: Central Narcotics Bureau).

(2021c) 'Down the Rabbit Hole' *Ads of the World*. www.adsoftheworld.com/campaigns/down-the-rabbit-hole.

(2023) *Statement in Response to Media Queries* (22 April). www.cnb.gov.sg/NewsAndEvents/News/Index/statement-in-response-to-media-queries-22Apr2023.

Chan, D. (2023) 'Zahid: About 1 Million Drug Addicts in the Country, Rising Trend Is Worrying' *New Straits Times* (10 July). www.nst.com.my/news/nation/2023/07/929373/zahid-about-1-million-drug-addicts-country-rising-trend-worrying.

Chok, S. (2017) 'Singapore's War on Drugs: A Historical Overview' *Lee Kuan Yew School of Public Policy*. https://lkyspp.nus.edu.sg/docs/default-source/case-studies/20180223_singapores_war_on_drugs_final.pdf?sfvrsn=5ec9c0b_2.

Coca, N. (2018) 'The War on Drugs in Southeast Asia' *New Naratif* (29 January). https://newnaratif.com/the-war-on-drugs-in-southeast-asia/.

Colman, A. M. and Gorman, L. P. (1982) 'Conservatism, Dogmatism, and Authoritarianism in British Police Officers' 16(1) *Sociology* 1.

Crofts, N., Monaghan, G., James, S., Turner, N. and Khan, M. Z. (2013) 'Law Enforcement and Drug Policy in Southeast Asia' in Rahman, F. and Crofts, N. (eds.), *Drug Law Reform in East and Southeast Asia* (Lanham: Lexington Books).

Cummings, A. D. P. (2012) '"All Eyez on Me": America's War on Drugs and the Prison-Industrial Complex' 15 *Journal of Gender Race and Justice* 417.

Dorabjee, J., Zakaria, M. F. and Lewis, D. (2013) 'The Asian Network of People Who Use Drugs' in Rahman, F. and Crofts, N. (eds.), *Drug Law Reform in East and Southeast Asia* (Lanham: Lexington Books).

Dupont, A. (2001) *East Asia Imperilled: Transnational Challenges to Security* (Cambridge: Cambridge University).

Ebay. (2022) *Singapore 2021 50th Anniv. of Central Narcotics Bureau First Day Cover 3 Stamps* (8 September). www.ebay.com/itm/304256951468.

Facebook. (2020) *Thai Youth League* (16 November). www.facebook.com/ThaiYouthLeague/posts/2826751937610613/.

Fagan, R. W. (1986) 'Police Attitudes Toward Capital Punishment' 14(3) *Journal of Police Science and Administration* 193.

Farrell, C. (2021) 'Judicial Caning in Singapore, Malaysia and Brunei' *World Corporal Punishment Research* (December). www.corpun.com/singfeat.htm.

Frankel, R. D. (2001) 'Thai Executions Meant to Shock' *Christian Science Monitor* (11 May). www.csmonitor.com/2001/0511/p6s1.html.

Freedom House. (2023) *Countries and Territories*. https://freedomhouse.org/countries/freedom-world/scores.

GlobalSecurity.org. (n.d.) 'Narcotics Suppression Bureau' *GlobalSecurity.org*. www.globalsecurity.org/intell/world/thailand/nsb.htm#:~:text=Narcotics%20Suppression%20Bureau%20is%20the,cracking%20down%20on%20illegal%20drugs.

Government of Malaysia. (2020) 'SKUAD ANTIDADAH' *Google Play* (23 December). https://play.google.com/store/apps/details?id=my.gov.onegovappstore.skuadaadk&hl=en_US.

Greenwald, G. (2009) *Drug Decriminalization in Portugal* (Washington: Cato Institute).

Gunawan, R. and Lai, G. (2018) 'Consensus and Contradictions in ASEAN: An Analysis of Southeast Asia At and After UNGASS 2016' in Klein, A. and Stothard, B. (eds.) *Collapse of the Global Order on Drugs: From UNGASS 2016 to Review 2019* (Leeds: Emerald Publishing).

Harring, S. (1991) 'Death, Drugs and Development: Malaysia's Mandatory Death Penalty for Traffickers and the International War on Drugs' 29 *Columbia Journal of Transnational Law* 365.

Havenhand, G. (2020) *Reorienting Drug Policy in Indonesia: Pathways to the Sustainable Development Goals* (Lembaga Bantuan Hukum Masyarakat and Reprieve). https://lbhmasyarakat.org/wp-content/uploads/2020/06/Pathways-to-the-Sustainable-Development-Goals-1.pdf.

Honna, J. (2011) 'Orchestrating Transnational Crime: Security Sector Politics as a Trojan Horse for Anti-Reformists' in Aspinall, E. and van Klinken, G. (eds.), *The State and Illegality in Indonesia* (Leiden: Brill).

Howe, S. W. and Haigh, Y. (2016) 'Anti-Corruption Watchdog Accountability: The Limitations of Judicial Review's Ability to Guard the Guardians' 75(3) *Australian Journal of Public Administration* 305.

Human Rights Watch. (2004) *Not Enough Graves: The War on Drugs, HIV/AIDS, and Violations of Human Rights.* www.hrw.org/report/2004/07/07/not-enough-graves/war-drugs-hiv/aids-and-violations-human-rights.

(2023) *Malaysia Repeals Mandatory Death Penalty.* www.hrw.org/news/2023/04/11/malaysia-repeals-mandatory-death-penalty#:~:text=Malaysia%20was%20one%20of%20only,use%20of%20the%20death%20penalty.

International Drug Policy Consortium. (2017) *Indonesia: More Humane Drug Policy Should Put Public Health First, Punitive Actions Second.* https://idpc.net/news/2017/08/indonesia-more-humane-drug-policy-should-put-public-health-first-punitive-actions-second.

International Society of Substance Abuse Professionals. (n.d.) *Malaysia Country Profile.* www.issup.net/national-chapters/issup-malaysia/country-profile.

Jelsma, M. and Armenta, A. (2015) 'The UN Drug Control Conventions: A Primer' *The Transnational Institute (TNI)* (8 October). www.tni.org/files/publication-downloads/primer_unconventions_24102015.pdf.

Johnson, D. T. and Zimring, F. E. (2009) *The Next Frontier: National Development, Political Change, and the Death Penalty in Asia* (Oxford: Oxford University Press).

Kantor Kementerian Agama Kabupaten Purbalingga. (2021) 'Guru Madin Diminta Ikut Sosialisasikan Bahaya Narkoba' *Kanwil Kemenag Jateng* (1 March). https://jateng.kemenag.go.id/berita/guru-madin-diminta-ikut-sosialisasikan-bahaya-narkoba/.

Kine, P. (2017) 'Philippine Drug Board Urges New Focus to Drug Campaign' *Human Rights Watch* (30 October). www.hrw.org/news/2017/10/30/philippine-drug-board-urges-new-focus-drug-campaign.

Kohli, A., Evans, P., Katzenstein, P. J., Przeworksi, A., Rudolph, S. H., Scott, J. C. and Skocpol, T. (1995) 'The Role of Theory in Comparative Politics: A Symposium' 48(1) *World Politics* 1.

Laohong, K. O. (2016) 'ONCB: Drug Smuggling Still Rampant' *Bangkok Post* (14 July). www.bangkokpost.com/thailand/general/1035649/oncb-drug-smuggling-still-rampant.

(2018) 'ONCB Backs Medicinal Cannabis Testing on Humans' *Bangkok Post* (18 May). www.bangkokpost.com/thailand/general/1467486/oncb-backs-medicinal-cannabis-testing-on-humans.

Lasco, G. (2020) 'Drugs and Drug Wars as Populist Tropes in Asia: Illustrative Examples and Implications for Drug Policy' 77 *International Journal of Drug Policy* 102668.

Lee, S. S., Jacka, D. and Crofts, N. (2013) 'Harm Reduction is Good Public Health' in Rahman, F. and Crofts, N. (eds.), *Drug Law Reform in East and Southeast Asia* (Lanham: Lexington Books).

Lilleker, D. G. (2003) 'Interviewing the Political Elite: Navigating a Potential Minefield' 23(3) *Politics* 207.

Lim, M. Z. (2022) 'SAF Scheme Allows Drug Users to Confess Once Without Being Punished: Ng Eng Hen' *The Straits Times* (13 September). www.straitstimes.com/singapore/politics/saf-scheme-allows-drug-users-to-confess-once-without-being-punished-ng-eng-hen.

Lindsey, T. and Nicholson, P. (2016) *Drugs Law and Legal Practice in Southeast Asia: Indonesia, Singapore and Vietnam* (Oxford: Hart Publishing).

Loader, I. and Mulcahy, A. (2003) *Policing and the Condition of England: Memory, Politics and Culture* (Oxford: Oxford University Press).

Loftus, B. (2009) *Police Culture in a Changing World* (Oxford: Oxford University Press).

Mapstone, R. (1992) 'The Attitudes of Police in a Divided Society: The Case of Northern Ireland' 32(2) *The British Journal of Criminology* 183.

Mayberry, K. (2018) 'Malaysia Death Penalty Abolition Opens Door to Drug Policy Review' *Al Jazeera* (29 November). www.aljazeera.com/news/2018/11/29/malaysia-death-penalty-abolition-opens-door-to-drug-policy-review.

McRae, D. (2013) 'Staying the Executioner's Guns?' *Inside Indonesia* (3 February). www.insideindonesia.org/staying-the-executioners-guns.

(2017) 'Indonesia's Fatal War on Drugs' *East Asia Forum* (28 November). www.eastasiaforum.org/2017/11/28/indonesias-fatal-war-on-drugs/.

Miao, M. (2017) 'The Penal Construction of Drug-Related Offenses in the Context of "Asian Values": The Rise of Punitive Anti-Drug Campaigns in Asia' 1(1) *International Comparative, Policy & Ethics Law Review* 46.

Miao, M. and Lai, G. (2023) 'Debunking the Three Myths About Reforming Asian Drug Policies' *Harvard-Yenching Institute Working Paper Series*. www.harvard-yenching.org/research/debunking-the-three-myths-about-reforming-asian-drug-policies/.

Ministry of Home Affairs. (2020) *Harm Prevention More Effective to Manage Drug Problem*. www.mha.gov.sg/docs/default-source/default-document-library/harm-prevention-is-more-effective-to-manage-the-drug-problem.pdf.

Ministry of Justice. (n.d.) *Office of the Narcotics Control Board*. https://web.archive.org/web/20220625234206/https://www.oncb.go.th/EN_ONCB/Pages/background.aspx.

Ministry of Social Affairs. (2019) *'Satria' BRSKPN Educate Public Through Broadcast 2019* (9 October). https://kemensos.go.id/en/satria-brskpn-educate-public-through-broadcast.

Muniandy, E. and Jalil, A. S. A. (2010) *Global Synthetics Monitoring: Analysis, Reporting and Trends (SMART) Programme Regional Workshop for East Asia 5–6 August 2010 Bangkok*. www.unodc.org/documents/southeastasiaandpacific/2010/08/smart-regional-workshop/Malaysia_-_National_ATS_Situations1.pdf.

National Anti-Drugs Agency. (n.d.a) *History of NADA*. https://web.archive.org/web/20230402091438/; www.adk.gov.my/en/corporate-info/history-of-nada/.

Vision, Mission and Objectives. https://web.archive.org/web/20230402082412/; www.adk.gov.my/en/corporate-info/vision-mission-and-objectives/.

Organisational Chart of National Anti-Drugs Agency. https://web.archive.org/web/20221128193222/; www.adk.gov.my/wp-content/uploads/Carta-Organisasi-AADK-2022_BI.pdf.

Nelken, D. (2011) 'Why Compare Criminal Justice' in Bosworth, M. and Hoyle, C. (eds.) *What Is Criminology?* (Oxford: Oxford University Press).

Office of the Narcotics Control Board. (n.d.a) 'About Us'. www.oncb.go.th/EN_ONCB/Pages/visionANDmission.aspx.

Narcotics Code. https://en.fda.moph.go.th/media.php?id=517578787425230848&name=NARCOTICS-CODE-ONCB120666.pdf.

Thailand Narcotics Control Annual Report 2020. https://www.oncb.go.th/EN_ONCB/Documents/Thailand%20Narcotics%20Control%20Annual%20Report%202020.pdf.

O'Sullivan, S. (2005) 'UK Policing and Its Television Portrayal: "Law and Order" Ideology or Modernising Agenda?' 44(5) *The Howard Journal of Crime and Justice* 504.

Pakes, F. (2015) *Comparative Criminal Justice* (3rd ed.) (New York: Routledge).

Pardo, B., Kilmer, B. and Huang, W. (2019) *Contemporary Asian Drug Policy: Insight and Opportunities for Change* (Santa Monica: RAND Corporation).

Pascoe, D. (2019) *Last Chance for Life: Clemency in Southeast Asia Death Penalty Cases* (Oxford: Oxford University Press).

(2023) 'Indonesia's Revised Criminal Code and the Death Penalty – Progress Amid the Gloom?' 24(1) *Australian Journal of Asian Law* 67.

Petcharamesree, S. (2023) '"Most Serious Crimes": Searching for a Common Interpretation in ASEAN' in Petcharamesree, S., Capaldi, M. and Collins, A. (eds.) *Unpacking the Death Penalty in ASEAN* (Singapore: Springer).

Ponsaers, P. (2001) 'Reading About "Community (Oriented) Policing" and Police Models' 24(4) *Policing: An International Journal* 470.

Prenzler, T. (1997) 'Is There a Police Culture?' 56(4) *Australian Journal of Public Administration* 47.

Quah, J. S. T. (2008) *Singapore's War on Drugs: Drawing Lessons from Success.* www.jonstquah.com/images/PHIL2008_QUAH.pdf.

(2014) 'Anti-Corruption Agencies in Four Asian Countries: A Comparative Analysis' 8(2) *International Public Management Review* 73.

Rahman, F. and Crofts, N. (2013) *Drug Law Reform in East and Southeast Asia* (Lanham: Lexington Books).

Rahman, F., Salleh, I. M., Golichenko, O. and Lunze, K. (2016) 'Public Health and Drug Policing in Malaysia: Using Empirical Evidence for Advocacy' 3(1) *APDR Working Paper Series.* www.academia.edu/46961465/Public_Health_and_Drug_Policing_in_Malaysia_Using_Empirical_Evidence_for_Advocacy.

Ritter, A. and Lancaster, K. (2013) 'Illicit Drugs, Policing and the Evidence-Based Policy Paradigm' 9(4) *Evidence and Policy* 457.

Sacco, L. N. (2014) 'Drug Enforcement in the United States: History, Policy, and Trends' *Congressional Research Service.* https://sgp.fas.org/crs/misc/R43749.pdf.

Sachsenröder, W. (2022) *From Opium to Methamphetamines: The Nine Lives of the Drug Industry in Southeast Asia* (Singapore: World Scientific).

Sarat, A. and Scheingold, S. (1998) 'Cause Lawyering and the Reproduction of Professional Authority: An Introduction' in Sarat, A. and Scheingold, S. (eds.) *Cause Lawyering* (Oxford: Oxford University Press).

Scorzelli, J. F. (1992) 'Has Malaysia's Antidrug Effort Been Effective?' 9(2) *Journal of Substance Abuse Treatment* 171.

Shofa, J. N. (2022) 'BNN Uncovers 23 International Drug Networks in 2022' *Jakarta Globe* (29 December). https://jakartaglobe.id/news/bnn-uncovers-23-international-drug-networks-in-2022.

Silvestri, M. (2003) *Women in Charge: Policing, Gender and Leadership* (Cullopton: Willan).

Steinmo, S. (2008) 'Historical Institutionalism' in Della Porta, D. and Keating, M. (eds.) *Approaches and Methodologies in the Social Sciences* (Cambridge: Cambridge University Press).

Taher, A. P. (2018) 'BNN Tetap Dukung Hukuman Mati untuk Kasus Narkoba' *Tirto* (19 January). https://tirto.id/bnn-tetap-dukung-hukuman-mati-untuk-kasus-narkoba-cDt8.

Tangsathaporn, P. (2022) 'UN Forges Bonds in War on Drugs' *Bangkok Post* (4 April). https://www.bangkokpost.com/thailand/general/2289686/un-forges-bonds-in-war-on-drugs.

Tanguay, P. (2011) 'Kratom in Thailand: Decriminalisation and Community Control' *Transnational Institute* (April). www.tni.org/files/download/kratom-briefing-dlr13.pdf.

The Jakarta Post. (2017) 'In a Drug Raid, It's Either Us or Them Who Die, Says BNN' (27 March). www.thejakartapost.com/news/2017/03/27/in-a-drug-raid-its-either-us-or-them-who-die-says-bnn.html.

The Malaysian Administrative Modernisation and Management Planning Unit. (n. d.) 'Drug Enforcement' *My Government.* www.malaysia.gov.my/portal/content/28901.

The Standard. (2023) 'Singapore Executes Second Prisoner in Three Weeks' (17 May). www.thestandard.com.hk/breaking-news/section/6/203831/Singapore-executes-second-prisoner-in-three-weeks%C2%A0.

United Nations. (1974) *Summary Record of the Seven Hundred and Fifty-Sixth Meeting* (20 February) UN Doc E/CH.7/SR.756. https://digitallibrary.un.org/record/1480206/files/E_CN-7_SR-756-EN.pdf?ln=fr.

United Nations Office of the High Commissioner for Human Rights. (2018) *Drug-Related Offences, Criminal Justice Responses and the Use of the Death Penalty in South-East Asia*. https://bangkok.ohchr.org/wp-content/uploads/2020/01/Drug-Related-Offences-2018.pdf.

United Nations Office on Drugs and Crime. (2008) *Drug-Free ASEAN 2015: Status and Recommendations*. www.unodc.org/roseap/uploads/archive/documents/Publications/ASEAN_2015.pdf.

US Department of Justice. (n.d.) *Federal Agencies & Related Links* www.deadiversion.usdoj.gov/links/index.html.

US Department of State. (2001) *Southeast Asia and the Pacific* (1 March). https://2009-2017.state.gov/j/inl/rls/nrcrpt/2000/891.htm.

Wallace, W. C. (2024) 'Police Recruits' Attitudes Towards the Death Penalty in Trinidad and Tobago' 76 *International Journal of Law, Crime and Justice* 100644. www.sciencedirect.com/science/article/pii/S1756061623000708.

Windle, J. (2016) 'Drugs and Drug Policy in Thailand' *Brookings Institution*. www.brookings.edu/wp-content/uploads/2016/07/windlethailand-final.pdf.

World Health Organization. (2017) *Alcohol Policy in the WHO South-East Asia Region: A Report* (New Delhi: World Health Organization). https://apps.who.int/iris/rest/bitstreams/1093193/retrieve.

Zulkifli, L. (2019) 'AADK, PDRM kekang kemasukan bekalan dadah di kawasan berisiko tinggi' *Malaysia Dateline* (13 February). www.malaysiadateline.com/aadk-pdrm-kekang-kemasukan-bekalan-dadah-di-kawasan-berisiko-tinggi/.

Appendix

List of Interviewees

Interview with Singaporean NGO Staff Member, 23 June 2023
Interview with Singapore-based Academic, 27 June 2023
Interview with Three Singaporean Criminal Lawyers, 28 June 2023
Interview with Singaporean Researcher, 30 June 2023
Interview with Malaysian Criminal Lawyer, 24 July 2023
Interview with Former Malaysian Prosecutor, 25 July 2023
Interview with Malaysian Criminal Lawyer, 26 July 2023
Interview with Malaysia NGO Staff, 27 July 2023a
Interview with Malaysian NGO Staff #2, 27 July 2023b
Interview with Malaysian NGO Staff #3, 28 July 2023a
Interview with Malaysian Academic and NGO Staff, 28 July 2023b
Interview with Malaysian Former Prosecutor and Malaysian Former AADK Staff, 29 July 2023a
Interview with Malaysia-based Academic, 29 July 2023b
Interview with Indonesian Civil Servant, 10 August 2023a

Interview with Indonesian Academic, 10 August 2023b
Interview with Indonesian Academic #2, 10 August 2023c
Interview with Indonesian NGO Staff, 11 August 2023
Interview with Indonesian former BNN Staff, 14 August 2023
Interview with Indonesian BNN Staff, 15 August 2023a
Interview with Indonesian NGO Staff #2, 15 August 2023b
Interview with Indonesian former BNN Staff #2, 18 August 2023
Interview with Thailand-based NGO Staff, 23 August 2023
Interview with Thai ONCB Officer, 24 August 2023
Interview with Malaysian Academic, 25 August 2023
Interview with Thailand-based IGO Staff, 28 August 2023
Interview with Indonesian NGO Staff #3, 5 September 2023

8

Leadership from Below?

Networked Governance in Preventing the Reintroduction of the Death Penalty in the Philippines

LEAVIDES DOMINGO-CABARRUBIAS AND MAI SATO

8.1 Introduction

The Philippine government has had a fragile relationship with the death penalty: its policy and practice have been characterised by ambivalence and repeated vacillations between retention and abolition.[1] After many years of using the death penalty throughout its long colonial history until the authoritarian years of President Ferdinand Marcos, the Philippines first abolished the death penalty in 1987. It was reinstated in 1993 and again abolished in 2006. Ten years later, calls for reimposition again surged. Upon his election as president in 2016, Rodrigo Duterte – whose campaign promise focused on ridding the nation of illegal drugs and criminality – vowed to reintroduce the death penalty.[2]

Duterte has been described as 'arguably the most dangerous figure to emerge on the Philippine scene' since Ferdinand Marcos.[3] Duterte's politics has been characterised by a proclivity for authoritarian rule and an easy resort to actions that violate basic human rights.[4] A day after he was sworn into office, he said: 'If you know of any addicts, go ahead and kill them yourself as getting their parents to do it would be too painful.'[5] In July 2016, more than a month after his proclamation, Duterte launched an anti-illegal drugs campaign, directing the Philippine National Police to implement measures to clear all drug-affected *barangays* (villages) across

[1] Johnson and Zimring (2009, p. 104).
[2] Chilkoti (2016).
[3] Bello (2017, p. 21).
[4] Ibid.
[5] Kine (2017).

the country.[6] Beyond this formal directive, Duterte's pronouncements and marching orders to kill drug dealers if they 'fight back' turned his drug policy into 'an unwritten state policy of extra-judicially killing people'.[7] His 'war on drugs' policy resulted in the death of 12,000 to 30,000 people from 2016 to 2019.[8] Duterte justified the killings as 'a war against the scum of society who should not be considered "human beings"'.[9]

As part of his punitive campaign to eradicate illicit drugs, Duterte vowed to reintroduce the death penalty.[10] During his yearly State of the Nation Addresses, he consistently urged the congress for 'the swift passage of the law reviving the death penalty by lethal injection for crimes specified under the Comprehensive Dangerous Drugs Act of 2002'.[11] The reimposition was supported by groups from across the socioeconomic spectrum and a large majority of legislators. In March 2017, the House of Representatives overwhelmingly passed *House Bill No. 4727* on the reimposition of the death penalty for drug-related offences and heinous crimes.[12] Under the bill, the discretionary death penalty is available as a punishment for the following offences: importation and/or sale of dangerous drugs regardless of quantity and purity; manufacture of dangerous drugs; and maintenance of a den where any dangerous drug is used or sold.[13] The death penalty may also be imposed where a serious crime (for example, murder) has been committed by a person under the influence of drugs; or when a public officer fails to account for confiscated drugs. Although the bill was stalled in the senate, legislators continued filing bills pushing for capital punishment in the succeeding years. In 2019 alone, 19 bills were filed and tabled in the House of Representatives. In March 2021, *House Bill No. 7814* was adopted, the second bill proposing the reimposition of capital punishment to have reached the senate in five years. The bill also added new capital offences such as possession of dangerous drugs during parties and social gatherings and importation/exportation of dangerous drugs using diplomatic passports/facilities. The

[6] Republic of the Philippines – National Police Commission, *Command Memorandum Circular No. 16-2016: PNP Anti-Illegal Drugs Campaign Plan – Project: Double Barrel* (1 July 2016).

[7] Bautista (2017, p. 2).

[8] International Criminal Court (2021, para. 67).

[9] Bautista (2017, p. 2).

[10] Chilkoti (2016).

[11] Seiff (2020).

[12] Amnesty International (2017).

[13] Congress of the Philippines, *House Bill No. 4727* (approved 7 March 2017).

bill also sought the mandatory death penalty for the planting of false evidence during the investigation of drug-related crimes.

8.2 Brief Review of Literature

The Philippines' vacillating death penalty policy and practice has been a subject of analysis by scholars. Tagayuna examines the various factors that led to the reinstatement of the death penalty in 1993, paying particular attention to the role of political agents from among the conservative, propertied class who had the capacity and resources to influence decision-makers to enact more punitive penalties.[14] Johnson and Zimring explain the events surrounding the first and second abolitions, identifying prominent themes such as volatility in the death penalty policy and ambivalence about its application.[15] Deinla *et al.* explore the potential drivers of the seemingly growing support for the death penalty revival during Duterte's administration, including the president's repeated pronouncements on the severity of the drug problem in the country and the necessity of the death penalty to address this problem.[16] These studies highlight the role of political elites in driving the trajectory of the death penalty in the country. Johnson and Zimring, for instance, assert that the first abolition was achieved through 'leadership from the front', in that although there was little pressure from the public, the members of the commission created by the president to amend the constitution – who were chosen almost exclusively from the upper class and were predominantly lawyers – decided to abolish it as a way of distancing the new government from Marcos' authoritarian regime.[17] The second abolition, according to them, was achieved through a combination of factors, including a change in the position of many legislators after being provided with more information by non-government organisations such as the Free Legal Assistance Group (FLAG).

The study by Colmenares focuses on the role of these non-government organisations.[18] He examines strategies and tactics used to resist efforts to reimpose the death penalty after its abolition in 2006 and up to the time of Duterte. He then compares these with those employed by

[14] Tagayuna (2004).
[15] Johnson and Zimring (2009).
[16] Deinla *et al.* (2021).
[17] Johnson and Zimring (2009, p. 113).
[18] Colmenares (2023).

transnational activists in campaigning for a United Nations moratorium on the death penalty. Colmenares identified 'coalition building' as one of the strategies successfully used in transnational campaigns:[19]

> [T]he coalition building strategy of the UN moratorium campaigns found its way into the Philippine campaigns, which made a conscious strategic decision to build a broad coalition emphasising the imperative of broad-based campaigning through a unified network of autonomous members. The coalition set aside substantial or residual differences in ideological, managerial, and resource mobilisation issues in order to strengthen the unity of the abolitionist camp in the face of a strong retentionist campaign.

This chapter expands on this observation by Colmenares and takes a closer look into how this strategy was operationalised in practice, looking at it through the 'networked governance' framework. Based on interviews with individuals involved in the abolitionist movement, it presents a case study of how small actors formed into a strong network to counter retentionist efforts. At the same time, in highlighting the pivotal role of the Philippines' anti-death penalty network in preventing reimposition, it expounds on the concept of 'leadership from the front' referred to by Johnson and Zimring.

Section 8.3 introduces the concept of 'networked governance' as a framework of analysis in understanding how the Philippine anti-death penalty movement worked to prevent the reimposition of the death penalty in the context of Duterte's autocratic rule. Section 8.4 discusses the methodology used in gathering data. Section 8.5 introduces the key actors in the anti-death penalty movement. Section 8.6 discusses the workings of the anti-death penalty movement as a network, and how the network members exploited their synergies and complementarities to amplify their voices and counter pro-death penalty narratives. Section 8.7 examines the role of the anti-death penalty network as a 'checks and balances' mechanism against an authoritarian rule that has spurred the passing of the death penalty bill in the House of Representatives. Section 8.8 analyses how this case study in the Philippines contextualises the 'leadership from the front' discourse in death penalty scholarship.

8.3 Analytical Framework: Networked Governance

In this chapter, we use the term 'networked governance' loosely to refer to political decision-making that involves a wide range of

[19] Ibid, p. 24.

participants – including both governmental and non-governmental actors – through a plethora of formal and informal mechanisms and processes.[20] It is used to understand how anti-death penalty actors in the Philippines worked collectively to prevent the reintroduction of the death penalty during Duterte's administration. As Houtzager notes, organisations which are isolated and disconnected from each other are unable to influence government behaviour, but once they coalesce into broad coalitions and networks, they are better able to influence policymaking.[21]

The term 'network' used in this chapter is broadly defined as 'a group of individuals from different institutions choosing to work together towards a common goal'.[22] According to network theorists, by combining their efforts, members of networks can have a greater impact on policy and practice because those from different backgrounds can contribute complementary skills, knowledge, and expertise.[23] Networks usually involve multiple stakeholders 'characterized by differences in access to information, methods of communication, and motivation'.[24] The purpose of these networks, therefore, is to gain critical mass, share information, knowledge, and skills, and increase legitimacy, among others. As explained by Huppé *et al.*:[25]

> These networks create bridges that enable various participants to exploit the synergies between the resources that they contribute, allowing for the pooling of knowledge, the exchange of experience, and for the generation of a feasible institutional framework for fruitful collaboration.

While the concept of networked governance has been defined and used in various settings, we are inspired by Braithwaite *et al.*'s use of this framework to examine the struggle for peace in Timor-Leste. They characterise the political project that led to the liberation of East Timor from Western and Indonesian power as networks among small, weak actors defeating the strong.[26] We borrow from Braithwaite *et al.*'s discussion of how networked governance provides a means of regulating authoritarian rule, including 'checking excesses of executive domination

[20] The definition is loosely adopted from Sørensen and Torfing (2005); Stoker (2006).
[21] Houtzager and Pattenden (2003, pp. 88–89).
[22] Creech *et al.* (2008, p. 2).
[23] Ibid.
[24] Caplan (2022, p. 543).
[25] Huppé, Creech, and Knoblauch (2012, p. 7).
[26] Braithwaite, Charlesworth, and Soares (2012, p. xi).

within a state'.[27] This is particularly relevant in the case of the Philippines during the time of Duterte, whose power over the legislative branch threatened to erode the separation of powers. We argue that the anti-death penalty network combined 'the voluntary energy and legitimacy of the civil society sector with the financial muscle and interest' of international organisations, and the coordination and capacity-building skills of the Commission on Human Rights of the Philippines (CHRP).[28]

The crucial role of the anti-death penalty network in preventing the reimposition of the death penalty will also be used to qualify the view that death penalty abolitions and moratoria are triggered by political leadership from the front, that is, leadership by political elites.[29] According to Johnson, the death penalty is always an exercise of state power, and the actors with the practical ability to secure abolition or a moratorium – or, in this case, the prevention of reimposition – are the elite decision-makers.[30] While this is true, this chapter puts a spotlight on the role of the anti-death penalty networks in the trajectory of capital punishment, using the Philippines as a case study. As noted by Chew in the case of Malaysia, the gradual move towards abolition, including the recent abolition of the mandatory death penalty, were not only driven exclusively by abolitionist lawmakers and policymakers but also by numerous abolitionist voices in Malaysia and around the world.[31] This chapter will highlight how the anti-death penalty network helped prevent the reimposition of the death penalty, which was being pushed by political elites.

8.4 Data

We interviewed twenty-one individuals involved in anti-death penalty advocacy: we carried out nine interviews from June 2019 to August 2019 when Duterte was in power,[32] and twelve interviews from January

[27] Ibid, p. xii.

[28] Loosely adopted from the definition of governance networks by Huppé, Creech, and Knoblauch (2012, p. 2).

[29] Johnson (2020, p. 104).

[30] Ibid, pp. 104 and 109.

[31] Chew (2023).

[32] The interviews were carried out under a project funded by the World Coalition Against the Death Penalty (WCADP) and implemented by the Australian National University (ANU). We received ethics approval from the ANU Human Research Ethics Committee to conduct interviews (protocol number: 2019/160).

2023 to February 2023 post-Duterte administration.[33] Appendix to this chapter provides a list of interviewees. For interviewees who did not wish to be identified by their names, we provided a description of their organisational affiliation only. Each interviewee has also been assigned a number (for example, I-5). These unique identifiers are used whenever we refer to the information provided by the interviewees. Based on the interviews, we analysed common themes arising from the experiences of interviewees in implementing various campaigns, participating in legislative advocacies, and collaborating with other organisations to come up with a strong voice that would oppose the attempts at reimposition.

8.5 Actors in the Anti-Death Penalty Movement

Many of the individuals and organisations that actively opposed the reimposition of the death penalty during the Duterte administration had been working in the area of human rights for a long time. One of the key actors in the anti-death penalty movement is the CHRP, an independent constitutional body created under the 1987 Constitution as a watchdog and protector against human rights abuses.[34] As a government entity independent from the other branches of the government and as a National Human Rights Institution (NHRI),[35] the CHRP is a relatively powerful institution in terms of both resources and reach of influence. However, circumstances during the Duterte administration put the CHRP in an extremely disadvantaged position. Duterte consistently disparaged the concept of human rights, thus blaming the CHRP for 'protecting the drug lords and causing the country's other problems'.[36] In a press conference following his State of the Nation Address in July 2017, Duterte declared that the CHRP would be 'better abolished', as he threatened to block all moves by the CHRP to investigate 'his men' – that is, Philippine soldiers and policemen – for the killing of alleged drug users and dealers.[37] This threat was part of Duterte's

[33] The interviews were carried out under a project funded by the European Commission with a sub-grant by the Capital Punishment Justice Project and implemented by Monash University. We received ethics approval from the Monash Human Research Ethics Committee to conduct interviews (Project ID: 34755).

[34] The 1987 Constitution of the Republic of the Philippines (ratified 2 February 1987; took effect 11 February 1987) Article XIII, ss. 17, and 18.

[35] Commission on Human Rights (n.d.).

[36] Smith (2017).

[37] Gavilan (2017).

ongoing tirade against human rights activists who had condemned his 'war on drugs' policy. In August 2017, Duterte called on police officers to shoot members of human rights organisations who are 'obstructing justice'.[38] Being a constitutional body, the CHRP cannot be abolished without a constitutional amendment, but its annual budget, which forms part of the government's overall yearly appropriations, needs to be approved by congress.[39] In September 2017, the House of Representatives voted to allocate a measly budget of Philippine Peso (PHP) 1,000.00 (about USD 20) to the CHRP, with the house speaker saying that the commission 'deserved a low budget for being a "useless" body and defending criminals' rights'.[40] Fortunately, the move failed to garner sufficient support from the senate.[41] However, the CHRP's power and legitimacy were continuously weakened by the administration, and it was but one of the small voices in the fight against reimposition.

A CHRP official described the abolitionist movement as 'coalitions within coalitions, networks coming together' (I-21). There are two umbrella organisations that have been leading the fight against the death penalty for years, including during the campaign that led to eventual abolition in 2006: the Coalition Against the Death Penalty (CADP) and the FLAG. The CADP, a coalition of church-based and civic groups and individuals that are opposed to the death penalty, was established in 1994 in response to the increasing number of individuals being sentenced to death after it was reimposed in 1993.[42] When the death penalty was abolished in 2006, the CADP continued its work by expanding its focus on prison reform more broadly (I-1). It holds monthly meetings and promotes 'restorative' interventions in the criminal justice system by campaigning for alternatives to imprisonment. During the Duterte administration, most of their works were done online, producing three- or four-minute films bringing awareness to the death penalty issue, which are available on their Facebook page (I-11).

The FLAG is a nation-wide organisation of human rights lawyers committed to the protection and promotion of human rights and civil liberties (I-2). The FLAG is also the largest human rights lawyers'

[38] Human Rights Watch (2017).

[39] 1987 Philippine Constitution of the Republic of the Philippines, Article VI, s. 29.

[40] Mogato (2017).

[41] After public backlash and senate opposition, the House of Representatives eventually approved a 508.5 million Peso budget for the CHRP, substantially lower than its 724.9 million Peso budget the previous year: Diaz (2017).

[42] Rappler.com (2021).

organisation, with 90 per cent of its members from outside Metro Manila (I-2). Lawyers from the FLAG had handled cases of individuals on death row when the death penalty was in effect, appealing death sentences and applying for a stay of executions.[43] In 1993, the FLAG spearheaded the creation of the Anti-Death Penalty Task Force (Task Force), a network of organisations and individuals opposed to the death penalty. The Task Force's membership includes the CADP (a coalition of NGOs), the CHRP (a State entity), a lawyers' group, academic institutions,[44] families of prisoners,[45] and other groups that were involved in abolition work (I-19). Religious organisations, particularly the Catholic Bishops Conference of the Philippines (CBCP) and the Philippine Jesuit Prison Service, played key roles as members of the Task Force, as they were able to mobilise many people within the Catholic church to attend hearings at the congress (I-20). Moreover, the voice of the Church carried considerable weight, considering that Filipinos are religious people (I-20).

In 2016, because of the increased focus on the issue of the death penalty in relation to illicit drugs, the Task Force expanded to broader efforts like partnering with NoBox Philippines Foundation, a non-profit organisation working in the area of drug policy and harm reduction (I-15). The presence of the NoBox in the Task Force gave 'the drug angle' to the abolitionist movement (I-5). Various human rights organisations also banded together to amplify their voices at the height of extrajudicial killings in 2016, calling on Duterte 'not to make his government's war on drugs a war on human rights'.[46] iDefend, a coalition of more than 30 non-governmental organisations of human rights defenders, actively campaigned against all violations of the right to life during Duterte's war on drugs, including extrajudicial killings and the reimposition of the death penalty.[47] In addition, international organisations such as the

[43] The FLAG represented, among others, Leo Echegaray, convicted in 1999 for repeatedly raping his 10-year-old stepdaughter and executed in February 1999; and Eduardo Agbayani, convicted in 1994 on two counts of incestuous rape of his daughter and executed in June 1999. They were the first and second individuals sentenced to death after the reintroduction of the death penalty in 1993: Amnesty International (1996; 1999); Bergonia (2019).

[44] University of the Philippines DNA Analysis Laboratory; University of the Philippines Paralegal Volunteers Organization; De La Salle University College of Law – Developmental Legal Advocacy Clinic.

[45] Samahan ng mga Pamilya ng mga Bilanggo [Association of Families of Persons Deprived of Liberty].

[46] iDefend (2016a).

[47] iDefend (2016b).

International Commission of Jurists actively supported legislators, especially those members of congress who were resisting the reimposition of the death penalty, by providing advice to the Philippine Government's obligations under international human rights laws and standards (I-3).

In the congress, although legislators against the death penalty were a minority during the Duterte administration, they were no less active in their advocacies. Long-time abolitionist Edcel Lagman, who principally authored the law that repealed the death penalty law in 2006, shared that he convened a human rights group called *Makatao* (Humane) in the House of Representatives which aimed, among others, to oppose the restoration of the death penalty (I-17). Former Representative Kit Belmonte, who was a member of the Justice Committee of the House of Representatives, actively opposed the passing of the bill, both in the Committee and plenary hearings (I-10). Representative France Castro of Alliance of Concerned Teachers (ACT) Party List, a member of the progressive *Makabayan* (Nationalist) Bloc, relayed that they reached out to their constituents, who are mostly from marginalised sectors, to conduct seminars explaining their position on the death penalty (I-12).[48]

8.6 The Anti-Death Penalty Network: Synergies and Complementarities

The members of the network come from different areas of expertise and are characterised by differences in access to information, knowledge, and other resources. As separate organisations, they have little influence over policymaking. Forming into networks gave them the advantage of being able to amplify their voices, benefit from each other's expertise, and increase the legitimacy of the movement. The extent to which these were accomplished is examined in the following subsections.

8.6.1 Amplifying Voices to Counter Dominant Narratives by the State

Duterte's repeated pronouncements and reiterated by his allies set the tone of discourse in traditional and social media on drug policy, the

[48] The *Makabayan* Bloc – a progressive bloc at the Lower House comprised of Representatives representing various marginalised sectors such as women, farmers, and labourers – coordinated with each other as well as with government agencies such as the CHRP on issues such as the death penalty (I-12).

death penalty, and human rights more generally. An army of Duterte netizens berated those who expressed any criticisms of Duterte, some even resorting to threats of bodily harm or rape against critics.[49] According to Bautista, '[t]he toxicity of the national discourse especially on social media on the issue of Duterte's war on drugs has stifled even the most rabid opposition who challenge the official narrative'.[50]

It took the concerted efforts of small groups that banded together to counter dominant narratives on issues such as the death penalty. A former CHRP Commissioner during the time of Duterte noted that 'because the death penalty had the backing of the highest office in the land, individuals and civil society organisations had to come together and had to be more purposive in their fight against the death penalty' (I-14).

By itself, the CHRP has been at the forefront of advancing human rights since its creation, and its efforts to oppose the death penalty included issuing advisories to counter assertions by pro-death penalty advocates; creating a microsite, The Right to Life,[51] containing all the documents about the stand of the CHRP on the death penalty; undertaking studies on the death penalty such as 'In Defense of the Right to Life: International Law and Death Penalty in the Philippines' with Dr Christopher Ward of the Australian National University (ANU)[52] and 'In Defense of the Right to Life: Analyzing Factors Affecting Filipino Opinion About Death Penalty' with Iremae D. Labucay of the Social Weather Stations;[53] and conducting information campaigns (I-18). Regional offices of the CHRP conduct community-based dialogues with stakeholders within their regions (I-13; I-16). At the same time, to ensure a wider reach, the CHRP has regularly collaborated with other organisations. In writing their advisories and other publications, they work with organisations such as the FLAG and international academics, which 'amplifies their campaign in the sense that they have more resources that support their arguments against the death penalty' (I-21). The CHRP also worked with the Right to Life Network to distribute information documents to communities;[54] and the World Coalition Against the Death Penalty (WCADP) to create infographics which were shared on social

[49] Bello (2017, p. 31).
[50] Bautista (2017, p. 2).
[51] The site may be found at www.righttolifeph.online/.
[52] Commission on Human Rights of the Philippines and Ward (2017).
[53] Commission on Human Rights of the Philippines and Labucay (2020).
[54] Gerzso (2017).

media.[55] Trying to replicate the Universities Against the Death Penalty,[56] a network of about 40 universities across the globe led by the University of Oslo, the CHRP started reaching out to students and faculty members in universities including the University of Santo Tomas, Ateneo De Manila University, De la Salle University, University of the Philippines, and universities in provinces such as Pampanga. Although the network remains unofficial, reaching out to students and academics 'sends a message that the anti-death penalty campaign is active not only within civil society but also in universities' (I-21).

The Task Force, in bringing together the various stakeholders and providing a platform for a unified campaign, succeeded in amplifying the voice of the anti-death penalty movement. When the attempts at reimposition started, the Task Force continued what it had been doing in the past to express its opposition, such as preparing position papers (I-19). The various groups contributed to all the initiatives of the Task Force, including the preparation of statements, policy briefs, and campaign materials, developing video materials, and organising conferences, and their discussions 'fed into each other's experiences and knowledge' (I-15). The Task Force regularly organised events in various provinces across the Philippines, such as the 'Tending Life' event in June 2019, in which local community groups, law students, and government agencies participated. Importantly, having NoBox as a member of the Task Force helped undermine the narrative that the use of the death penalty is a solution to drug-related problems.

8.6.2 *Sharing Information and Expertise*

Uniting into a network is important because there are groups that have expertise in particular areas that others do not. According to a CHRP official, working with various organisations is a 'force multiplier' because they can accomplish more and reach a wider audience as the different organisations have different focus, expertise, and constituents: 'some of the things that we [CHRP] can't do, they do things well, given our limitations' (I-18). For example, the lawyers' groups 'are the ones with evidence-based justifications and rationale why we should not go back to death penalty' (I-20). Lawyers from the FLAG contributed their

[55] Commission on Human Rights, #nodeathpenalty and World Coalition Against the Death Penalty (2017).

[56] The Nordic Page (n.d.).

experience on the ground regarding the cases they have handled and their experiences in strategic lawyering, which was 'valuable information that gives us confidence and credibility in pushing for our advocacy' (I-18). The FLAG also released studies on prosecution and detention rates, experiences of prisoners on death row, costs of the death penalty, and related topics.

The CADP comprised largely of grassroots workers and those visiting prisons and detention centres became first-hand sources of information (I-21). A CADP official remarked that their members are always on the ground, so their inputs have significant bearings on any discussion, and they 'have a privileged position to pursue the discussion for abolition' – in fact, the campaigns spearheaded by the Task Force, have utilised much of their inputs (I-11). As a coalition of organisations focusing on penal reform, the CADP's activities included organising death row inmates and their families, helping inmates draft letters, training the families on how to lobby; lobbying in congress; appearing in media, and engaging people in discussion in television shows, organising forums, and conducting option for life seminars in school (I-11). Through this network, each organisation in the Coalition has a vast network of organisations they can rely on, and they have also been 'blessed with talented individuals' (I-11).

The focus of NoBox on harm reduction and its different approaches towards drug use opened up more avenues to show that the death penalty is not a solution to illicit drugs (I-19). The attendance of NoBox in regular meetings allowed them to contribute information and data in relation to drugs (I-15). At the same time, the Task Force helped the organisation gain knowledge and experience in engaging with different legislators (I-15). The Task Force benefitted from the coordination and capacity-building skills of the CHRP. The CHRP helped put together information and prepare advisories, and served as a link between the government and the Task Force (I-21):

> [W]e complement each other's work. For example, many of the members are from the Church and then from the prison reform NGOs. So, they . . . are experts in the situation of persons deprived of liberty. They've encountered persons who use drugs and then FLAG, mainly because the members are lawyers, so, we get the legal expertise in that. And then we have civil society organisations as well, human rights defenders, so we complement each other's work. And then of course, the CHR, we're NHRI, and we balance the positions because we have to bridge government and civil society and we're an NHRI (I-21).

Within the group, their assigned work depended on their own expertise on particular issues, and they complemented each other (I-21).

8.6.3 *Increasing Legitimacy and Improving Access to Finance*

Separately, the organisations each have sources of funding and different levels of recognition locally and internationally. The CHRP, for instance, has undertaken projects funded by the European Commission, Australian Aid, US Aid, and embassies.[57] The FLAG, in the past years, has 'received hundreds of thousands of dollars from the European Union and its members to support the organisation's advocacy in capital cases and to underwrite a wide variety of death penalty workshops and publications'.[58] The funding support helped the FLAG become the country's foremost source of information on capital punishment and enabled it to have a significant impact on many key decision-makers before the abolition in 2006.[59] One interviewee declined to disclose their funding source but shared that the organisation receives both domestic and international funding (interviewee's identity withheld).

During Duterte's administration, however, almost all organisations interviewed expressed a lack of funding as a key barrier to implementing their activities. Working together as a group helped maximise their resources – they could have more workforce, pool their funds, or reach out to personalities that are beyond the ability of any one organisation alone. It also increased the reach of each organisation as each member can promote the activities of the others. For the Tending Life event, for example, member organisations of the Task Force were responsible for inviting participants and working together in putting up the event (I-1). Government agencies, such as the Drug Enforcement Agency, the Parole and Probation Service, the Bureau of Jail Management and Penology, and the National Bureau of Investigation, attended the event. Working together, therefore, also increases the legitimacy of the movement as the members of the network are well-recognised locally and internationally in their own rights. The Task Force has established strong links with some government agencies, including criminal justice agencies, such as the prison service. Even before the death penalty was abolished, for instance, prison officers used to get in touch with FLAG lawyers to assist death row inmates (I-2).

[57] Commission on Human Rights website (www.righttolifeph.online/category/studies).
[58] Johnson and Zimring (2009, p. 136).
[59] Ibid.

8.7 The Role of Anti-Death Penalty Network as a Check against Abuse of Power

The Duterte administration showed strong tendencies for authoritarian rule and the violation of separation of powers. Duterte's power over the legislature became very pronounced even before congress convened in July 2016, as a large majority of legislators, even those previously belonging to opposing parties, allied themselves with Duterte – partly out of fear of retribution from the president or his 'more rabid supporters'.[60] Duterte thus gained a 'supermajority' in congress, both in the House of Representatives, and the senate. Of the 297 members of the House of Representatives, only eight remained as genuine members of the opposition; of the twenty-four senators, three remained in the opposition.[61] The passage of *House Bill No. 4727* – with 216 votes in favour, fifty-four against, and one abstention – came after repeated expressions of support by Duterte's allies in the House of Representatives, who described the death penalty as 'killing that goes through a process'.[62] The speaker of the house reportedly openly 'threatened to strip members of congress of key positions if they dared to vote against the bill'.[63]

The anti-death penalty network, in registering its strong opposition to the bill became one of the few voices of resistance to Duterte's power. The role of the network was crucial because, 'in the same way that congress was united in coming out with a death penalty law, it was important to show that it's not just specific people, or the "usual suspects" opposing the death penalty' (I-19). According to an officer of FLAG, it was important to show that a group that was organised specifically to campaign for abolition to stop the death penalty (I-19). Even just attending congressional hearings and expressing a clear position against the death penalty sent a message that there were people standing up against it. The human rights groups attended because they wanted to send the message '*na may nagbabantay*' [that there are people who are vigilantly watching] (I-20). At the height of campaigns against the death penalty in the lower house, they were able to mobilise many people, and they almost filled the whole second floor of the House of Representatives (I-20). International

[60] According to Bello (2017, p. 31), some of the legislators had joined the majority out of loyalty; some to get committee chairmanships or access funds; and some out of fear of retribution.

[61] Ibid.

[62] Former House Speaker Pantaleon Alvarez quoted in iDefend (2016b).

[63] Amnesty International (2017).

advocates also attended plenary hearings and actively lobbied members of Committees who were not yet clear on their position, including members of the Justice Committee, the Charter Change Committee, and the Dangerous Drugs Committee, aiming to convince them to vote against the death penalty provisions (I-10).

Braithwaite *et al.* highlighted the importance of 'networks of checks and balances from civil society outside the state'.[64] The anti-death penalty network played an important part in Philippine history as a check against Duterte's power: one of the forces that resisted attempts during the Duterte administration to corrupt democratic institutions and principles.

8.8 Leadership from Below?

'Leadership from the front', a well-known phrase in death penalty scholarship, suggests that the trajectory of capital punishment is steered by the leadership of political elites.[65] Johnson states that 'public education campaigns are a hollow hope' though not irrelevant.[66] This does not discount, however, the vital part that the anti-death penalty movement plays in steering the trajectory of death penalty policy and practice. Information and education campaigns can be crucial in changing the views of decision-makers.[67] This has been proven in the case of the Philippines during the 2006 abolition when information campaigns, mostly by the FLAG, succeeded in convincing key decision-makers to vote for abolition, even those lawmakers who were previously in favour of capital punishment.[68]

When the attempts at reimposition started in 2016, the Task Force vigilantly monitored bills that were being filed in congress that have any relation to the death penalty and set meetings to strategise about how to handle these (I-19). They targeted legislators that they may be able to sway by providing them research materials, and provided support to legislators that were going to be a part of interpellation – not just by compiling research materials but by simplifying these, even making cue cards for them (I-21). The International Commission of Jurists responded to queries from senators who were thinking of opposing the

[64] Braithwaite, Charlesworth, and Soares (2012, p. xiii).
[65] Johnson (2020, pp. 104 and 109).
[66] Ibid, 104.
[67] Ibid, p. 106.
[68] Johnson and Zimring (2009, p. 136).

bill and intend to continue working with legislators (I-3). After the death penalty bill was passed in the House of Representatives, there was a groundswell of public protests and mobilisations (I-10). Anti-death penalty legislators at the lower house continued working by coordinating with senators to convince them to either not act on the bill or to reject it (I-17).

Certainly, it was the senators' decision not to act favourably on the death penalty bills that ultimately stalled the attempts at reimposition. In this sense, one could argue that senators exercised their 'leadership from the front'. However, this analysis ignores the pivotal role of networked governance exercised by small groups in the Philippines. As observed by Colmenares, pressure from abolitionist groups greatly influenced the decisions of senators:[69]

> The bills, however, did not get past the Senate . . ., which succumbed to the effective and focused campaigning of both domestic and international abolitionists. It is worth noting that Senators, elected at large nationally, are often concerned with wider national and international issues that may affect their electoral fortunes and are, therefore, susceptible to lobbying by civil society organisations.

The anti-death penalty movement failed to prevent the move by political elites at the lower house to reintroduce the death penalty; however, strong advocacy by the anti-death penalty network was crucial in bringing a spotlight to the issue and in sending the message that there is a robust opposition from different groups in the entire socioeconomic spectrum as well as from international bodies.

8.9 Conclusion

Braithwaite and Drahos note that 'weak single strands in webs of influence often become strong by being tied to other weak strands'.[70] This notion is similar to the famous Philippine metaphor about the *walis-tingting* (broom) – a bundle of broomsticks derived from coconut leaves, tied together to be used in sweeping the yard. The broomstick has long been perceived as a symbol of strength in unity: it is easy to break one or two sticks, but tied together, they are formidable, and they serve their purpose effectively – one or two sticks cannot clean as effectively as when bundled together.[71]

[69] Colmenares (2023, p. 23).
[70] Braithwaite and Drahos (2000, p. 31).
[71] Reyes (2000).

This case study has shown that networked governance by small organisations was key in preventing the reimposition of the death penalty. However, the extent to which the Philippine experience can provide important lessons for consolidating abolitionist organisations in other jurisdictions is less clear. In the case of the Philippines, many of the actors comprising the network, such as the CBCP, the CHRP, and the FLAG, have been active in their anti-death penalty advocacy since the late 1980s. They continued their advocacy through the years, 'establishing an institutional continuity that reinforced campaigns every time reimposition bills were filed in congress'.[72] The Task Force has been instrumental in the 2006 abolition but has again come to the fore when the threats for reimposition arose during the time of Duterte. The network has thus gained substantial experience and has proven that it is a force to be reckoned with, even in the face of threats of authoritarian rule. In addition, about 81 per cent of the Philippine population are Catholics, which explains the wide reach of the Catholic church as mentioned in this chapter. The CBCP has a vast network of grassroots organisations in almost every municipality in the country. These factors need to be considered if the networked governance experience of the Philippines is to be considered for replication elsewhere.

Although the senate has not acted favourably on any death penalty bills to date, the possibility of reimposition remains. Currently, under the administration of Ferdinand Marcos, Jr., there are at least four bills pending in the House of Representatives seeking to reintroduce the death penalty for 'heinous crimes' including drug-related offences. Duterte's long-time ally Ronald de la Rosa also filed a similar bill in the senate. Historical and contemporary examples confirm that death penalty abolition can be fragile, challenged by changing political alignments, including populist invocations of law-and-order remedies to address social disorder and crime. As one of the interviewees asserts, the fight against the death penalty, particularly in the context of the association made with drugs, needs to be an ongoing endeavour (I-15).

References

Amnesty International. (1996) *Philippines: Further Information on Death Penalty: Leo Pilo Echegaray*. www.amnesty.org/en/documents/asa35/007/1996/en/.

(1999) *Philippines: Imminent Execution: Eduardo Agbayani*. www.amnesty.org/en/documents/asa35/020/1999/en/.

[72] Colmenares (2023, p. 25).

(2017) *Philippines: The Death Penalty Is an Inhumane, Unlawful and Ineffective Response to Drugs.* www.amnesty.org.au/philippines-death-penalty-inhumane-unlawful/.

Bautista, L. B. (2017) 'Duterte and His Quixotic War on Drugs' 20 *Thinking ASEAN* 2.

Bello, W. (2017) 'The Spider Spins His Web: Rodrigo Duterte's Ascent to Power' 65 *Philippine Sociological Review* 31.

Bergonia, T. S. (2019) 'The Death Penalty Debate: Comedic Episode, Studies Show Risks' *Inquirer.net* (6 July). https://newsinfo.inquirer.net/1146785/the-death-penalty-debate-comedic-episode-studies-show-risks.

Braithwaite, J., Charlesworth, H. and Soares, A. (2012) *Networked Governance of Freedom and Tyranny: Peace in Timor-Leste* (Canberra: Australian National University Press).

Braithwaite, J. and Drahos, P. (2000) *Global Business Regulation* (Cambridge: Cambridge University Press).

Caplan, R. (2022) 'Networked Governance' 24 *Yale Journal of Law & Technology* 543.

Chew, D. (2023) 'A New Chapter: Malaysia's Journey Toward Abolition' *Eleos Justice* (11 May). www.monash.edu/law/research/eleos/blog/eleos-justice-blog-posts/a-new-chapter-malaysias-journey-toward-abolition.

Chilkoti, A. (2016) 'Rodrigo Duterte Vows to Restore Death Penalty in the Philippines' *Financial Times* (16 May). www.ft.com/content/7cc28c6c-1b56-11e6-8fa5-44094f6d9c46.

Colmenares, N. J. (2023) 'Analysing the Success of Death Penalty Campaigns in the Philippines: Strategies, Tactics and Framing' 24(1) *Australian Journal of Asian Law* 19.

Commission on Human Rights. (n.d.) 'About the Commission'. https://chr.gov.ph/about-us/#:~:text=The%20Commission%20on%20Human%20Rights.

Commission on Human Rights of the Philippines and Labucay, I. D. (2020) *In Defense of the Right to Life: Analyzing Factors Affecting Filipino Opinion About Death Penalty* (Philippines: CHRP).

Commission on Human Rights of the Philippines and Ward, C. (2017) *In Defense of the Right to Life: International Law and Death Penalty in the Philippines* (Philippines: CHRP).

Commission on Human Rights, #nodeathpenalty and World Coalition Against the Death Penalty. (2017) 'Poverty and the Death Penalty in the Philippines: A Deadly Mix' *Piktochart* (10 October). https://create.piktochart.com/output/25003946-philippines.

Creech, H., Vetter, T., Matus, K. and Seymour, I. R. (2008) *The Governance of Non-Legal Entities: An Exploration Into the Challenges Facing Collaborative, Multistakeholder Enterprises That Are Hosted by Institutions* (Winnipeg: International Institute for Sustainable Development).

Deinla, I., Mendoza, R. U., Pizzaro, A. and Santiago, R. P. R. (2021) 'Death Penalty in the Philippines: Evidence on Economics and Efficacy' Ateneo School of Government Working Paper. https://papers.ssrn.com/sol3/papers.cfm?abstract_id=3763271.

Diaz, J. (2017) 'House OKs Budget; CHR Gets P500 M' *The Philippine Star* (26 September). www.philstar.com/headlines/2017/09/26/1743094/house-oks-budget-chr-gets-p500-m.

Gavilan, J. (2017) '"My Men" Can Snub Your Probe, Duterte Tells CHR, Ombudsman' *Rappler* (24 July). www.rappler.com/nation/176597-sona-2017-duterte-chr-ombudsman/.

Gerzso, T. (2017) 'The Commission on Human Rights of the Philippines Launches a Campaign Against the Reinstatement of the Death Penalty in the Country' *World Coalition Against the Death Penalty* (26 October). https://worldcoalition.org/2017/10/26/the-commission-on-human-rights-of-the-philippines-launches-a-campaign-against-the-reinstatement-of-the-death-penalty-in-the-country/.

Houtzager, P. P. and Pattenden, J. (2003) 'Coalition Building from Below' in Houtzager, P. P. and Moore, M. (eds.) *Changing Paths: International Development and the New Politics of Inclusion* (Ann Arbor: University of Michigan Press).

Human Rights Watch. (2017) 'Philippines: Duterte Threatens Human Rights Community'. www.hrw.org/news/2017/08/18/philippines-duterte-threatens-human-rights-community.

Huppé, G. A., Creech, H. and Knoblauch, D. (2012) *The Frontiers of Networked Governance* (Winnipeg: International Institute for Sustainable Development).

iDefend. (2016a) 'Don't Make the War on Drugs a War on Human Rights, New HR Group Told President Duterte' (11 August). https://idefend.ph/news/statements/dont-make-war-drugs-war-human-rights-new-hr-group-told-president-duterte.

(2016b) 'Defend the Right to Life, Resist Institutionalised Violence' (9 December). https://idefend.ph/news/statements/defend-right-life-resist-institutionalised-violence.

International Criminal Court. (2021) *Situation in the Philippines: Decision on the Prosecutor's Request for Authorisation of an Investigation Pursuant to Article 15(3) of the Statute* (No. ICC-01/21). www.icc-cpi.int/sites/default/files/CourtRecords/CR2021_08044.PDF.

Johnson, D. T. (2020) *The Culture of Capital Punishment in Japan* (Cham: Palgrave McMillan).

Johnson, D. T. and Zimring, F. E. (2009) 'A Lesson Learned? The Philippines' in Johnson, D. T. and Zimring, F. E. (eds.) *The Next Frontier: National Development, Political Change, and the Death Penalty in Asia* (Oxford: Oxford University Press).

Kine, P. (2017) 'The Philippines' Duterte Incites Vigilante Violence' *Human Rights Watch* (19 April). www.hrw.org/news/2017/04/19/philippines-duterte-incites-vigilante-violence.

Mogato, M. (2017) 'Philippine Congress Backs Annual Budget of Just $20 for Agency Probing Drugs War' *Reuters* (12 September). www.reuters.com/article/us-philippines-drugs-rights-idUSKCN1BN1JV.

Rappler.com. (2021) 'Human Rights Groups Coalesce, Go Digital to Fight Death Penalty' (7 May). www.rappler.com/video/act-one/coalition-against-death-penalty-panibagong-pagkakataon-film-series/.

Reyes, E. A. C. (2000) *Brooms & Mats, Ducks & Magnets: Metaphors for Synergism.* http://saniblakas.faithweb.com/metaphors.htm.

Seiff, A. (2020) 'Philippine President and Politicians Push for Return of Death Penalty Amid "War on Drugs"' *International Bar Association* (17 August). www.ibanet.org/article/B041B93E-63C5-4361-8997-3D83C10E22FB.

Smith, T. (2017) 'Duterte's Latest Target: The Commission on Human Rights' *The Diplomat* (8 August). https://thediplomat.com/2017/08/dutertes-latest-target-the-commission-on-human-rights/.

Sørensen, E. and Torfing, J. (2005) 'Network Governance and Post-Liberal Democracy' 27(2) *Administrative Theory & Praxis* 199.

Stoker, G. (2006) 'Public Value Management: A New Narrative for Networked Governance?' 36(1) *American Review of Public Administration* 41.

Tagayuna, A. (2004) 'Capital Punishment in the Philippines' 5(1) *Explorations in Southeast Asian Studies – A Journal of the Southeast Asian Studies Student Association* 1.

The Nordic Page. (n.d.) 'University of Oslo Calls World Universities Against Death Penalty'. www.tnp.no/norway/panorama/4100-university-of-oslo-norway-calls-world-universities-against-death-penalty/.

Appendix

List of Interviewees

Assigned number	Name	Organisational affiliation
From June 2019 to August 2019		
I-1	Rodolfo (Rudy) Diamante	Secretary General, Catholic Bishops Conference of the Philippines (CBCP) – Episcopal Commission on Prison Pastoral Care
I-2	Cookie Diokno	Secretary General, Free Legal Assistance Group (FLAG)

(*cont.*)

Assigned number	Name	Organisational affiliation
I-3	Emerlynne Gil	Senior International Legal Adviser, International Commission of Jurists
I-4	Ray Paolo J. Santiago	Executive Director, Ateneo Human Rights Center, School of Law, Ateneo de Manila University
I-5	Anonymous	Officer, NoBox
I-6	Anonymous	Officer, Coalition Against the Death Penalty
I-7	Anonymous	Staff, Commission on Human Rights of the Philippines (CHRP)
I-8	Anonymous	Staff, Commission on Human Rights of the Philippines (CHRP)
I-9	Anonymous	Staff, Commission on Human Rights of the Philippines (CHRP)
From January 2023 to February 2023		
I-10	Jose Christopher 'Kit' Belmonte	Former Member, House of Representatives of Philippines
I-11	Fr. Silvino Borres	President, Coalition Against the Death Penalty (CADP)
I-12	France Castro	Member, House of Representatives of Philippines (Alliance of Concerned Teachers (ACT) Teachers Party List)
I-13	Atty. Romel P. Daguimol	Regional Director, Commission on Human Rights of the Philippines (CHRP) – Cordillera Administrative Region
I-14	Karen Gomez-Dumpit	Former Commissioner, Commission on Human Rights of the Philippines (CHRP)
I-15	Inez Feria	Chairperson, NoBox
I-16	Atty. Rexford Guevarra	Regional Director, Commission on Human Rights of the Philippines (CHRP) – Region IV-A
I-17	Edcel Lagman	Member, House of Representatives of Philippines
I-18	Atty. Francis Tom Temprosa	Director IV, Commission on Human Rights of the Philippines (CHRP)
I-19	Atty./Assistant Professor Theodore Te	Regional Coordinator, Free Legal Assistance Group (FLAG)
I-20	Rosemarie R. Trajano	Former Secretary General, Philippine Alliance of Human Rights Advocates Convenor, iDefend
I-21	Anonymous	Staff, Commission on Human Rights of the Philippines (CHRP)

PART IV

States in Transition

9

The New Narcotics Code of Thailand

A Promising Law?

RONNAKORN BUNMEE

9.1 Introduction

The story of control of illegal drugs in modern Thailand has been marked by extremes. In 2003, Thailand launched a bloody 'war on drugs' which led to the extrajudicial killing of more than 2,800 people, many of them innocent.[1] Almost twenty years later, it became the first country in Asia to legalise the cultivation and consumption of domestically-grown cannabis in 2022.[2] In September 2023, the Government of Thailand announced that it would – once again – make the fight against narcotics part of the national agenda.[3]

The experience in Thailand has shown that harsh penalties and all-out efforts to eradicate this persistent issue have not only failed to curb the drug problem[4] but also bred a fresh challenge: the drastic overpopulation of prisons. Thailand ranks among the top ten countries in the world for the highest number of people in prison,[5] with more than 80 per cent of the total prison population convicted of drug-related offences ranging from personal consumption to drug trafficking.[6]

[1] Human Rights Watch (2008).

[2] However, there are plans afoot to ban its recreational use soon: Thepgumpanat and Wongcha-um (2024).

[3] Editorial (2023).

[4] For the experience in other countries, refer to Degenhardt *et al.* (2008). Ever-increasing quantity of illegal drugs have been seized in Thailand, for example, refer to Chongcharoen (2023); Saksornchai (2023).

[5] Refer to World Population Review (n.d.).

[6] Those convicted of narcotics offences comprised 82 per cent of the 285,182 total prison population (or 234,666 inmates) two months before the implementation of the new Narcotics Code: see www.correct.go.th/rt103pdf/report_result.php?date=2021-10-01&report=drug.

The punitive approach towards drug offenders also reflects poorly on Thailand's penal institutions. There are few successful rehabilitation programmes to guide convicted offenders towards reformation. As a result, there is a high recidivism rate among released prisoners: in the fiscal year of 2019 (from 1 October 2018 to 30 September 2019), 73 per cent of the 106,000 released prisoners reoffended within three years.[7] Consequently, a distressing cycle transpires offenders – upon release – revert to crime, leading to inevitable re-incarceration. This cycle, in turn, accentuates the problem of prison overcrowding, underlining the deficiencies within the legal system and policy measures.

A radical revision of the country's approach to drug control was undertaken in recognition of the urgent need to rethink the laws regulating drug use and treatment alternatives. In November 2021, two new drug laws – the Narcotics Code and the Narcotics Procedure Act (No. 2) B.E. 2564 (2021) (NPA 2021) – were passed, heralding a conceptual shift in how drug-related issues are dealt with. Instead of branding drug users, particularly small-scale offenders as criminals, the new laws aim to provide them with second chances by adopting a public health approach to drug control rather than a purely punitive one.[8] The Narcotics Code replaces all existing drug-related substantive pieces of legislation, twenty-four of them to be precise, which were sometimes inconsistent and out of date. In addition, because some pharmaceutical drugs are essential for the advancement of medical, scientific, and industrial innovations, an efficient licensing regulation is enacted to prevent the abuse of these substances. Simultaneously, the NPA 2021 amends the existing drug procedural law, updating it to synchronise with the current socio-legal landscape and the new Narcotics Code.

Section 9.2 will examine both the Narcotics Code and the NPA 2021 to highlight their innovative aspects. Section 9.3 will discuss its challenges.

9.2 The Innovations

The innovative aspects of the new laws can be categorised into five key points. First, they consolidate legislation into a comprehensive, systematic Code. Second, they introduce various committees for improved enforcement. Third, they legalise certain drugs for medical, research,

[7] See www.correct.go.th/recstats/index.php/th/sumReportCondition. This may be compared with a worldwide reconviction rate of between 18 and 55 per cent within two years of the prisoners' release: Yukhnenko, Farouki, and Fazel (2023).

[8] Dickinson (2023).

and economic purposes, heralding a new era in which narcotics are no longer demonised but can be used for beneficial ends. Fourth, the laws make crucial alterations to sentencing policy, ensuring that the brunt of punitive action is felt by drug traffickers who perpetrate and profit from the drug trade rather than the victims of substance abuse. Lastly, the legislation propounds a shift towards public health initiatives for treating and rehabilitating drug users, recognising their needs as patients rather than their wrongs as offenders. Whether the transition from punitive action to public health initiatives will be the panacea to Thailand's drug conundrum remains to be seen. However, one thing is certain: this holistic approach marks a significant step towards a more compassionate, and hopefully more effective, resolution to the country's drug dilemma.

9.2.1 Unified Law

Numerous laws have been introduced in the past to combat drug-related offences. Regrettably, these myriad pieces of legislation have proven difficult to navigate owing to their disparate nature. Over twenty pieces of legislation existed, scattered across the legal landscape, causing a labyrinthine challenge in understanding and implementing the country's drug-related law. The new Narcotics Code consolidates the existing laws pertaining to narcotics into a unified system. This systematic and unified approach not only simplifies the laws for better comprehension but also eliminates conflicting provisions to ensure smoother implementation.

However, the legislative overhaul does not come without its complexities. As part of this transition, all secondary laws previously repealed under the Narcotics Code will have to remain operational until new secondary legislation is enacted. A careful cross-referencing of existing secondary legislation vis-à-vis the new narcotics laws during the transitional period is therefore needed to maintain the effectiveness of narcotics control during this transitional period. It is critical to ensure that the new primary laws and existing secondary laws do not result in incongruity or legal loopholes that could potentially undermine the national narcotics control strategy. In this context, it is equally essential to enact new secondary laws promptly that align with the overarching ethos and provisions of the Narcotics Code and the NPA 2021.

9.2.2 Systematic Committees

In an innovative manoeuvre, the Narcotics Code establishes a quadripartite committee structure to manage drug-related affairs. This new structure recognises the multifaceted nature of drug control and the need for diverse expertise and perspectives. The first committee is the Narcotics Control Board (NCB), operating under the prime minister's leadership, which serves as the linchpin in the formulation of drug policies.[9] In addition, the NCB has been endowed with the authority to modify the classification of specific substances as illicit drugs. Further powers granted to the NCB include the delineation of zones specifically allocated for the cultivation, manufacture, testing, consumption, and possession of drugs.

The second committee is the Narcotics Commission, chaired by the secretary-general of the ministry of public health, which is entrusted with the responsibility of actual drug control, highlighting the specificity and practical focus required in enforcement actions.[10] The third committee is the Property Examination Committee, under the stewardship of the secretary-general of the ministry of justice, which has the mandate to inspect and seize assets associated with drug offences.[11] This committee adds a financial disincentive to drug trafficking, augmenting punitive measures.

The last committee is the Narcotics Addiction Treatment and Rehabilitation Committee, which embodies the shift in perspective towards treating illicit drug users as patients rather than criminals. This committee, led by a deputy prime minister, is tasked with the treatment and care of illicit drug users, underlining the emphasis on rehabilitation.[12]

Through the committee system, the new legislation fosters comprehensive cooperation, incorporating both public and private sector perspectives. This approach enables systematic consideration and implementation of various strategies, from prevention, suppression, and control, to punishment and rehabilitation, illustrating a holistic approach to tackling the drug issue in Thailand.

9.2.3 Allowing Drug Use and Possession

The Narcotics Code has introduced significant changes to drug use and possession where drugs can be used without requiring prior authorisation under some circumstances. According to section 32 and an

[9] The Narcotics Code, s. 4.
[10] The Narcotics Code, s. 25.
[11] The Narcotics Code, s. 63.
[12] The Narcotics Code, s. 109.

announcement by the ministry,[13] state agencies and the Thai Red Cross are permitted to produce, import, export, and possess psychotropic substances listed in Categories 3 and 4 and narcotic drugs in Category 3.[14] These activities are sanctioned solely for the purposes of treatment or prevention of diseases, analysis, research, or educational use, or for any benefit of the state but must not serve any commercial interests. In terms of distributing these controlled substances, this is permitted only for the treatment or prevention of diseases in patients or ill animals within legally recognised medical institutions.

The Narcotics Code also recognises the potential necessity or benefit of specific substances when used medically by legalising the possession of certain types and quantities of drugs for treatment purposes. Section 33 permits patients to possess a necessary quantity of narcotic drugs listed in Category 2,[15] or psychotropic substances in Categories 2, 3, or 4 for personal medical treatment as prescribed by a doctor. Furthermore, section 33(2) allows vehicles that are not registered in Thailand and

[13] Ministry of Public Health Announcement regarding the criteria, methods, and conditions for the production, import, export, distribution, or possession of drugs or psychotropic substances without requiring permission, BE 2566 (2023) issued on 29 November 2023.

[14] Psychotropic substances are classified into four categories by the Narcotics Code, s. 30:

(a) Category 1 are psychotropic substances which have no medical use and have a high likelihood or potential for abuse, such as mescaline, psilocybin, DMT, DET, and cathinone.
(b) Category 2 are psychotropic substances which have medical use and have a high likelihood or potential for abuse, such as phentermine, midazolam, zolpidem, methylphenidate, ketamine, and pseudoephedrine.
(c) Category 3 are psychotropic substances which have medical use and have a likelihood or potential for abuse, such as amobarbital, pentobarbital, and pentazocine.
(d) Category 4 are psychotropic substances which have medical use and have a lower likelihood or potential for abuse than that of category 3, such as diazepam, lorazepam, clorazepate, and chlordiazepoxide.

[15] Narcotic drugs are classified into five categories by the Narcotics Code, s. 29:

(a) Category 1 are serious narcotic drugs such as heroin.
(b) Category 2 are general narcotic drugs such as morphine, cocaine, codeine, or medical opium.
(c) Category 3 are narcotic drugs in the form of medicinal preparations and mix of narcotic drugs in Category 2, in accordance with the rules prescribed by the Minister of Public Health as suggested by the Narcotics Commission.
(d) Category 4 are chemicals used for production of narcotic drugs in Category 1 or 2 such as acetic anhydride.
(e) Category 5 are narcotic drugs not included in Category 1 to 4 such as opium poppy plant.

engaged in international public transport,[16] to carry narcotic drugs listed in Categories 2 or 5, including certain species of opium poppy (*Papaver somniferum* L. and *Papaver bracteatum* Lindl.),[17] or psychotropic substances in Categories 2, 3 or 4, limited to quantities essential for routine first aid or emergency situations. The individual in charge of these vehicles is required to implement suitable safeguards to prevent the loss or unauthorised use of these narcotics or controlled substances.

In addition to medical use, the Narcotics Code also acknowledges the responsible recreational use of certain drugs. Some drugs, such as Kratom (*Mitragyna speciosa*), have been removed from the list of illicit drugs. However, while it is widely thought that cannabis consumption became completely legal in Thailand from 9 June 2022, cannabis, in fact, remains a drug listed in Category 5. The Ministry of Public Health Announcement on Specifying Drugs in Category 5, B.E. 2565 (2022)[18] only exempts cannabis substances extracted from domestically grown cannabis or hemp plants, provided they meet one of the following criteria: extracts with a tetrahydrocannabinol (THC) content not exceeding 0.2 per cent by weight, and extracts derived from hemp seeds. However, these two exemptions cover almost all cannabis products available in Thailand.

Nevertheless, in other circumstances, the use of controlled substances requires official authorisation. For instance, section 34 of the Narcotics Code stipulates that the importation, exportation, and possession of narcotic drugs in Category 1[19] always require a permit from the minister of public health and can only be undertaken for the benefit of the state in preventing or suppressing drug offences; international cooperation; use

[16] If the vehicle is registered in Thailand, the types and doses of the controlled substances are limited by the Ministry of Public Health Announcement on Specifying Names and Quantities of Controlled Substances in Categories 2, 3, or 4 for Exclusive Use on Aircraft Registered in the Kingdom Engaged in International Public Transport, B.E. 2563 (2020), issued on 22 December 2020 and the Ministry of Public Health Announcement on Specifying Names and Quantities of Controlled Substances in Categories 2, 3, or 4 for Exclusive Use on Ships Registered in the Kingdom Engaged in International Public Transport, B.E. 2563 (2020), issued on 22 December 2020.

[17] The Ministry of Public Health Announcement on Specifying Drugs in Category 5, B.E. 2565 (2022) which was issued on 9 February 2022 and in force from 9 June 2022.

[18] Issued on 9 February 2022 and in force from 9 June 2022.

[19] For the comprehensive enumeration of fifty-two types of drugs listed in Category 1, refer to the Ministry of Public Health Announcement on Specifying Drugs in Category 1, B.E. 2565 (2022), promulgated on 5 August 2022, and the Ministry of Public Health Announcement on Specifying Drugs in Category 1 (Second Issue), B.E. 2566 (2023), issued on 29 November 2023.

in research studies; or medical, scientific and industrial purposes. Moreover, according to section 35, narcotic drugs in Category 5 can be produced, imported, or exported, with the aforementioned exemptions for international transport, with a permit from the director of the Thai Food and Drug Administration.

This distinction illustrates a balanced approach towards drug regulation, acknowledging their potential benefits whilst mitigating the risks of misuse. Furthermore, the Narcotics Code provides the NCB with the authority to contribute to research aimed at reducing harm from drug use and devising strategies for prevention, suppression, and solution of drug problems. The latitude of the Board's powers extends to the issuance of a Royal Decree, stipulating a designated area for specific activities if it deems such a move beneficial. Upon receiving authorisation, for example, a person may conduct experimental cultivation of crops that yield drugs or active substances which may be used in the production of such substances. This provision indicates an openness towards exploring alternative uses and sources of potentially beneficial substances within a controlled environment.

9.2.4 *Targeted Criminal Sanctions*

One of the principal issues which led to overcrowding in Thailand's prisons is the lack of distinction between drug users and drug dealers, coupled with the excessive reliance on presumptions in the law. This has resulted in disproportionate punishment, with a broad range of offenders invariably sent to prison, regardless of their offence severity.

A significant amendment made is the alteration of presumptions regarding the intent to traffic a drug. Previously, mere possession of drugs was unequivocally equated with an intent to traffic it. An amendment in 2017, effected through the Narcotics Act (sixth Amendment) B.E. 2560 (2017), refined this assumption by considering the quantity of narcotics in possession as a critical factor. An intention to traffic would now be inferred only if an individual was found with narcotics exceeding specified quantities. However, this change had minimal effect on alleviating the issue of prison overcrowding.

Consequently, section 107 of the Narcotics Code introduced a shift from a simplistic reliance on the quantity of narcotics possessed to an analysis of behaviour. Practically, this meant requiring proof that an individual's possession of narcotics is with the intention of either personal consumption or trafficking it. Furthermore, the presumption has been inverted. Where previously possession of a specific quantity of narcotics led to an irrefutable presumption of an intent to traffic it, the current legislation assumes that possession of a minimal quantity indicates personal use only. Prosecutors now have the task to prove an intent to traffic the drugs should they wish to pursue such charges. Additionally, the legislation reduced the quantities of drugs needed to infer intent. For instance, possession of fifteen tablets of methamphetamine previously indicated an intent to traffic it;[20] but under the new law, possession of five or fewer tablets suggests personal use.[21] This refined approach facilitates a better differentiation between consumers and traffickers, tailored to the nuances of individual cases.

Addressing past concerns of disproportionate penalties, the updated narcotics legislation has refined sanctions to correspond with the severity of offences more closely. For example, for the offence of possessing narcotic drugs in Category 1, such as heroin, for personal consumption, which is a non-serious offence,[22] the penalty has been reduced from a previously harsh one to ten years' imprisonment and/or a fine of Thai baht (THB) 20,000 to THB 200,000,[23] to a more proportionate sentence of not more than two years' imprisonment and/or a fine not exceeding THB 40,000.[24] Additionally, for consuming narcotic drugs in Category 1, the penalty has been adjusted from the former six months to three years' imprisonment and/or a fine ranging from THB 10,000 to THB 60,000,[25] to a new maximum of one year's imprisonment and/or a fine up to THB 20,000.[26] Importantly, even for serious offences such as distributing Category 1 narcotic drugs, the legislation has lessened the penalty by eliminating the mandatory minimum sentence of four years' imprisonment,[27] even though the same maximum penalty of fifteen years still applies.[28]

[20] The repealed Narcotics Act B.E. 2522 (1979), s. 15(2).

[21] Ministerial Regulation Specifying the Quantities of Narcotics and Controlled Substances Presumed to be Possessed for Consumption, B.E. 2567 (2024), s. 2(1).

[22] The definition of a serious drug-related offence is provided in the Narcotics Code, s. 1, which encompasses offences concerning the production, importation, exportation, sale, or possession of illicit drugs, except in the case of possession for personal consumption. Additionally, conspiracy, aiding and abetting, or an attempt to commit a serious drug-related offence is also regarded as a serious drug-related offence.

[23] The repealed Narcotics Act B.E. 2522 (1979), s. 67.

[24] The Narcotics Code, s. 164.

[25] The repealed Narcotics Act B.E. 2522 (1979), s. 91.

[26] The Narcotics Code, s. 162.

[27] The repealed Narcotics Act B.E. 2522 (1979), s. 65.

[28] The Narcotics Code, s. 145.

The new Code provides judges more leeway to impose penalties tailored to the unique circumstances of each offender. Section 152 introduces a remarkable degree of judicial discretion for serious offences. This provision permits the court to consider the gravity of the offence, the financial situation of the accused, and their behaviour to decide if special circumstances justify a lesser sentence than what the law statutorily mandates. This flexibility to reduce sentences based on individualised factors, including financial status, is a distinct approach that is not found in other areas of criminal law in Thailand. Ordinarily, in standard criminal cases, the maximum sentence reduction a court can apply is up to half of the prescribed penalty,[29] and the financial status of the defendant is not usually considered for reducing a sentence below the statutory minimum. However, it is important to point out that the Narcotics Code is not necessarily more lenient than the general criminal law. According to section 20 of the Thailand Penal Code, courts have the discretion to impose only imprisonment on an offender, even in cases where the law requires both imprisonment and a fine. In contrast, section 152, paragraph one, of the Narcotics Code specifies that for serious offences, offenders must receive both imprisonment *and* a fine.

Moreover, in cases of non-serious offences involving drug consumption or possession for personal use, section 165 outlines that the court's approach should prioritise rehabilitation over punishment, aiming to encourage defendants to overcome illicit drug use through appropriate treatment. When deciding on the penalty to be imposed, the court must tailor its judgment to fit the circumstances of each individual involved, even in instances where the offence was committed jointly.[30] This entails assessing the offence's gravity, which can vary significantly from case to case, and the potential harm depending on the type and quantity of drugs involved. It also requires a thorough examination of the defendant's background, including their age, past conduct, lifestyle, cognitive abilities, educational background, familial obligations, and reasons for drug use (whether for medical treatment, pain management, or other necessities) as well as their physical and mental health, social environment, instances of coercion, intimidation, fraud in drug consumption, exploitation by drug dealers, and any other extenuating factors. Furthermore, the nature and quantity of the drugs consumed or possessed, the

[29] The Thailand Penal Code, s. 78.

[30] The Narcotics Code, s. 165, paragraph one.

frequency of drug use, and whether the drugs were used to help them perform their work can also influence the sentencing decision.[31]

If the accused has no prior history of imprisonment, the court may opt for alternatives to incarceration.[32] These alternatives can include protective measures[33] such as placing the individual in protective custody, banning them from entering specified areas, requiring them to post a bond with security, restraining them in a medical facility, or barring them from practising certain professions. Alternatively, the court may decide to place the accused on probation,[34] during which they must report regularly to a designated official or participate in specific training programmes. Apart from protective measures and probation, the court may also offer the accused a choice to undergo rehabilitation which will be discussed in this chapter.

The more favourable provisions in the Narcotics Code extend to individuals who committed offences before the enactment of the new Code. If they have been convicted and received a more severe punishment than what the Code stipulates, they can petition the court, invoking section 3 of the Penal Code, to seek a reduction in their sentence or to be released. However, the reduction of punishment in such cases is not automatically applied. Additionally, if their cases are still under trial, the new law becomes immediately applicable. However, there is one exception: if the case is not yet finalised but the court of first instance has already issued a judgment, the presumption of intent to traffic drugs remains in effect.[35] Thus, if the accused had in their possession quantities of drugs exceeding the specified limits, they would still be presumed to have the intent to traffic those drugs. This provision faced challenges regarding its constitutionality, as it applied different laws to individuals accused of the same offence. Nonetheless, the Constitutional Court determined that this provision did not breach the Constitution.[36]

The new Narcotics Code provides more explicit and rational guidelines for penalising drug traffickers and those involved in drug syndicates. For instance, it provides a clear framework for confiscation of assets resulting from drug trafficking. Suppose a drug dealer accumulates

[31] The Narcotics Code, s. 165, paragraph two.
[32] The Narcotics Code, s. 166.
[33] The Narcotics Code, s. 166 in conjunction with the Thailand Penal Code, s. 39.
[34] The Narcotics Code, s. 166 in conjunction with the Thailand Penal Code, s. 56.
[35] Act Promulgating the Narcotics Code B.E. 2564 (2021), s. 21.
[36] The Constitutional Court Ruling No. 15/2566 (2023).

assets worth THB 10 million from the drug trade but only has THB 6 million worth of assets at the time of the arrest. In such a scenario, the authorities could previously confiscate only the remaining THB 6 million. Section 79, paragraph three, of the Narcotics Code, however, now allows the confiscation of property equal in value to the property that the convicted offender actually acquired from the drug trade. Thus, additional assets not directly derived from drug trafficking can be seized to meet this value – including assets acquired through legitimate work, inherited property, or marital assets. However, this value-based confiscation is available only to serious offences and the prosecutor may petition the court to enforce the judgment against other assets of the convicted offender within ten years from the date the court issued the judgment.[37]

The new legislation also introduces new offences related to drug trafficking, such as the creation of 'mule' accounts. Section 129 imposes penalties on individuals who permit others to use their identity, documents, or other evidence to establish or register bank accounts, electronic cards, and Subscriber Identity Module (SIM) cards, or to allow the use of such accounts or registrations they have already made, knowing or having reasonable grounds to know that this is to facilitate the commission of a serious drug-related crime. The consequences include up to three years' imprisonment and/or a fine not exceeding THB 60,000. Furthermore, in 2023, the government enacted the Emergency Decree on Measures for the Prevention and Suppression of Technological Crimes, B.E. 2566 (2023), targeting cybercrimes. Section 9 of this decree outlines an offence similar to that of a mule account. Under this section, knowingly opening a mule account or having reasonable grounds to know that the account will be used to facilitate any form of criminal offence constitutes an offence. It carries the same potential imprisonment period as section 129 of the Narcotics Code, but with a significantly higher fine of THB 300,000, which is five times the fine stipulated for the narcotics-related offence.

In summary, the revamped drug laws mark a significant departure from previous legislation in Thailand, placing emphasis on the severity and nature of offences while balancing the need to punish perpetrators with efforts to rehabilitate offenders. It provides a more coherent and thoughtful approach to drug control, aiming to reduce prison overcrowding and align punishments with the realities of drug use and trafficking in Thailand.

[37] The Narcotics Code, ss. 79 and 85.

9.2.5 *Criminals vs Patients*

A notable advancement within Thailand's new drug laws is the reimagining of drug users as patients rather than criminals, echoing approaches adopted in countries such as Portugal. This represents a significant paradigm shift in addressing the country's drug problem, moving away from punitive measures towards therapeutic and rehabilitative interventions. Specifically, this approach is available only for those who are merely drug users but not for those who traffic drugs. Section 108 provides definitions for certain terms used in the Narcotics Act as follows:[38]

> 'Addiction' means the habitual and continuous use of drugs, leading to a state of dependency on such substances, which is a condition that can be diagnosed according to scientific principles.
>
> 'Treatment' means the process of treating individuals addicted to drugs, encompassing screening, assessing the severity of the addiction, medical treatment, rehabilitation, harm reduction from drug use, and follow-up after treatment.
>
> 'Rehabilitation' means any action aimed at treating the behaviour related to drug use and restoring the physical and mental health of the addicted individual to a normal state.
>
> 'Social rehabilitation' means any action aimed at supporting and aiding individuals who are addicted to drugs or who have undergone treatment, to improve their quality of life in terms of housing, education, and employment, as well as providing ongoing care and assistance to enable them to lead a normal and healthy life in society.

Consuming narcotic drugs in Categories 1, 2, or 5, or psychotropic substances in Categories 1 or 2, may result in a sentence of one year in prison and/or a fine.[39] Possession of these substances for personal use can lead to a two-year prison sentence and/or a fine.[40] However, if the accused successfully completes a rehabilitation programme, sections 113, 114, and 169 dictate that it will be as though the accused never committed the offence, meaning that they will not have a criminal record. This lack of a criminal record significantly aids in their successful reintegration into society after treatment, reducing the likelihood of reoffending.

[38] Author's translation.
[39] The Narcotics Code, s. 162.
[40] The Narcotics Code, s. 164.

Individuals using illicit drugs have three potential pathways to undergo treatment in a rehabilitation programme. Upon successful completion of the programme, they will be issued with a certificate and the law will regard them as not guilty of the drug offences.[41] The first pathway is through their own initiative before their illicit drug use is discovered. Under section 113, an illicit drug user can approach a drug treatment facility to seek treatment. Thailand has over 140 such facilities, some of which are operated by the government and others by Civil Society Organisations (CSOs).[42]

In the second scenario, individuals apprehended for consuming or possessing narcotic drugs in Categories 1, 2, or 5, or psychotropic substances in Categories 1 or 2, police or Office of the Narcotics Control Board (ONCB) officials have the authority under Section 114 to refer them to a drug treatment facility. This route is contingent upon two prerequisites: the individual's agreement to engage in the treatment programme and their legal status of neither awaiting trial for an offence warranting imprisonment nor currently serving a sentence. A history of imprisonment or previous treatment does not disqualify them from undergoing treatment again. However, failure to complete or flee from the programme could adversely affect their eligibility for future treatment referrals.[43]

Third, if the police or the ONCB official do not refer the accused to the facility, the court may undertake this referral themselves.[44] However, in addition to the same conditions being applicable, namely, the aforementioned individual's willingness and their status, section 168 also stipulates that for the court to refer the accused to a facility, it must be convinced by the circumstances of the case that the accused does not deserve punishment and is remorseful.

The therapeutic approach of the new laws not only involves interventions such as regular reporting and travel restrictions but also encourages the involvement of the individual's family and community in their rehabilitation.[45] These provisions allow individuals to maintain a semblance of a normal life while undergoing treatment, apart from mandatory appointments with healthcare professionals.

41 The Narcotics Code, ss. 113 and 114, paragraph two.

42 https://ncmc.moph.go.th/home/upload/web_news_files/my64sx04myo4wwc8gw.pdf.

43 The Narcotics Code, s. 114, paragraph three.

44 The Narcotics Code, s. 167.

45 The Narcotics Code, s. 120.

The laws further stipulate comprehensive guidelines for the treatment and rehabilitation process for drug users. A key feature of the new framework includes the establishment of screening centres tasked with assessing the severity of a person's illicit drug use and potential health risks.[46] This assessment helps to determine the appropriate level of intervention and treatment, thus tailoring care to individual needs. The process also incorporates a structured referral system, directing drug users to appropriate treatment and rehabilitation facilities.[47] To ensure continuity of care and monitoring of their progress, periodic follow-up measures are also instituted for individuals who have undergone treatment.[48]

9.3 The Challenges Ahead

9.3.1 Operational Aspects

While the new Narcotics Code has brought several commendable benefits, it is crucial to acknowledge and address the challenges that lie ahead. First, during this transitional period of legislation, it is important to note that while many of the primary drug laws have been repealed, their ancillary statutes will remain in force until new comprehensive legislation is introduced. Consequently, these laws necessitate careful examination to ensure their compatibility with the overarching legal framework. Failure to do so may lead to initial confusion and potential conflicts, particularly regarding the cultivation of cannabis. The abrupt liberalisation of cannabis cultivation, distribution, and consumption without appropriate regulation has caused confusion among police officers and the public alike.[49] Despite being portrayed as a harmful substance for decades, individuals have started cultivating cannabis at home, cannabis shops have sprung up nationwide, and consumption for leisure, including by children, has occurred without restrictions. A bill proposed by the Bhumjaithai Party, a leading advocate for the legalisation of cannabis, aimed at regulating the cultivation and distribution of cannabis was rejected in parliament on 15 September 2022. As of now (25 February 2024), no law directly controls the use of cannabis, except for extracts

[46] The Narcotics Code, s. 116.
[47] The Narcotics Code, s. 117.
[48] Ibid.
[49] Laohong (2022); Peter (2022).

derived from plants cultivated overseas or those containing THC content exceeding 0.2 per cent by weight.[50]

Second, the court can choose to lower the punishment below that stipulated by law or may opt for alternatives to incarceration, such as putting the offender on probation, or referring the offender to undergo rehabilitation at a drug treatment facility. This expanded discretion allows for penalties that are proportionate to the gravity of the offences committed, however, it is imperative to monitor the application of this discretion closely to ensure that it does not lead to inconsistencies or subjective judgments within the legal system.

Third, while the new drug law demonstrates a commendable shift towards treating drug users as patients and distinguishing between non-serious offenders (who consume drugs or possess drugs for personal consumption) and serious offenders (who produce, import, export, distribute, or possess drugs for the purposes of trafficking), it is imperative to assess whether the prosecutors have the requisite knowledge and understanding of the new legal provisions to implement the law. Moreover, special attention must be given to the treatment and rehabilitation programmes for drug offenders. The availability of adequate resources within the justice system, public health services, and the broader community is paramount in executing this aspect of the legislation successfully.

9.3.2 *Death Penalty as Sentencing Option*

A greater challenge is the use of the death penalty as a sentencing option in the Narcotics Code. Before discussing this issue in detail, it will be useful to give some background on the death penalty in Thailand.

Despite international trends towards its abolition, Thailand has retained the death penalty for crimes such as murder, corruption, bribery, and drug offences.[51] As of 22 January 2024, there were 325 individuals awaiting execution in Thailand, comprising 297 males and 28 females. Of this number, 199, or 61 per cent of those on death row, are

[50] The Ministry of Public Health Announcement on Specifying Drugs in Category 5, B.E. 2565 (2022) which was issued on 9 February 2022 and came into force on 9 June 2022.

[51] Since 2003, the method of execution used has been by lethal injection: The Thailand Penal Code, s. 19. There are 'some 60 offences' punishable with the death penalty: Muntarbhorn (2021).

convicted for drug-related offences.[52] This fails to comply with the requirement in international law that retentionist countries apply the death penalty to the 'most serious crimes' only since drug offences do not fall within this category.[53]

On the other hand, in a public opinion survey conducted in 2018, it was found that only 2 per cent of the respondents supported the use of the death penalty for drug offences.[54] Of all the executions between 1935 and 2006, only less than 9 per cent were for drug offences.[55] Furthermore, the most recent execution in the country took place in 2018 (for aggravated murder), and there have not been any executions since then.[56]

However, section 145 of the Narcotics Code reiterates Thailand's retentionist stance by expressly allowing the court to impose the death penalty. The section reads as follows:[57]

> Whoever produces, imports, exports, sells, or possesses narcotic drugs falling under Category 1, which contravene section 90, shall be sentenced to a prison term not exceeding fifteen years and a fine not exceeding one million five hundred thousand Baht.
>
> If the commission of the offence meets any of the following criteria, the offender shall be sentenced to a prison term ranging from two to twenty years and a fine ranging from two hundred thousand to two million Baht:
>
> (1) Offences committed for commercial purposes;
> (2) Offences that cause widespread distribution among the public;
> (3) Offences involving the sale to a person under the age of eighteen;
> (4) Offences committed within an educational institution, places of religious significance, or government facilities;
> (5) Offences committed through the use or threat of force;
> (6) Offences committed while in possession of or using weapons.
>
> If the commission of the offence falls under either paragraph one or paragraph two of this section and meets either of the following criteria, the offender shall be sentenced to a prison term ranging from five years to life imprisonment and a fine ranging from five hundred thousand to five million pounds or the death penalty:

52 Department of Correction of Thailand (n.d.).

53 International Covenant on Civil and Political Rights, Article 6(2); Human Rights Committee (2017, paras. 17 and 18).

54 Online reporters (2018).

55 Homicide offences comprised 81 per cent, offences against the King or the Kingdom comprised 10 per cent: Johnson and Zimring (2009, p. 403).

56 Giorgetta (2023).

57 Author's translation.

(1) Offences committed by leaders, persons in command, or persons managing criminal networks;
(2) Offences that pose a threat to the stability of the state or public safety.

One could argue that Thailand's stance on the death penalty has undergone a positive change since the enactment of the Code. Previously, the death penalty applied to the production, importation, exportation, and possession of narcotic drugs in Category 1, which are drugs causing severe harm such as heroin, or Category 2, which are drugs causing general harm such as morphine, cocaine, codeine, or medicinal opium, without the requirement that the offence be committed by a leader, person in command, or a person managing criminal networks, or that it posed a threat to state security or public safety as stipulated in the Code currently. Furthermore, the criteria under the Code that the offence be committed by a leader, person in command, or a person managing criminal networks aligns with what the 1988 United Nations Convention Against Illicit Traffic in Narcotic Drugs and Psychotropic Substances considers as 'particularly serious' drug offences.[58]

In contrast, the inclusion of the stability of the state and public safety as criteria to elevate drug offences to the level of the most serious crimes lacks any direct authority or precedents. Moreover, these criteria are broad and vague, potentially violating the principle of *lex certa*, which demands that criminal provisions be precisely defined. The precise threshold or extent of production, importation, exportation, sale, or possession of illicit drugs that would impact the stability of the state or the security of the people is unclear. The Constitutional Court of Thailand has emphasised the requirement of legal certainty, asserting that citizens must be able to understand which behaviours are prohibited.[59] It is well recognised that a degree of flexibility is acceptable as long as citizens can ascertain the boundaries of the criminal law. However, the terms 'stability of the state' and 'public safety' are beyond the margin of flexibility. A similar term, 'substantial economic loss', is employed in section 135/1 of the Thailand Penal Code concerning offences related to terrorism. The interpretation of what constitutes a 'substantial' economic loss has yielded divergent rulings, as seen in cases

[58] United Nations Convention Against Illicit Traffic in Narcotic Drugs and Psychotropic Substances 1988, Article 3(5). However, this is not to suggest that the death penalty is supported by any of the international drug control conventions, refer to the United Nations Office on Drugs and Crime (2016).

[59] The Constitutional Court Judgment No. 4/2559 (2016).

involving riots and the destruction of department stores and residential areas in Bangkok in 2010, raising questions about whether such acts qualify as terrorism. The civil court's rulings in cases 4326/2554 (2011) and 1212/2555 (2012) determined that burning down a major department store in the centre of Bangkok did not constitute a substantial economic loss; therefore, it was not considered a terrorist act. Conversely, the Southern Bangkok Civil Court, in case 1007/2554 (2010), ruled that the act of burning down department stores following a riot was carried out for political impact, thereby classifying it as a terrorist act. These contrasting judgments highlight the complexities and challenges in interpreting and applying the law, underscoring the need for clear guidelines and consistent legal standards. It is, therefore, doubtful if section 145, paragraph three (2) is in compliance with the international law.[60]

The second concern is the 'death row phenomenon' where inmates wait for an inordinate length of time pending their execution. Since 61 per cent of death penalty inmates are convicted of drug offences,[61] it can be expected that the availability of the death penalty in the Code will exacerbate the phenomenon.

Various courts around the world have recognised that a prolonged period on death row constitutes cruel, inhuman or degrading treatment where the delay is attributable to the State. Protection from cruel, inhuman or degrading treatment is enshrined in Article 7 of the International Covenant on Civil and Political Rights[62] as well as in Article 28, paragraph four of Thailand's Constitution. There are different ways to determine when the protection is violated. One way is to use a fixed period of time spent on death row, beyond which will be considered cruel or inhuman treatment;[63] while another way is to adopt a multifactorial approach based on not just the time spent on its own but also other considerations such as the conditions on death row,[64] and the inmate's age and mental state at the time of the offence.[65]

[60] International Covenant on Civil and Political Rights, Arts. 6(2) and 15.

[61] See note 52.

[62] Thailand acceded to the International Covenant on Civil and Political Rights on 29 October 1996.

[63] Refer to, for example, *Pratt and Morgan v. The Attorney General for Jamaica and another (Jamaica)* [1993] UKPC 1; *Henfield v. Attorney General of the Commonwealth of The Bahamas; Farrington v. The Minister of Public Safety and Immigration and Others* [1996] UKPC 4; *Attorney General v. Susan Kigula & 417 Ors* (Constitutional Appeal No. 3 of 2006) [2009] UGSC 6.

[64] *Soering v. the United Kingdom* (1989) (Application No. 14038/88) para. 107.

[65] Ibid, para.111.

It is not the intention of this chapter to argue which approach is better in dealing with the death row phenomenon. Both approaches have their own difficulties. Nor is it intended to say that prison conditions in Thailand need to be improved to meet international standards. However, if Thailand wishes to retain the death penalty and yet abide by international norms, it would have to confront the issue of the death row phenomenon. As pointed out in *Cox v. Canada*:[66]

> ... imposing rigid time limits for the conclusion of all appeals and requests for clemency is dangerous and may actually work against the person on death row by accelerating the execution of the sentence of death. It is generally in the interest of the petitioner to remain alive for as long as possible. Indeed, while avenues of appeal remain open, there is hope, and most petitioners will avail themselves of these possibilities, even if doing so entails continued uncertainty. This is a dilemma inherent in the administration of justice within all those societies that have not yet abolished capital punishment.

9.4 Conclusion

In conclusion, while the new drug laws in Thailand have made important advances, it is important to address the remaining challenges. By tackling issues related to transitional legislation, ensuring equitable application of penalties, reviewing excessively harsh punishments, promoting legal professionals' understanding of the law, providing adequate resources for treatment and rehabilitation, and involving the community, the new legislation can have a truly positive impact.

Overall, the new drug law in Thailand demonstrates a progressive approach to dealing with drug users, moving away from punitive measures towards a more compassionate and rehabilitative approach. This shift aligns with international best practices, humanises individuals struggling with illicit drug use, and addresses the underlying causes of the problem. It fosters a healthier society and promotes sustainable solutions to the nation's drug issues.

Furthermore, the Narcotics Code makes a notable change in the application of the death penalty by introducing additional criteria for its imposition. However, the lack of clear definitions of the criteria may still render Thai law inconsistent with international standards. There is

[66] *Cox v. Canada*, Communication No. 539/1993, U.N. Doc. CCPR/C/52/D/539/19930 (1994), concurring opinion of Kurt Herndl and Waleed Sadi.

also a need to tackle the potential problem of the death row phenomenon in Thailand so long as the death penalty is retained.

References

Chongcharoen, P. (2023) '50 Million Meth Pills Seized, Couple Arrested' *Bangkok Post* (13 December). www.bangkokpost.com/thailand/general/2704604/50-million-meth-pills-seized-couple-arrested.

Degenhardt, L., Chiu, W. T., Sampson, N., Kessler, R. C., Anthony, J. C., Angermeyer, M., Bruffaerts, R., de Girolamo, G., Gureje, O., Huang, Y., Karam, A., Kostyuchenko, S., Lepine, J. P., Mora, M. E., Neumark, Y., Ormel, J. H., Pinto-Meza, A., Posada-Villa, J., Stein, D. J., Takeshima, T. and Wells, J. E. (2008) 'Toward a Global View of Alcohol, Tobacco, Cannabis, and Cocaine Use: Findings from the WHO World Mental Health Surveys' 5(7) *PLoS Medicine* e141. https://journals.plos.org/plosmedicine/article?id=10.1371%2Fjournal.pmed.0050141.

Department of Correction of Thailand. (n.d.) *Statistics About Death Penalty*. www.correct.go.th/executed/filepdf/1706085243.pdf.

Dickinson, D. (2023) 'Thailand: Moving from Punishment to Treatment of People Who Use Drugs' *UN News* (25 June). https://news.un.org/en/story/2023/06/1137927.

Editorial. (2023) 'The Fight Against Drugs' *Bangkok Post* (19 September). www.bangkokpost.com/opinion/opinion/2649362/the-fight-against-drugs.

Giorgetta, A. (2023) 'Time to Ditch the Death Penalty' *Bangkok Post* (10 October). www.bangkokpost.com/opinion/opinion/2661008/time-to-ditch-the-death-penalty.

Human Rights Committee. (2017) *Concluding Observations on the Second Periodic Report of Thailand* (CCPR/C/THA/CO/2). www.ohchr.org/en/documents/concluding-observations/ccprcthaco2-concluding-observations-second-periodic-report.

Human Rights Watch. (2008) *Thailand's 'War on Drugs'*. www.hrw.org/news/2008/03/12/thailands-war-drugs.

Johnson, D. T. and Zimring, F. E. (2009) *The Next Frontier: National Development, Political Change and the Death Penalty in Asia* (Oxford: Oxford University Press).

Laohong, K. O. (2022) 'Drug Code Sows Cannabis Confusion' *Bangkok Post* (19 January). www.bangkokpost.com/thailand/general/2249635/drug-code-sows-cannabis-confusion.

Muntarbhorn, V. (2021) 'Slowly Moving Away from the Death Penalty' *Bangkok Post* (22 April). www.bangkokpost.com/opinion/opinion/2103711/slowly-moving-away-from-the-death-penalty.

Online reporters. (2018) "Majority Want Continued Enforcement of Death Penalty: Nida Poll' *Bangkok Post* (24 June). www.bangkokpost.com/thailand/general/1491530/majority-want-continued-enforcement-of-death-penalty-nida-poll.

Peter, Z. (2022) 'Thailand's Legalization of Cannabis Sparks Health Concerns, Confusion' *Voice of America* (22 June). www.voanews.com/a/thailand-s-legalization-of-cannabis-sparks-health-concerns-confusion/6627940.html.

Saksornchai, J. (2023) 'Thai Police Say Drug Bust Nets Methamphetamine, Crystal Meth and Heroin Worth $8.2 Million' *Associated Press* (28 September). https://apnews.com/article/drugs-thailand-police-crystal-methamphetamine-heroin-myanmar-cd590bdc548de7564eb5c38fe79ea410.

Thepgumpanat, P. and Wongcha-um, P. (2024) 'Thailand to Ban Recreational Cannabis Use by Year-End, Health Minister Says' *Reuters* (29 February). www.reuters.com/world/asia-pacific/thailand-ban-recreational-cannabis-use-by-year-end-says-health-minister-2024-02-29/.

United Nations Office on Drugs and Crime. (2016) *Statement by the UNODC Executive Director on the Recent Executions in Indonesia* (29 July). www.unodc.org/unodc/en/press/releases/2016/July/statement-by-the-unodc-executive-director-on-the-recent-executions-in-indonesia.html.

World Population Review. (n.d.) *Incarceration Rates by Country 2023*. https://worldpopulationreview.com/country-rankings/incarceration-rates-by-country.

Yukhnenko, D., Farouki, L. and Fazel, S. (2023) 'Criminal Recidivism Rates Globally: A 6-Year Systemic Review Update' 88 *Journal of Criminal Justice*102115.

10

The Undercurrent of the Death Penalty for Drug Trafficking in Southeast and East Asia for Abolitionist States

The Case of Hong Kong

KAREN JOE-LAIDLER AND KATE LOWE

10.1 Southeast Asia Penal Responses: Drugs, Death Penalty, and Imprisonment

Globally, illicit drug production and trafficking are rising annually, and illicit drug markets are becoming more diverse and complex in terms of size, product, and logistics. The trafficking of illicit drugs within East and Southeast Asia is at record levels, with quantities and types of drugs increasing within and around Thailand, Laos, and Myanmar, areas historically known as the 'golden triangle' and associated with opium production.[1] According to the United Nations Office of Drugs and Crime's latest regional report, this growth has largely involved synthetic drugs, particularly methamphetamine, but also ketamine and several new psychoactive substances (NPS), facilitated, in part, by the availability of related chemicals as well as the expansion of trafficking routes.[2] In response to these market shifts and increasing international concerns over the scale of trafficking, the region has held steadfast in its 'war on drugs' with some of the harshest and most punitive responses for possession, trafficking, and production globally, including the use of mandatory

This research is funded by the Hong Kong Research Grants Council's Research Impact Fund, project R7031-21.

We would like to thank Leona Li, Velda Chui, and Jack Ng Chun Wai for their assistance in the analysis and preparation of this chapter.

[1] Wojcik (2020).

[2] United Nations Office of Drugs and Crime (2023).

and minimum sentences and lengthy periods of pretrial detention.[3] East Asia includes seven countries and territories. While Hong Kong and Macau do not have the death penalty, South Korea has had a moratorium on executions since 1998. China, Taiwan, and Japan are retentionist states although the latter's is restricted to murder. North Korea is a retentionist state and executes for drug-related crimes. Although eight of the eleven countries in the Southeast Asia region retain the death penalty for drug-related crimes, Brunei and Lao People's Democratic Republic (PDR) are abolitionist in practice, having not carried out any executions in at least the past ten years. The remaining six countries are retentionist states and have the death penalty for the manufacturing, importation, and trafficking of drugs. In Lao PDR, Myanmar, and Singapore, the death penalty is mandatory for certain drug-related offences.[4]

Although data accessibility and transparency issues hinder our understanding of judicial and prison experiences within the region, we do know that the use of the death penalty, as the most punitive response to drug trafficking, has been gaining momentum. Such a focus is perhaps explained by the 'stronghold' of retentionist countries, which still actively operate the death penalty for drug offences to maintain the 'war on drugs'. The effect of the 'stronghold' has recently drawn international attention with Singapore's role (along with Iran) in reversing the decline of the use of the death penalty globally, as there was a 336 per cent increase in executions in 2021 for drug-related offences.[5] Many, if not most, of the people sentenced to death within the region for drug offences are from marginalised populations.[6] Individuals from ethnic minority backgrounds, women, foreign nationals, and members of vulnerable groups remain disproportionately affected by the imposition of the death penalty for drug offences.[7] The increase in executions illustrates that progress regarding the death penalty can often be 'fragile and often temporary'.[8] The death penalty represents what Hoyle refers to as the 'tip of the iceberg – most visible element of a broader punitive system'.[9] As countries such as Indonesia and Malaysia take pause with

[3] Hoyle (2022).
[4] Amnesty International (2023); Harm Reduction International (2023); Luong (2021).
[5] Harm Reduction International (2022).
[6] Ibid.
[7] Ibid.
[8] Ibid, p. 13.
[9] Hoyle (2022).

moratoriums on the imposition of the death penalty, increasing numbers of those convicted of trafficking face long prison sentences, including life terms.

This chapter focuses on the context and presence of the death penalty in the region in relation to abolitionist states. We are specifically concerned with the undercurrent caused by retentionist states and the 'war on drugs' on its regional abolitionist neighbours. Do the presence and deterrence ethos of retentionist states play a role in sentencing drug trafficking among abolitionist states, and to what effect? We draw on the case of Hong Kong, examining court cases as indicators of the key issues in the legal rationales and response to drug trafficking.[10] Hong Kong is an important case to consider as it is a locale which has had a historical reputation as a major international transshipment site for illicit drugs, and authorities view recent large seizures of drugs destined for elsewhere in the region as effective enforcement efforts.[11] Although many of its neighbours in the region support the death penalty, Hong Kong has not done so for quite a while. The death penalty, prescribed for murder, kidnapping resulting in murder, and piracy, was officially abolished in 1993, and the last execution was in 1965.

10.1.1 Regional Context and Trends

Discourse concerning the increase in long-term imprisonment for drug-related offences has been associated with a previous decline in the use of the death penalty, with 2020 seeing the lowest number of executions worldwide.[12] Several countries have formally or informally replaced the death penalty with life imprisonment as the harshest penalty, and death

[10] The data for this analysis are drawn from legal judgments of the Hong Kong's District Court and High Court, where drug trafficking cases, given their sentence, are normally brought. We also followed those cases which moved onto the Court of Appeal, where cases are reviewed and guidelines can be set, and the Final Court of Appeal, the highest court in Hong Kong, which considers questions of law relating to sentencing. From the Hong Kong Judiciary's online archive of judgments, reasons for verdicts, and sentences, we drew on the search terms – drug trafficking and death penalty ($n = 23$); death penalty; drug trafficking and double jeopardy ($n = 5$); and drug trafficking and death penalty ($n = 23$). After screening out duplications ($n = 3$), cases where drug trafficking was referenced but the defendant was not charged with such an offence ($n = 2$) and a case involving the defendant's claim of police intimidation (repatriation to his home country where there is the death penalty), the total number of cases for this analysis was 17.

[11] Lo (2021).

[12] Harm Reduction International (2022).

sentences have been commuted to life imprisonment.[13] An example of this is Thailand where the death penalty is no longer mandatory. Research illustrates that between 2014 and 2020, the number of people serving a life sentence has increased by 50 per cent in Thailand, further suggesting but not necessarily confirming that these two trends may be connected.[14] For those countries that retain the death penalty, research indicates that there is an increasing reluctance to carry out executions for trafficking even though formal death sentences continue to be issued.[15] Yet recently we have witnessed 'renewed vigour' for the use of the death penalty within the region, particularly in Singapore and Iran in 2021.[16] Within Southeast Asia, The Global Drug Policy Index reports that within the region, life sentences, without the possibility of parole, are 'frequently' imposed (in 16–30 per cent of cases) in Nepal and Thailand and 'very frequently' (in 41–81 per cent of cases) in Indonesia.[17] Such stark figures do not consider sentences not formally defined as life sentences, but the person is detained in prison for life. These 'de facto life sentences'[18] can arise through the application of a fixed sentence where the person is likely to die in prison, or through indeterminate detention on mental health grounds following a conviction in countries such as Hong Kong.[19]

Within the region, research indicates there has been an increase in formal life sentences for drug-related offences in certain countries, yet if we take a broader, inclusive view of all crimes, we see a regional increase in the use of both the death penalty and a rise of 46 per cent in prison populations in Asia 2021.[20] While not conclusive in rebutting or reaffirming the assumption, the statistics suggest that the penal landscape in Southeast Asia for drug-related offences may be more nuanced than originally presumed. For example, as we will note in Section 10.1.2, policies such as the use of mandatory minimum sentences across a range of drug-related offences have contributed to the growth in imprisonment.

[13] Ibid.
[14] Penal Reform International (2022).
[15] Leechaianan and Longmire (2013).
[16] Penal Reform International (2022, p. 7).
[17] The Global Drug Policy Index (2021).
[18] van Zyl Smit and Appleton (2019).
[19] Pascoe (2023).
[20] Penal Reform International (2022).

10.1.2 Mandatory Minimum Sentences for Drug-Related Offences

International non-governmental organisations (NGOs) have called for the removal of mandatory minimum sentences for drug offences within the region and globally.[21] Within East and Southeast Asia, many countries have established comparatively high mandatory minimum sentences for relatively low-level offences including drug possession and use, and life imprisonment is increasingly imposed for drug trafficking and manufacturing offences, such as in the Philippines.[22] In such circumstances, mandatory minimum sentencing enables judges to only consider the quantity and type of drug during sentencing procedures, narrowing the possibilities of mitigation through judicial discretion in sentencing. Within such legal and sentencing frameworks, cases may become oversimplified and yield an unfair and harsh penal response which does not consider coercion, drug dependence, or the experience of trauma or abuse. Research also illustrates that punitive policies are not effective in deterring crime and impact women and communities marginalised on the basis of ethnicity and race, resulting in international NGOs calling for the removal of mandatory minimum sentences for drug offences within the region and globally.[23]

10.1.3 Processes: Navigating Criminal Justice Systems Abroad

Whilst sentencing and legalisation frameworks are important in shaping prison sentences so too is a person's wider experience of the criminal justice system, such as their ability to access their rights during arrest, arraignments, pre-trial, plea bargaining, and the trial itself. Research has highlighted that, for many facing the death penalty or long prison sentences, their marginalised status in society may also impede the exercise of a person's legal rights. For example, foreign nationals may find themselves navigating a legal system within a different country, culture, and language. The lack of legal knowledge and limited understanding of the criminal justice system in which they are detained further hinder their ability to navigate the system. Foreign nationals may also

21 Penal Reform International (2019).

22 Penal Reform International (2022).

23 Eisen (2015); Penal Reform International (2019).

have limited financial means to secure bail or legal counsel, consular assistance, and little family support during detention and incarceration.[24]

10.2 Hong Kong's Legal Response to Drug Trafficking

Unlike many of its neighbouring countries, Hong Kong does not have the death penalty. Yet its legal response is framed within the broader prohibitionist drug policy and consistent with the generally punitive approach within the region.[25] Hong Kong lies within a region in which a significant number of countries continue to actively operate the death penalty for drug trafficking. The courts have noted this, and that Hong Kong also shares a border with, and is a part of, China where the death penalty is used, although the extent is not known with any degree of certainty. Such geopolitical factors shape Hong Kong's approach to sentencing traffickers. This can be witnessed in the case of *HKSAR v. Kilima Abubakar Abbas*,[26] which currently is one of the landmark precedents in drug trafficking cases and involves drug importation by a foreign national. Macrae VP described the regional context of Hong Kong in this manner:[27]

> The practice and policy of sentencing will vary from country to country. It will necessarily take into account the prevalence of the particular offence in that country, the attitudes of the general public, the culture and traditions of its people and any other economic, social and political considerations peculiar to that community. In the context of Hong Kong, sentencing practice and policy will also have to reflect the fact that this is a city with its own legal system, whilst nevertheless part of a large country with a different legal system; and it will, as a matter of comity, want to bear in mind the attitudes of its neighbours to particular crimes and the seriousness with which those crimes are regarded by its neighbours.
>
> And since in this jurisdiction we do not have the death penalty for drug trafficking, unlike almost all of our neighbours, that position is in no small measure due to our own particular policy of law enforcement, backed up by harsh, but consistent, sentencing for drug trafficking.

He went on to state that:[28]

> Many countries in this region employ the death penalty for drug trafficking and I am not at all persuaded that traffickers are unaware of that

[24] Hoyle and Harry (2020).
[25] Kong and Laidler (2020).
[26] *HKSAR v. Kilima Abubakar Abbas* [2018] HKCA 602.
[27] Ibid, pp. 28 and 29.
[28] Ibid, p. 37.

ultimate punishment in some of the countries through which they pass, or that the offence of drug trafficking carries very severe sentences of imprisonment in Hong Kong.

It is, in fact, the issue of consistency that the courts have continued to reiterate as one of the fundamental principles in sentencing of drug trafficking cases. The court has repeated in appeal cases that its sentencing guidelines provide this consistency.[29] At the same time, sentencing guidelines are not a 'straitjacket' requiring a purely mathematical approach as judges must consider not only the quantity but also assess the defendant's role and culpability.

In *HKSAR v. Herry Jane Yusup*[30] the Court of Appeal clarified the process and the principles to be adopted in sentencing drug trafficking cases. The arithmetical starting point should be calculated for a notional sentence and fall within the sentencing guidelines according to the following steps.

10.2.1 Step One: An Assessment of the Gravity of the Offence

In drug trafficking cases, judges typically assess gravity by focusing on the harm caused or created by the offence. The first step is an assessment of the type and quantity of the drug concerned and to identify the relevant guidelines.[31]

10.2.2 Step Two: An Assessment of Role and Culpability

The next step in the process of determining the appropriate sentence for drug trafficking is an assessment by the judge of the role and culpability of the defendant based on the evidence before the court. The court has identified the more common classifications of trafficking. In particular, the guidelines for trafficking in dangerous drugs are based upon

[29] See Appendix to this chapter.

[30] *HKSAR v. Herry Jane Yusuph* [2020] HKCA 974, p. 7.

[31] For sentencing guidelines, see *HKSAR v. Abdallah Anwar Abbas* [2009] 2 HKLRD 437 (an enhancement of at least 2 years is appropriate for trafficking more than 1 kg of heroin or cocaine across borders); *HKSAR v. Dewi Kartika Sari Binti Musli* [2012] HKCU 2453 (29 November 2012, unreported) (for a case involving less than 1 kg of the same drugs, the level of enhancement is at the judge's discretion); and *HKSAR v. Chung Ping Kun* [2014] HCCC 519 (2 July 2014, unreported) (introducing a three-tier guideline under which a 1–2-year enhancement is appropriate for drugs falling within the 500–1,000 g band).

categorisation as a courier or storekeeper, that is, the person who is delivering, distributing or conveying the drugs in question for a dealer; or storing the consignment of drugs on behalf of himself or someone else. However, the court is aware of the distinctions and hierarchy of roles in drug trafficking, identifying the 'actual (or direct) trafficker (often where there is evidence of equipment and large sums of cash), the manager or organiser, operator or financial controller, and the international operator or financial controller'. Those at these higher levels will face enhanced sentences.[32]

10.2.3 Step Three: Reference Bands in Guidelines

The judge will identify the relevant band of the guidelines applicable to the defendant given the circumstance of the commission of the offence and the roles of the defendant:[33]

> The offender's role in the drugs trade is, however, a highly relevant factor in deciding *at what point within the tariff* his sentence should be.

10.2.4 Step Four: Aggravating Factors

Having identified the 'notional starting point' by reference to the quantity of the dangerous drugs and the role and culpability of the defendant, the judge will then consider factors which aggravate the offence.[34] In addition to these guidelines, the courts have also established that a previous conviction for trafficking in dangerous drugs,[35] the carrying of dangerous drugs across the border or with an 'international element',[36] the dealing in more than one type of dangerous drug,[37] and the use of young persons or minors to carry or deal with dangerous drugs will justify an enhancement of the sentence.[38]

10.2.5 Step Five: Mitigating Factors

The judge will consider mitigating circumstances which will justify a discount from the normal starting point of the sentence. An example of a

[32] See details on categories in *HKSAR v. Herry Jane Yusuph* [2020] HKCA 974, pp. 33–38.
[33] *HKSAR v. Leung Kwai Ping* [2001] 4 HKC 383.
[34] *R v. Lau Tak-ming & Others* [1990] 2 HKLR 370, [1990] HKCU 399.
[35] Ibid.
[36] *HKSAR v. Abdallah Anwar Abbas* [2009] 2 HKLRD 437.
[37] Ibid.
[38] *HKSAR v. Lam Kam-kwong* [2002] 1 HKC 541.

mitigating circumstance is the tendering of a guilty plea at the earliest opportunity, in which case the court will usually award a third of a discount, although 'the one-third discount was not intended to be an impenetrable ceiling beyond which a judge cannot go if he has good reasons in the proper exercise of his discretion for doing so'.[39]

In *HKSAR v. Henry Jane Yusup* the court affirmed that other forms of mitigation should be taken into consideration before the discount for the guilty plea is considered.[40] In drug trafficking cases, judges should consider that personal circumstances will count for little unless they are exceptional, as the court emphasised in *HKSAR v. Abdallah Anwar Abbas*:[41]

> As for mitigation, the grievousness of the offence – a description that is born of the recognition of the dreadful misery caused to victims and their families and the serious harm to society generally – dictates that meaningful mitigation, apart from the plea of guilty, is rarely available.

10.2.6 Step Six: Totality

The final stage of the sentencing process is for the judge to stand back and look at the overall sentence passed to ensure that it is a fair, just, and balanced sentence in all the circumstances of the offence and the offender. Where there is more than one count or charge involved, or more than one aggravating feature justifying enhancement of the starting point, the sentencing judge must be careful that the ultimate sentence is not out of proportion to the defendant's overall criminality.

10.3 The Influence of the 'Death Penalty' in Court of Appeal Cases

In our review of cases, where the death penalty is referenced, sixteen of the seventeen defendants were foreign nationals and suggests that the protection of Hong Kong's borders from the importation of drugs and deterrence are paramount in meting out consistent and harsh punishment.[42]

[39] *HKSAR v. Herry Jane Yusuph* [2020] HKCA 974, p. 42.

[40] Ibid.

[41] *HKSAR v. Abdallah Anwar Abbas* [2009] 2 HKLRD 437, p. 19.

[42] *Secretary for Justice v. Tang King Wa* [2023] 2 HKLRD 1440 is the only case involving a local resident convicted for his role as a courier of cocaine. This case involved an appeal of the perceived leniency of a sentence to a training school given the defendant's age and circumstances. On appeal, the court reviewed the original sentence, noting the quantity of drugs and the gravity of the offence and referenced *HKSAR v. Herry Jane Yusuph* [2021] 1 HKLRD 290.

10.3.1 Protect and Deter Drug Trafficking in Hong Kong

The judiciary holds firmly to the view that drug trafficking is a serious crime with a maximum penalty of a life sentence and a Hong Kong Dollar (HKD) 5 million fine and has stated on more than one occasion that it has the 'function of denunciation, deterrence and punishment of drug traffickers' to safeguard the community[43] and protect Hong Kong and its citizens from the 'evils' of drugs.[44] The court's strict adherence to the sentencing guidelines goes beyond the issue of consistency and includes a deterrence message to those who might believe trafficking is a fast and low-risk route to making money, as underscored by McWalters J:[45]

> ... trafficking in drugs is such an evil trade. The harm these drugs cause to the societies in which they are consumed is enormous and there is the further harm, as you now feel, to the accused, their families and societies from which they come as they are often from impoverished families in third world countries. The drug trade is all about exploitation, exploitation of the consumers and exploitation of the couriers and the low-ranking people involved in it.

Cases involving the importation of drugs also indicate that such lengthy sentences serve to protect Hong Kong's borders.[46] Accordingly, Hong Kong's ability and success to control, deter, and contain drug trafficking within Hong Kong is, in part, due to 'harsh, but consistent, sentencing for drug trafficking'.[47] The judiciary has expressed confidence in this 'sentencing regime':[48]

> The one thing that has struck me, having had to consider in the past few months the trends and statistics for the seizures, arrests and convictions in respect of a wide spectrum of dangerous drugs in Hong Kong since January 2015 is that rather than being swamped by a problem which is out of control, as other countries seem to have been, the problem in Hong Kong is being steadily contained, if not, in certain respects, reduced. And since in this jurisdiction we do not have the death penalty for drug trafficking unlike almost all of our neighbours, that position is in no small measure due to our own particular policy of law enforcement, backed up by harsh, but consistent, sentencing for drug trafficking.

[43] See *HKSAR v. Nwadiuto Samuel Joseph* [2017] HKCA 64 and *HKSAR v. Herry Jane Yusuph* [2020] HKCA 974, p. 25.

[44] *HKSAR v. Raja Rajeswary P Kagasfaron* [2020] HKCFI 2981.

[45] *HKSAR v. Osisioma Emmanuel Emeka* [2011] HKCFI 1428, p. 3.

[46] *HKSAR v. Kilima Abubakar Abbas* [2018] HKCA 602, p. 9.

[47] Ibid, pp. 28–29.

[48] Ibid.

Such rationales can be frequently witnessed in the sentencing rationales for foreign nationals such as in the case of *HKSAR v. Torres Gomez Marino Enrique*.[49] In this case, a male Colombian citizen was sentenced to a fourteen-year imprisonment term for trafficking 0.60 kg of cocaine into Hong Kong. Toh J elaborated on the sentencing rationale:[50]

> It is all too common in Hong Kong these days for defendants to come from Colombia with financial difficulties and who are forced into carrying drugs to Hong Kong for the sake of repaying their debt. In some countries, very often drug traffickers get the death penalty. In Hong Kong, we visit these kind of offences with heavy sentences, and the reason is to try and deter other people who are tempted for the sake of easy money to bring drugs into Hong Kong.

More recently, in the case of *HKSAR v. Raja Rajeswary P Kagasfaron*,[51] a female Malaysian citizen was sentenced to twenty-one years and one month for trafficking 853 g of methamphetamine into Hong Kong. As Campbell-Moffat J remarked during sentencing:[52]

> You are extremely lucky, Ms Rajeswary, that you chose to traffic in dangerous drugs outside of Malaysia. You told the court you knew that it was a capital offence in your own country and yet you willingly took the risk in our jurisdiction and you must therefore suffer the consequences. There is a significant deterrent factor in sentencing international drug trafficking. It is an evil which we do not wish to encourage and cannot be seen to be undermined by lenient sentences.

Such sentiments have been raised by the prosecution against lenient sentences which might take into consideration the culpability of a defendant. In the case of *Kilima*, Macrae VP wrote:[53]

> Having noted that, in not having the death penalty as a sentence for unlawfully trafficking in dangerous drugs, the sentencing regime in Hong Kong was already less harsh than in other Southeast Asian countries, Ms Lai (the prosecuting counsel) expressed the concern that if the sentences of imprisonment imposed on couriers were to be reduced there was the risk of Hong Kong 'becoming a haven for drug traffickers'.

[49] *HKSAR v. Torres Gomez Marino Enrique* [2013] HKCFI 1653.

[50] Ibid, p. 2.

[51] *HKSAR v. Raja Rajeswary P Kagasfaron* [2020] HKCFI 2981.

[52] Ibid, p. 4.

[53] *HKSAR v. Kilima Abubakar Abbas* [2018] HKCA 602, p. 9.

This discussion has considered how the death penalty, although not operational in Hong Kong, plays a role in shaping and justifying long-term prison sentences, and notably sentences involving foreign nationals. While its presence in the judicial consciousness can perhaps be explained by the international element of the trafficking and Hong Kong's proximity to regions where capital punishment is a reality, closer inspection of judgments may suggest other factors are at play.

10.3.2 National and Regional: Being a 'Good Neighbour'

One narrative present in sentencing is that of being a 'good neighbour'. Here, the outcome is the same; it is a justification for long prison sentences for drug trafficking. Yet the narrative is slightly different in the context of the death penalty. The focus lies not locally but rather regionally, and perhaps internationally, on Hong Kong seeking to align itself with countries (neighbours) which operate harsh punitive measures in an effort to deter drug trafficking. This message of a united and committed front in fighting the 'war on drugs' goes beyond Hong Kong's borders, to the region and is a symbol for the international community. This is apparent in the case of *HKSAR v. Osisioma Emmanuel Emeka*[54] where the offender was intercepted at the Hong Kong airport with 4.75 kg of cocaine and sentenced to eighteen years and six months. McWalters J remarked in sentencing:[55]

> Because the drug trade is international, Hong Kong must do all it can to support the efforts of all countries in combating it. For some countries, punishment will involve the imposition of the death penalty and you are fortunate, indeed, that Hong Kong is not such a country. Nevertheless Hong Kong courts must show to the international community that in its punishment of drug-traffickers it is standing side-by-side with other countries in its efforts to deter persons from engaging in this trade.

10.3.3 China: 'One Country Two Systems' and a Border

Such sentencing rationales have importance in the context of Hong Kong being a Special Administrative Region of China. While the Mainland has

[54] *HKSAR v. Osisioma Emmanuel Emeka* [2011] HKCFI 1428.
[55] Ibid, p. 3.

the death penalty for drug trafficking, Hong Kong operates under its own sentencing policies within the common law system. As Macrae VP noted in *Kilima*:[56]

> Hong Kong is part of a large country with a different legal system; and it will, as a matter of comity, want to bear in mind the attitudes of its neighbours to particular crimes and the seriousness with which those crimes are regarded by its neighbours.

Hong Kong's close proximity to mainland China has played a role in courts highlighting offenders' 'near miss' with the death penalty, and emphasising how close the defendant came to being prosecuted in a jurisdiction where capital punishment operates. In the *HKSAR v. Conde Mamady*, as Lugra-Mawson DHCJ noted during sentencing:[57]

> You must have been very well aware of the dangers that you ran and the risk that if you were found you would receive a very heavy sentence. In fact, in some parts of East Asia your sentence would have been the death penalty. Had you been found 20 miles further North from Hong Kong it certainly would have been. Here we do not have death penalties. The maximum penalty for the offence you have committed is life imprisonment.

In *HKSAR v. Herico Elsa Valencia*, Line J stated just before passing a sentence of twenty-three years of imprisonment that:[58]

> [i]t is a long sentence, but those who carry drugs know the stakes that are played for, and indeed it is right to point out that if you had been stopped at the commencement of your journey, or if you had carried those drugs on back into China, in either of those other places you would have faced the death penalty.

10.4 The Death Penalty as a Tool to Convey a Consistent Message: Tough Yet Fair

The death penalty is frequently drawn upon by judges when passing a long prison sentence for drug trafficking. Its repeated mention in judgments is curious given that Hong Kong does not have capital punish-

[56] *HKSAR v. Kilima Abubakar Abbas* [2018] HKCA 602, p. 28.
[57] *HKSAR v. Conde Mamady* [2012] HKCFI 508, p. 2.
[58] *HKSAR v. Herico Elsa Valencia* [2012] HKCFI 1706, p. 2.

ment, and raises the question as to why judges reference the death penalty in neighbouring countries at this stage in the proceedings. Two trends emerge. First, the death penalty is mentioned just before or after the passing of the sentence. Such was the case in *HKSAR v. Jitsatta Chosita* who was sentenced to twenty-five years by Line J.:[59]

> For drug trafficking on this scale, the sentence has to be a very long one and it doesn't need me to say – and it is a sobering thought – that if you had done this and been caught in another country in South-East Asia, you may well have faced the death penalty.

Another example is the case of *HKSAR v. Zuberi Zuberi Mussa*[60] where the offender was sentenced to seven years imprisonment for trafficking 380 g of heroin into Hong Kong. McWalters J addressed the offender as follows:[61]

> For the reasons which you have just heard me read out, you are sentenced to 9 years' imprisonment. . .You may feel this sentence is harsh, but you will understand that in some countries you would face the death penalty.

Second, defendants at the point of sentencing are often asked by the judge to reflect on the fact that they could have been facing the death penalty. This is illustrated in Line J's comments in *HKSAR v. Nganga Halfani Abdallah*:[62]

> In the circumstances, the sentence of 15 years and 4 months is the least one I can pass consistent with the public duty I have to perform. It is a long sentence but you might just reflect on this, that if you had crossed other borders in South-East Asia you would not have been facing imprisonment. You would have been facing the death penalty. That is a sobering thought.

The reference to the death penalty in the sentencing process appears to be made frequently in cases involving foreign nationals. While the unexpressed intention of the judges can never be known with certainty, its frequency of use suggests that the death penalty is being used as a vehicle to convey a larger message and principle. Perhaps it is to encourage the offender to look upon a long prison sentence more favourably.

[59] *HKSAR v. Jitsatta Chosita* [2013] HKCFI 1658, p. 1.
[60] *HKSAR v. Zuberi Zuberi Mussa* [2012] HKCFI 1028.
[61] Ibid, p. 3.
[62] *HKSAR v. Nganga Halfani Abdallah* [2010] HKCFI 2250, p. 2.

It also suggests that the judiciary is keen to be seen as being tough on drug trafficking but also fair, just, balanced and not out of proportion to the defendants' criminality and crime committed.

Two narratives are apparent. The first is local and fuelled by a desire to protect Hong Kong from becoming a 'safe haven' for drug traffickers in view of the absence of the death penalty. This is to be achieved through consistently giving long prison sentences for trafficking. The second is regional and global, with Hong Kong as a key part of the international community 'standing side-by-side' in the fight against the international drug trade and consistently giving long-term prison sentences to demonstrate such a commitment. Underpinning both narratives is a message of deterrence through harsh and consistent sentencing. Increasingly caught in this punitive policy in Hong Kong are foreign nationals. Yet there are also more local legal issues at play, too, in increasing the prison sentence of foreign nationals in Hong Kong which mirror the trends that research studies have illustrated in other neighbouring regions.

10.5 Conclusion

While the death penalty for drug trafficking remains a key issue for the region, it is also the case that long-term prison sentences are increasing. Our review of the legal responses and sentencing practices in Hong Kong underscores how the presence of the death penalty in the region plays an important role in legitimating long prison sentences in general, and in abolitionist states in particular. Its salience appears to be drawn upon and clearly articulated in cases involving foreign nationals. Emphasis is placed on the leniency of an abolitionist state. While consistency, proportionality and deterrence appear as the main justifications for strict and long sentences, ever-present is the reminder of the borders – to protect those within and to be situated in the larger regional 'war on drugs'.

References

Amnesty International. (2023) *Amnesty International Global Report: Death Sentences and Executions 2022.* www.amnesty.org/en/documents/act50/6548/2023/en/.

Eisen, L. B. (2015) 'Mandatory Minimum Sentences – Time to End Counterproductive Policy' *Brennan Centre for Justice* (9 June). www.brennancenter.org/our-work/analysis-opinion/mandatory-minimum-sentences-time-end-counterproductive-policy.

Harm Reduction International. (2022) *The Death Penalty for Drug Offences: Global Overview 2021*. https://hri.global/flagship-research/death-penalty/the-death-penalty-for-drug-offences-global-overview-2021/.

(2023) *The Death Penalty for Drug Offenses: Global Overview 2022*. https://hri.global/wp-content/uploads/2023/03/HRI_DeathPenalty_Report2022_REV.pdf.

Hoyle, C. (2022) *Dealing with Punishment: Risks and Rewards in Indonesia's Illicit Drug Trade* (London: The Death Penalty Project).

Hoyle, C. and Harry, L. (2020) 'Compounded Vulnerability: Foreign National Women and the Death Penalty in Southeast Asia' 40 *Amicus Journal* 15.

Kong, T. S. K. and Laidler, K. J. (2020) 'The Paradox for Chem-Fun and Gay Men: A Neoliberal Analysis of Drugs and HIV/AIDS Policies in Hong Kong' 52(1) *Journal of Psychoactive Drugs* 77.

Leechaianan, Y. and Longmire, D. R. (2013) 'The Use of the Death Penalty for Drug Trafficking in the United States, Singapore, Malaysia, Indonesia and Thailand: A Comparative Legal Analysis' 2(2) *Laws* 115.

Lo, C. (2021) 'Hong Kong Seizes Record HK$2.2 Billion Worth of Narcotics in 2020 as COVID-19 Forces Syndicates to Send Drugs by Air Cargo' *South China Morning Post* (30 January). www.scmp.com/news/hong-kong/law-and-crime/article/3119919/hong-kong-seizes-record-hk22-billion-worth-narcotics.

Luong, H. T. (2021) 'Why Vietnam Continues to Impose the Death Penalty for Drug Offences: A Narrative Commentary' 88 *International Journal of Drug Policy* 103043.

Pascoe, D. (2023) 'Life Imprisonment in Hong Kong' in van Zyl Smit, D., Appleton, C. and Vucong, G. (eds.) *Life Imprisonment in Asia* (Singapore: Palgrave Macmillan).

Penal Reform International. (2019) *Global Prison Trends* (London: Penal Reform International).

(2022) *Global Prison Trends 2022* (London: Penal Reform International).

The Global Drug Policy Index. (2021) *The Global Drug Policy Index 2021*. https://globaldrugpolicyindex.net/wp-content/themes/gdpi/uploads/GDPI%202021%20Report%20EN.pdf.

United Nations Office of Drugs and Crime. (2023) *Synthetic Drugs in East and Southeast Asia: Latest Developments and Challenges*. www.unodc.org/roseap/uploads/documents/Publications/2023/Synthetic_Drugs_in_East_and_Southeast_Asia_2023.pdfch_10_foot_5.

Van Zyl Smit, D. and Appleton, C. (2019) *Life Imprisonment: A Global Human Rights Analysis* (Cambridge: Harvard University Press).

Wojcik, J. (2020) 'Southeast Asia Has a Synthetic Drug Problem China Has Key Stake in Fixing It' *Oxford Political Review* (15 August). https://oxfordpoliticalreview.com/2020/08/15/southeast-asia-has-a-synthetic-drug-problem-china-has-key-stake-in-fixing-it/.

Appendix

Sentencing guidelines for drug offences

Drug	Quantity of drug involved	Tariff	Cases
Heroin and Cocaine	Up to 10 g	2–5 years	(a) *The Queen v. Lau Tak-ming* [1990] HKCA 96 – for heroin (b) *AG v. Pedro Nel Rojas* [1994] HKCA 54 as read with (a) – for cocaine (c) *HKSAR v. Abdallah Anwar Abbas* [2009] HKCA 115
	10–50 g	5–8 years	
	50–200 g	8–12 years	
	200–400 g	12–15 years	
	400–600 g	15–20 years	
	600–1,200 g	20–23 years	
	1,200–4,000 g	23–26 years	
	4,000–15,000 g	26–30 years	
	Over 15,000 g	At the court's discretion	
Ice (methamphetamine)	Up to 10 g	3–7 years	*HKSAR v. Tam Yi-chun* [2014] HKCA 279; *HKSAR v. Abdallah Anwar Abbas* [2009] HKCA 115
	10–70 g	7–11 years	
	70–300 g	11–15 years	
	300–600 g	15–20 years	
	600–1,200 g	20–23 years	
	1,200–4,000 g	23–26 years	
	4,000–15,000 g	26–30 years	
	Over 15,000 g	At the court's discretion	

(*cont.*)

Drug	Quantity of drug involved	Tariff	Cases
Ketamine and Ecstasy	Up to 1 g	Within the court's	*Secretary for Justice v. Hii Siew-cheng* [2008]
(3,4-methylenedioxymethampheta	1–10 g	discretion	HKCA 197; *HKSAR v. Wong Yat-san* [2008]
mine (MDMA))	10–50 g	2–4 years	HKCA 200
	50–300 g	4–6 years	
	600–1,200 g	6–9 years	
	300–600 g	9–12 years	
	Over 1,000 g	12–14 years	
		14 years upwards	
Cannabis resin	Under 2,000 g	Up to 16 months	*The Queen v. Tuen Shui-ming* [1995] HKCA 36
	Over 2,000 g	16–24 months	(herbal cannabis – a discount of up to a year
	Over 3,000 g	24–36 months	of similar amount of cannabis resin)
	Over 6,000 g	36–48 months	(cannabis oil – an increase of at least a year of
	Over 9,000 g	4 years upwards	similar amount of cannabis resin)
Methaqualone (powder)	Under 500 g	As the court thinks	*The Queen v. Chan Chi-man* [1986] HKCA 15
	Over 500 g	fit	
	Over 1,000 g	6–12 months	
	Over 2,000 g	12–24 months	
	Over 3,000 g	2–3 years	
	Over 6,000 g	3–4½ years	
	Over 9,000 g	4½–6 years	
		6 years upwards	

Methaqualone (tablet)	Up to 2,000 tablets	As the court thinks	*The Queen v. Chan Chi-man* [1986] HKCA 15
	Over 2,000 tablets	fit	
	Over 4,000 tablets	6–12 months	
	Over 8,000 tablets	12–24 months	
	Over 12,000 tablets	2–3 years	
	Over 24,000 tablets	3–4½ years	
	Over 36,000 tablets	4½–6 years	
		6 years upwards	
Morphine and barbiturates	Up to 30 g	2–3 years	*The Queen v. Chan Chi-ming* [1979] HKCA 25– for morphine and barbiturates
	30–150 g	3–5 years	
	150–1,000 g	5–8 years	
	Over 1,00 g	8–12 years	
Opium	Under 500 g	As the court thinks	*The Queen v. Lau Yiu-nam* [1986] HKCA 88
	Over 500 g	fit	
	Over 1,000 g	6–12 months	
	Over 2,000 g	12–24 months	
	Over 3,000 g	2–3 years	
		3 years upwards	

INDEX

acts of merit, 26
  penalties, and, 27
  subsequent to commission of offence, 27
Agensi Antidadah Kebangsaan (AADK), 168
  Director General, appointment of, 180
  education and rehabilitation, 175, 180–181
  establishment, 174
  harm reduction strategy, 181
  law enforcement, 180
  mission statement, 181
aggravating circumstances
  China, 24
  Hong Kong, 253
Amnesty International, 83, 111
appeals
  death penalty, 254
  right to appeal, 129
Association of Southeast Asian Nations (ASEAN), 167
  anti-drug education, 173
  Declaration of Principles to Combat the Abuse of Narcotics Drugs, 188
  war on drugs, 137, 173
Atma Jaya Catholic University, 143

Badan Narkotika Nasional (BNN, National Narcotics Board), 168
  establishment, 175–176
  founding purposes, 176, 182
  functions and powers, 181
  independence, 182
  law enforcement, 182
  organisational structure, 182
  rehabilitation and treatment programmes, 182
Bangladesh, 139
  war on drugs, 9
Barisan Nasional, 119
Belmonte, Kit, 209
black market, 3
Brunei, 168, 247
Bumiputera, 118
  London Dawn Raid, 120
  special privileges and affirmative action programmes, 119
burden of proof
  Death Penalty Evidence Rules (China), 45
  Iran, 70–72
  possession and knowledge, 94
  Provisions on Eliminating Illegally Obtained Evidence (China), 45
  reasonable doubt, 45

Cambodia, 168
caning, 138
cannabis, 2
  cannabis mixture, 99–101
  decriminalisation, 4, 88, 137, 174, 225, 230
  generational change in attitudes, 88
  Singaporean swimming team, 88
Castro, France, 209
Catholic Bishops Conference of the Philippines (CBCP), 208
  Task Force, membership of, 208
Central Narcotics Bureau (CNB), 168
  anti-drug education, and, 177
  Director, appointment of, 178

establishment, 173
functions and powers, 177–178
original organisational structure, 177
other agencies, relationship with, 178
China, 10–11
Adjudication Committee, role of, 37
death penalty, 1, 6, 9–10, 21–23, 247
burden of proof, 48
knowledge of presence of drugs, 40–44
most heinous criminals, redefining, 23–36
purity of drugs, 38–40
restriction and reduction of, 48
threshold quantities, 36–38
drug mules, 31–34
drug smugglers, 24
habitual offenders, 24
ICCPR, and, 4
judicial reform, 49
organised crime, 24
professional drug traffickers, 24
recidivists, 24
rule of law, 49
searches and arrests, resisting, 24
sentencing guidelines, 11
Strike Hard anti-crime campaign, *See* Strike Hard anti-crime campaign
trafficking, 7
circumstantial evidence
use of, 46
class
colonial rubber plantations, 115–117
Malaysian ghettos, 121–124
postcolonial rubber plantations, 117–121
class-based grievances, 113
Coalition Against the Death Penalty (CADP)
establishment, 207
first-hand sources of information, 212
Task Force, membership of, 208
Commission on Human Rights of the Philippines (CHRP), 205, 217
counter-narratives, 210–211
Duterte, relationship with, 206
establishment, 206
funding, 213
resources and influence, 206
Right to Life Network, 210
Task Force, membership of, 208, 212
The Right to Life, 210
competence, 62
selection of judges, 63–64
confessions
miscarriage of justice, and, 73
retraction of, 65, 74
use of
Iran, 65, 71–72, 74
constitutive theory of rights, 113
Corruption Eradication Commission (KPK), 182
criminal justice
navigating the system, 250
strategies, 3
cultivation
personal use, for, 2

Dalian Conference Summary 2008, 24
aggravating circumstances, 25
knowledge of presence of drugs, 40–42
mitigating circumstances, 26–35
purity of drugs, 38–40
types of offenders, 23
de la Rosa, Ronald, 217
death penalty, 5–6, 260, *See also by country*
abolition of, 138, 171
accessibility and transparency issues, 247
appeals, 254
burden of proof, 48
deterrence, and, 84–86
drug offending, and, 1
drug-related crime, impact on, 5
good neighbour narrative, 257
judicial tool, as, 258–260
litigation, 86
long term imprisonment, and, 248
retentionist and abolitionist states, 247–248
serious crimes and, 4
state power, and, 205
UNODC on, 5

death row, 6
  death row phenomenon, 129, 242
  drug couriers/mules, *See* drug couriers/mules
  Indonesia, *See* Indonesia
  Malaysia, *See* Malaysia
  probationary death sentence, 89
  Thailand, 239
decriminalisation, 3
  cannabis
    Thailand, 4, 88, 137, 174, 225, 230
  medical cannabis, 88
  minor drug possession, 180
  recreational cannabis, 88
delay
  right to be tried without, 129
detention
  drug users, 137
  rehabilitative, 180
deterrence, 260
  death penalty and, 84–86
  punitive polices, and, 250
  rational-choice theory, 135
  restrictive, 85
  sentencing role of, 255–257
  studies on, 135
  theory, 135
drug couriers/mules, 6
  burden of proof, 32
  China, 31–34
  death row, on, 113
  innocent carriers, 114, 126
  marginalised and vulnerable people, 33, 111
  socioeconomic social status, consideration of, 126
drug crime
  agency, and, 145
  case study sample, 144–145
  colonial history, impact of, 138
  control, focus on, 171
  economic motivations, 149–152, 156
  Malaysian ghettos, 121–124
  marginalised and vulnerable people, 33, 111, 139, 146–149, 247
  pathways, 145–146, 152–155
  personal motivations, 146, 156
  recruitment, 153
  relational motivations, 146, 152–156
  research design, 143–144
  social conditions, 146–149, 156
drug offences
  public safety, 241
  stability of the state, 241
drug offenders
  recidivism, 226
  unique circumstances, 233
drug policy
  national, *See* national drug policy
drug production
  statistics, 136
Duterte, Rodrigo, 205
  anti-death penalty movement, and, 206–209, 213
  authoritarian power, 205
    countering, 214–215
  CHRP, relationship with, 206
  death penalty, 200–202, 217
    scholarship, 202–203
  drug policy discourse, 209
  human rights, 206
  war on drugs, 8–9, 187

East Timor, 204
evidence
  collection of, 47
  conclusive and sufficient, 45
  Sharia-based evidentiary requirements, 71
extradition, 2
extrajudicial killings, 8, 189, 201, 208, 225
  state-sanctioned, 8, 186

Free Legal Assistance Group (FLAG), 202, 217
  death row inmates, 213
  functions and powers, 207
  funding, 213
  information campaigns, 215
  legal assistance, 211

Global Drug Policy Index, 249
global war on drugs, 3–4
Golden Triangle, 136, 139, 173, 246
group-differentiated rights theory, 112–114

Guangdong, 11, 22, 36, 50
Guangxi, 36, 47

Hasina, Sheikh, 9
Henan, 36
Hindraf (Hindu Rights Action Force) 2007, 113, 122
Hong Kong
  abolition of death penalty, 9–10, 14
  China, relationship to, 257–258
  death penalty, 247
  trafficking, legal response to, 251–252
    aggravating factors, 253
    gravity of offence, 252
    guidelines, 253
    mitigating factors, 253
    role and culpability, 252
    totality, 254
Hubei, 36, 50
human rights, 155
  abuses, 138
  jus cogens, 55
  violations, 1

iDefend, 208
impartiality, 62
independence
  institutional guarantees, 63
  judicial, 62
Indonesia, 135, 139, 168
  Badan Narkotika Nasional (BNN, National Narcotics Board), *See* Badan Narkotika Nasional (BNN, National Narcotics Board)
  case study sample, 144–145
  death penalty, 1, 7, 9–10, 89, 175, 189, 247
  death row, 12
  extrajudicial killing, 187
  harm reduction approaches, 6
  life imprisonment, 249
  methadone programme, 190
  prison overcrowding, 137
  probationary death sentence, 89
  research design, 143–144
  war on drugs, 9, 139–143, 155
input legitimacy
  definition, 62
International Commission of Jurists, 209, 215
International Covenant on Civil and Political Rights (ICCPR), 73
  fair and public hearing, 64, 128
  international normative standard, as, 55–56
  judicial independence, 62
  public judgments, 68
  torture, use of, 65
international drug policy, 156
  treaties, 1–3, 168, 173, 185
investitive criteria, 113
Iran, 11
  appeals, 66
  death penalty, 1, 5, 9–11, 56, 247, 249
    judicial discretion, 74
    restriction and reduction of, 73
  execution statistics, 60–61
  fair and public hearing, 64–66
  fair trial guarantees, 11
  hudud offences, 70
  ICCPR, ratification of, 55–56
  independence and selection of judges, 63–64
  judicial discretion, 74
  Law for Combating Illicit Drugs, *See* Law for Combating Illicit Drugs (Iran)
  most serious crimes, defining, 56–57
  Revolutionary Court, 64
    judgments, brevity of, 68–70
  torture, use of, 65

Jahanabadi, Jalil Rahimi, 67
Japan, 247
joint crime
  criminal responsibility, determination of, 34
  principals and accomplices, 34–35
judgment
  access to, 68

Kampung Medan, 121
  race riots (2001), 121
Khomeini, Ayatollah, 64

Klang Strikes (1941), 113, 116
knowledge
  wilful blindness, 94–97
Kraivichien, Thanin, 174
Kratom (*Mitragyna speciosa*), 230
Kunming, 37

Lagman, Edcel, 209
Lao PDR, 247
Laos, 139, 168, 246
Law for Combating Illicit Drugs (Iran)
  2017 amendment, 57–60
    impact of, 60–61
Lee Kuan Yew, 174, 184
legal rights
  group-differentiated rights theory, *See* group-differentiated rights theory
legitimacy
  definition, 53
  empirical, 53
  input. *See* input legitimacy
  normative. *See* normative legitimacy
  output. *See* output legitimacy
  state institutions, 72
Li Xiao, 49
London Dawn Raid, 120

Macau, 247
Mahathir Mohamad, 175, 180, 184
Makabayan (Nationalist) Bloc, 209
Makatao (Humane), 209
Malaysia, 168
  1971 New Economic Policy, 112
  1990 National Development Policy, 112
  Agensi Antidadah Kebangsaan (AADK). *See* Agensi Antidadah Kebangsaan (AADK)
  Bar Council Legal Aid Centre, 129
  corporal punishment, 185
  death penalty, 1, 7, 9–10, 89, 112, 138, 247
    abolition of, 90, 129–130, 138, 187, 189, 205
  death row, 12, 111, 122–123, 130
  demographics, 111
  double presumption rule, 112, 114, 125–128
    self-incrimination, and, 129
  drug control legislation, 174
  fair trial rights, 127–129, 131
  ICCPR, and, 4
  independence from colonial rule, 117
  Indian agricultural/indentured labour, 113, 115
  kangany system of recruitment, 115
  labour movement (1940s), 116
  legal aid schemes, 128
  marginalisation of Indian ethnic minority, 12
  National Development Policy (NDP), 120
  National Legal Aid Foundation, 129
  New Economic Policy (NEP), 118–119
  palm oil industry, 120
  postcolonial multicultural milieu, 118
  racial equality, 117
  racial politics, 118
  trafficking, 7
  war on drugs, 12, 125
Malaysian Indians, 112
  anti-caste and anti-colonial movement, 117
  colonial rubber plantations, 115–117
  double discrimination, 114
  drug-related offences, 124
  ghettos, 121–124
  historical origins, 112
  language difficulties, 128
  Malaysian Indian Congress (MIC) Blueprint (1974), 119
  marginalisation, 130
  NDP, and, 120
  NEP, and, 119
  non-rights bearer group, as, 114
  postcolonial rubber plantations, 117–121
  racial stigmatisation, 121
  victims of deaths in custody, 122
mandatory sentencing, 1
Marcos, Ferdinand, 200, 202
Marcos, Ferdinand Jr., 217

medical treatment
  controlled substances, 229
mitigating circumstances
  China, 24
  Hong Kong, 253
Mitnick, Eric, 112–114
Mohseni-Ejei, Gholamhossein, 63
Myanmar, 36–37, 139, 141, 151, 160, 168, 246

Narcotics Addiction Treatment and Rehabilitation Committee
  functions and powers, 228
Narcotics Commission
  functions and powers, 228
Narcotics Control Board (NCB), 178, 228
  authority, 228
  drug research, 231
Narcotics Suppression Bureau (NSB), 179
national drug policy
  agencies, 167–170
  law enforcement, and, 170–172, 176
  non-state actors, 13
  politics, and, 13
  priorities, setting, 171
  self-interest, role of, 171
National Human Rights Institution (NHRI), 206
National Intelligence Coordination Agency (Badan Koordinasi Intelijen Negara - BAKIN), 176
national narcotics agencies, 13, 167–170
  bureaucratic bodies, as, 188
  capital punishment, 185–187, 190
  common themes, 183–185
  functions and powers, 176–185
  future directions, 189
  historical background, 172–176
  law enforcement bodies, cooperation with, 184
  legislative regulation, 184
  ministerial or presidential appointments, 184
  mission confusion, 172
  multidimensional role, 188
  national health ministries, working with, 187
  organisational missions, 172
  politics, and, 183
  scholarship, 170–172
National Narcotics Coordinating Board (Badan Koordinasi Narkotika Nasional - BKNN), 176
Nepal, 249
network theory, 204
networked governance, 13, 203, 217
  analytical framework, 203–205
  data, 205
  force multiplier, 211
new drugs, 30
Nixon, Richard, 8
NoBox Philippines Foundation
  harm reduction, focus on, 212
  Task Force, partnership with, 208, 211
non-rights bearer group, 112, 131
  creation of, 113
normative legitimacy
  death penalty, and, 53–54
  ICCPR as international standard, 55–56
North Borneo, 118
North Korea, 247

offenders
  joint crime, *See* joint crime
  motivations, 1, 13
  types of, 24
Office of the Narcotics Control Board (ONCB). 168
  establishment, 173
  extrajudicial killing schemes, 186
  functions and powers, 178–179
  law enforcement, 179
  narcotics policy implementation, 179
  other agencies, relationship with, 179
output legitimacy
  definition, 62
  reasoned judgments, 68–70
  standard of proof, 70–72
  transparency, 66–68

Pakistan
  death penalty, 7
Patto, Kasthuriraani, 123

Permodalan Nasional Berhad, 120
Philippine Jesuit Prison Service Task Force, membership of, 208
Philippines, 139, 168, 187
  anti-death penalty movement, 206–209
    abuse of power, countering, 214–215
    dominant state narratives, countering, 209–211
    funding, 213
    information and expertise, sharing, 211–213
    leadership from below, 215–216
  Anti-Death Penalty Task Force, 208
    counter narratives, 211
  death penalty, 200
    abolition of, 9–10, 13, 200
    politics, and, 202
    reinstatement, 202
    scholarship, 202–203
  Option for Life seminars, 212
  prison overcrowding, 137
  sentencing trends, 250
  war on drugs, 1, 201, 207
possession
  definition, 91
  knowledge, and, 94–97
  legislative reform in Thailand, 228–231
  mens rea, 91–94
  personal use, for, 2
  safe-keeping defence, 97–99
poverty
  drug crime, and, 13, 60, 73, 139, 142, 147, 149, 151
  feminisation of, 139
  NEP and eradication of, 119
  socioeconomic disparities in Malaysia, 113
  urban, 120, 122
  war on drugs, and, 6
precursor chemicals
  manufacture and distribution, 2
presumption of innocence
  drug trafficking laws, 114, 128
procedural rights, 1
proceeds of crime
  confiscation, 2
public education campaigns, 215
public health initiatives, 8
punishment
  threat of, 3
purchase
  personal use, for, 2
purity of drugs
  China, 38–40
    cost of testing, 30

quantity of drugs
  additional crimes, confessing to, 28
  cannabis dual charging practice, 100
  first-time drug offender, 31
  intent, inferring, 231
  market value, and, 30
  procedural irregularities, 47
  purity, considerations of, 28–30
  threshold, raising the, 36–38, 73
  undercover enticement, and, 30

race
  colonial rubber plantations, 115–117
  Malaysian ghettos, 121–124
  postcolonial rubber plantations, 117–121
race-based grievances, 113
racial discrimination
  drug offences, and, 101–103
rational-choice theory, 135
reasonable doubt
  circumstantial evidence, and, 46
  elements, 45
  types of evidence, 70
  wilful blindness, 96
recreational drug use, 12
  decriminalisation, and, 88
  Singapore, 103
re-examination
  application for, 29
  authority, 29
rehabilitation, 123, 187, 228, 235, 243
  drug treatment facility, 8, 25, 239
  drug users, 6, 173, 177, 185, 189–190, 243
  national narcotics agencies, 168, 172, 174–176, 179–181

patients rather than offenders, 227, 236–238
prioritising, 233
recidivism, and, 226
remorse, and, 140
right to legal counsel, 64
risk environment, 149
drug use, 154
risk individualisation, 145–146

Sabah, 117–118
Sarawak, 117–118
scheduled drugs, 2
self-incrimination
privilege against, 129
right against, 11
sentencing, *See also by country*
China and Hong Kong, 257–258
deterrence, 255–257
discretionary, 1
disproportionate penalties, reconciling, 232
good neighbour narrative, 257
guidelines, 260–265
judicial discretion, 29
life imprisonment, 248
removal of mandatory minimum sentences, 250
serious crimes
death penalty, and, 4, 56
ICCPR definition, 56
shared identity, 113
absence/denial of rights, 113
Shinawatra, Thaksin, 184, 186
Singapore, 12, 168
anti-death penalty activism, 83, 87, 103
cannabis and cannabis mixture, 99–101
Central Narcotics Bureau (CNB), *See* Central Narcotics Bureau (CNB)
corporal punishment, 185
death penalty, 1, 5, 9–10, 12, 83, 103, 138, 189, 247, 249
deterrence, and, 84–86
public opinion, 84
racial minorities, 101–103
societal resistance, 86–88
death row, 131
drug control legislation, 173
ICCPR, and, 4
knowledge and possession, 94–97
possession and *mens rea*, 91–94
presumption of innocence, 96
safe-keeping defence, 97–99
split from Malaysia, 118
trafficking, 7
war on drugs, 125
Singapore Anti-Narcotics Association (SANA), 177
Sirisena, Maithripala, 9
social harm, 25, 27
South Korea, 247
spheres of membership, 113
Sri Lanka
war on drugs, 9
Straits Settlements, 115
Strike Hard anti-crime campaign, 22, 25, 32, 35
wrongful convictions and executions, 44
subjective malice, 25
substantial economic loss
defining, 241
Suharto, 175
supplementary examination
application for, 29
authority, 29
Supreme People's Court, 23
due process, 11
Sutherland, Edwin, 146

Taiwan, 247
Taman Permata, 121
Thailand, 139, 168, 246
anti-illicit drugs legislation, 14
death penalty, 8–10
abolition of, 187, 189
arbitrary executions, 174
sentencing option, 239–243
decriminalisation of cannabis, 4, 88, 137, 174, 225, 230
drug control legislation, 173
extrajudicial killing schemes, 186
incarceration statistics, 225

Thailand (cont.)
legislative reform, 226, 243–244
committee structure, 227–228
criminals as patients, rebranding, 236–238
drug use and possession, 228–231
operational challenges, 238–239
targeted criminal sanctions, 231–235
unified law, 227
life imprisonment, 249
Office of the Narcotics Control Board (ONCB), *See* Office of the Narcotics Control Board (ONCB)
prison overcrowding, 137
war on drugs, 1, 225
Thomas, Sir Shenton, 116
trafficking, 2, 14, *See also by country*
deterrence, and, 84–86, 255–257
double presumption rule, 112, 114, 125–128
self-incrimination, and, 129
drug couriers/mules. *See* drug couriers/mules
drug user, by, 6, 30
fair trial rights, 127–129
presumptions regarding the intent, 231
safe-keeping defence, 97–99
statistics, 136, 246
war on drugs, 125
transparency
administration of justice, 66–68

United Nations, 188
General Assembly Special Session on the World Drug Problem (2016), 174
International Conference on Drug Abuse and Illicit Trafficking (1987), 175
international treaties. *See* international drug policy
moratorium on the death penalty, 203
United Nations Human Rights Committee
death penalty, on, 4
United Nations Office on Drugs and Crime (UNODC), 3, 57
death penalty, and, 5
regional report, 246
Universal Periodic Review (UPR) processes, 55
Universities Against the Death Penalty, 211

Vietnam, 168
harm reduction interventions, 7
voluntary confession of guilt, 27
voluntary surrender, 26
circumstances, 26
penalties, and, 27

walis-tingting (broom), 216
war on drugs, 9, 112, 125, 131, 137, 173, 187, 248, 260
Bangladesh, 9
Indonesia, 139–143, 155
Malaysia, 12, 125
Philippines, 1, 201, 207
political legitimacy, and, 188
poverty, and, 6
Singapore, 125
Sri Lanka, 9
Thailand, 1, 225
USA, 8
Widodo, Joko, 89, 184, 187
World Coalition Against the Death Penalty, 210
Wuhan Conference Summary 2015, 24
knowledge of presence of drugs, 42–44
mitigating circumstances, 26–35

Xi Jinping, 49
Xishuangbanna, 37

Yunnan, 11, 22, 34, 36–37, 43, 50

www.ingramcontent.com/pod-product-compliance
Lightning Source LLC
LaVergne TN
LVHW011808200926
848484LV00005B/1111
* 9 7 8 1 0 0 9 5 1 3 5 1 7 *